TOKYO GHOUL:re

2

SU
ISHIDA

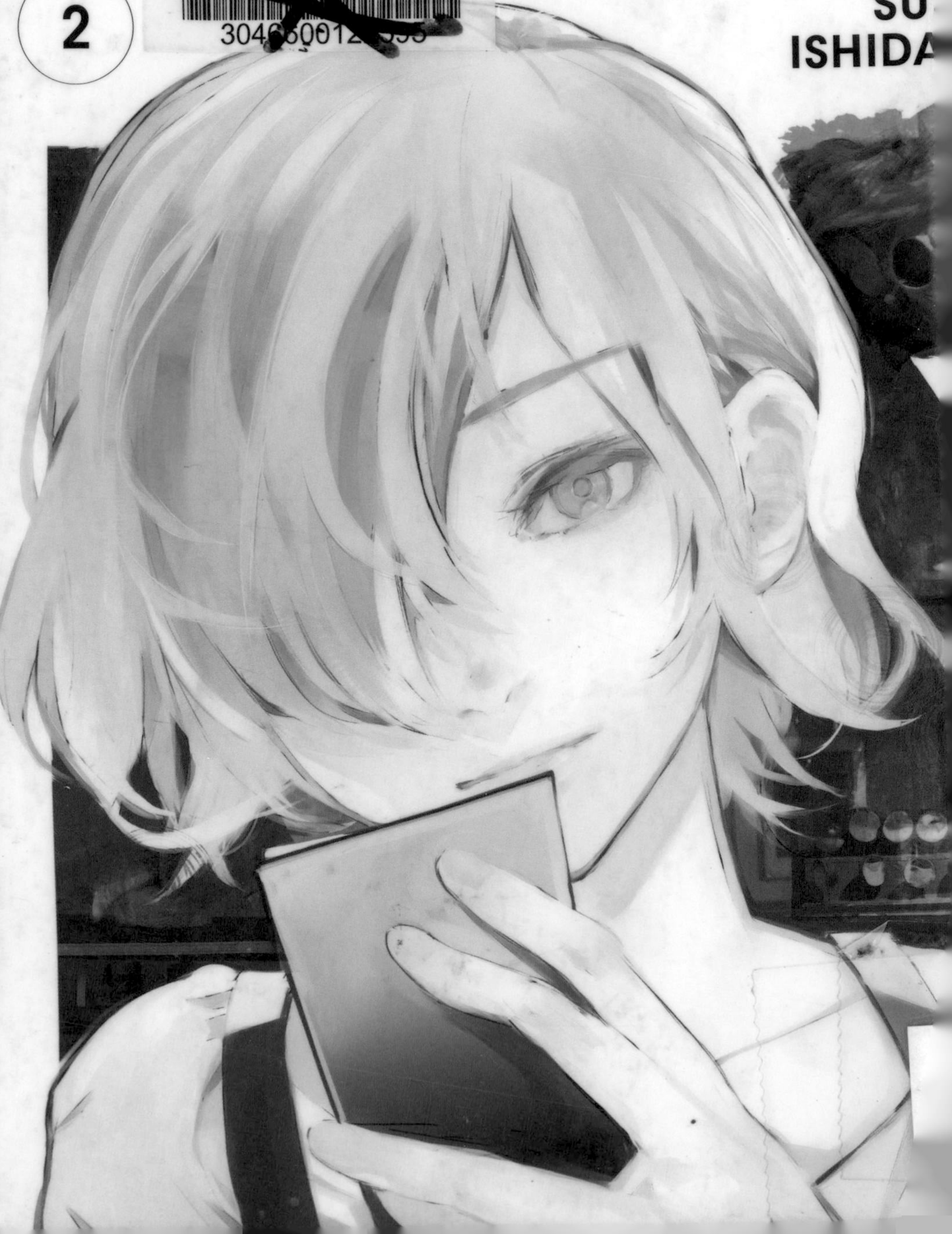

TOKYO GHOUL:re 2

東京喰種

SUI ISHIDA

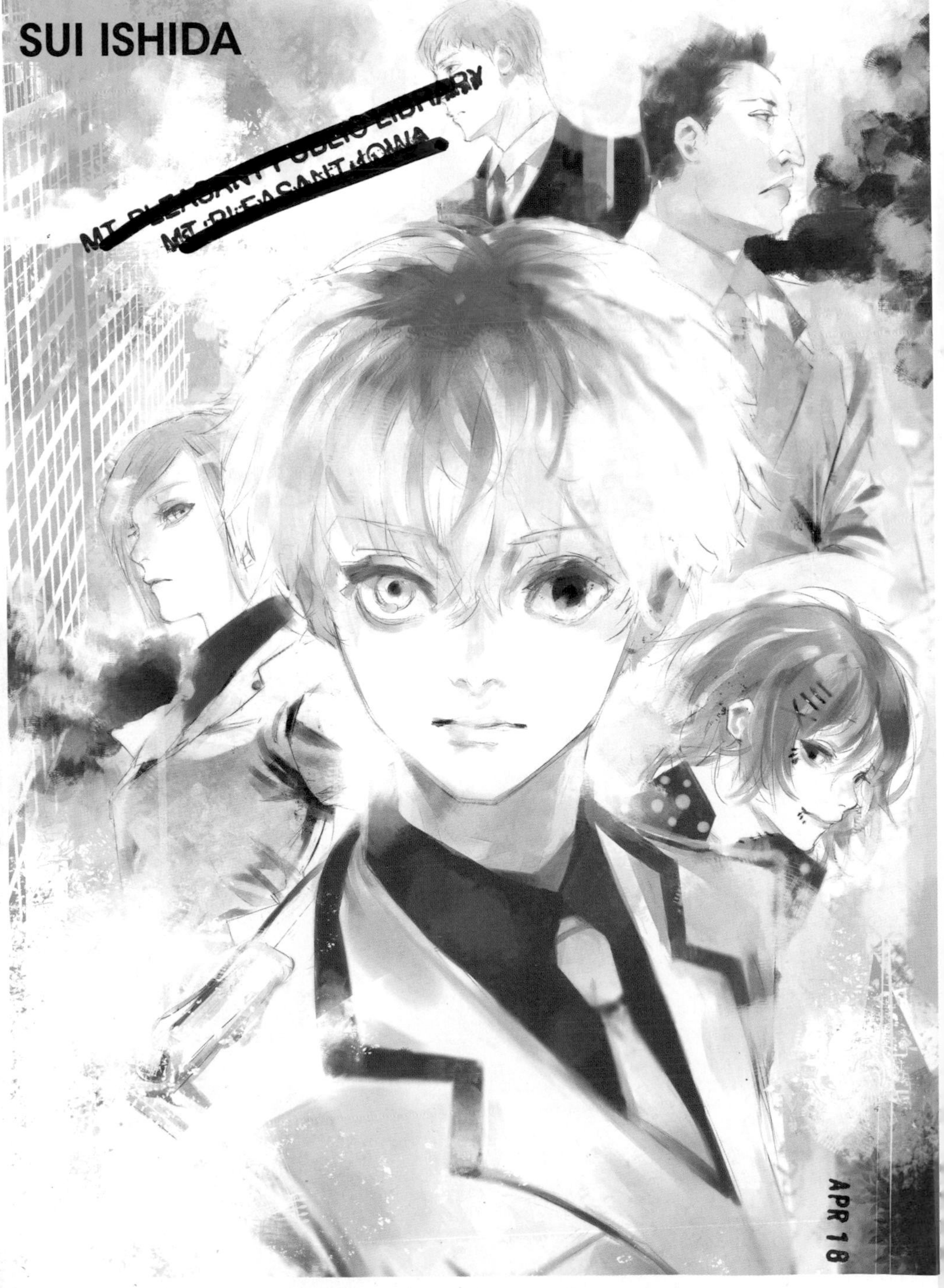

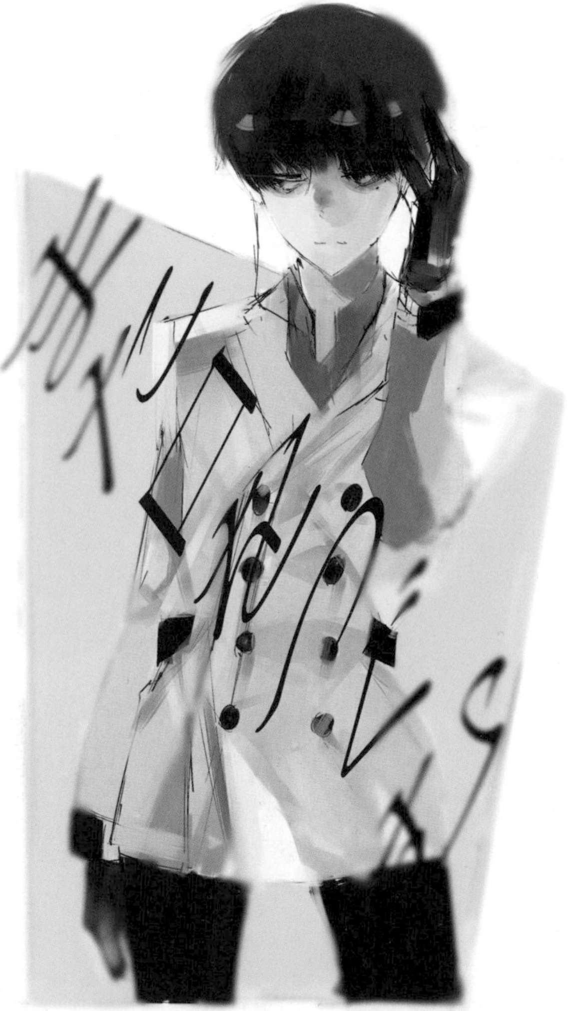

Shut your mouth again

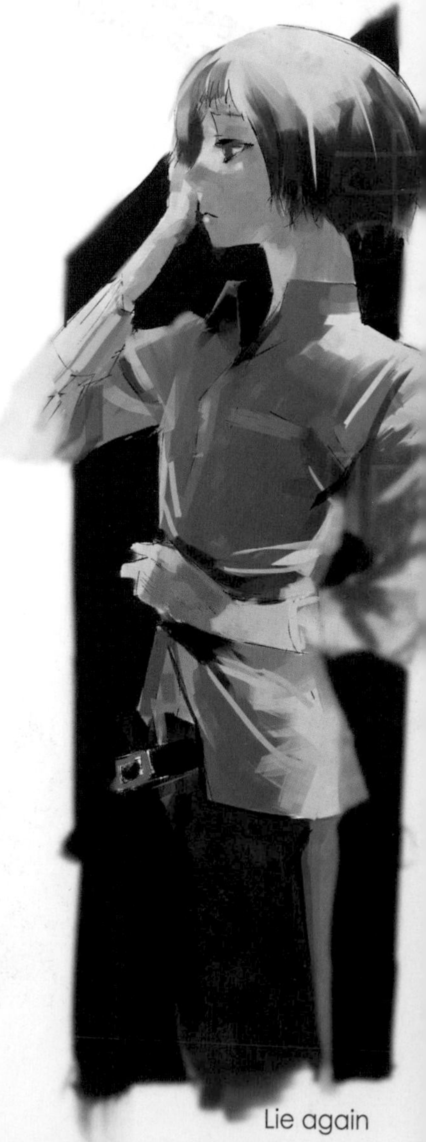

Lie again

TOKYO GHOUL:re ②

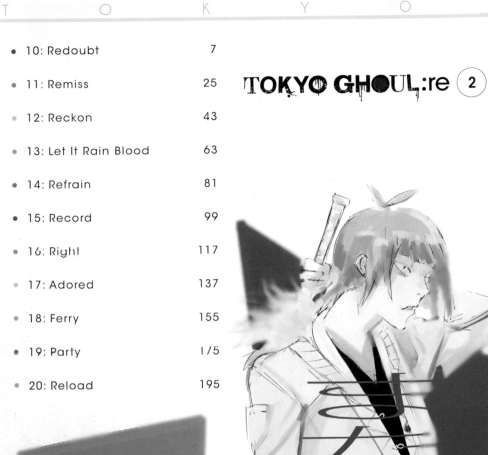

Bear it again

Asleep again

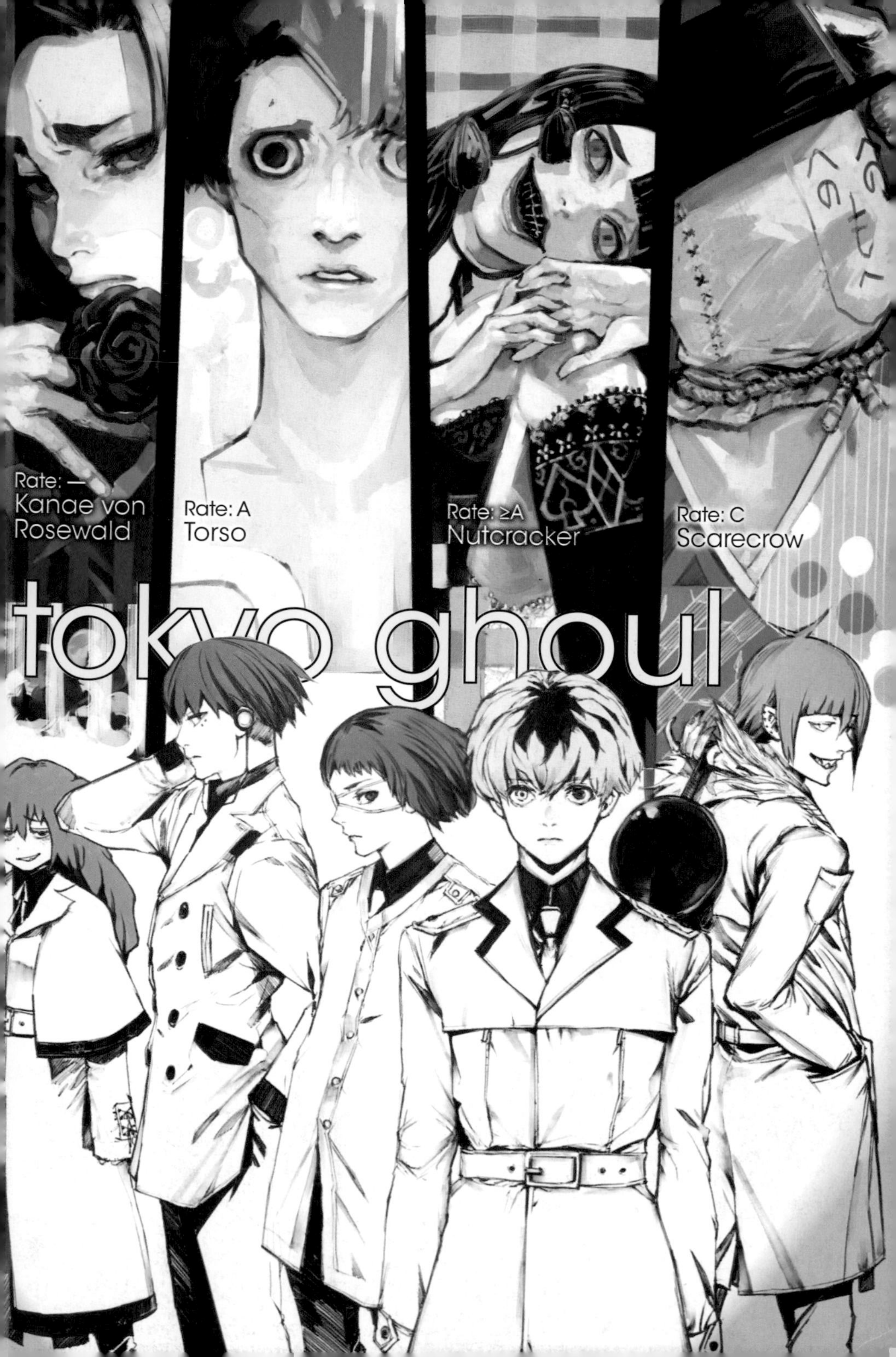
Rate: —
Kanae von Rosewald
Rate: A
Torso
Rate: ≥A
Nutcracker
Rate: C
Scarecrow
tokyo ghoul

CCG Ghoul Investigators / Tokyo Ghoul : re

The CCG is the only organization in the world that investigates and solves Ghoul-related crimes. Founded by the Washu Family, the CCG developed and evolved Quinques, a type of weapon derived from Ghouls' Kagune. Quinx, an advanced, next-generation technology where humans are implanted with Quinques, is under development.

Mado Squad

Qs (Quinx): Investigators implanted with Quinques. They all live together in a house called the **Chateau** with Investigator Sasaki.

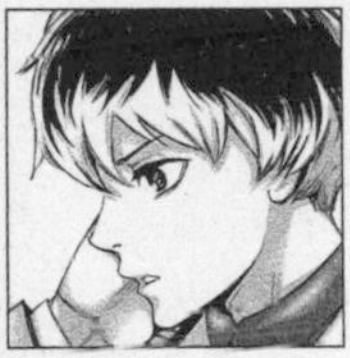

● Haise Sasaki
佐々木琲世
Rank 1 Investigator
Mentor to the Quinx Squad. Despite being half-Ghoul, he is passionate about guiding the Quinxes. He has no memory of his past. And whose voice sometimes echoes in his head...?!

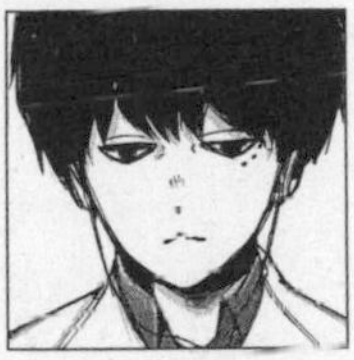

● Kuki Urie
瓜江久生
Rank 2 Investigator
Former Quinx Squad leader. The most talented fighter in the squad. His father, a special investigator, was killed by a Ghoul. Urie seeks to avenge his death.

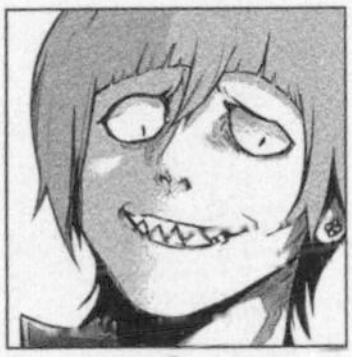

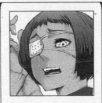

● Ginshi Shirazu
不知吟士
Rank 3 Investigator
Current squad leader of the Quinx Squad. Agreed to the Quinx procedure for mainly financial reasons. Despite his thuggish appearance, he has a very caring side.

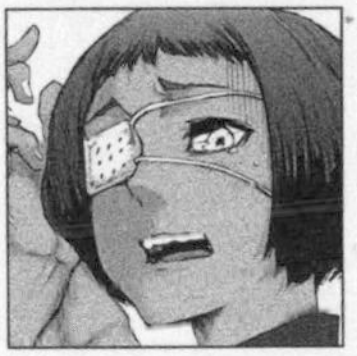

● Toru Mutsuki
六月 透
Rank 3 Investigator
His parents were killed by a Ghoul and he decided to become a Ghoul Investigator. Assigned female at birth, he decided to transition after undergoing the Quinx procedure.

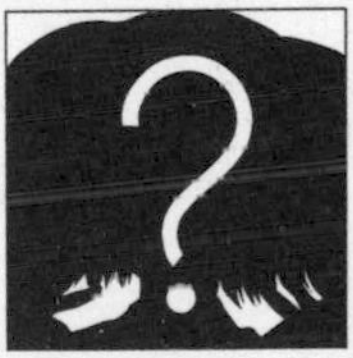

● Saiko Yonebayashi
米林才子
Rank 3 Investigator
Unknown

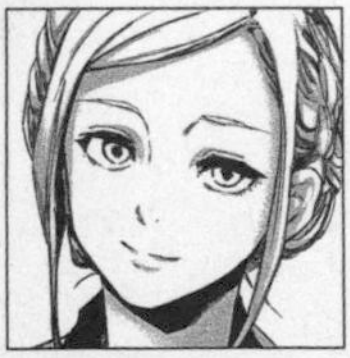

● Akira Mado
真戸 暁
Senior Investigator
Mentors Haise. Takes after her father and is determined to eradicate Ghouls. Investigating the Aogiri Tree.

Hirako Squad

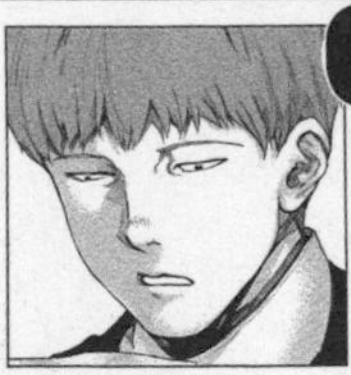

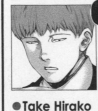

● Take Hirako
平子 丈
Senior Investigator
In pursuit of the Orochi. A reticent investigator.

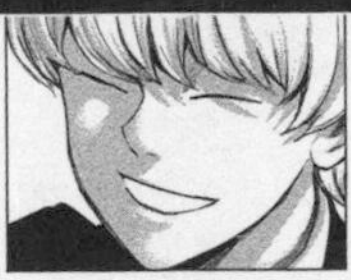

● Kuramoto Ito
伊東倉元
Rank 1 Investigator
Member of the Hirako Squad. Has a cheerful disposition.

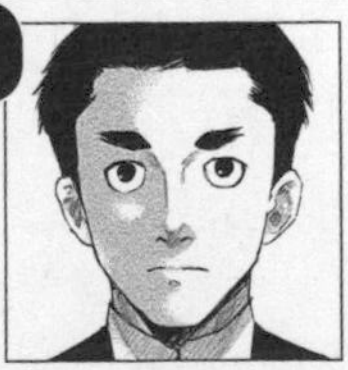

● Takeomi Kuroiwa
黒磐武臣
Rank 2 Investigator
The son of Special Investigator Iwao Kuroiwa.

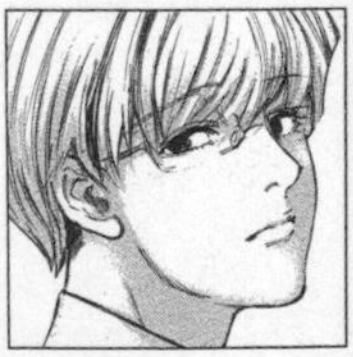

● Kisho Arima
有馬貴将
Special Investigator
An undefeated investigator who is respected by many at the CCG.

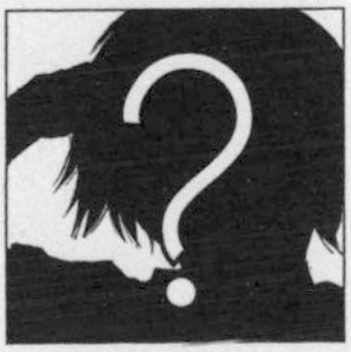

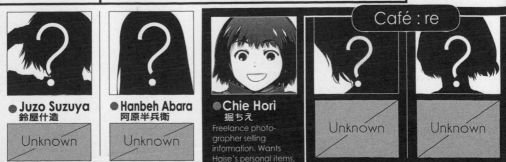

● Juzo Suzuya
鈴屋什造
Unknown

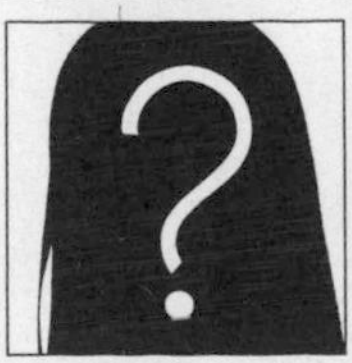

● Hanbeh Abara
阿原半兵衛
Unknown

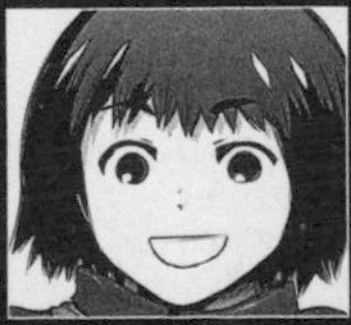

● Chie Hori
掘ちえ
Freelance photographer selling information. Wants Haise's personal items.

Café : re

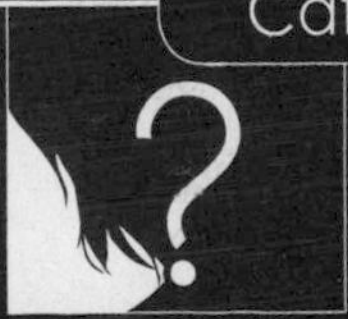

Unknown

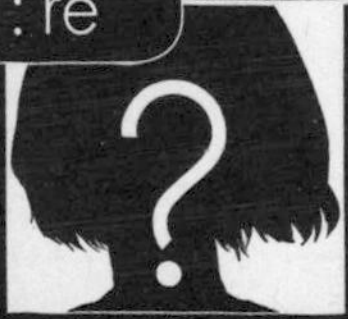

Unknown

Tokyo Ghoul :re ● Ghouls

They appear human, but have a unique predation organ called a Kagune and can only survive by feeding on human flesh. They are the nemesis of humanity. Besides human flesh, the only other thing they can ingest is coffee. Ghouls can only be wounded by a Kagune or a Quinque made from a Kagune. One of the most prominent Ghoul factions is the Aogiri Tree, a hostile organization that is expanding its numbers.

Aogiri Tree

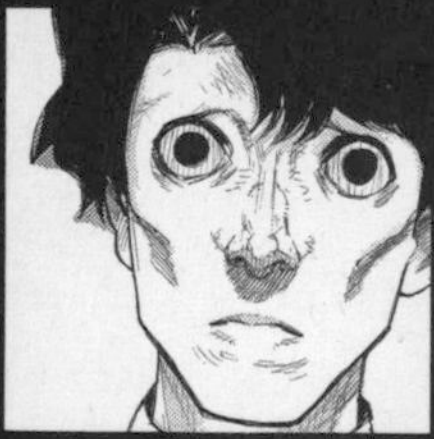

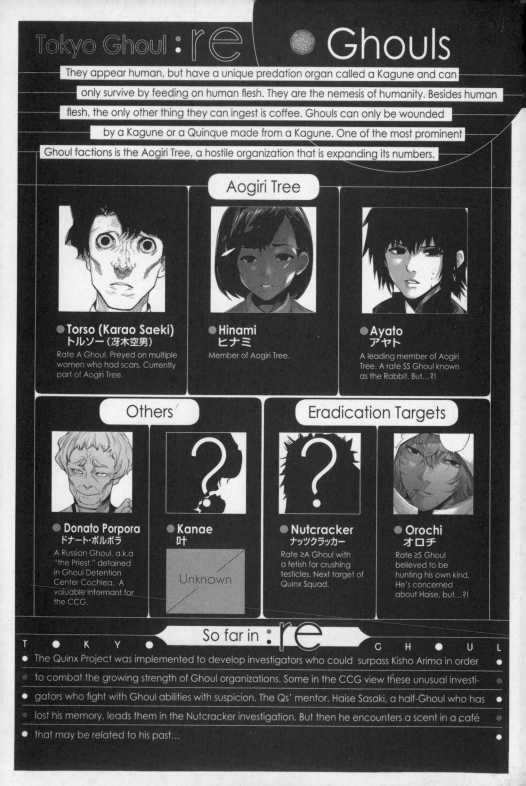

● Torso (Karao Saeki)
トルソー（冴木空男）

Rate A Ghoul. Preyed on multiple women who had scars. Currently part of Aogiri Tree.

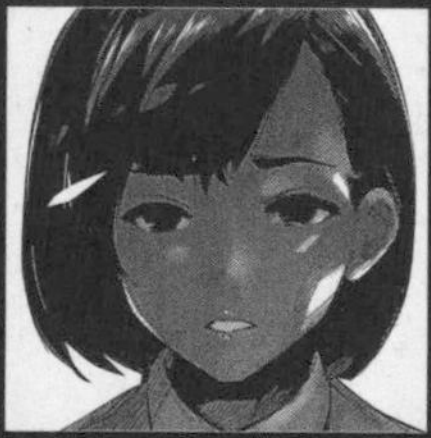

● Hinami
ヒナミ

Member of Aogiri Tree.

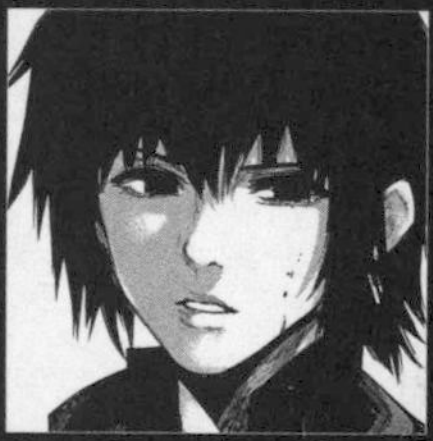

● Ayato
アヤト

A leading member of Aogiri Tree. A rate SS Ghoul known as the Rabbit. But…?!

Others

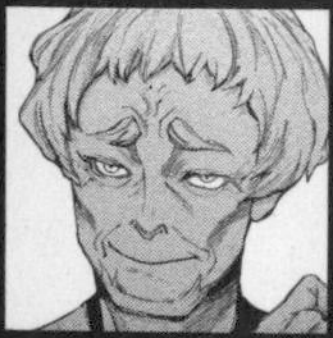

● Donato Porpora
ドナート・ポルポラ

A Russian Ghoul, a.k.a "the Priest," detained in Ghoul Detention Center Cochlea. A valuable informant for the CCG.

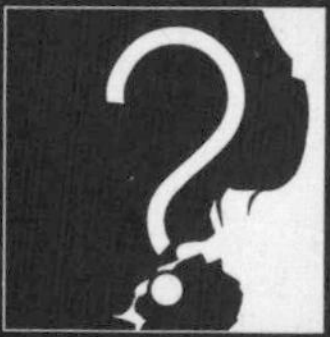

● Kanae
叶

Unknown

Eradication Targets

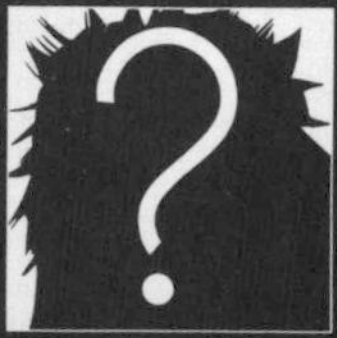

● Nutcracker
ナッツクラッカー

Rate ≥A Ghoul with a fetish for crushing testicles. Next target of Quinx Squad.

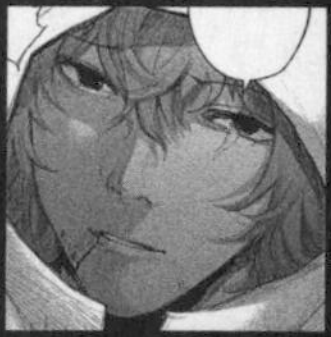

● Orochi
オロチ

Rate ≥S Ghoul believed to be hunting his own kind. He's concerned about Haise, but…?!

So far in :re

T ● K Y ● G H ● U L

The Quinx Project was implemented to develop investigators who could surpass Kisho Arima in order to combat the growing strength of Ghoul organizations. Some in the CCG view these unusual investigators who fight with Ghoul abilities with suspicion. The Qs' mentor, Haise Sasaki, a half-Ghoul who has lost his memory, leads them in the Nutcracker investigation. But then he encounters a scent in a café that may be related to his past…

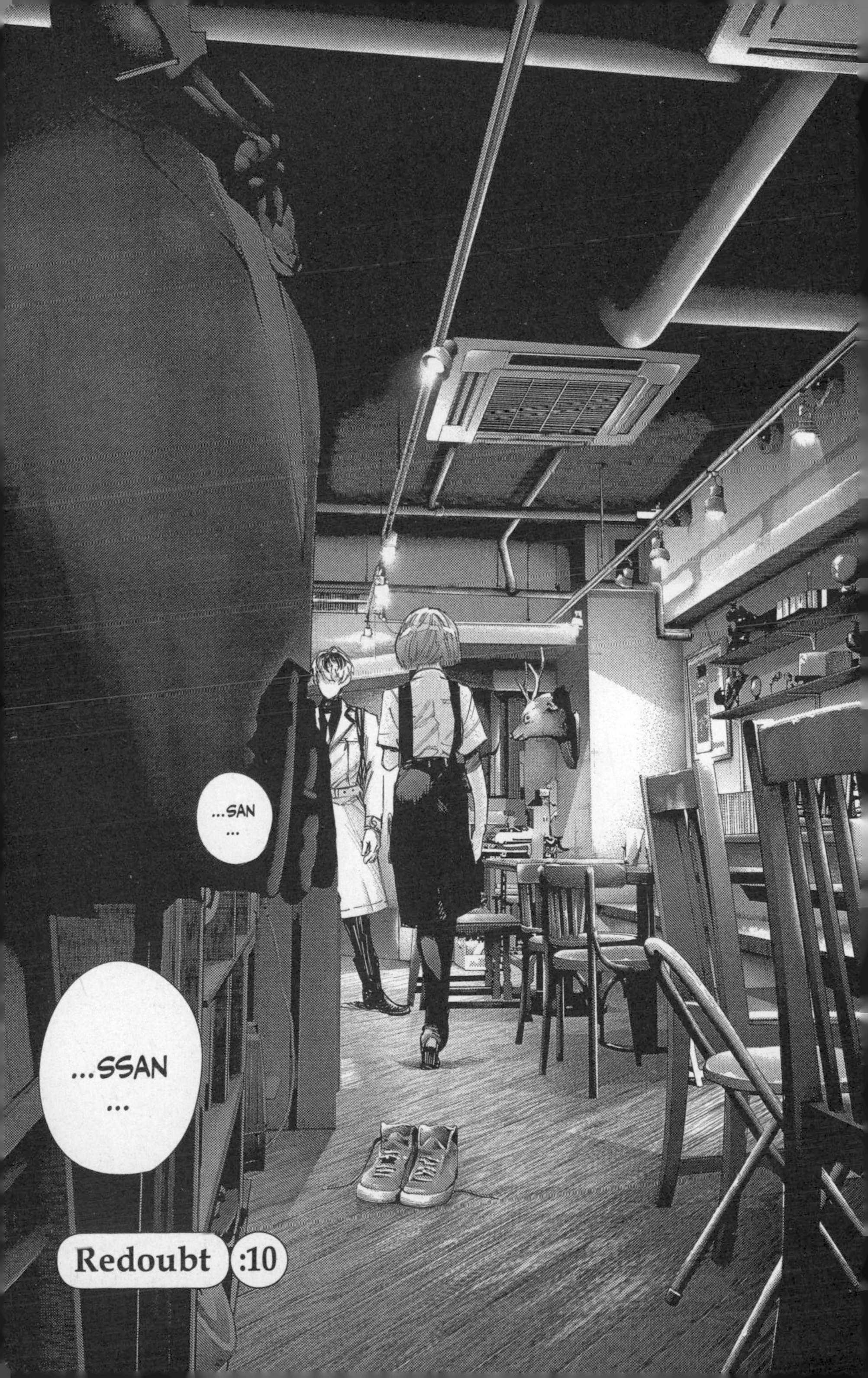
...SAN ...
...SSAN ...
Redoubt :10

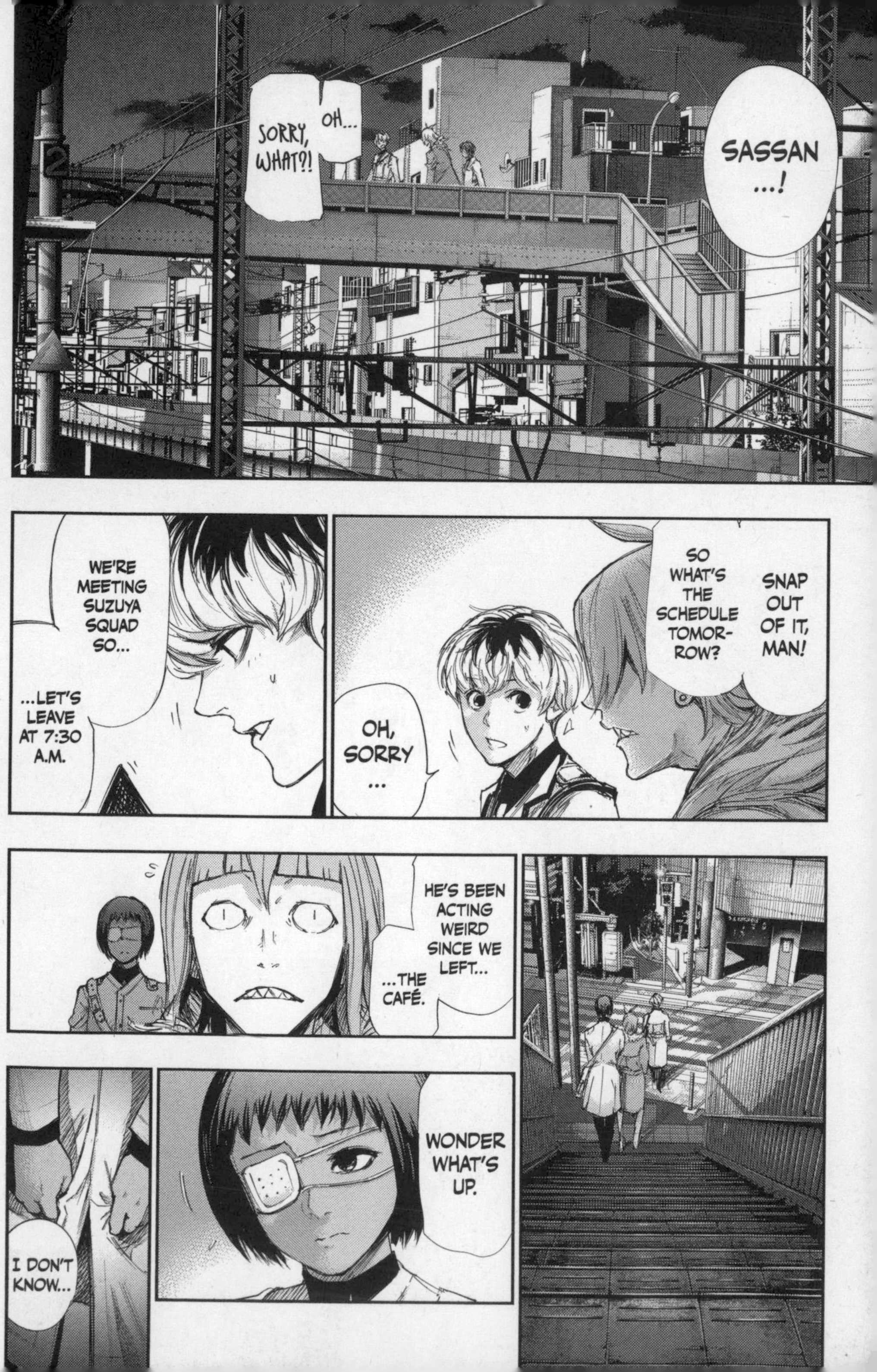
SASSAN ...!
OH...
SORRY, WHAT?!
SNAP OUT OF IT, MAN!
SO WHAT'S THE SCHEDULE TOMORROW?
OH, SORRY ...
WE'RE MEETING SUZUYA SQUAD SO...
...LET'S LEAVE AT 7:30 A.M.
HE'S BEEN ACTING WEIRD SINCE WE LEFT...
...THE CAFÉ.
WONDER WHAT'S UP.
I DON'T KNOW...

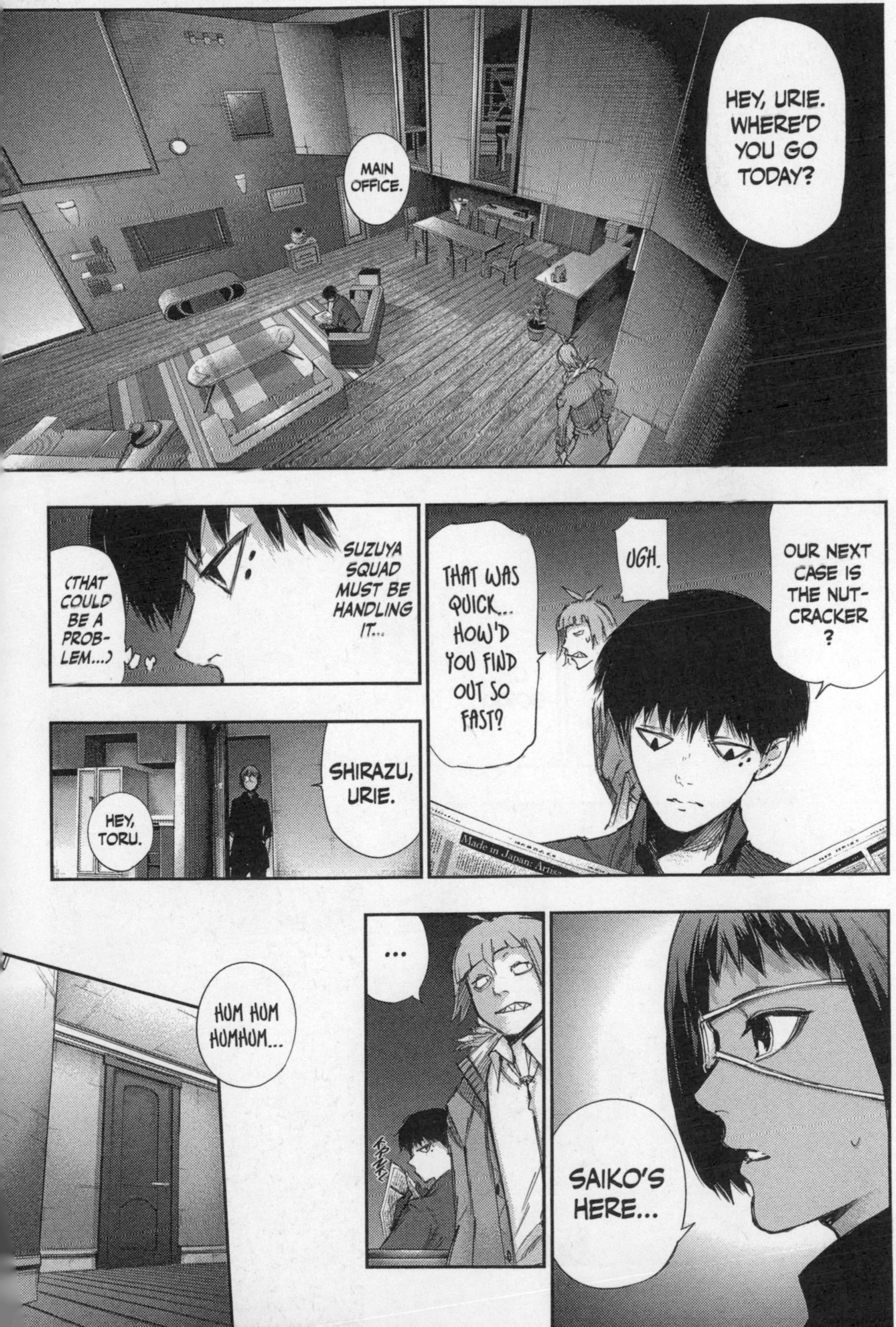
HEY, URIE. WHERE'D YOU GO TODAY?
MAIN OFFICE.
OUR NEXT CASE IS THE NUT-CRACKER?
UGH.
THAT WAS QUICK... HOW'D YOU FIND OUT SO FAST?
SUZUYA SQUAD MUST BE HANDLING IT...
(THAT COULD BE A PROB-LEM...)
SHIRAZU, URIE.
HEY, TORU.
SAIKO'S HERE...
...
KRNK!
HUM HUM HUMHUM...

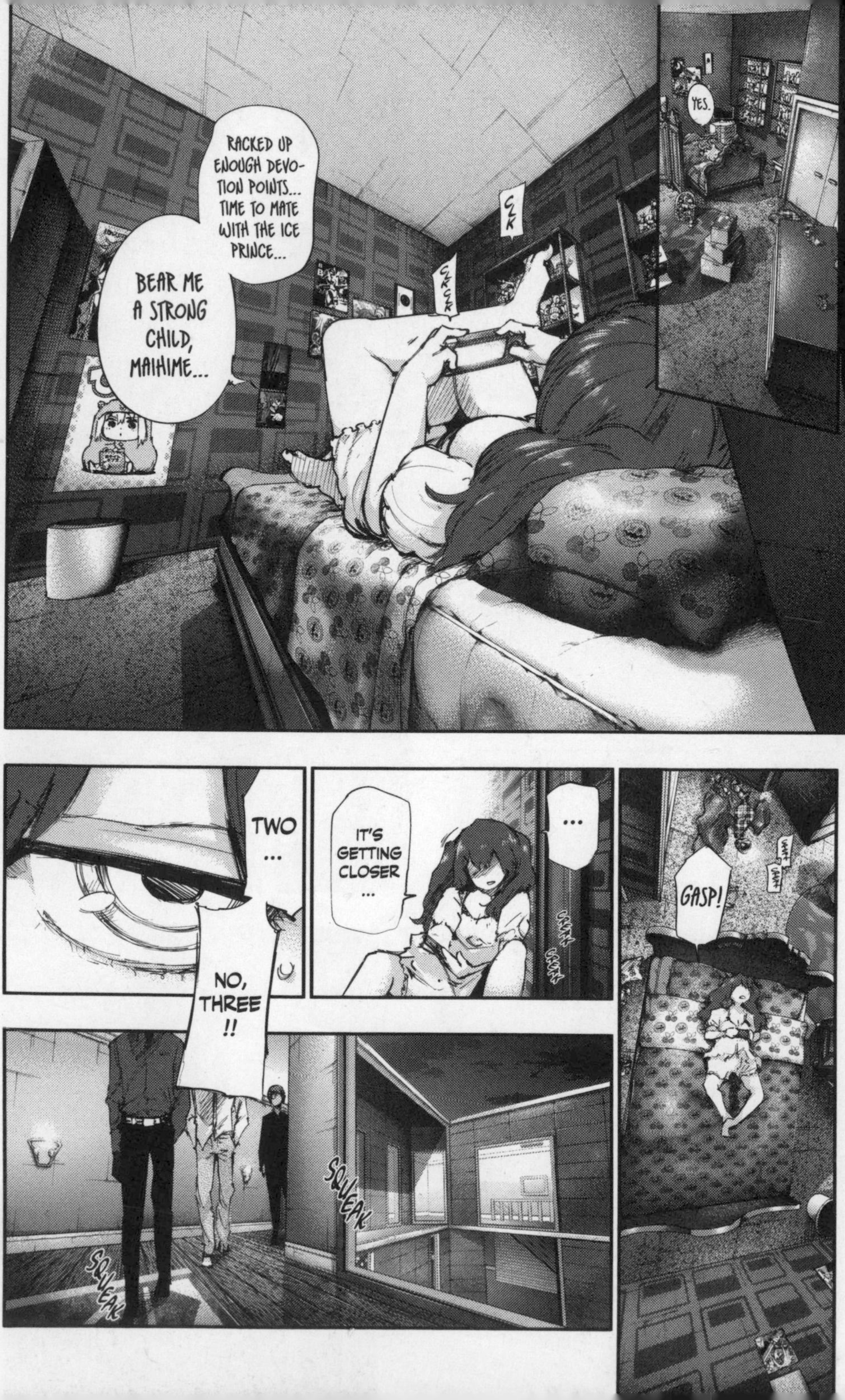
YES.
CLK
RACKED UP ENOUGH DEVOTION POINTS... TIME TO MATE WITH THE ICE PRINCE...
CLKCLK
BEAR ME A STRONG CHILD, MAIHIME...
GASP!
...
CREAK
CREAK
IT'S GETTING CLOSER ...
TWO ...
NO, THREE !!
SQUEAK
SQUEAK

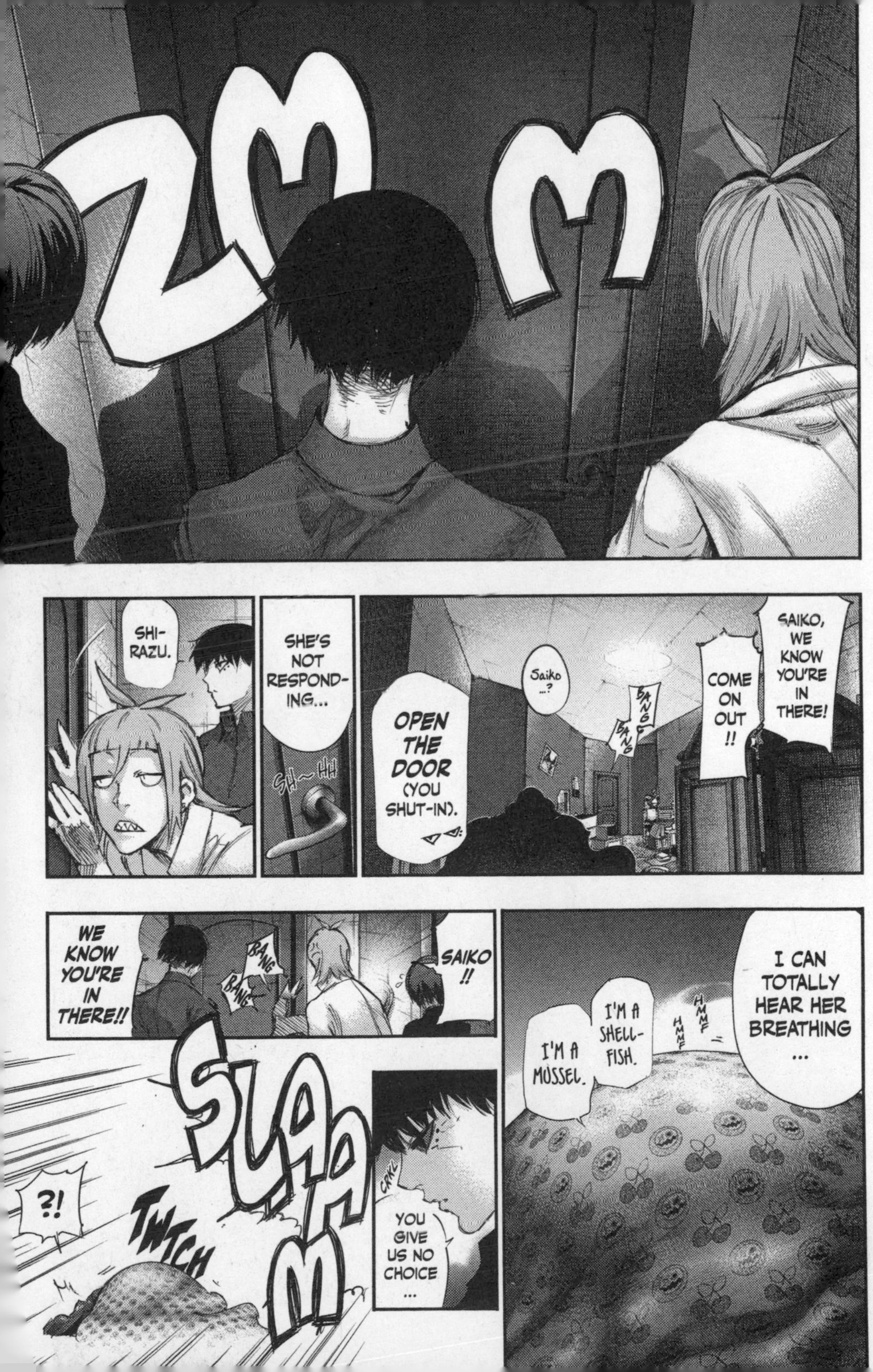
ZMM
SAIKO, WE KNOW YOU'RE IN THERE!
COME ON OUT !!
BANG BANG
Saiko ...?
SHE'S NOT RESPONDING...
OPEN THE DOOR (YOU SHUT-IN).
SHI-RAZU.
I CAN TOTALLY HEAR HER BREATHING ...
HMMF HMMF
I'M A SHELL-FISH.
I'M A MUSSEL.
SAIKO !!
BANG BANG
WE KNOW YOU'RE IN THERE!!
CRKL
YOU GIVE US NO CHOICE ...
SLAMM
TWITCH
?!

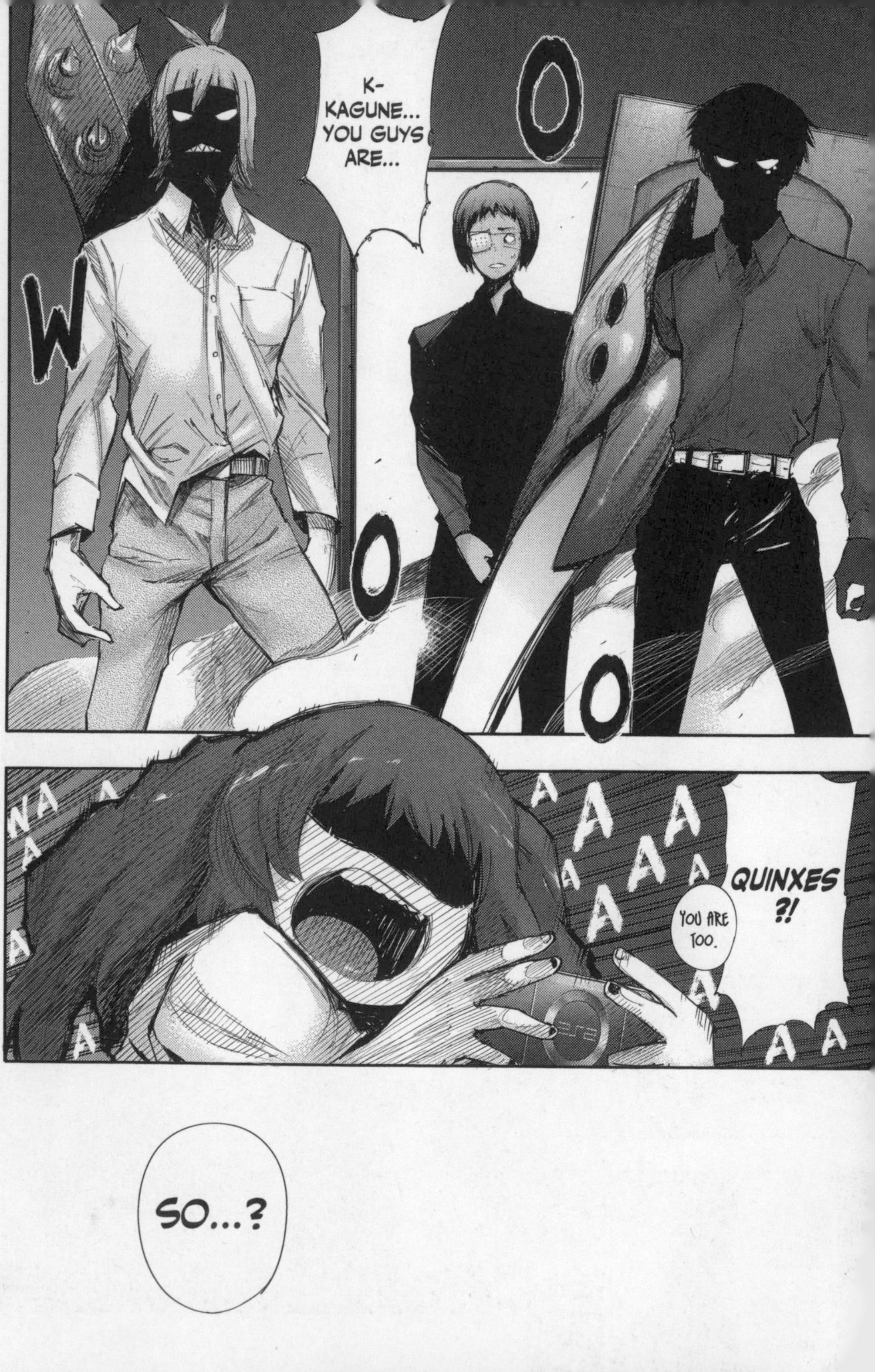
K-KAGUNE... YOU GUYS ARE...
WOOO
QUINXES?!
YOU ARE TOO.
WAAAAAAAAAAAAA
SO...?

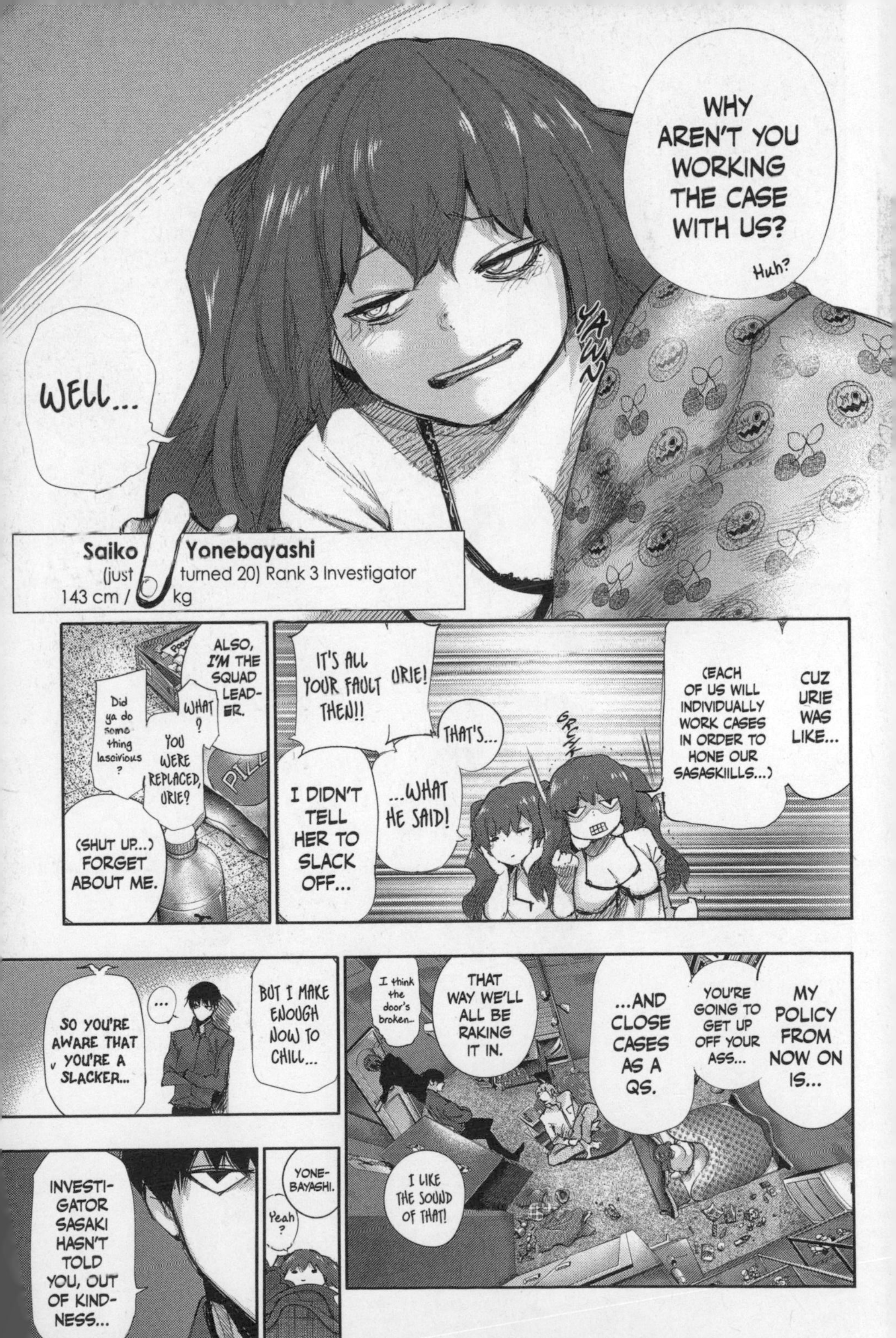
WHY AREN'T YOU WORKING THE CASE WITH US?
Huh?
YAWN
WELL...
Saiko Yonebayashi
(just turned 20) Rank 3 Investigator
143 cm / kg
CUZ URIE WAS LIKE...
(EACH OF US WILL INDIVIDUALLY WORK CASES IN ORDER TO HONE OUR SASASKIILLS...)
GRCH
URIE! IT'S ALL YOUR FAULT THEN!!
THAT'S...
...WHAT HE SAID!
I DIDN'T TELL HER TO SLACK OFF...
ALSO, I'M THE SQUAD LEADER.
WHAT?
YOU WERE REPLACED, URIE?
Did ya do some thing lascivious?
(SHUT UP...) FORGET ABOUT ME.
MY POLICY FROM NOW ON IS...
YOU'RE GOING TO GET UP OFF YOUR ASS...
...AND CLOSE CASES AS A QS.
THAT WAY WE'LL ALL BE RAKING IT IN.
I think the door's broken...
I LIKE THE SOUND OF THAT!
BUT I MAKE ENOUGH NOW TO CHILL...
...
SO YOU'RE AWARE THAT YOU'RE A SLACKER...
YONE-BAYASHI.
Yeah?
INVESTIGATOR SASAKI HASN'T TOLD YOU, OUT OF KINDNESS...

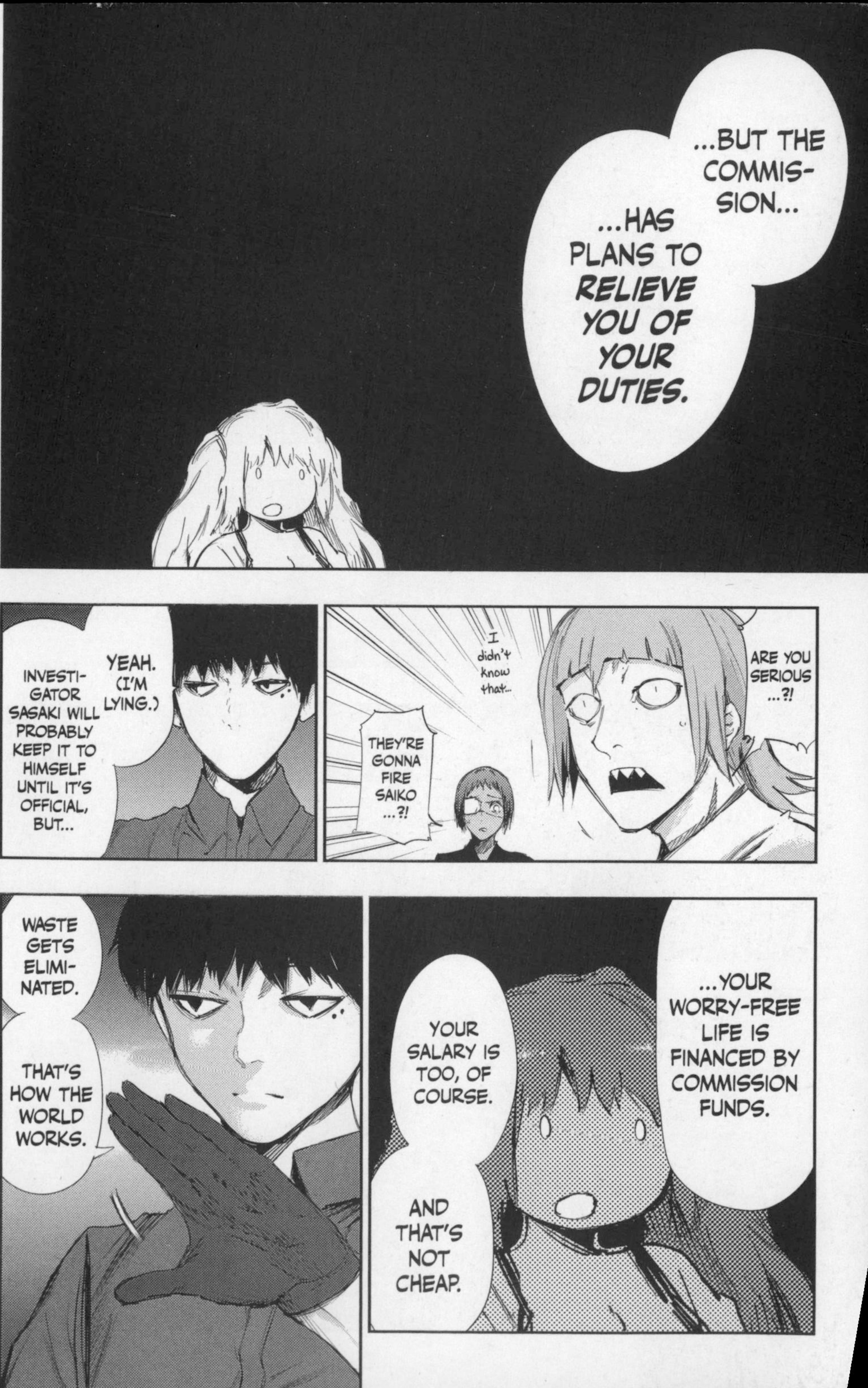
...BUT THE COMMISSION...
...HAS PLANS TO RELIEVE YOU OF YOUR DUTIES.
ARE YOU SERIOUS ...?!
I didn't know that...
THEY'RE GONNA FIRE SAIKO ...?!
YEAH. (I'M LYING.)
INVESTIGATOR SASAKI WILL PROBABLY KEEP IT TO HIMSELF UNTIL IT'S OFFICIAL, BUT...
...YOUR WORRY-FREE LIFE IS FINANCED BY COMMISSION FUNDS.
YOUR SALARY IS TOO, OF COURSE.
AND THAT'S NOT CHEAP.
WASTE GETS ELIMINATED.
THAT'S HOW THE WORLD WORKS.

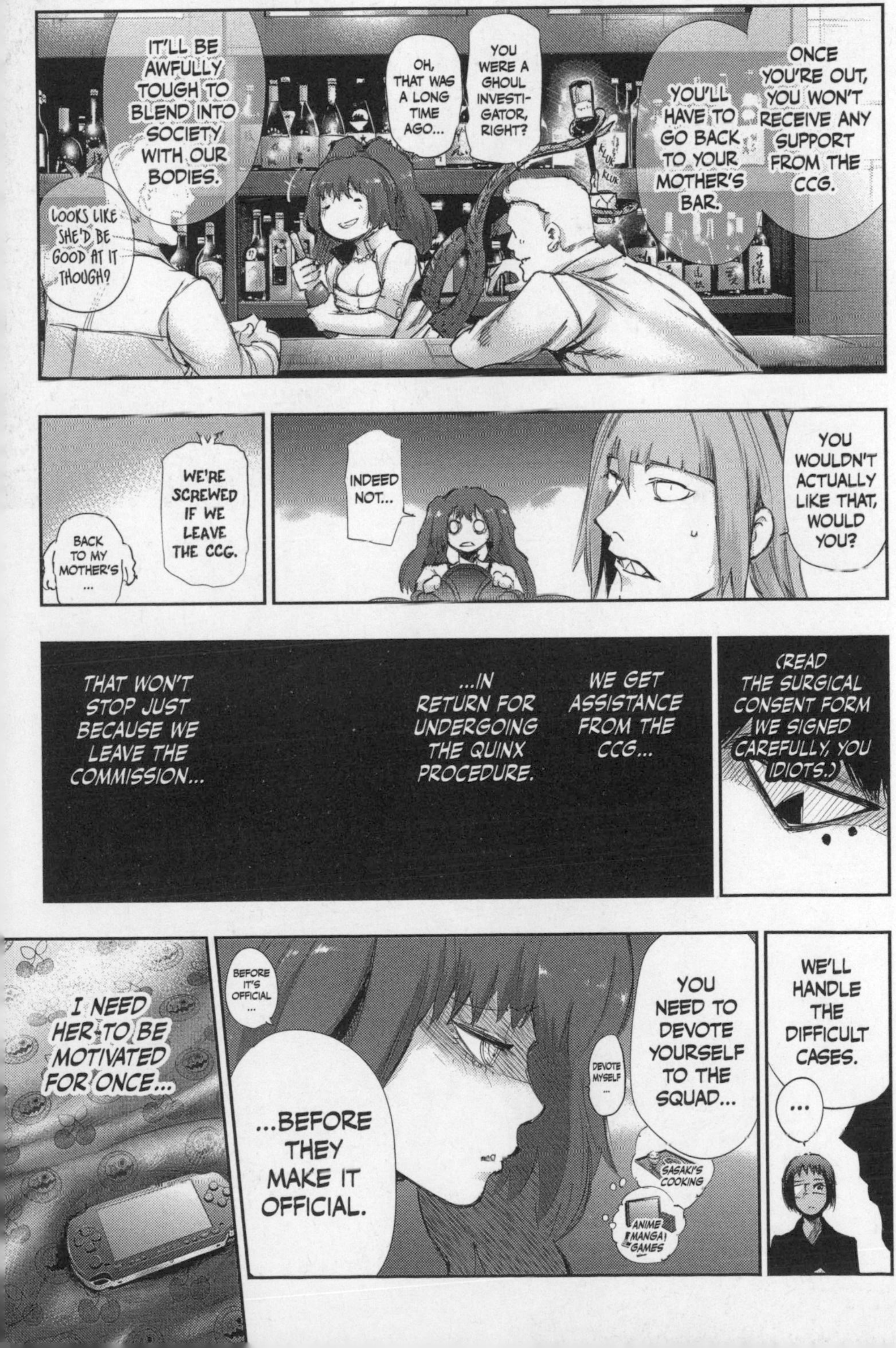
ONCE YOU'RE OUT, YOU WON'T RECEIVE ANY SUPPORT FROM THE CCG.
YOU'LL HAVE TO GO BACK TO YOUR MOTHER'S BAR.
KLUK KLUK
YOU WERE A GHOUL INVESTIGATOR, RIGHT?
OH, THAT WAS A LONG TIME AGO...
IT'LL BE AWFULLY TOUGH TO BLEND INTO SOCIETY WITH OUR BODIES.
LOOKS LIKE SHE'D BE GOOD AT IT THOUGH?
YOU WOULDN'T ACTUALLY LIKE THAT, WOULD YOU?
INDEED NOT...
WE'RE SCREWED IF WE LEAVE THE CCG.
BACK TO MY MOTHER'S ...
(READ THE SURGICAL CONSENT FORM WE SIGNED CAREFULLY, YOU IDIOTS.)
WE GET ASSISTANCE FROM THE CCG...
...IN RETURN FOR UNDERGOING THE QUINX PROCEDURE.
THAT WON'T STOP JUST BECAUSE WE LEAVE THE COMMISSION...
WE'LL HANDLE THE DIFFICULT CASES.
...
YOU NEED TO DEVOTE YOURSELF TO THE SQUAD...
DEVOTE MYSELF ...
SASAKI'S COOKING
ANIME MANGA GAMES
BEFORE IT'S OFFICIAL ...
...BEFORE THEY MAKE IT OFFICIAL.
I NEED HER TO BE MOTIVATED FOR ONCE...

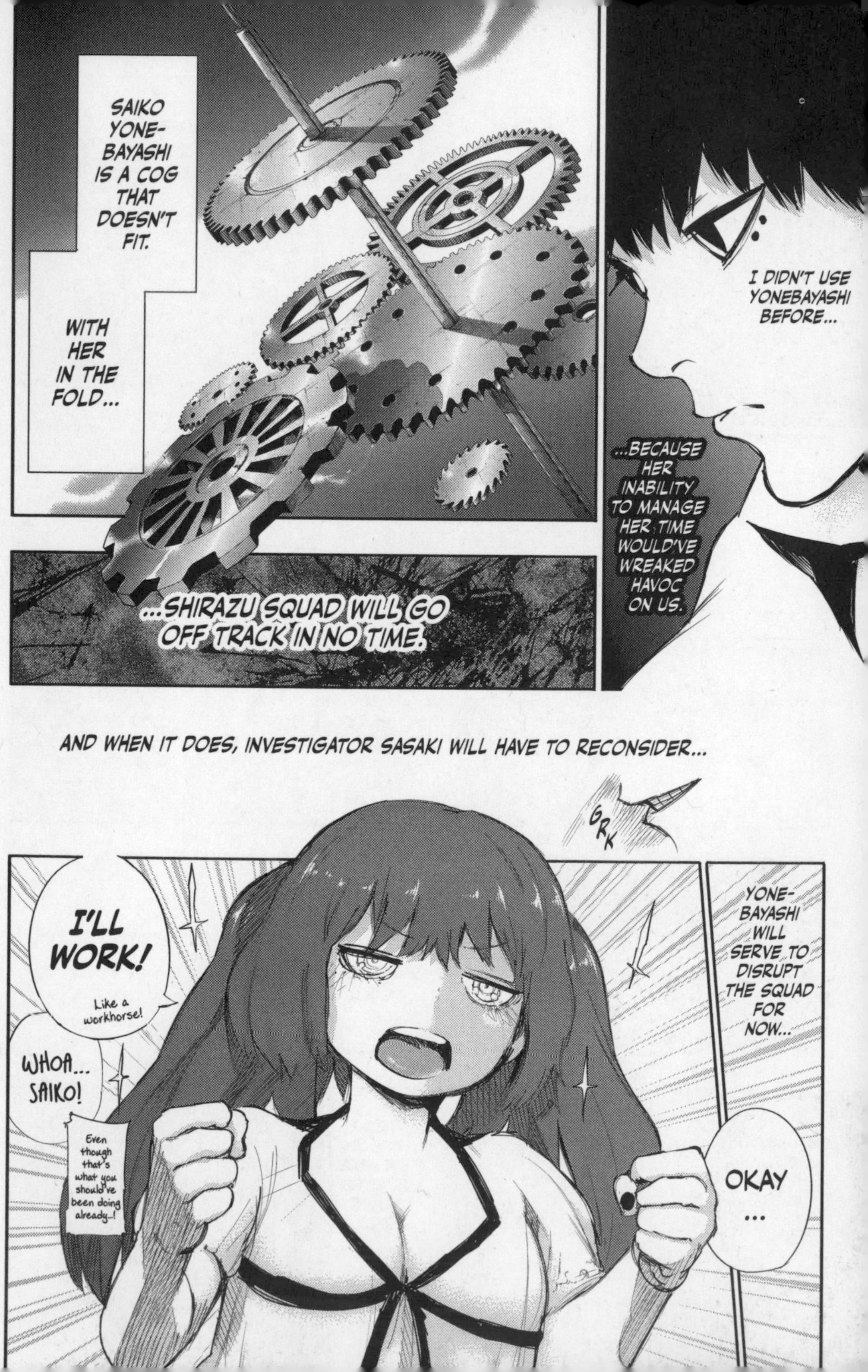
I DIDN'T USE YONEBAYASHI BEFORE...
...BECAUSE HER INABILITY TO MANAGE HER TIME WOULD'VE WREAKED HAVOC ON US.
SAIKO YONE-BAYASHI IS A COG THAT DOESN'T FIT.
WITH HER IN THE FOLD...
...SHIRAZU SQUAD WILL GO OFF TRACK IN NO TIME.
AND WHEN IT DOES, INVESTIGATOR SASAKI WILL HAVE TO RECONSIDER...
GRK
YONE-BAYASHI WILL SERVE TO DISRUPT THE SQUAD FOR NOW...
OKAY...
I'LL WORK!
Like a workhorse!
WHOA... SAIKO!
Even though that's what you should've been doing already...!

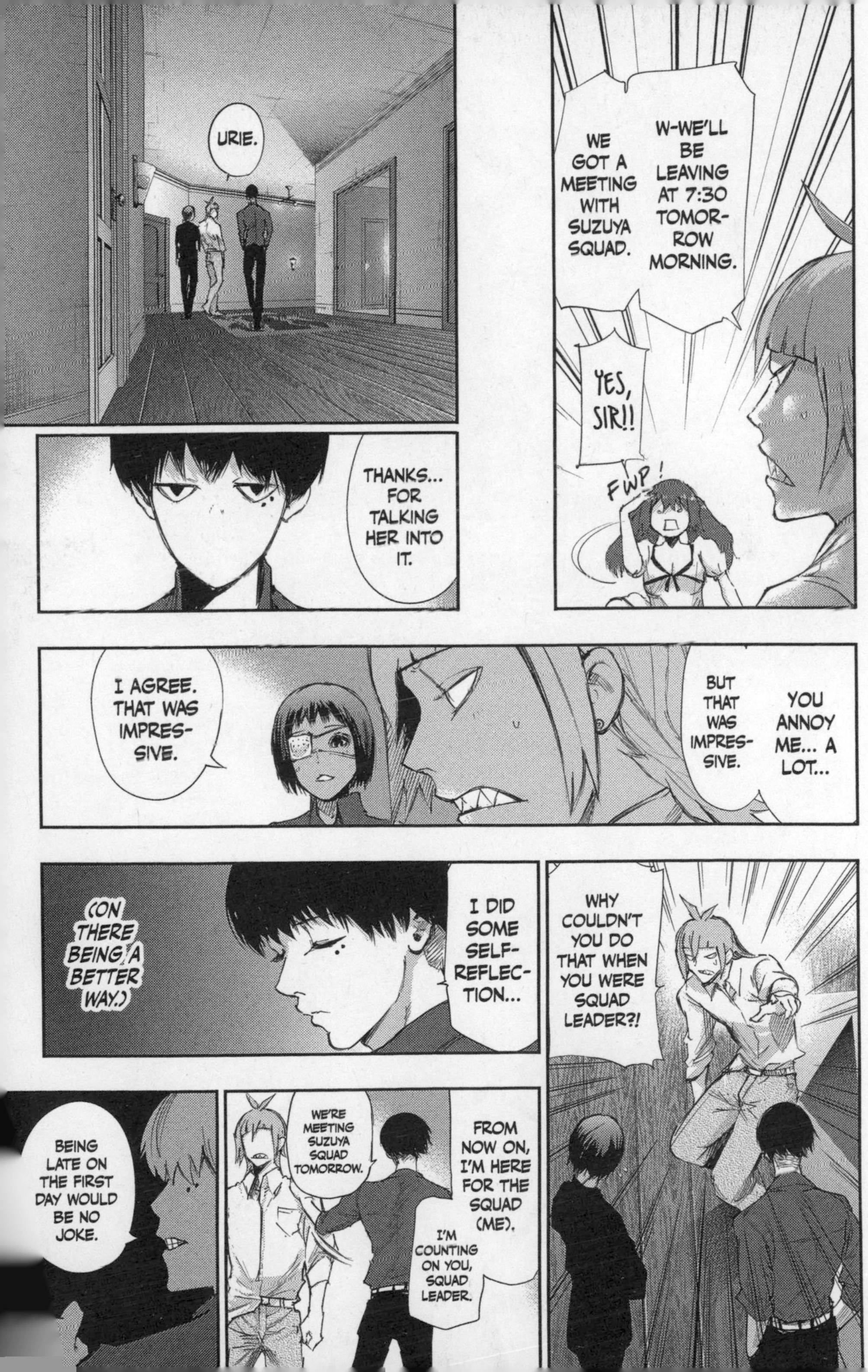
W-WE'LL BE LEAVING AT 7:30 TOMORROW MORNING.
WE GOT A MEETING WITH SUZUYA SQUAD.
YES, SIR!!
FWP!
URIE.
THANKS... FOR TALKING HER INTO IT.
YOU ANNOY ME... A LOT...
BUT THAT WAS IMPRESSIVE.
I AGREE. THAT WAS IMPRESSIVE.
WHY COULDN'T YOU DO THAT WHEN YOU WERE SQUAD LEADER?!
I DID SOME SELF-REFLECTION...
(ON THERE BEING A BETTER WAY.)
FROM NOW ON, I'M HERE FOR THE SQUAD (ME).
WE'RE MEETING SUZUYA SQUAD TOMORROW.
I'M COUNTING ON YOU, SQUAD LEADER.
BEING LATE ON THE FIRST DAY WOULD BE NO JOKE.

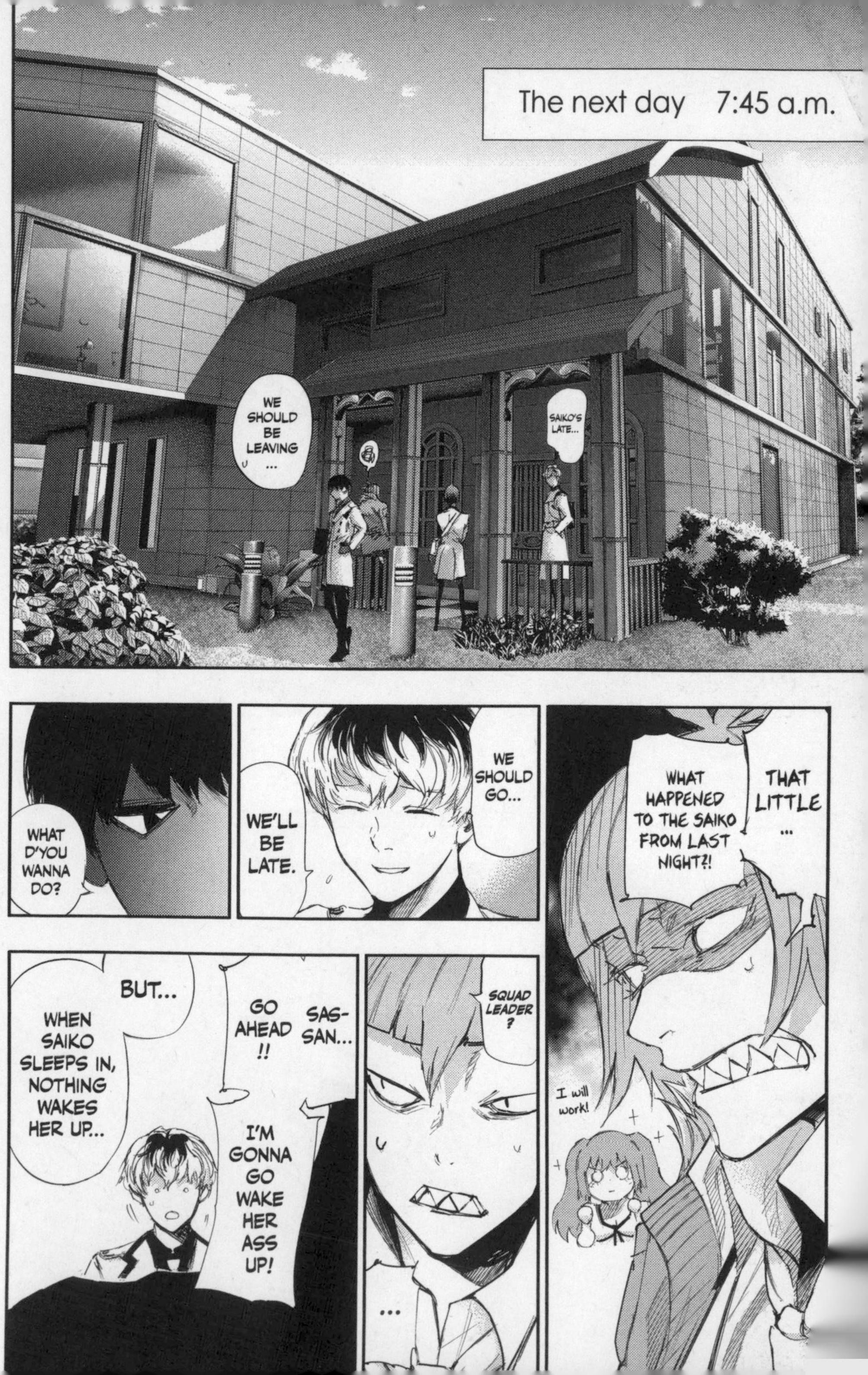

The next day 7:45 a.m.
SAIKO'S LATE...
WE SHOULD BE LEAVING ...
THAT LITTLE ...
WHAT HAPPENED TO THE SAIKO FROM LAST NIGHT?!
I will work!
WE SHOULD GO...
WE'LL BE LATE.
WHAT D'YOU WANNA DO?
SQUAD LEADER ?
...
SAS-SAN...
GO AHEAD !!
I'M GONNA GO WAKE HER ASS UP!
BUT...
WHEN SAIKO SLEEPS IN, NOTHING WAKES HER UP...

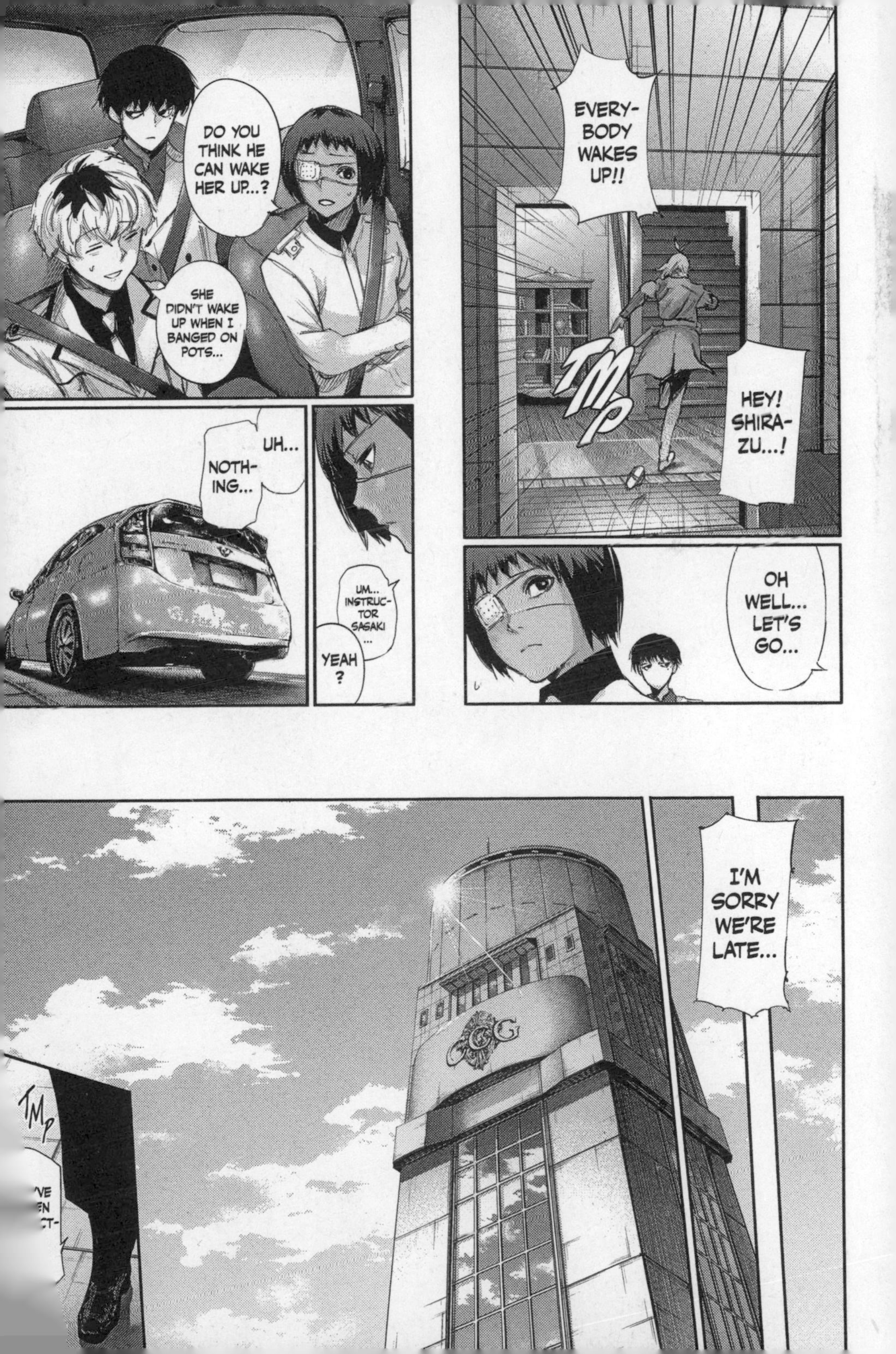
EVERY-BODY WAKES UP!!
TMP
HEY! SHIRA-ZU...!
OH WELL... LET'S GO...
DO YOU THINK HE CAN WAKE HER UP...?
SHE DIDN'T WAKE UP WHEN I BANGED ON POTS...
UM... INSTRUCTOR SASAKI...
YEAH?
UH...
NOTHING...
I'M SORRY WE'RE LATE...
CCG
TMP

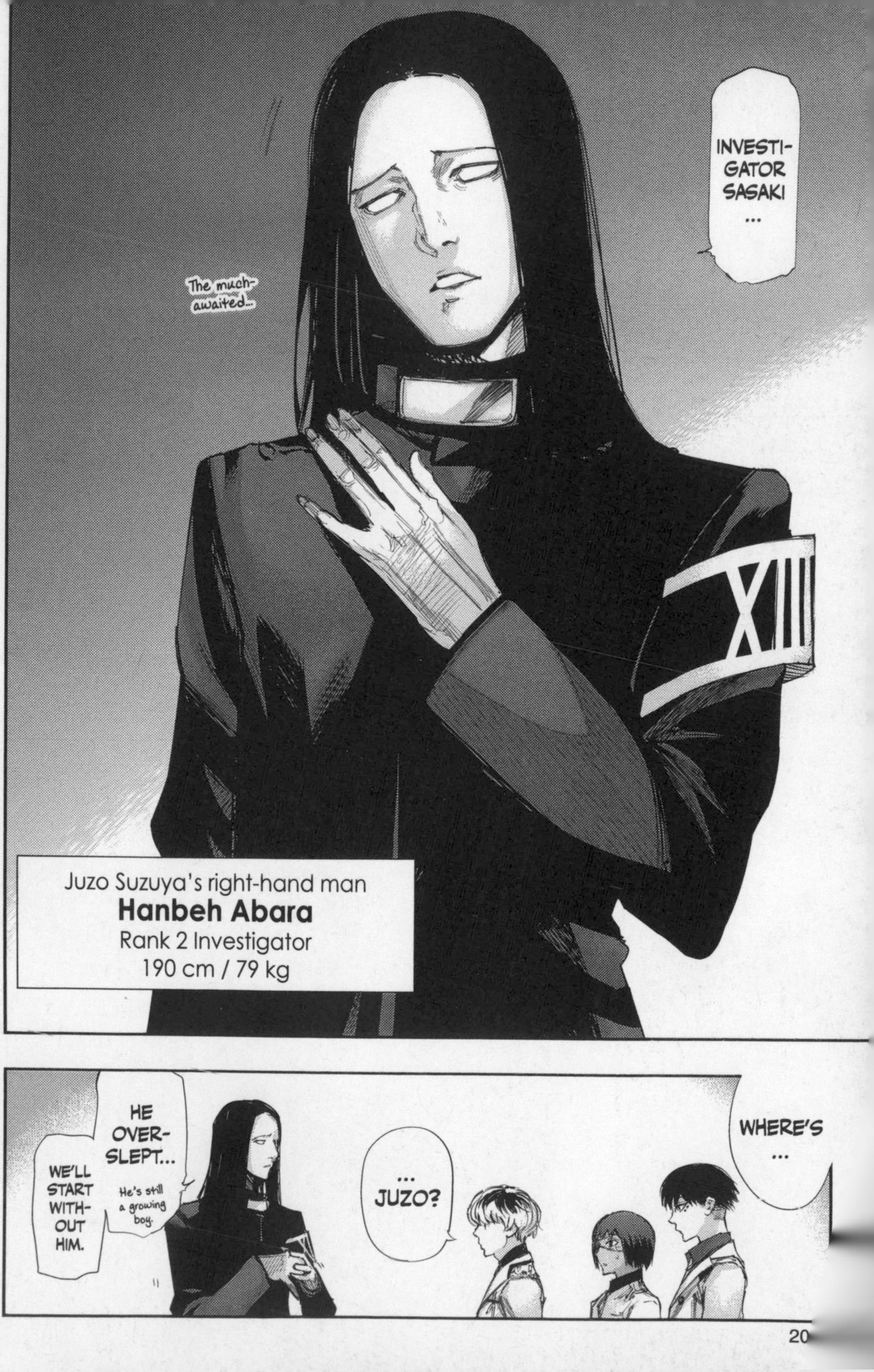
INVESTI-GATOR SASAKI ...
The much-awaited...
Juzo Suzuya's right-hand man
Hanbeh Abara
Rank 2 Investigator
190 cm / 79 kg
WHERE'S ...
... JUZO?
HE OVER-SLEPT...
He's still a growing boy.
WE'LL START WITH-OUT HIM.

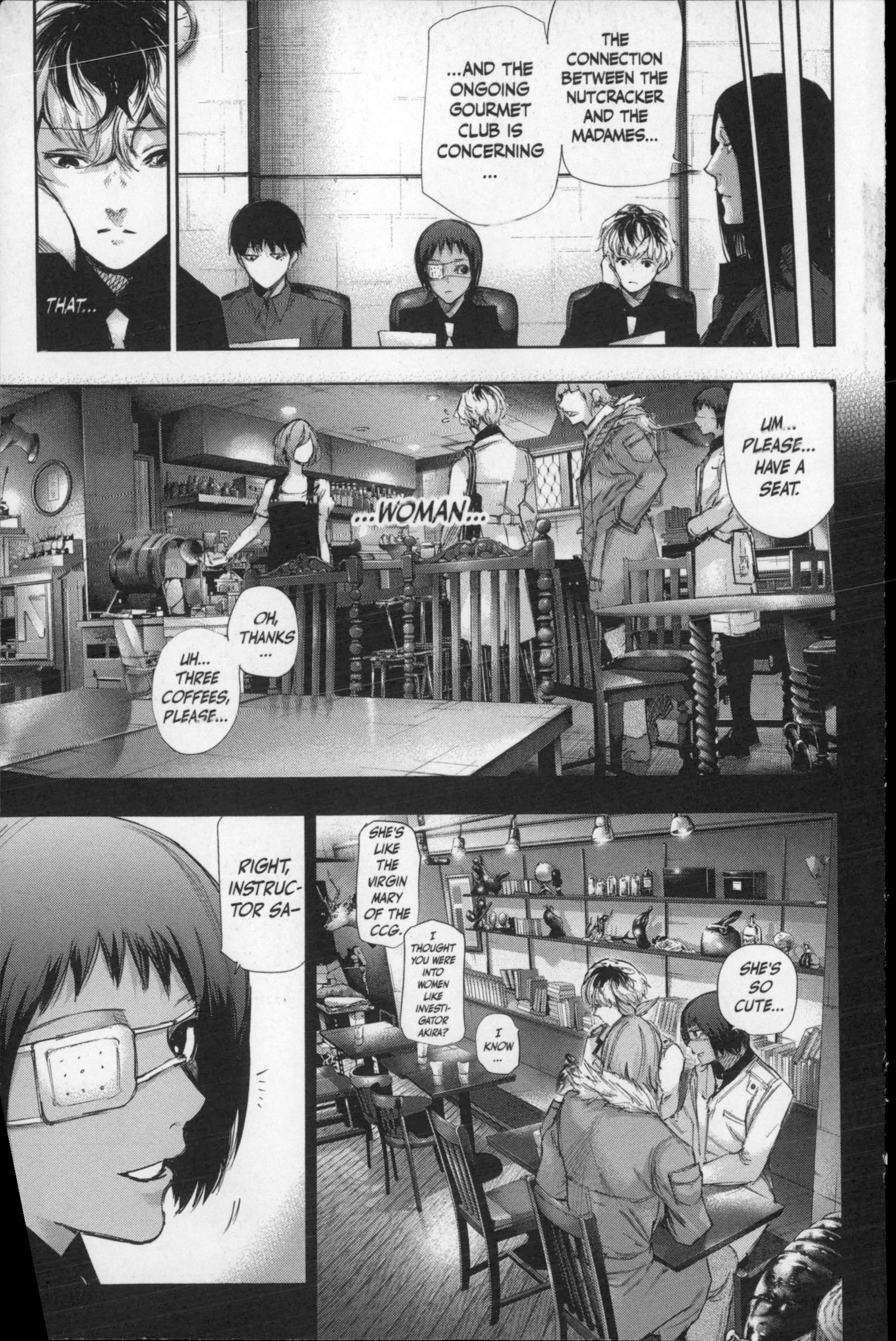
THE CONNECTION BETWEEN THE NUTCRACKER AND THE MADAMES...
...AND THE ONGOING GOURMET CLUB IS CONCERNING ...
THAT...
UM... PLEASE... HAVE A SEAT.
...WOMAN...
OH, THANKS ...
UH... THREE COFFEES, PLEASE...
SHE'S SO CUTE...
I KNOW ...
I THOUGHT YOU WERE INTO WOMEN LIKE INVESTI-GATOR AKIRA?
SHE'S LIKE THE VIRGIN MARY OF THE CCG.
RIGHT, INSTRUC-TOR SA-

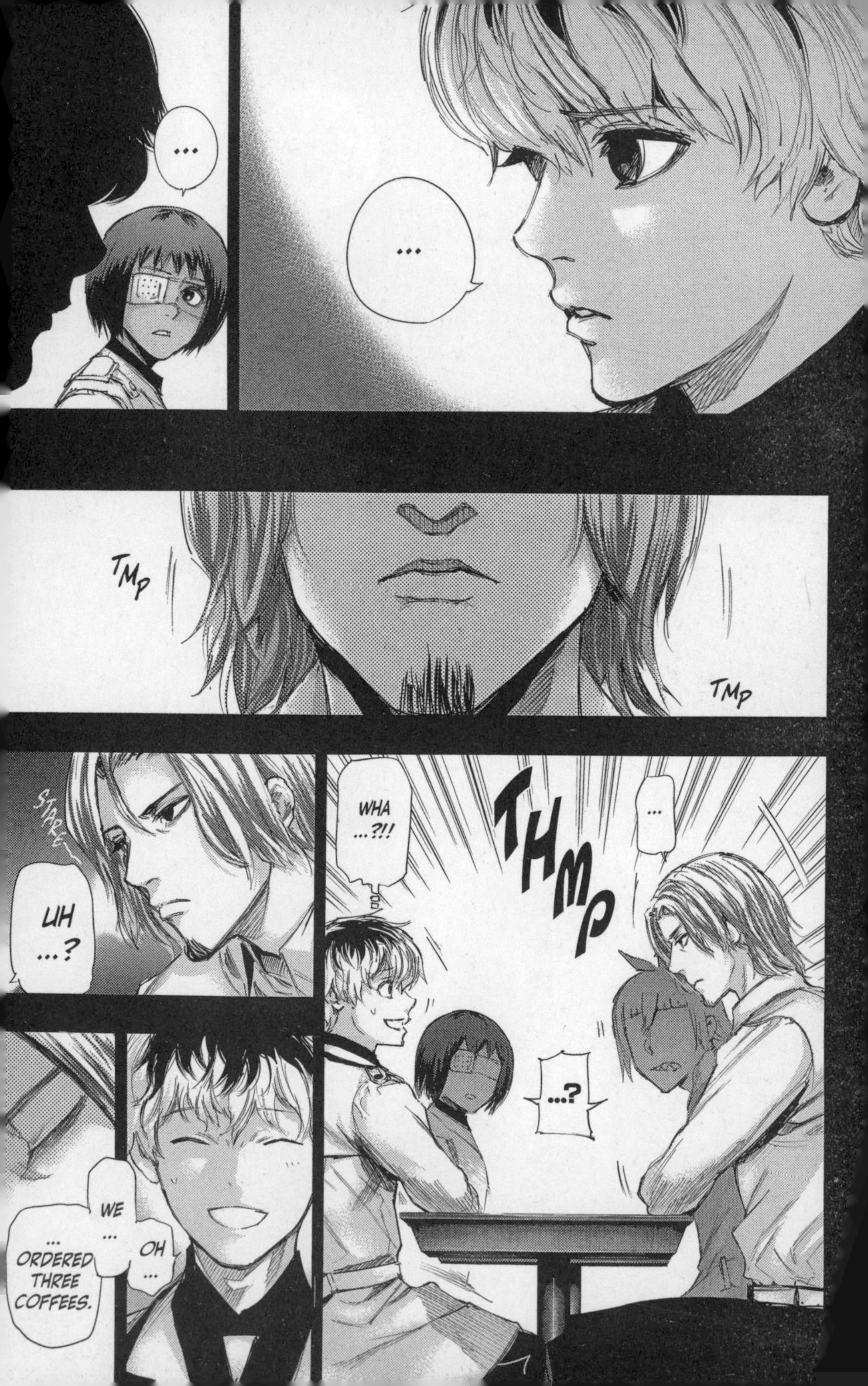
...
...
TMP
TMP
...
THMP
WHA ...?!!
...?
STARE
UH ...?
OH ...
WE ... ... ORDERED THREE COFFEES.

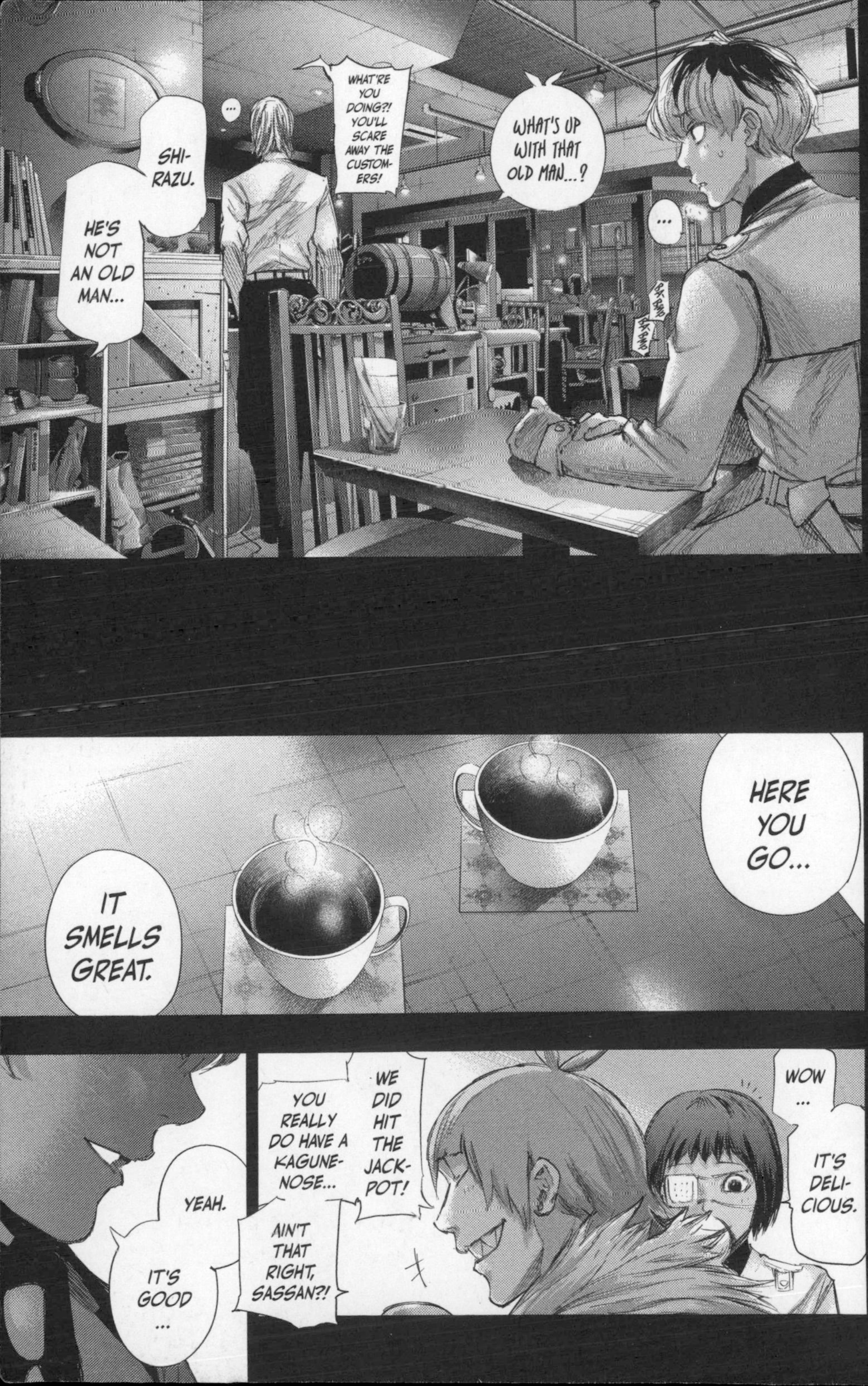
WHAT'S UP WITH THAT OLD MAN...?
...
BA-BUMP
BA-BUMP
WHAT'RE YOU DOING?! YOU'LL SCARE AWAY THE CUSTOMERS!
...
SHI-RAZU.
HE'S NOT AN OLD MAN...
HERE YOU GO...
IT SMELLS GREAT.
WOW ...
IT'S DELICIOUS.
WE DID HIT THE JACKPOT!
YOU REALLY DO HAVE A KAGUNE-NOSE...
AIN'T THAT RIGHT, SASSAN?!
YEAH.
IT'S GOOD ...

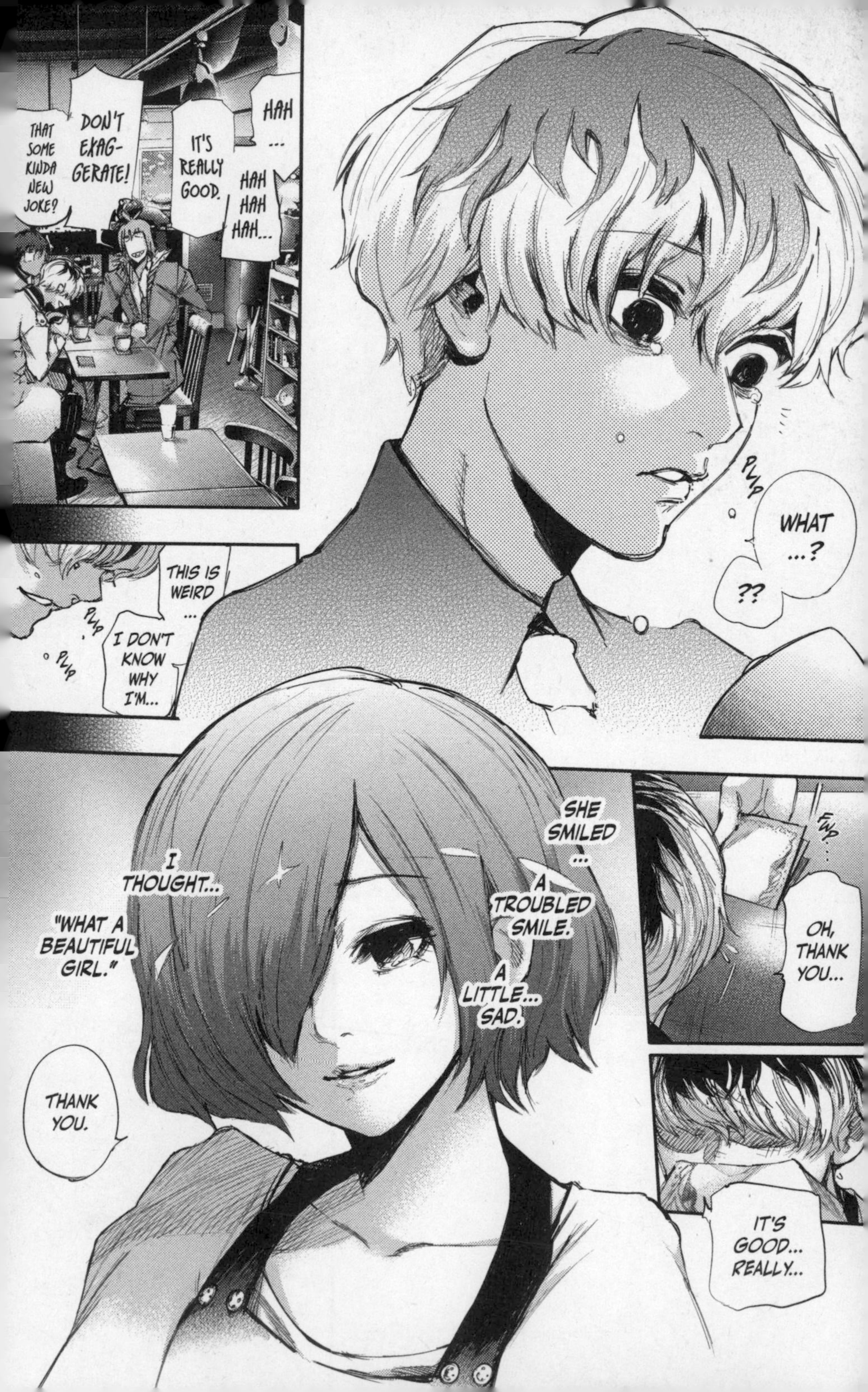
PLIP
WHAT ...?
??
HAH ... HAH HAH HAH...
IT'S REALLY GOOD.
DON'T EXAG-GERATE!
THAT SOME KINDA NEW JOKE?
THIS IS WEIRD ...
I DON'T KNOW WHY I'M...
PLIP
PLIP
FWIP...
OH, THANK YOU...
IT'S GOOD... REALLY...
SHE SMILED ...
A TROUBLED SMILE.
A LITTLE... SAD.
I THOUGHT...
"WHAT A BEAUTIFUL GIRL."
THANK YOU.

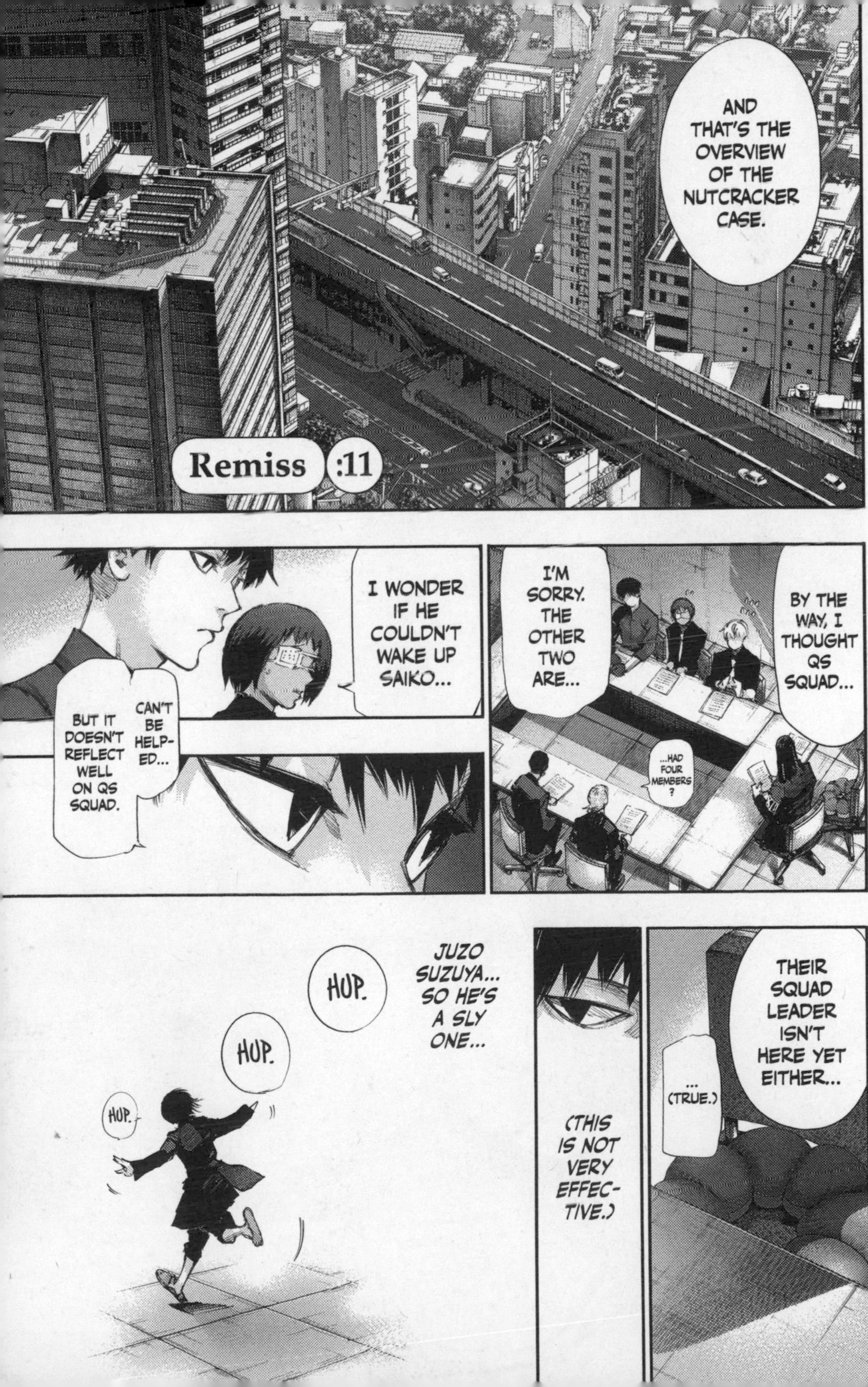AND THAT'S THE OVERVIEW OF THE NUTCRACKER CASE.
Remiss :11
BY THE WAY, I THOUGHT QS SQUAD...
...HAD FOUR MEMBERS?
I'M SORRY. THE OTHER TWO ARE...
I WONDER IF HE COULDN'T WAKE UP SAIKO...
CAN'T BE HELPED...
BUT IT DOESN'T REFLECT WELL ON QS SQUAD.
THEIR SQUAD LEADER ISN'T HERE YET EITHER...
... (TRUE.)
(THIS IS NOT VERY EFFECTIVE.)
JUZO SUZUYA... SO HE'S A SLY ONE...
HUP.
HUP.
HUP.

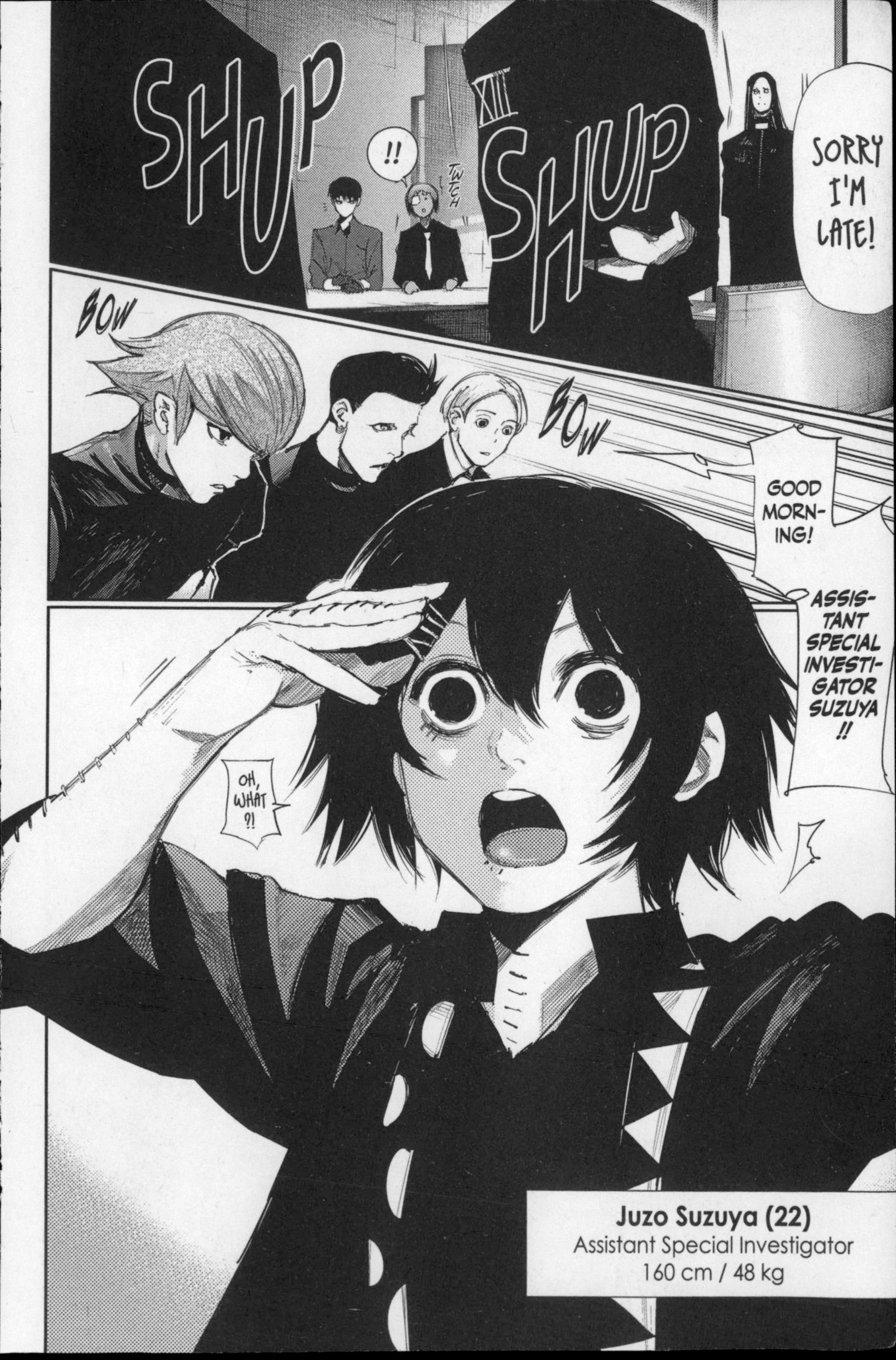
SORRY I'M LATE!
SHUP
!!
TWITCH
SHUP
BOW
GOOD MORNING!
BOW
ASSISTANT SPECIAL INVESTIGATOR SUZUYA!!
OH, WHAT?!
Juzo Suzuya (22)
Assistant Special Investigator
160 cm / 48 kg

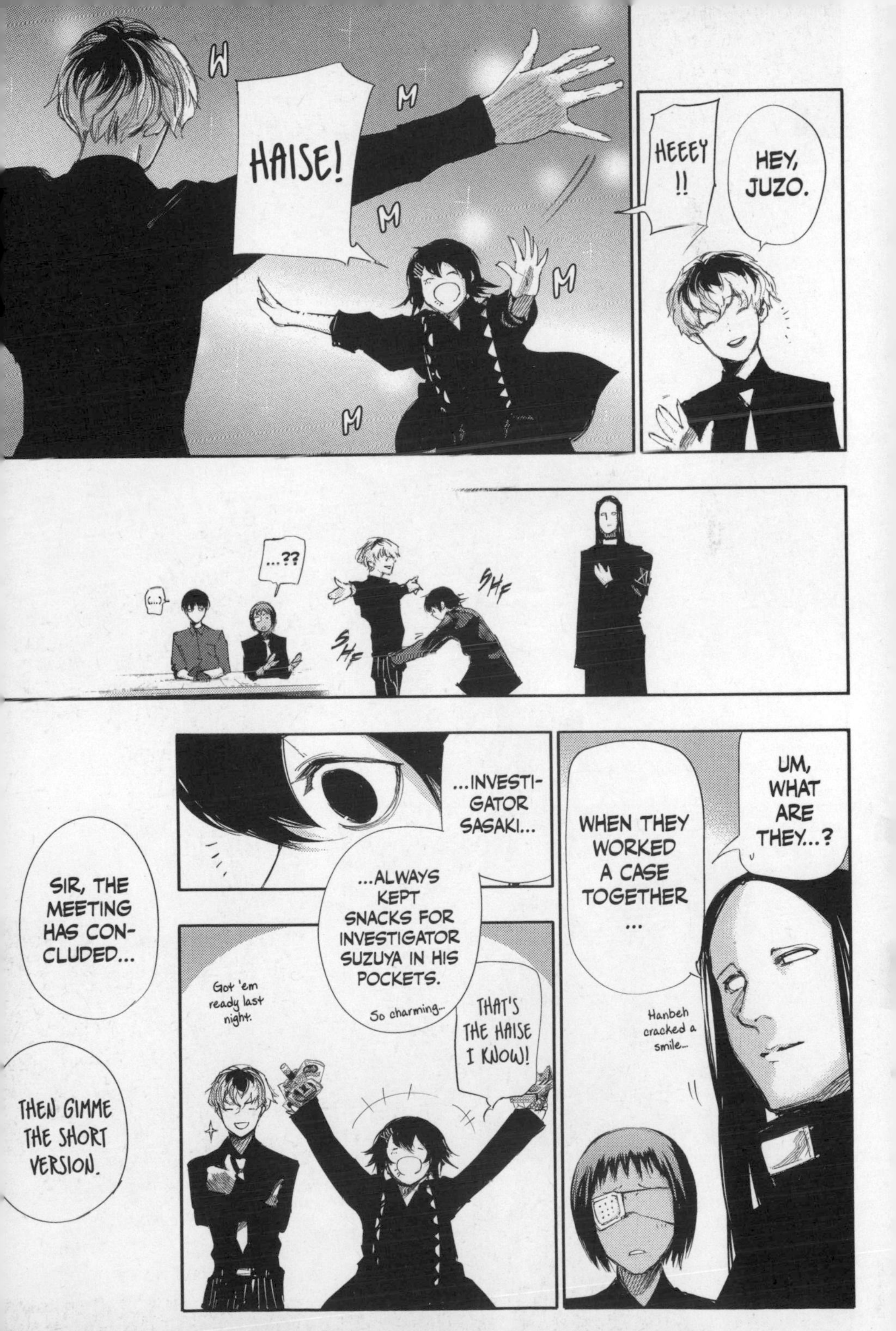
HEY, JUZO.
HEEEY !!
HAISE!
W
M
M
M
M
SHF
SHF
...??
(...)
UM, WHAT ARE THEY...?
WHEN THEY WORKED A CASE TOGETHER ...
Hanbeh cracked a smile...
...INVESTI-GATOR SASAKI...
...ALWAYS KEPT SNACKS FOR INVESTIGATOR SUZUYA IN HIS POCKETS.
So charming...
THAT'S THE HAISE I KNOW!
Got 'em ready last night.
SIR, THE MEETING HAS CON-CLUDED...
THEN GIMME THE SHORT VERSION.

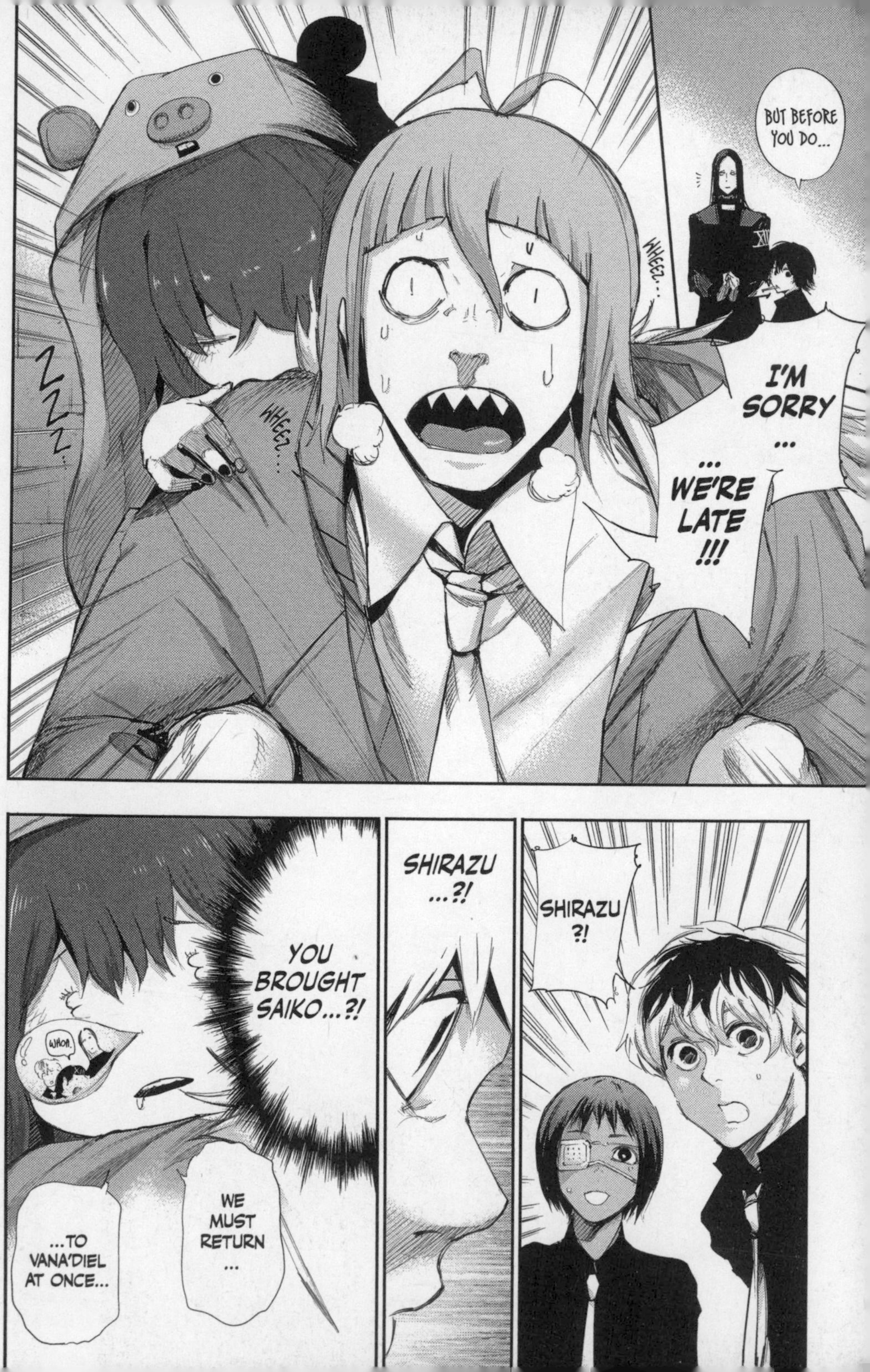
BUT BEFORE YOU DO...
WHEEZ...
I'M SORRY ...
... WE'RE LATE !!!
WHEEZ...
ZZZ...
SHIRAZU ?!
SHIRAZU ...?!
YOU BROUGHT SAIKO...?!
WE MUST RETURN ...
...TO VANA'DIEL AT ONCE...

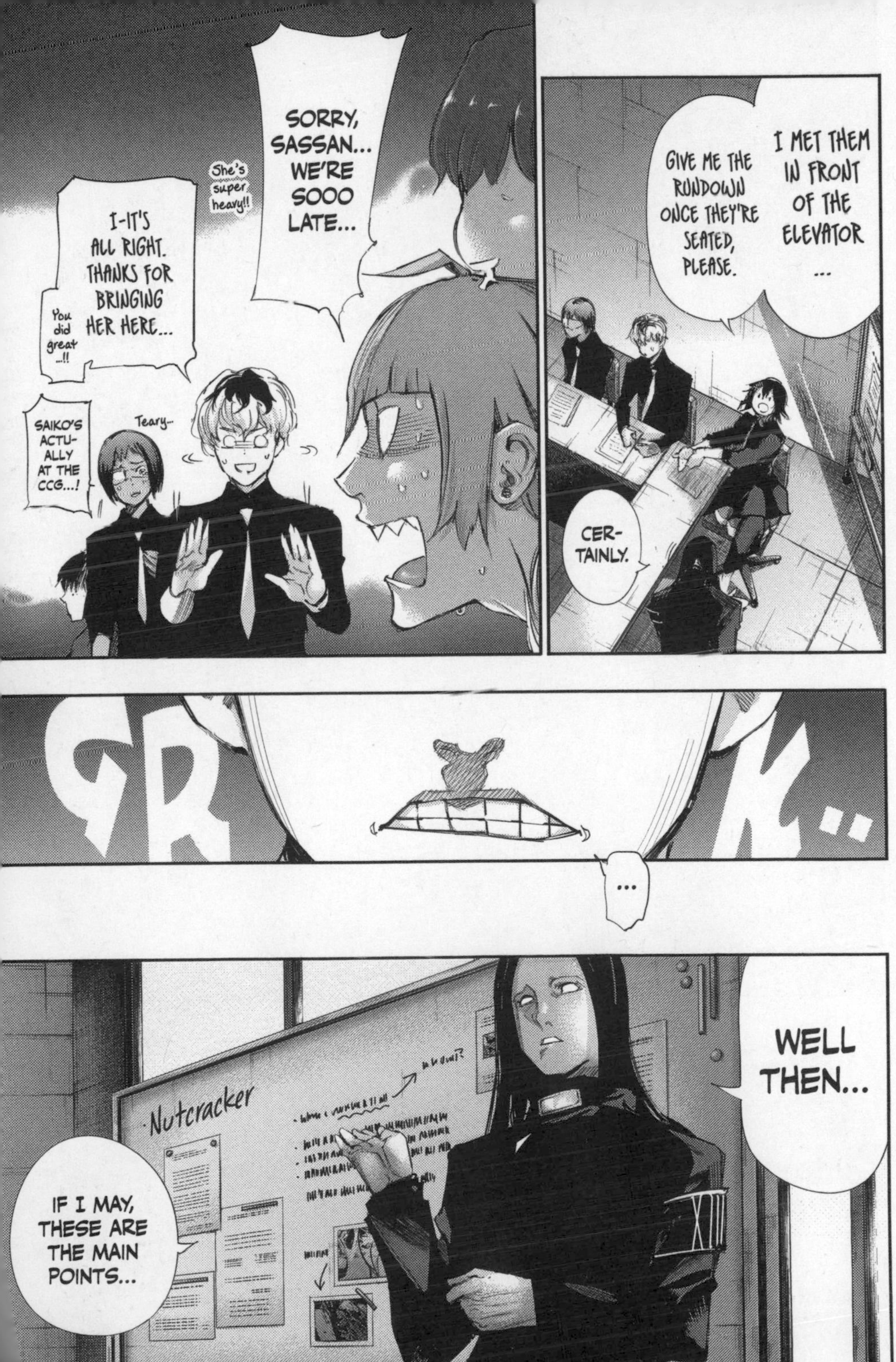
I MET THEM IN FRONT OF THE ELEVATOR ...
GIVE ME THE RUNDOWN ONCE THEY'RE SEATED, PLEASE.
CER-TAINLY.
SORRY, SASSAN... WE'RE SOOO LATE...
She's super heavy!!
I-IT'S ALL RIGHT. THANKS FOR BRINGING HER HERE...
You did great ...!!
Teary...
SAIKO'S ACTU-ALLY AT THE CCG...!
GR... K...
...
WELL THEN...
Nutcracker
IF I MAY, THESE ARE THE MAIN POINTS...

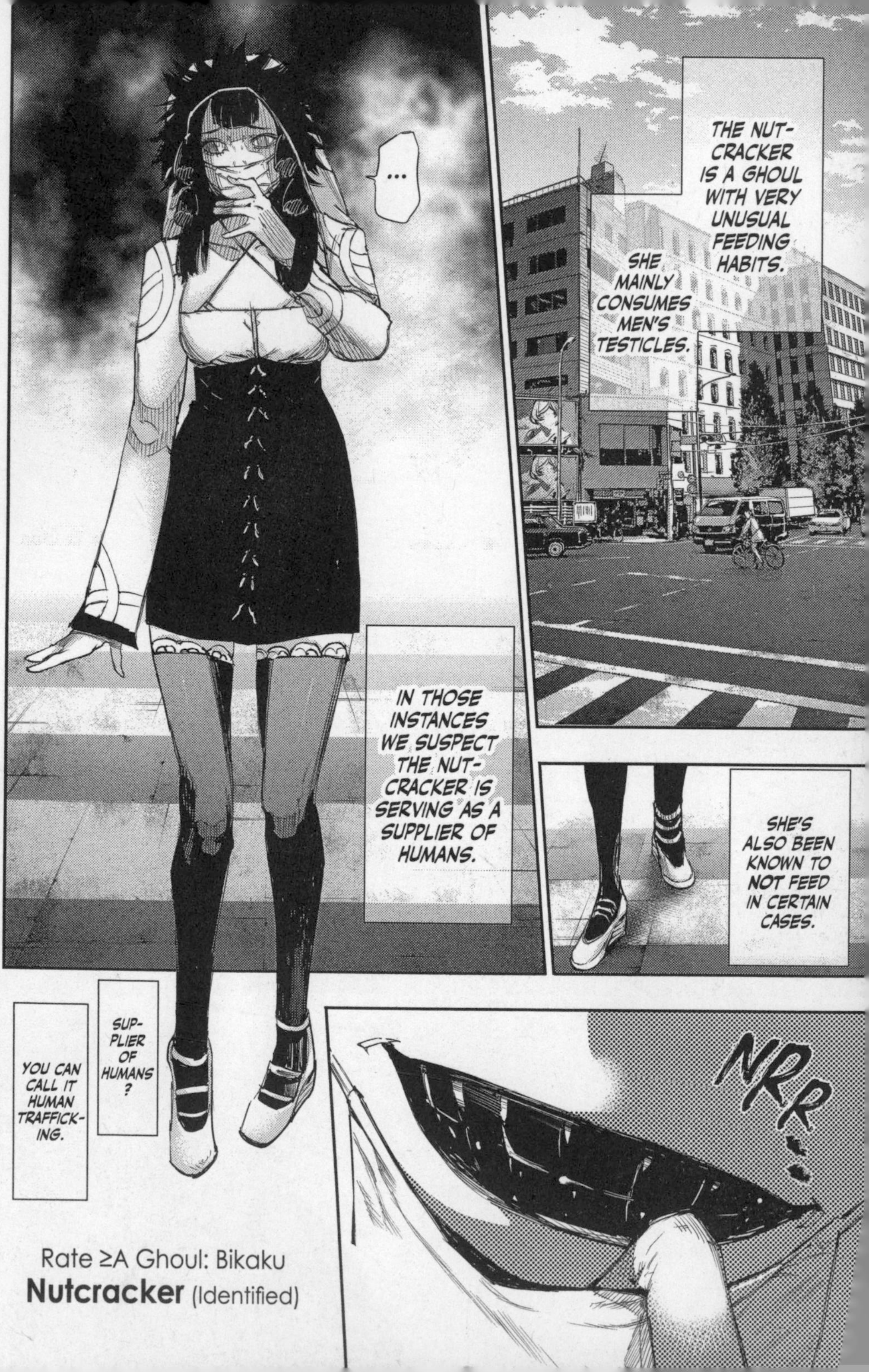
THE NUT-CRACKER IS A GHOUL WITH VERY UNUSUAL FEEDING HABITS.
SHE MAINLY CONSUMES MEN'S TESTICLES.
SHE'S ALSO BEEN KNOWN TO NOT FEED IN CERTAIN CASES.
...
IN THOSE INSTANCES WE SUSPECT THE NUT-CRACKER IS SERVING AS A SUPPLIER OF HUMANS.
NRR
SUP-PLIER OF HUMANS?
YOU CAN CALL IT HUMAN TRAFFICK-ING.
Rate ≥A Ghoul: Bikaku
Nutcracker (Identified)

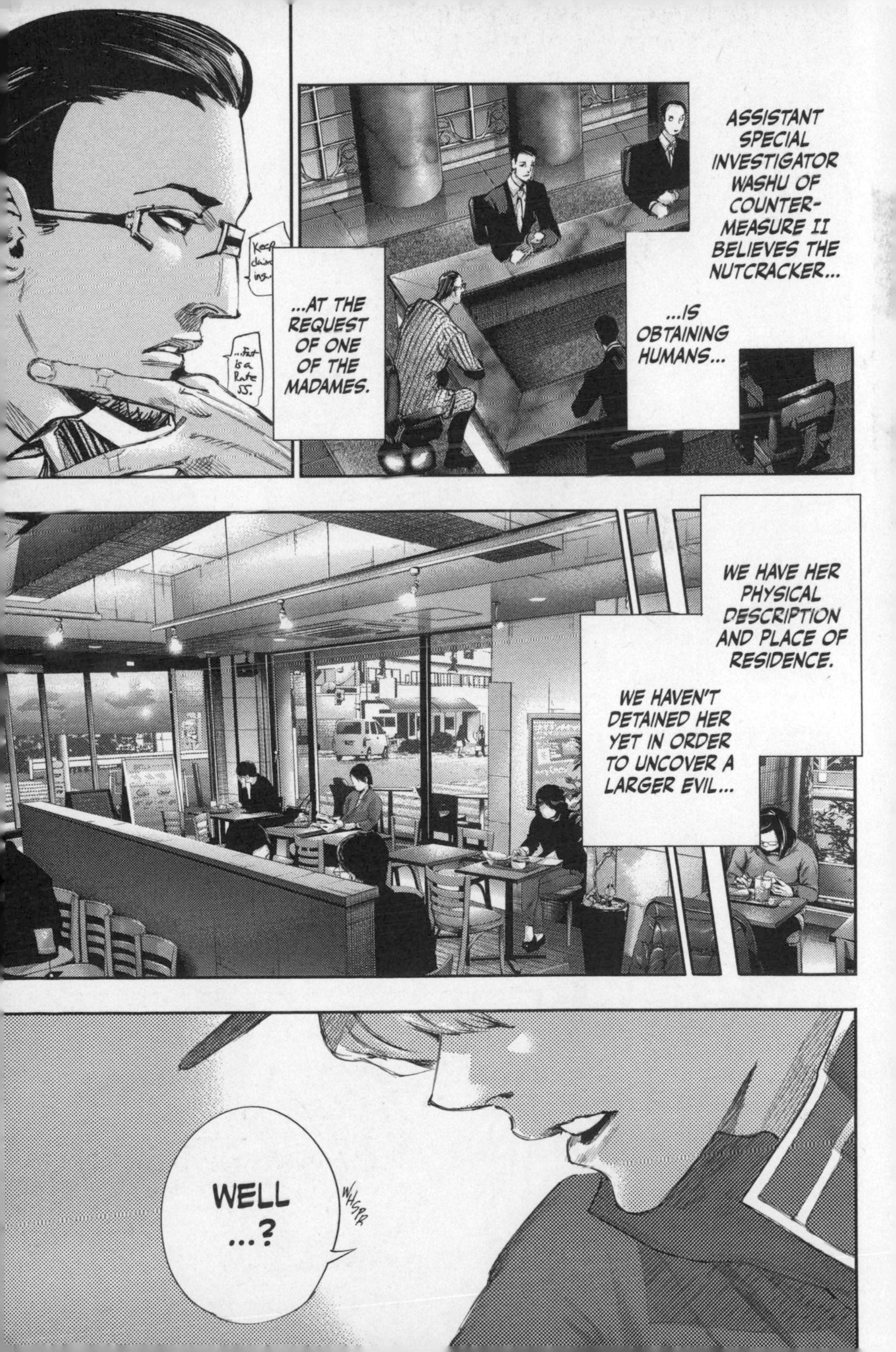

ASSISTANT SPECIAL INVESTIGATOR WASHU OF COUNTER-MEASURE II BELIEVES THE NUTCRACKER...
...IS OBTAINING HUMANS...
...AT THE REQUEST OF ONE OF THE MADAMES.
Keep claim ings...
...Fast is a Rate SS.
WE HAVE HER PHYSICAL DESCRIPTION AND PLACE OF RESIDENCE.
WE HAVEN'T DETAINED HER YET IN ORDER TO UNCOVER A LARGER EVIL...
WELL ...?
WHSPR

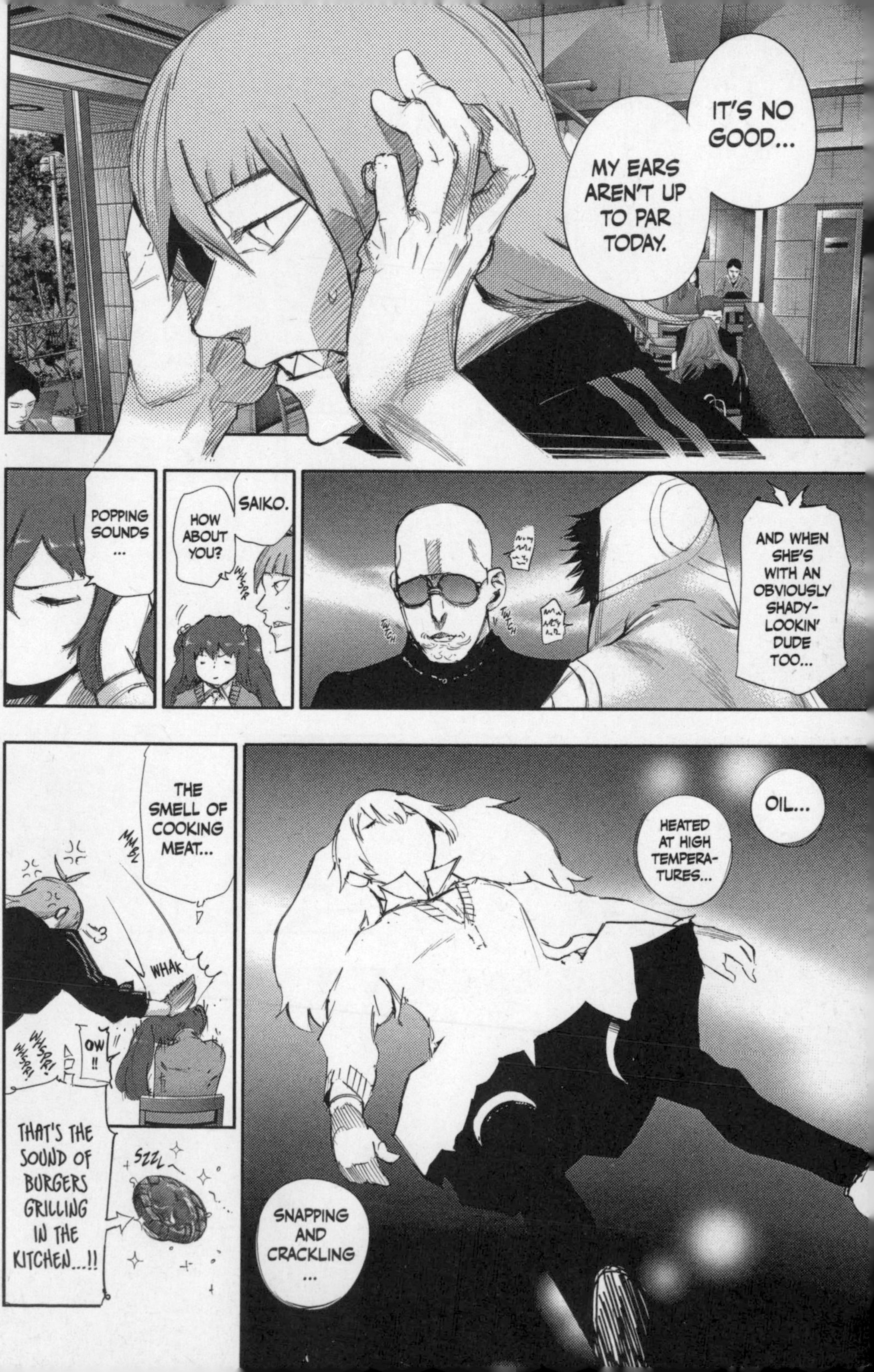
IT'S NO GOOD...
MY EARS AREN'T UP TO PAR TODAY.
AND WHEN SHE'S WITH AN OBVIOUSLY SHADY-LOOKIN' DUDE TOO...
TWITCH
TWITCH
SAIKO.
HOW ABOUT YOU?
WHSPR
POPPING SOUNDS ...
OIL...
HEATED AT HIGH TEMPERA-TURES...
SNAPPING AND CRACKLING ...
THE SMELL OF COOKING MEAT...
MMBL
WHAK
OW !!
WHSPR! WHSPR!
THAT'S THE SOUND OF BURGERS GRILLING IN THE KITCHEN...!!
SZZL

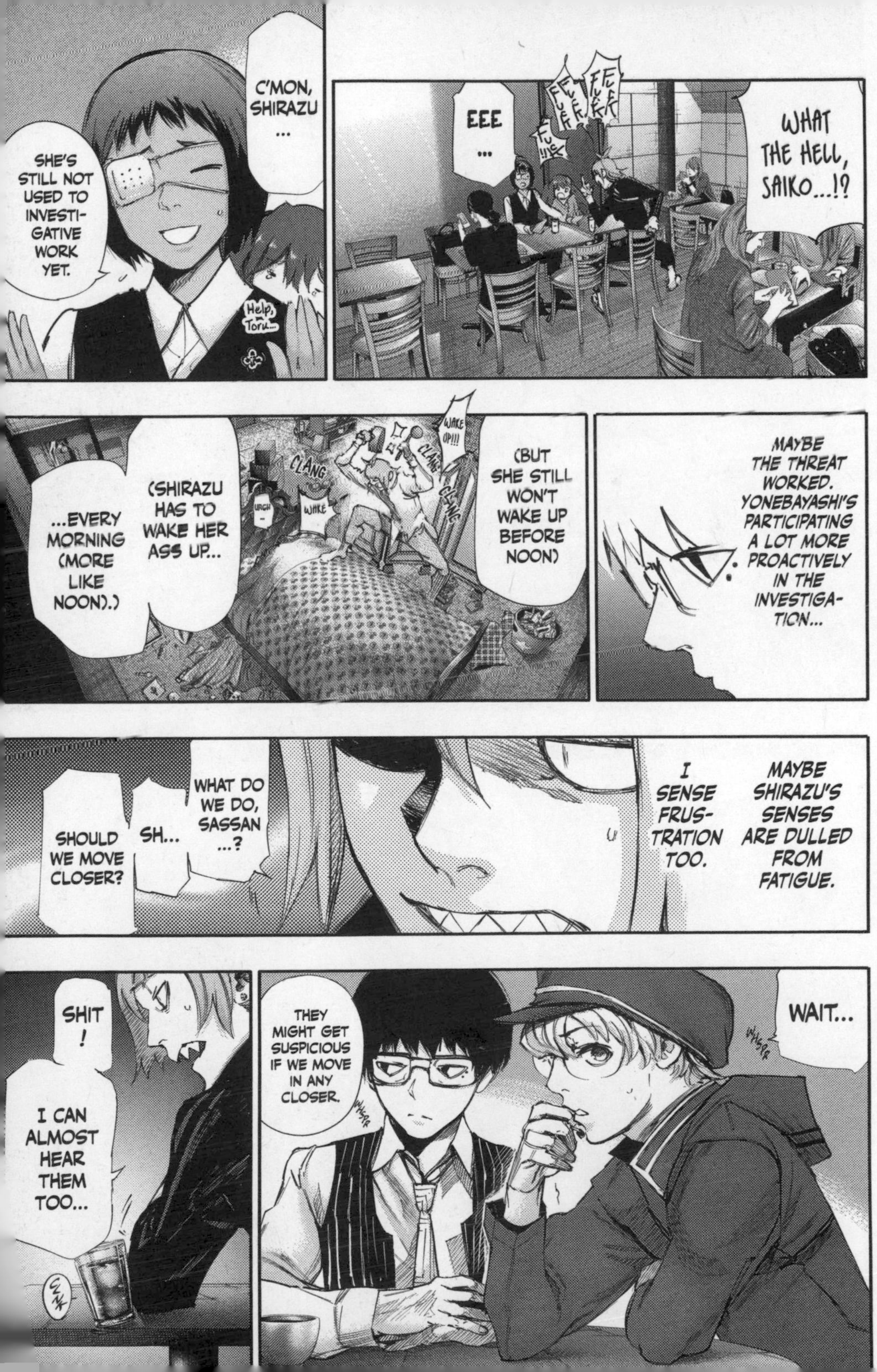
WHAT THE HELL, SAIKO...!?
EEE ...
C'MON, SHIRAZU ...
SHE'S STILL NOT USED TO INVESTI-GATIVE WORK YET.
Help, Toru...
MAYBE THE THREAT WORKED. YONEBAYASHI'S PARTICIPATING A LOT MORE PROACTIVELY IN THE INVESTIGA-TION...
(BUT SHE STILL WON'T WAKE UP BEFORE NOON)
WAKE UP!!!
CLANG
CLANG
CLANG
CLANG
WAKE
URGH
(SHIRAZU HAS TO WAKE HER ASS UP...
...EVERY MORNING (MORE LIKE NOON).)
MAYBE SHIRAZU'S SENSES ARE DULLED FROM FATIGUE.
I SENSE FRUS-TRATION TOO.
WHAT DO WE DO, SASSAN ...?
SH...
SHOULD WE MOVE CLOSER?
WAIT...
THEY MIGHT GET SUSPICIOUS IF WE MOVE IN ANY CLOSER.
SHIT!
I CAN ALMOST HEAR THEM TOO...

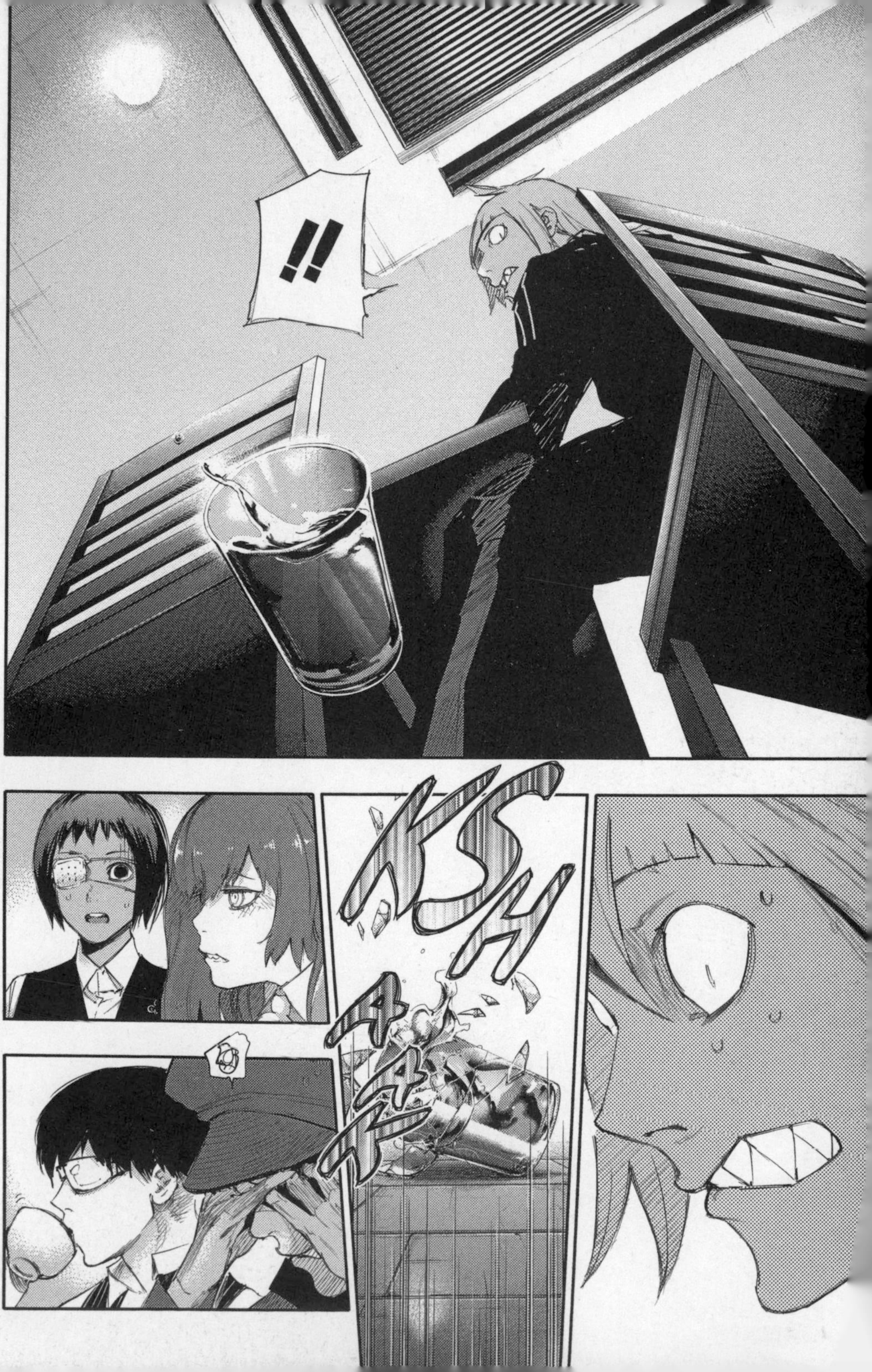
!!
KSH
AAK

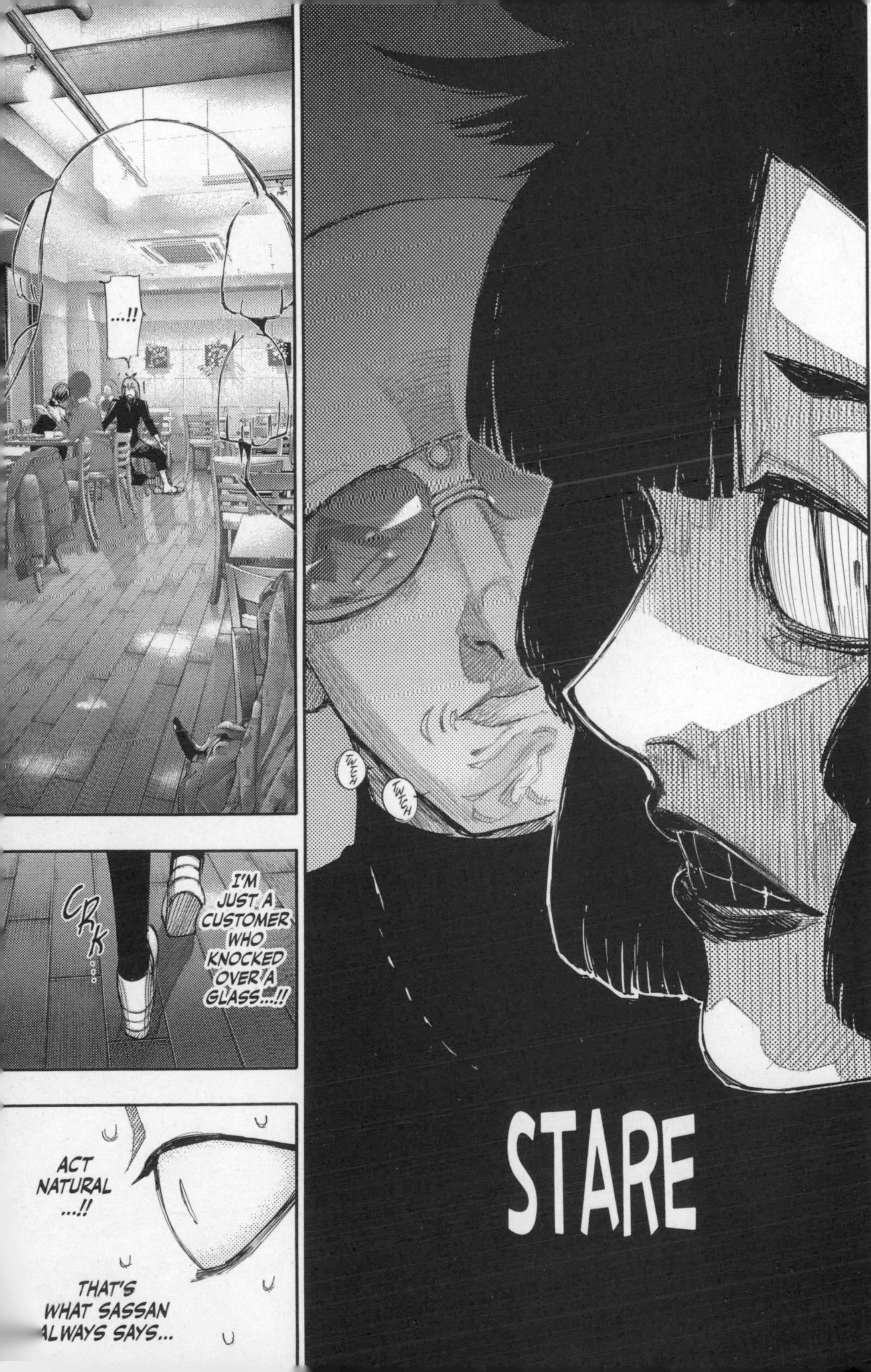
STARE
...!!
I'M JUST A CUSTOMER WHO KNOCKED OVER A GLASS...!!
CRK...
ACT NATURAL ...!!
THAT'S WHAT SASSAN ALWAYS SAYS...

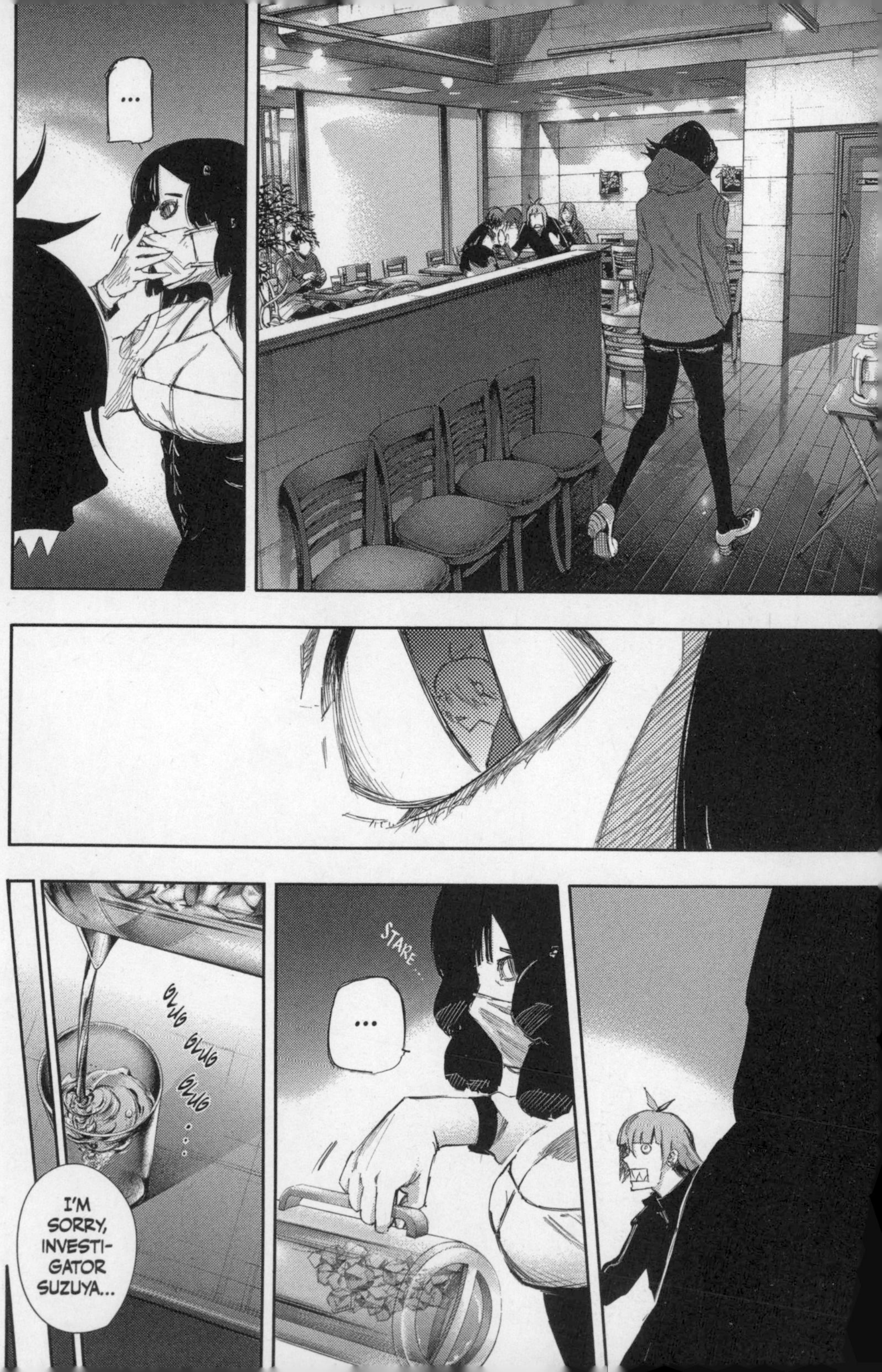
...
STARE...
...
GLUG GLUG GLUG...
I'M SORRY, INVESTIGATOR SUZUYA...

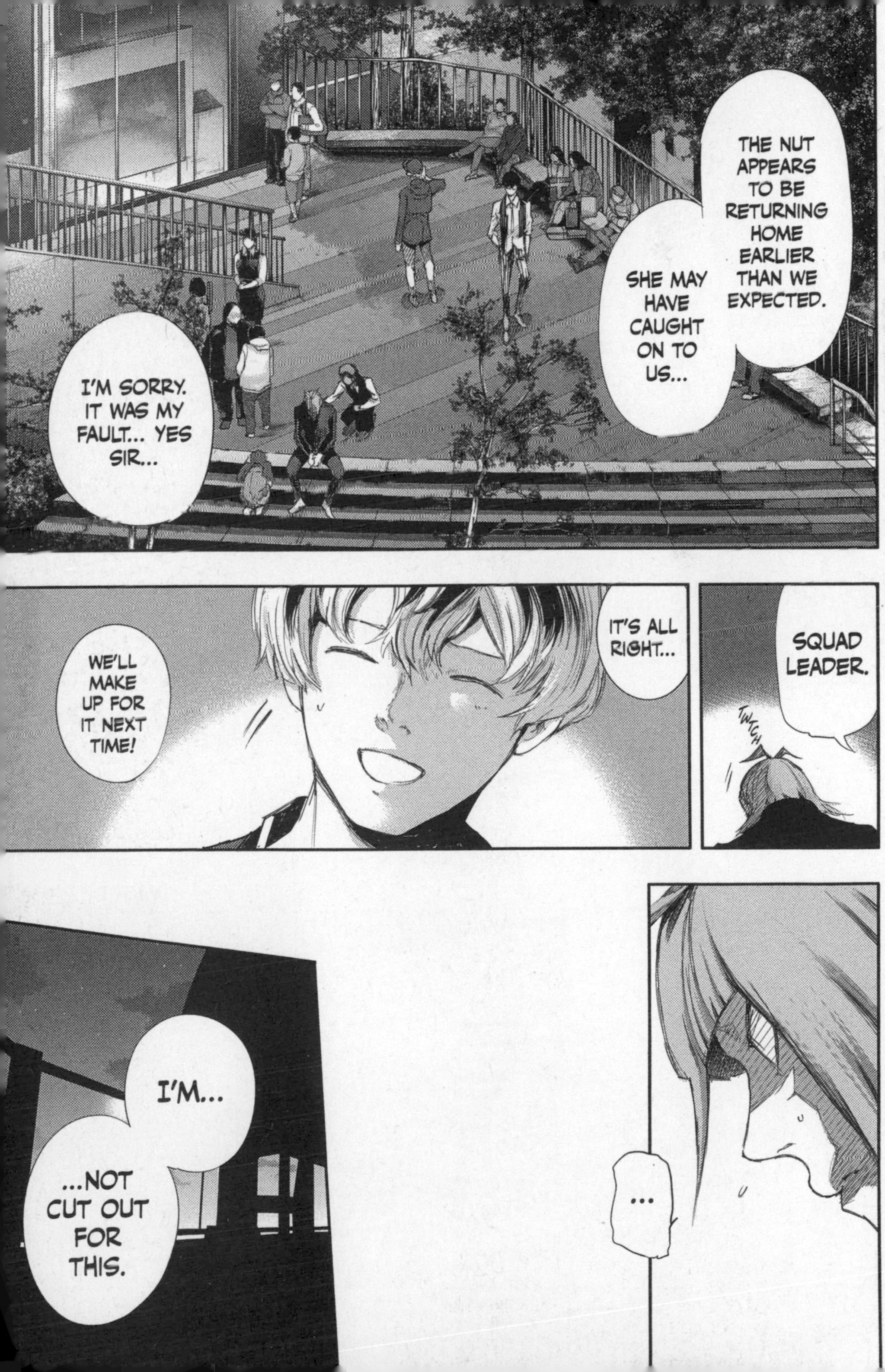
THE NUT APPEARS TO BE RETURNING HOME EARLIER THAN WE EXPECTED.
SHE MAY HAVE CAUGHT ON TO US...
I'M SORRY. IT WAS MY FAULT... YES SIR...
SQUAD LEADER.
TWITCH
IT'S ALL RIGHT...
WE'LL MAKE UP FOR IT NEXT TIME!
...
I'M...
...NOT CUT OUT FOR THIS.

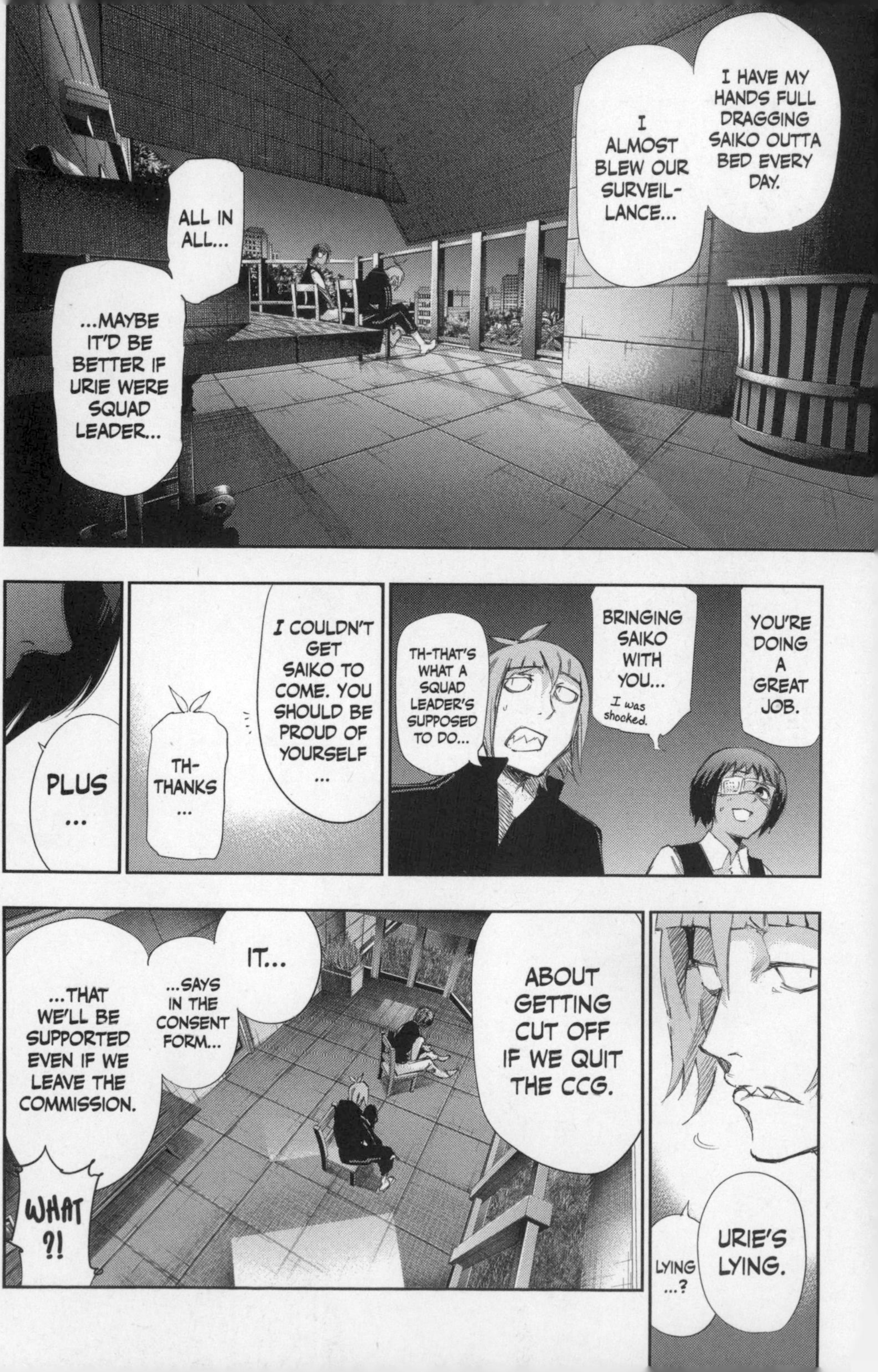
I HAVE MY HANDS FULL DRAGGING SAIKO OUTTA BED EVERY DAY.
I ALMOST BLEW OUR SURVEIL-LANCE...
ALL IN ALL...
...MAYBE IT'D BE BETTER IF URIE WERE SQUAD LEADER...
YOU'RE DOING A GREAT JOB.
BRINGING SAIKO WITH YOU...
I was shocked.
TH-THAT'S WHAT A SQUAD LEADER'S SUPPOSED TO DO...
I COULDN'T GET SAIKO TO COME. YOU SHOULD BE PROUD OF YOURSELF...
TH-THANKS...
PLUS...
URIE'S LYING.
LYING...?
ABOUT GETTING CUT OFF IF WE QUIT THE CCG.
IT...
...SAYS IN THE CONSENT FORM...
...THAT WE'LL BE SUPPORTED EVEN IF WE LEAVE THE COMMISSION.
WHAT?!

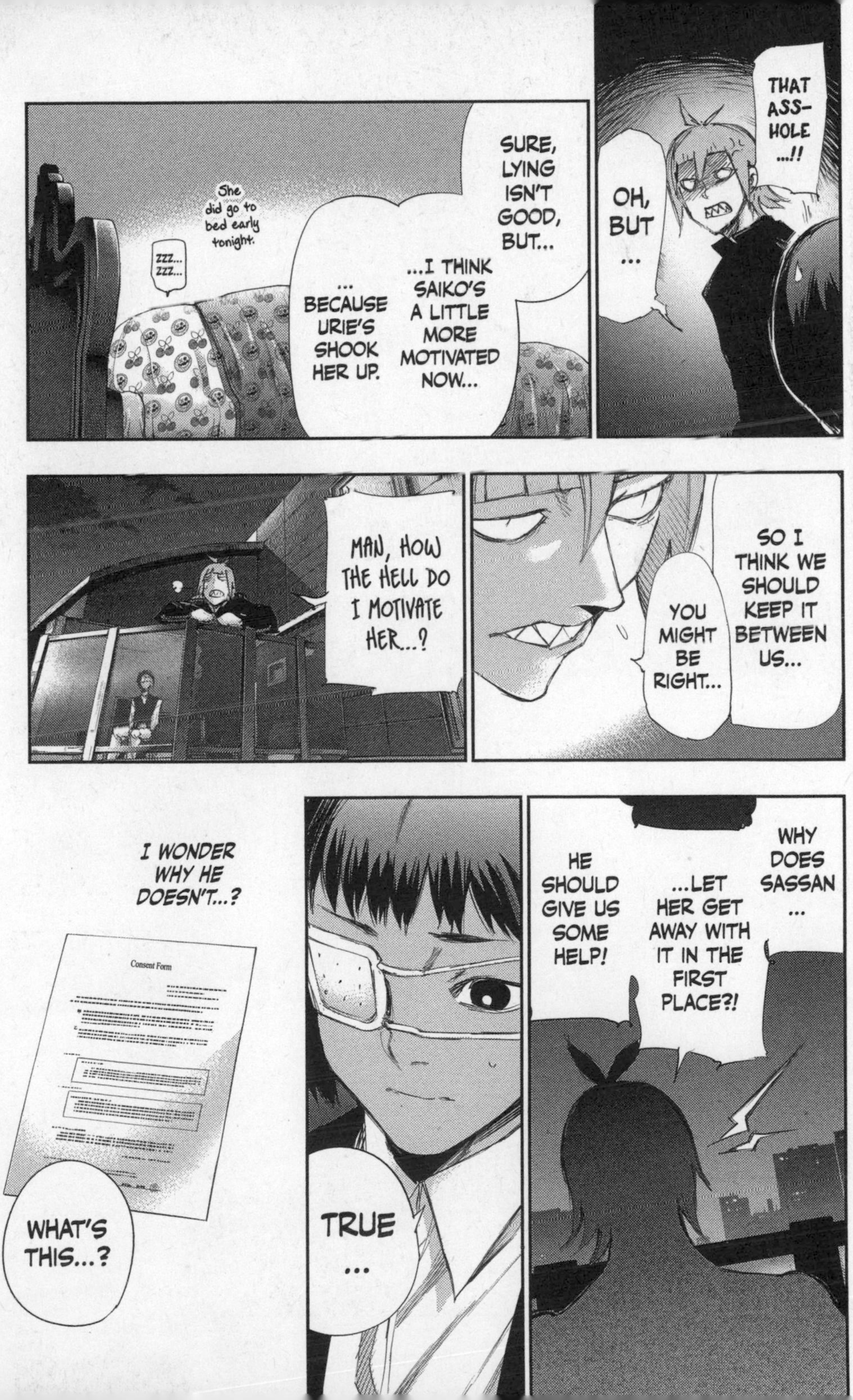
THAT ASS-HOLE ...!!
OH, BUT ...
SURE, LYING ISN'T GOOD, BUT...
...I THINK SAIKO'S A LITTLE MORE MOTIVATED NOW...
...BECAUSE URIE'S SHOOK HER UP.
She did go to bed early tonight.
zzz... zzz...
SO I THINK WE SHOULD KEEP IT BETWEEN US...
YOU MIGHT BE RIGHT...
MAN, HOW THE HELL DO I MOTIVATE HER...?
WHY DOES SASSAN ...
...LET HER GET AWAY WITH IT IN THE FIRST PLACE?!
HE SHOULD GIVE US SOME HELP!
TRUE ...
I WONDER WHY HE DOESN'T...?
Consent Form
WHAT'S THIS...?

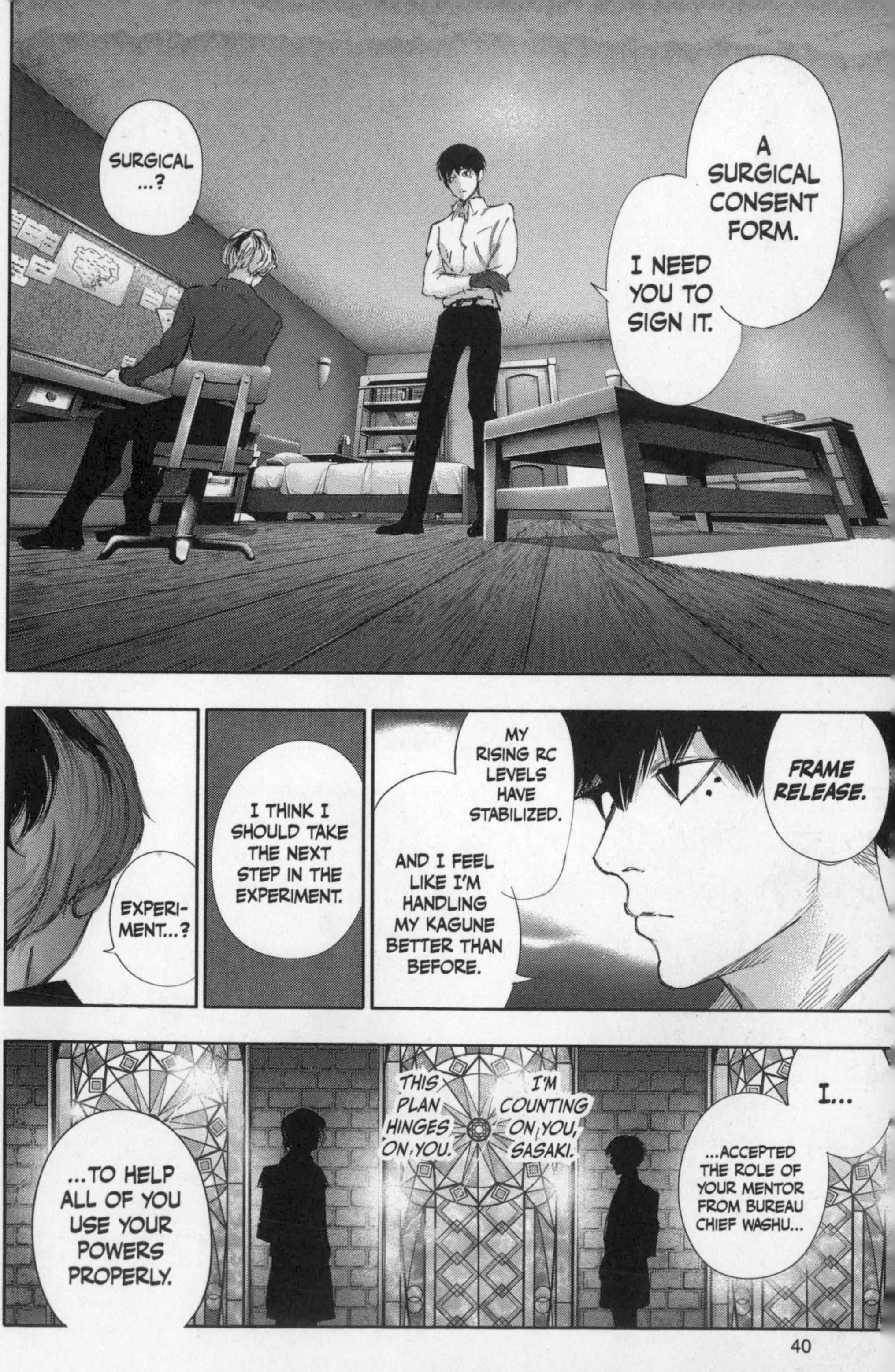
A SURGICAL CONSENT FORM.
I NEED YOU TO SIGN IT.
SURGICAL ...?
FRAME RELEASE.
MY RISING RC LEVELS HAVE STABILIZED.
AND I FEEL LIKE I'M HANDLING MY KAGUNE BETTER THAN BEFORE.
I THINK I SHOULD TAKE THE NEXT STEP IN THE EXPERIMENT.
EXPERI-MENT...?
I...
...ACCEPTED THE ROLE OF YOUR MENTOR FROM BUREAU CHIEF WASHU...
I'M COUNTING ON YOU, SASAKI.
THIS PLAN HINGES ON YOU.
...TO HELP ALL OF YOU USE YOUR POWERS PROPERLY.

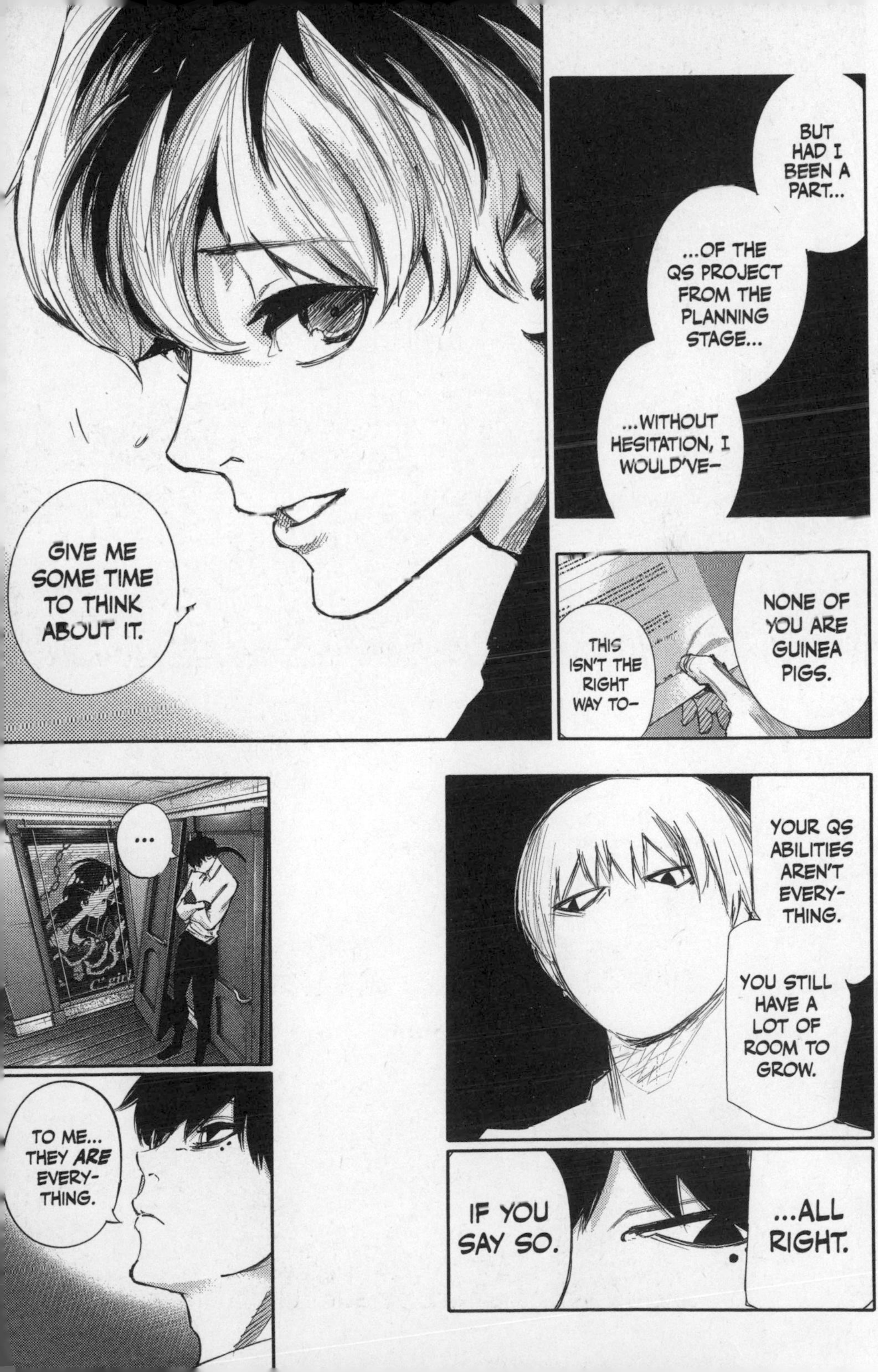
BUT HAD I BEEN A PART...
...OF THE QS PROJECT FROM THE PLANNING STAGE...
...WITHOUT HESITATION, I WOULD'VE–
NONE OF YOU ARE GUINEA PIGS.
THIS ISN'T THE RIGHT WAY TO–
GIVE ME SOME TIME TO THINK ABOUT IT.
YOUR QS ABILITIES AREN'T EVERYTHING.
YOU STILL HAVE A LOT OF ROOM TO GROW.
...ALL RIGHT.
IF YOU SAY SO.
...
TO ME... THEY *ARE* EVERYTHING.

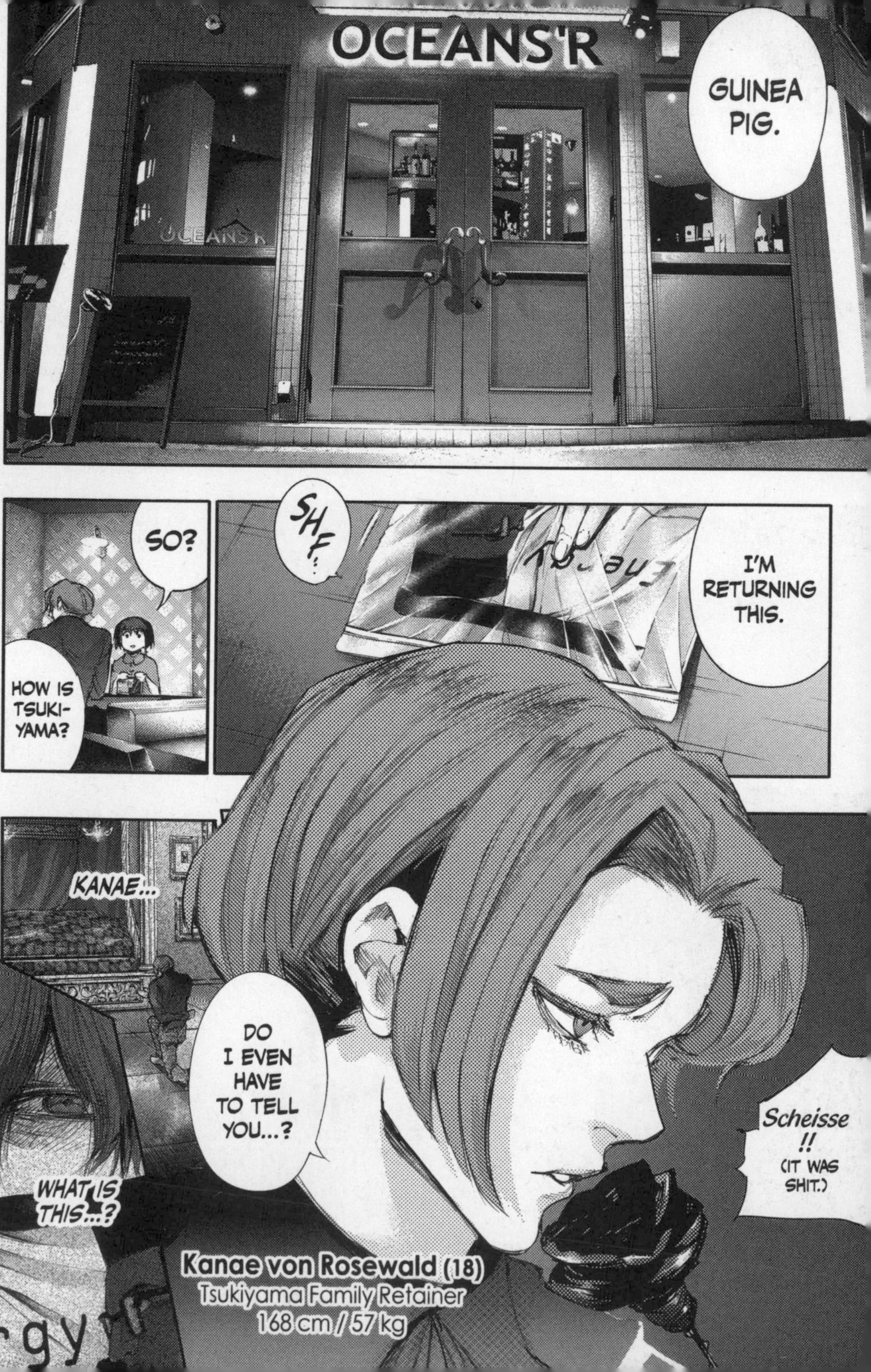
OCEANS'R
GUINEA PIG.
SHF..
I'M RETURNING THIS.
SO?
HOW IS TSUKIYAMA?
Scheisse!! (IT WAS SHIT.)
DO I EVEN HAVE TO TELL YOU...?
Kanae von Rosewald (18)
Tsukiyama Family Retainer
168 cm / 57 kg
KANAE...
WHAT IS THIS...?

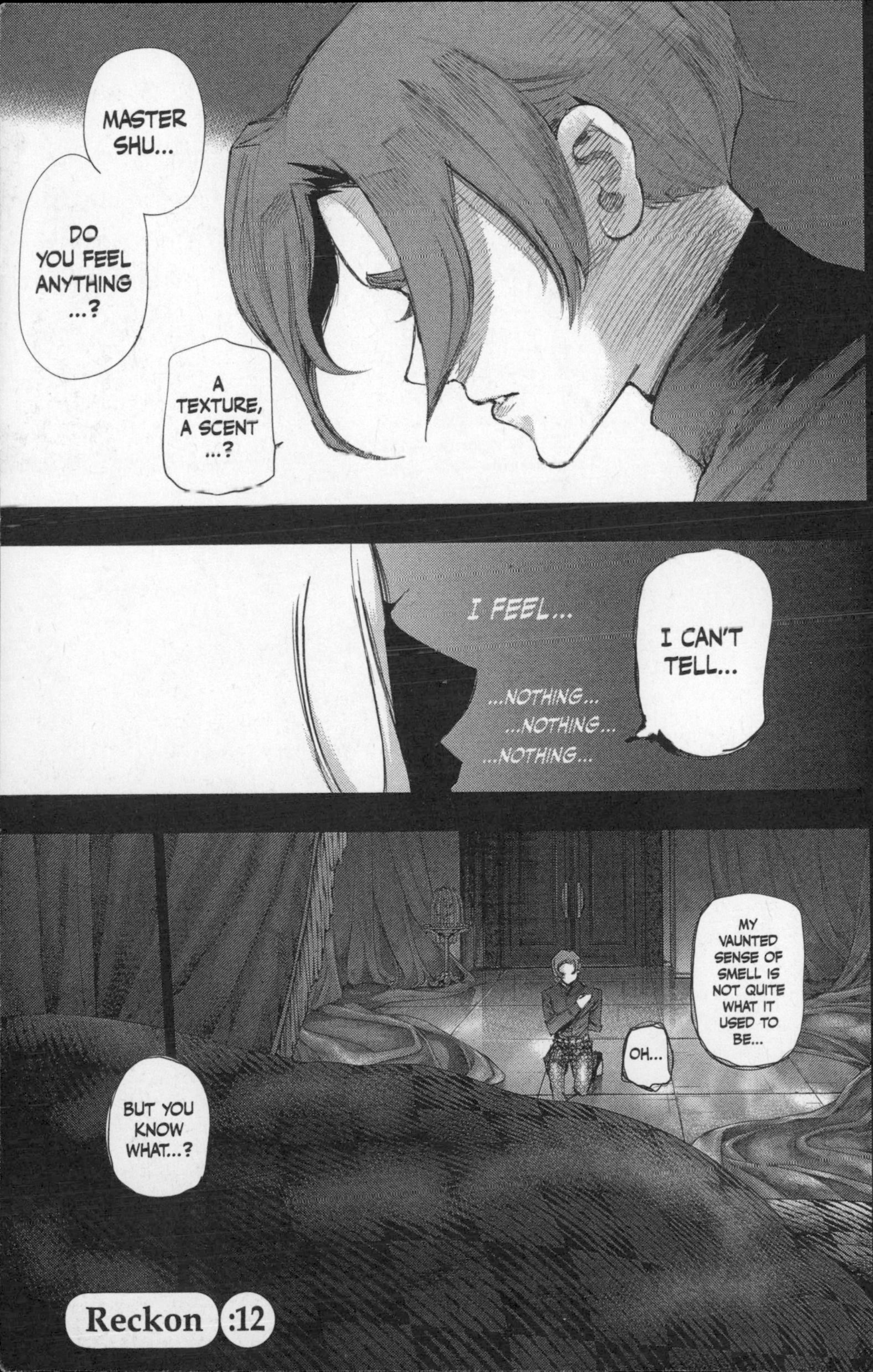
MASTER SHU...
DO YOU FEEL ANYTHING ...?
A TEXTURE, A SCENT ...?
I CAN'T TELL...
I FEEL...
...NOTHING...
...NOTHING...
...NOTHING...
MY VAUNTED SENSE OF SMELL IS NOT QUITE WHAT IT USED TO BE...
OH...
BUT YOU KNOW WHAT...?
Reckon :12

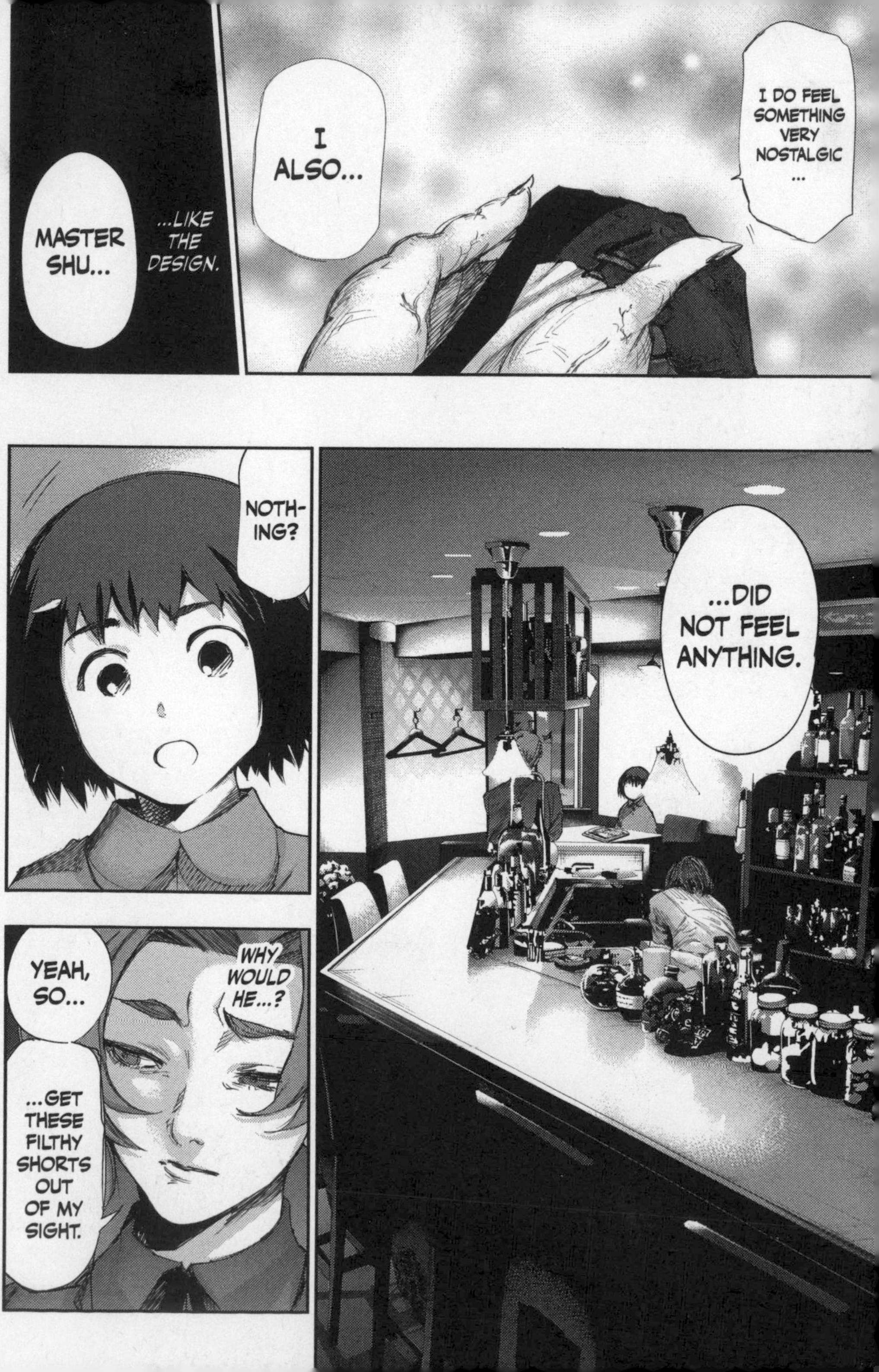
I DO FEEL SOMETHING VERY NOSTALGIC ...
I ALSO...
...LIKE THE DESIGN.
MASTER SHU...
...DID NOT FEEL ANYTHING.
NOTH-ING?
WHY WOULD HE...?
YEAH, SO...
...GET THESE FILTHY SHORTS OUT OF MY SIGHT.

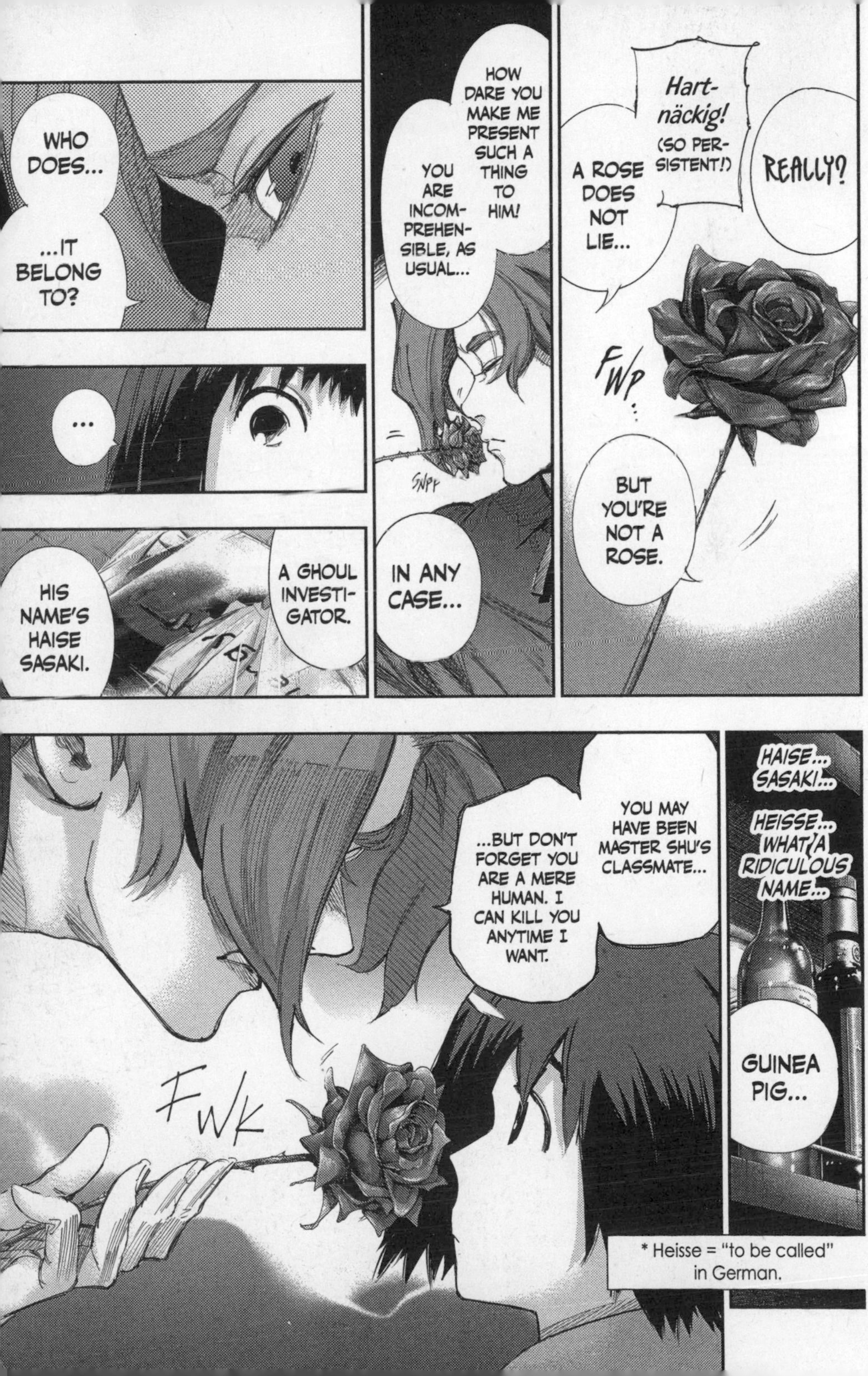
REALLY?
Hart-näckig! (SO PERSISTENT!)
A ROSE DOES NOT LIE...
FWP
BUT YOU'RE NOT A ROSE.
HOW DARE YOU MAKE ME PRESENT SUCH A THING TO HIM!
YOU ARE INCOMPREHENSIBLE, AS USUAL...
SNFF
IN ANY CASE...
WHO DOES...
...IT BELONG TO?
...
A GHOUL INVESTIGATOR.
HIS NAME'S HAISE SASAKI.
HAISE... SASAKI...
HEISSE... WHAT A RIDICULOUS NAME...
GUINEA PIG...
YOU MAY HAVE BEEN MASTER SHU'S CLASSMATE...
...BUT DON'T FORGET YOU ARE A MERE HUMAN. I CAN KILL YOU ANYTIME I WANT.
FWK
* Heisse = "to be called" in German.

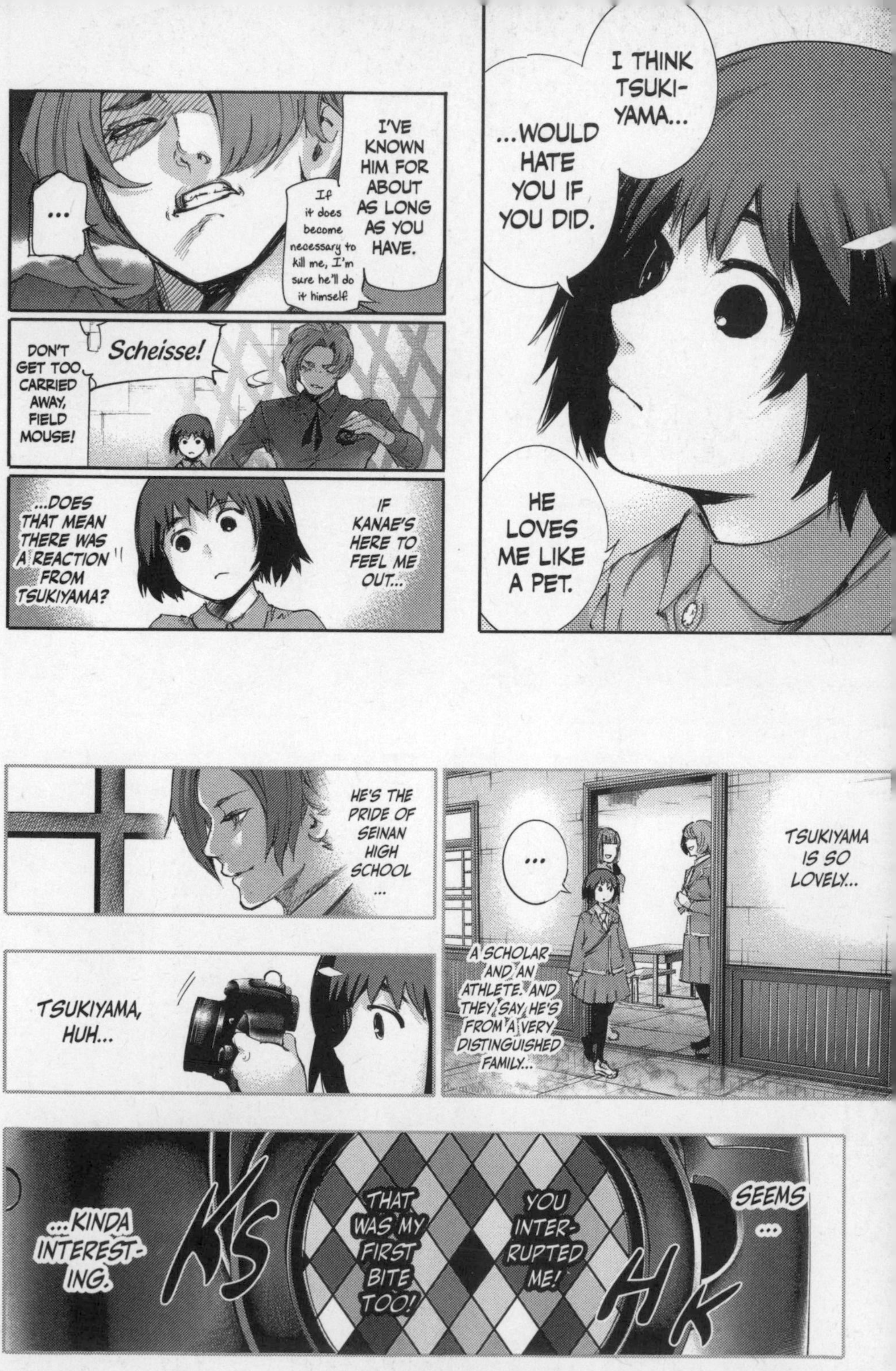
I THINK TSUKIYAMA...
...WOULD HATE YOU IF YOU DID.
HE LOVES ME LIKE A PET.
I'VE KNOWN HIM FOR ABOUT AS LONG AS YOU HAVE.
If it does become necessary to kill me, I'm sure he'll do it himself.
...
Scheisse!
DON'T GET TOO CARRIED AWAY, FIELD MOUSE!
IF KANAE'S HERE TO FEEL ME OUT...
...DOES THAT MEAN THERE WAS A REACTION FROM TSUKIYAMA?
TSUKIYAMA IS SO LOVELY...
...
A SCHOLAR AND AN ATHLETE. AND THEY SAY HE'S FROM A VERY DISTINGUISHED FAMILY...
HE'S THE PRIDE OF SEINAN HIGH SCHOOL...
TSUKIYAMA, HUH...
SEEMS...
HK
YOU INTER-RUPTED ME!
THAT WAS MY FIRST BITE TOO!
KS
...KINDA INTEREST-ING.

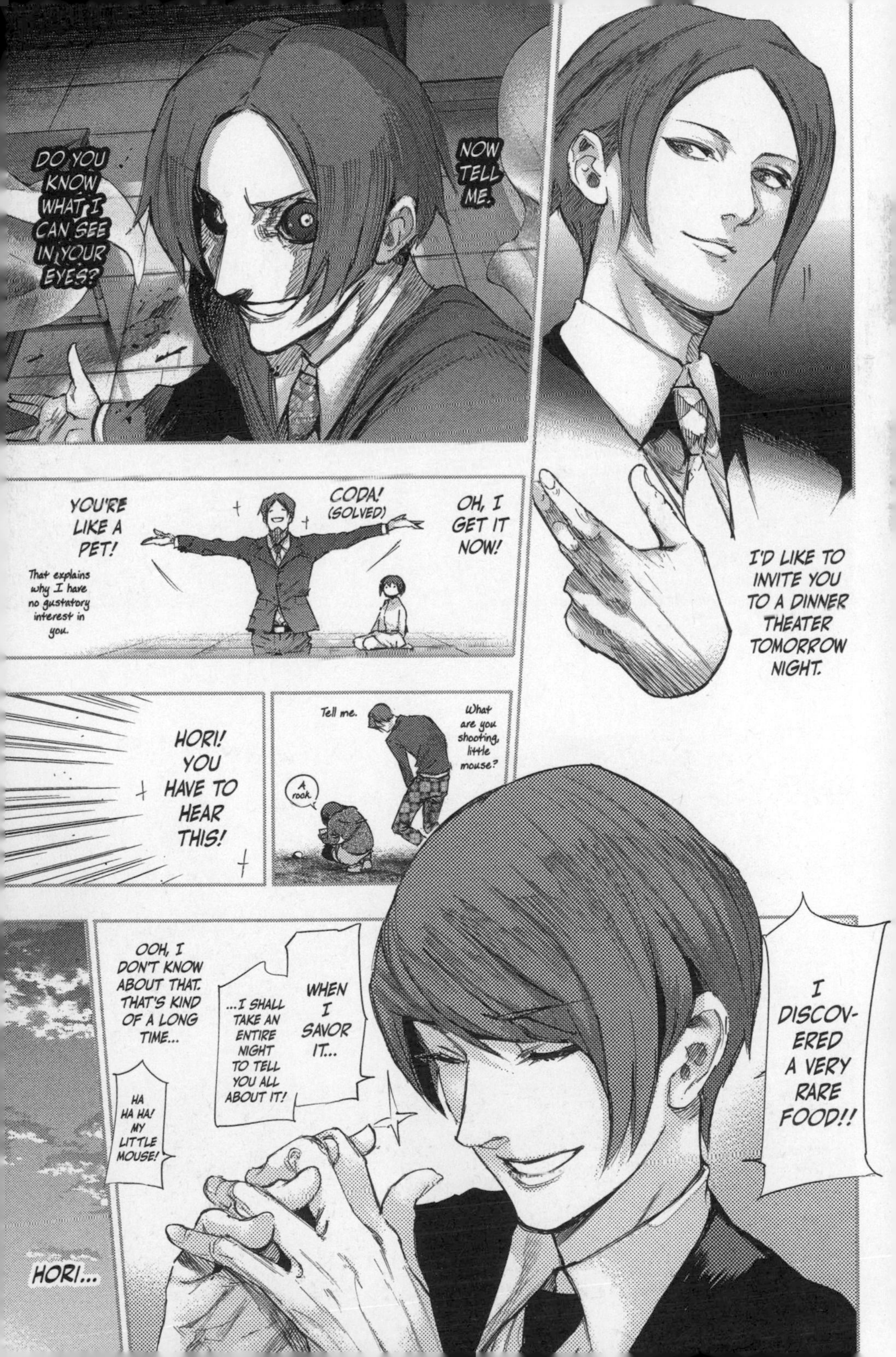
I'D LIKE TO INVITE YOU TO A DINNER THEATER TOMORROW NIGHT.
NOW TELL ME.
DO YOU KNOW WHAT I CAN SEE IN YOUR EYES?
OH, I GET IT NOW!
CODA! (SOLVED)
YOU'RE LIKE A PET!
That explains why I have no gustatory interest in you.
What are you shooting, little mouse?
Tell me.
A rock.
HORI! YOU HAVE TO HEAR THIS!
I DISCOVERED A VERY RARE FOOD!!
WHEN I SAVOR IT...
...I SHALL TAKE AN ENTIRE NIGHT TO TELL YOU ALL ABOUT IT!
OOH, I DON'T KNOW ABOUT THAT. THAT'S KIND OF A LONG TIME...
HA HA HA! MY LITTLE MOUSE!
HORI...

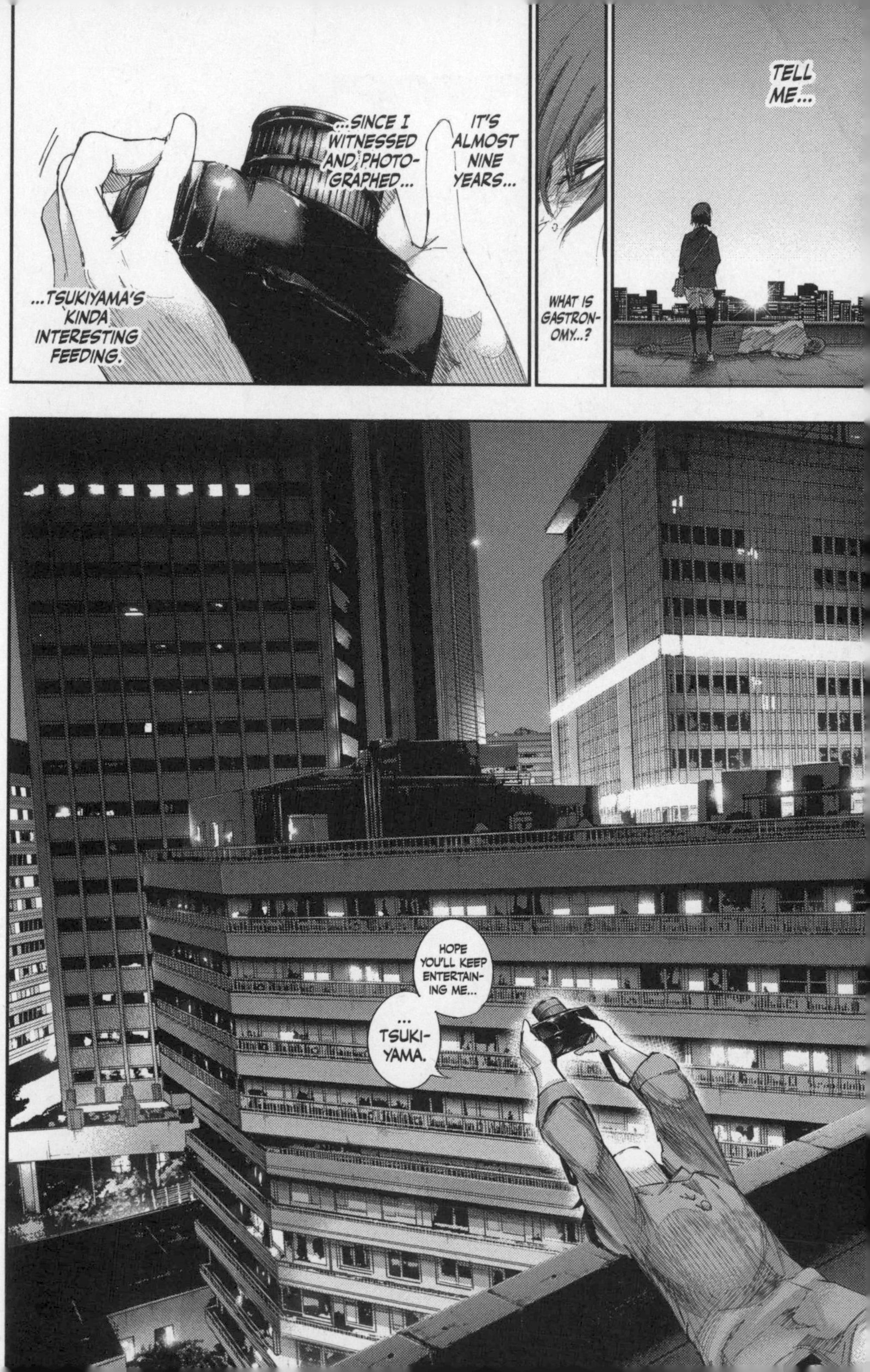
TELL ME...
WHAT IS GASTRONOMY...?
IT'S ALMOST NINE YEARS...
...SINCE I WITNESSED AND PHOTOGRAPHED...
...TSUKIYAMA'S KINDA INTERESTING FEEDING.
HOPE YOU'LL KEEP ENTERTAINING ME...
...TSUKIYAMA.

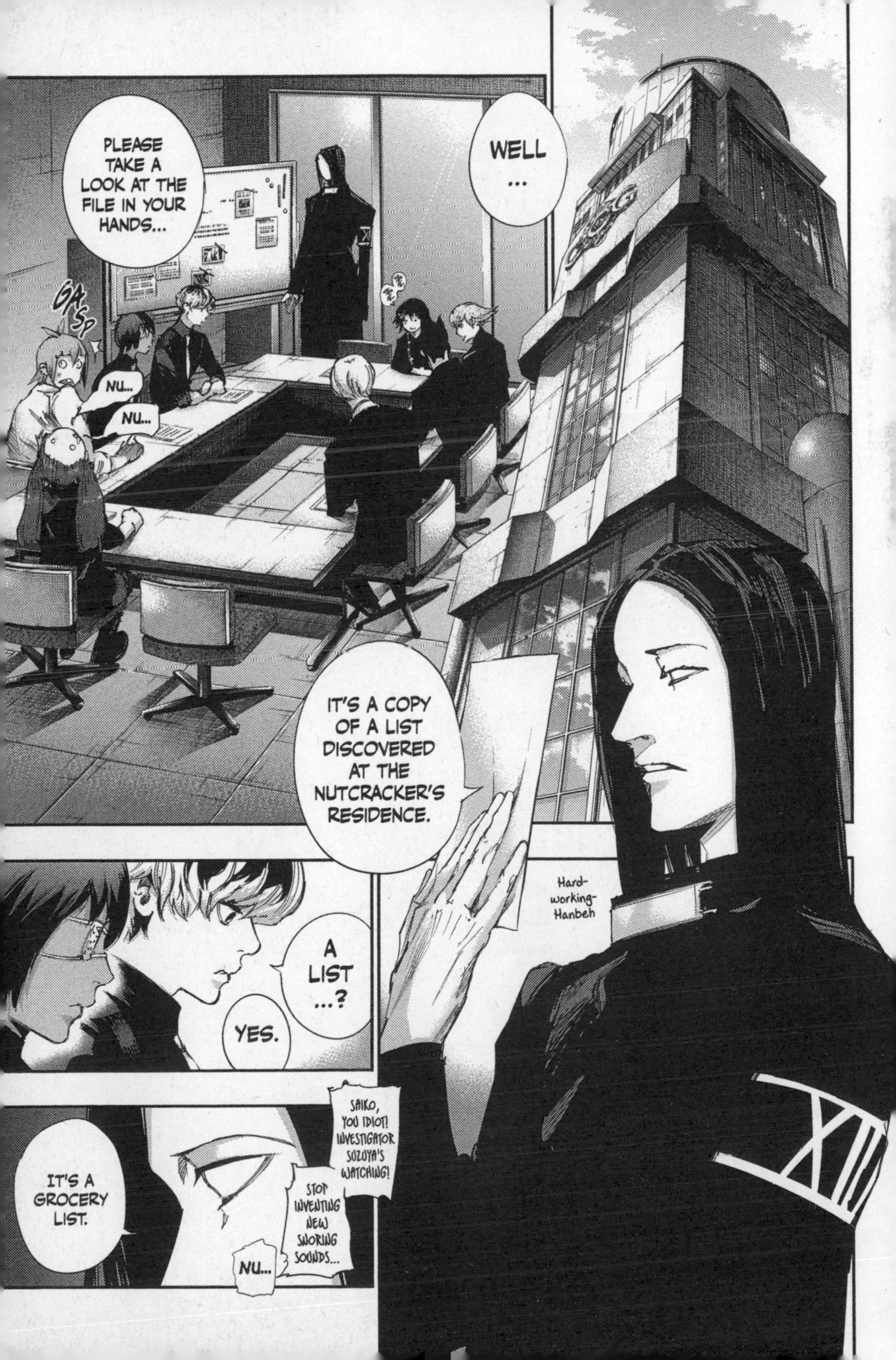
WELL ...
PLEASE TAKE A LOOK AT THE FILE IN YOUR HANDS...
GASP
NU...
NU...
IT'S A COPY OF A LIST DISCOVERED AT THE NUTCRACKER'S RESIDENCE.
Hard-working-Hanbeh
A LIST ...?
YES.
IT'S A GROCERY LIST.
SAIKO, YOU IDIOT! INVESTIGATOR SUZUYA'S WATCHING!
STOP INVENTING NEW SNORING SOUNDS...
NU...

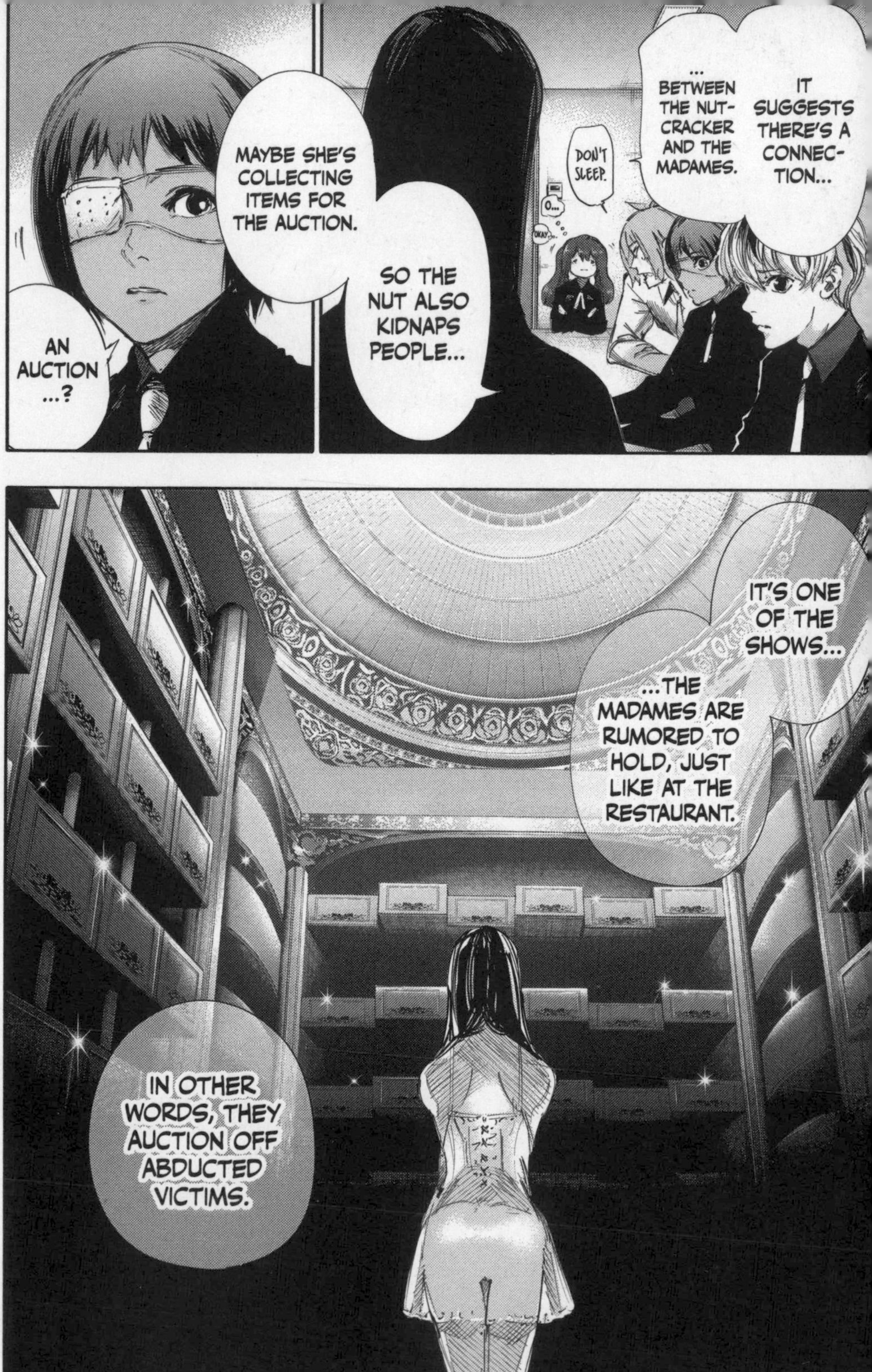
IT SUGGESTS THERE'S A CONNECTION...
...BETWEEN THE NUTCRACKER AND THE MADAMES.
DON'T SLEEP.
O...
OKAY...
SO THE NUT ALSO KIDNAPS PEOPLE...
MAYBE SHE'S COLLECTING ITEMS FOR THE AUCTION.
AN AUCTION ...?
IT'S ONE OF THE SHOWS...
...THE MADAMES ARE RUMORED TO HOLD, JUST LIKE AT THE RESTAURANT.
IN OTHER WORDS, THEY AUCTION OFF ABDUCTED VICTIMS.

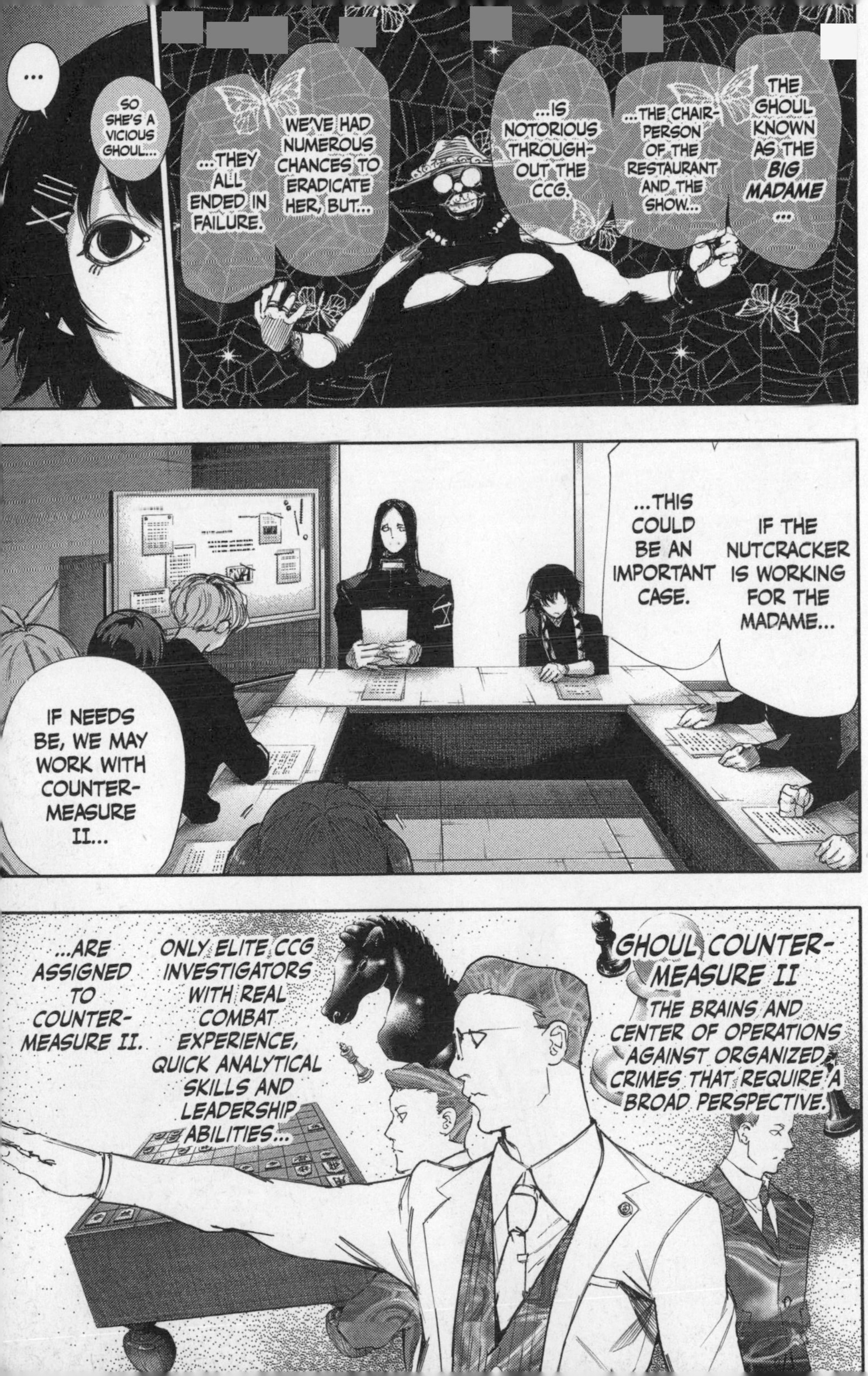
THE GHOUL KNOWN AS THE BIG MADAME...
...THE CHAIRPERSON OF THE RESTAURANT AND THE SHOW...
...IS NOTORIOUS THROUGHOUT THE CCG.
WE'VE HAD NUMEROUS CHANCES TO ERADICATE HER, BUT...
...THEY ALL ENDED IN FAILURE.
SO SHE'S A VICIOUS GHOUL...
...
IF THE NUTCRACKER IS WORKING FOR THE MADAME...
...THIS COULD BE AN IMPORTANT CASE.
IF NEEDS BE, WE MAY WORK WITH COUNTER-MEASURE II...
GHOUL COUNTER-MEASURE II
THE BRAINS AND CENTER OF OPERATIONS AGAINST ORGANIZED CRIMES THAT REQUIRE A BROAD PERSPECTIVE.
ONLY ELITE CCG INVESTIGATORS WITH REAL COMBAT EXPERIENCE, QUICK ANALYTICAL SKILLS AND LEADERSHIP ABILITIES...
...ARE ASSIGNED TO COUNTER-MEASURE II.

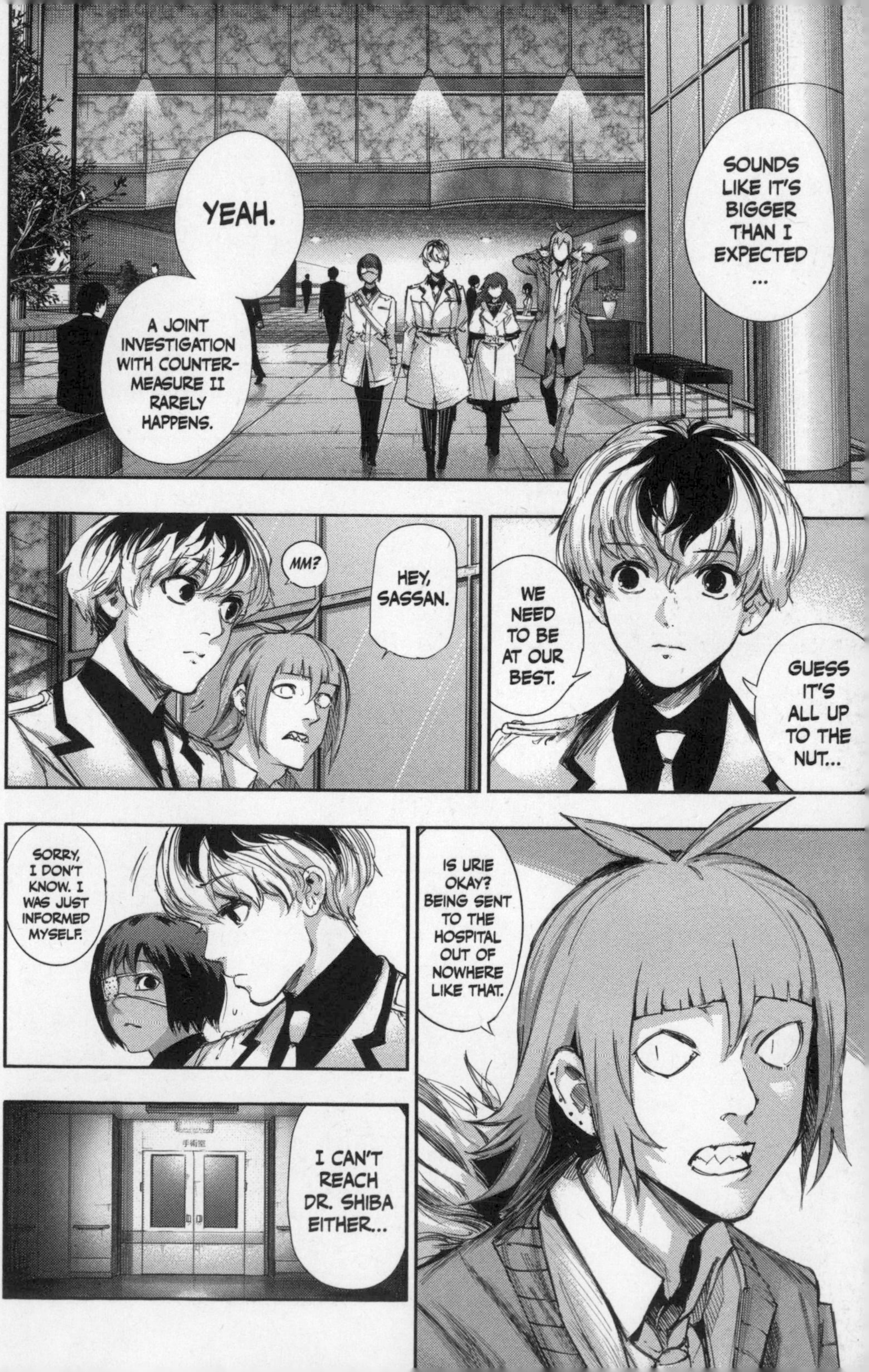
SOUNDS LIKE IT'S BIGGER THAN I EXPECTED...
YEAH.
A JOINT INVESTIGATION WITH COUNTER-MEASURE II RARELY HAPPENS.
WE NEED TO BE AT OUR BEST.
GUESS IT'S ALL UP TO THE NUT...
HEY, SASSAN.
MM?
IS URIE OKAY? BEING SENT TO THE HOSPITAL OUT OF NOWHERE LIKE THAT.
SORRY, I DON'T KNOW. I WAS JUST INFORMED MYSELF.
手術室
I CAN'T REACH DR. SHIBA EITHER...

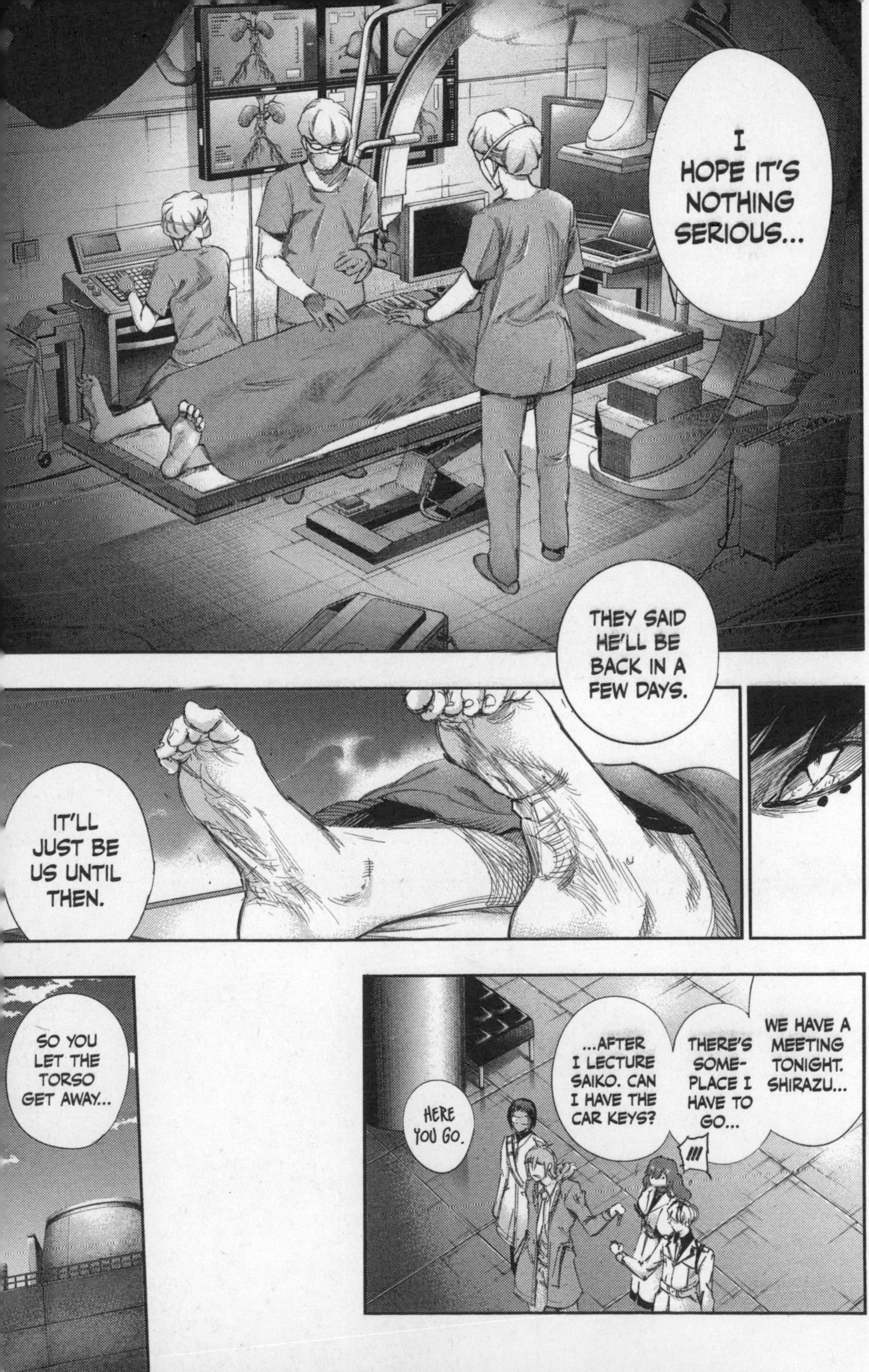
I HOPE IT'S NOTHING SERIOUS...
THEY SAID HE'LL BE BACK IN A FEW DAYS.
IT'LL JUST BE US UNTIL THEN.
WE HAVE A MEETING TONIGHT. SHIRAZU...
THERE'S SOME-PLACE I HAVE TO GO...
!!!
...AFTER I LECTURE SAIKO. CAN I HAVE THE CAR KEYS?
HERE YOU GO.
SO YOU LET THE TORSO GET AWAY...

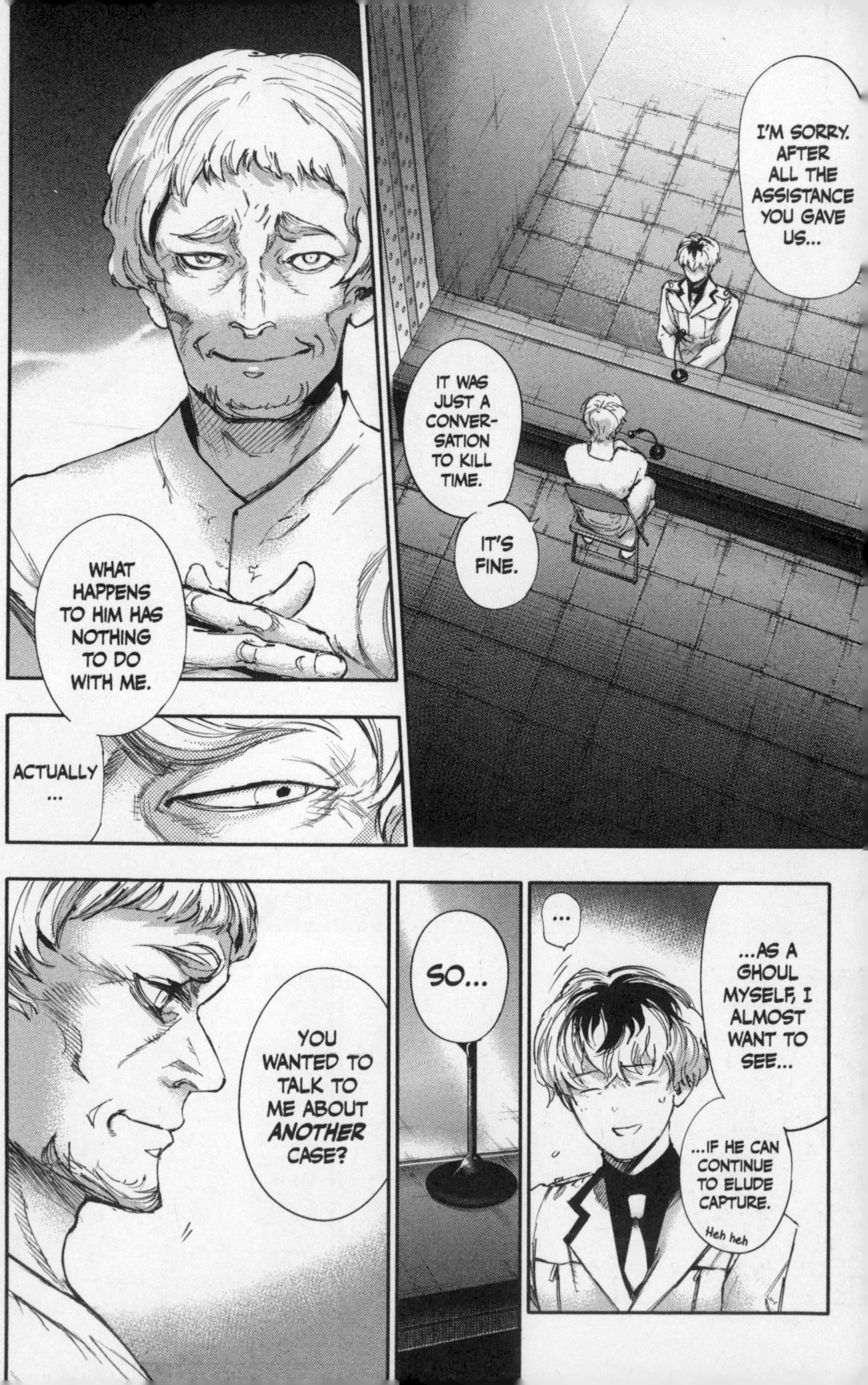
I'M SORRY. AFTER ALL THE ASSISTANCE YOU GAVE US...
IT WAS JUST A CONVER-SATION TO KILL TIME.
IT'S FINE.
WHAT HAPPENS TO HIM HAS NOTHING TO DO WITH ME.
ACTUALLY ...
...
...AS A GHOUL MYSELF, I ALMOST WANT TO SEE...
...IF HE CAN CONTINUE TO ELUDE CAPTURE.
Heh heh
SO...
YOU WANTED TO TALK TO ME ABOUT *ANOTHER* CASE?

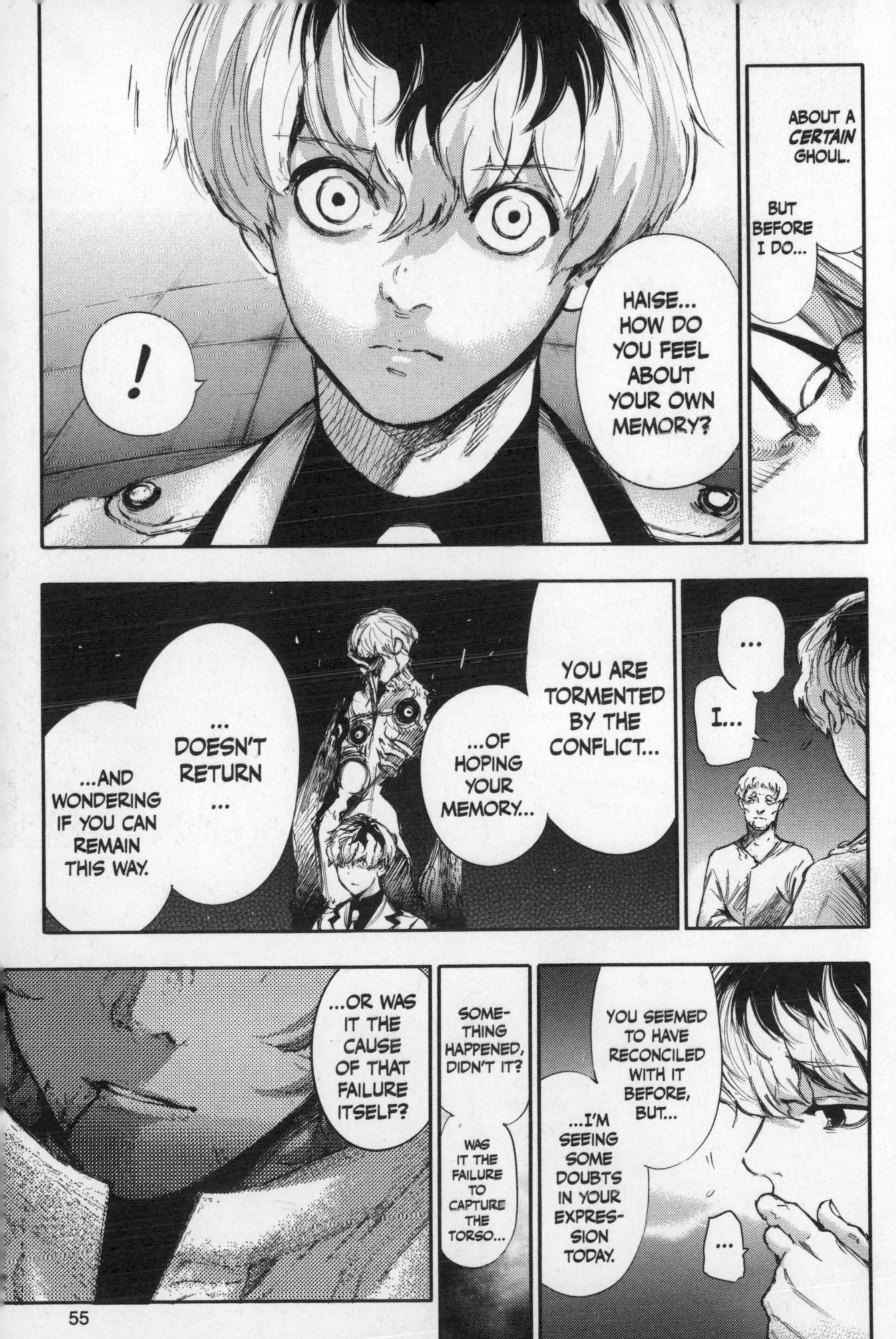
ABOUT A *CERTAIN* GHOUL.
BUT BEFORE I DO...
HAISE... HOW DO YOU FEEL ABOUT YOUR OWN MEMORY?
!
...
I...
YOU ARE TORMENTED BY THE CONFLICT...
...OF HOPING YOUR MEMORY...
...DOESN'T RETURN...
...AND WONDERING IF YOU CAN REMAIN THIS WAY.
YOU SEEMED TO HAVE RECONCILED WITH IT BEFORE, BUT...
...I'M SEEING SOME DOUBTS IN YOUR EXPRESSION TODAY.
...
SOMETHING HAPPENED, DIDN'T IT?
WAS IT THE FAILURE TO CAPTURE THE TORSO...
...OR WAS IT THE CAUSE OF THAT FAILURE ITSELF?

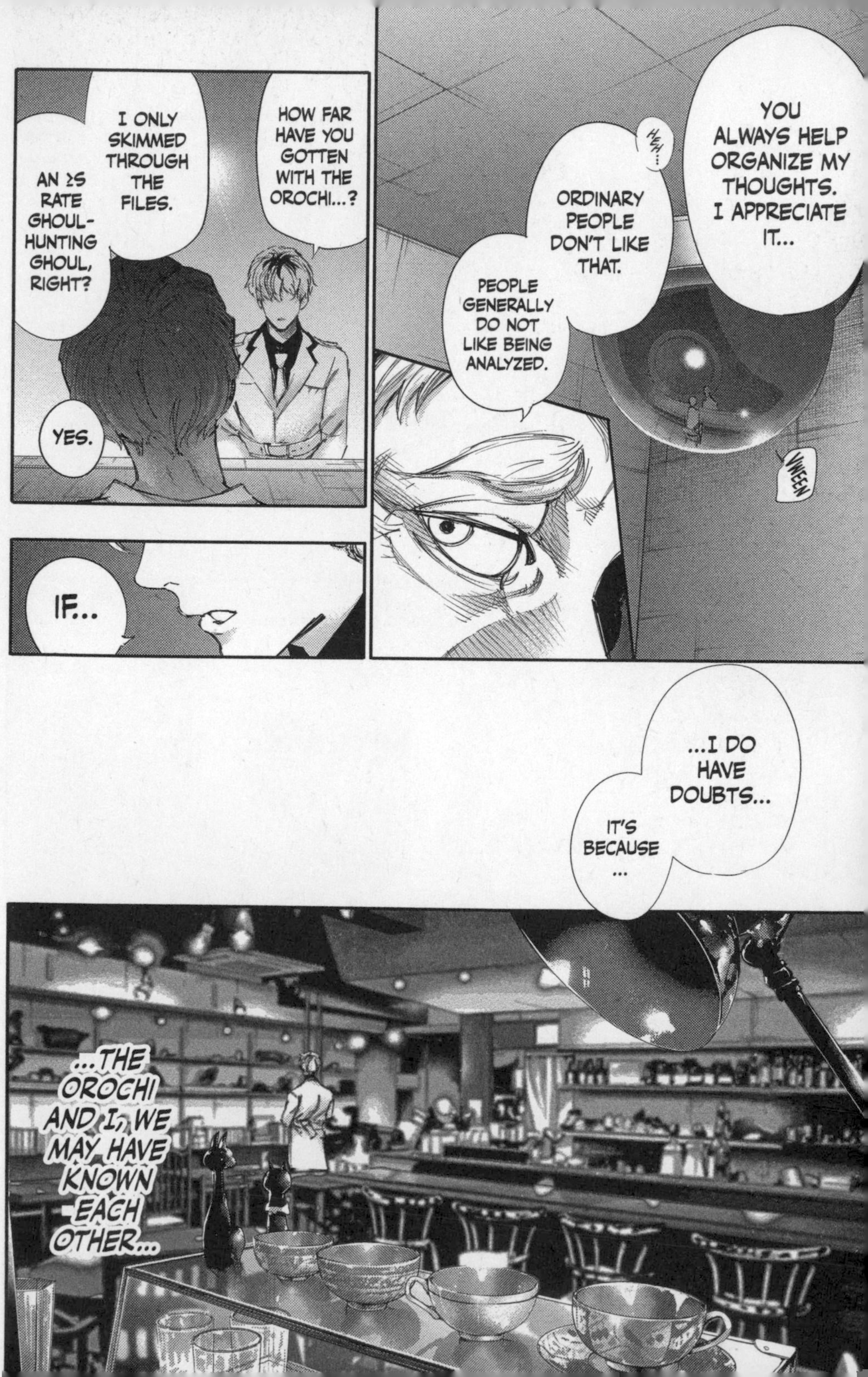
YOU ALWAYS HELP ORGANIZE MY THOUGHTS. I APPRECIATE IT...
HEH...
ORDINARY PEOPLE DON'T LIKE THAT.
PEOPLE GENERALLY DO NOT LIKE BEING ANALYZED.
VWEEN
HOW FAR HAVE YOU GOTTEN WITH THE OROCHI...?
I ONLY SKIMMED THROUGH THE FILES.
AN ≥S RATE GHOUL-HUNTING GHOUL, RIGHT?
YES.
IF...
...I DO HAVE DOUBTS...
IT'S BECAUSE ...
...THE OROCHI AND I, WE MAY HAVE KNOWN EACH OTHER...

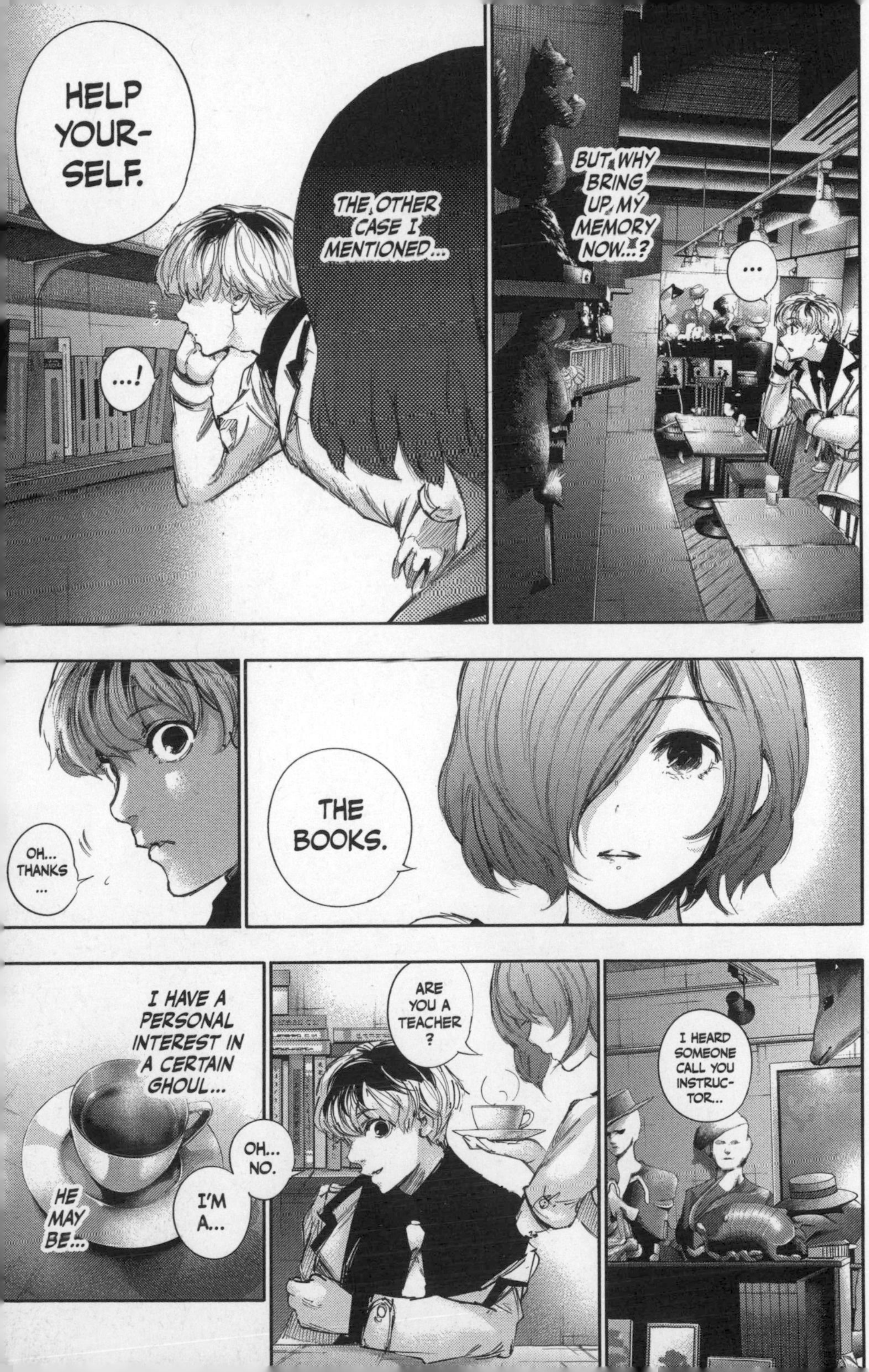
BUT WHY BRING UP MY MEMORY NOW...?
...
THE OTHER CASE I MENTIONED...
HELP YOURSELF.
...!
THE BOOKS.
OH... THANKS ...
I HEARD SOMEONE CALL YOU INSTRUCTOR...
ARE YOU A TEACHER?
OH... NO.
I'M A...
I HAVE A PERSONAL INTEREST IN A CERTAIN GHOUL...
HE MAY BE...

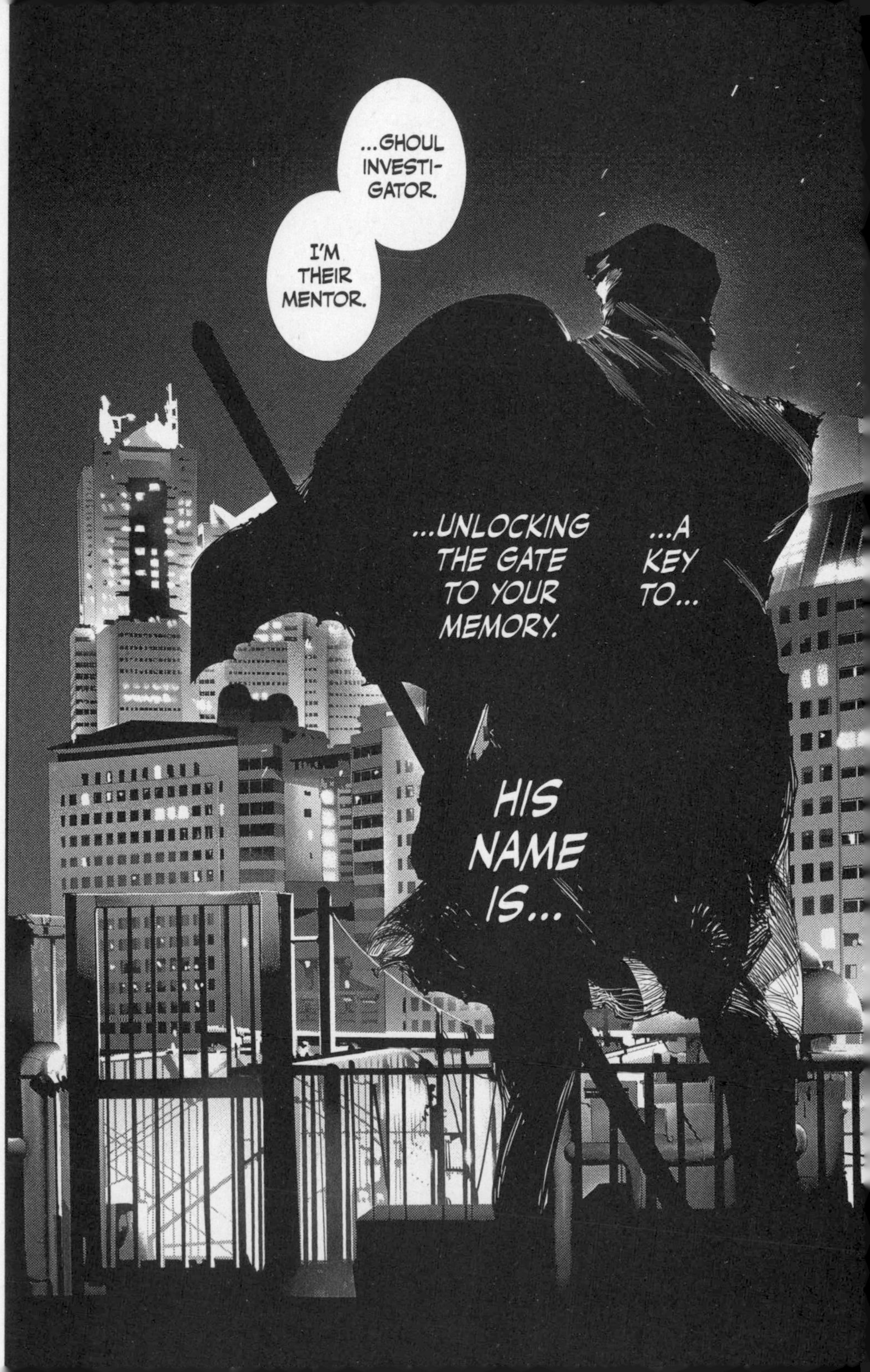
...GHOUL INVESTIGATOR.
I'M THEIR MENTOR.
...A KEY TO...
...UNLOCKING THE GATE TO YOUR MEMORY.
HIS NAME IS...

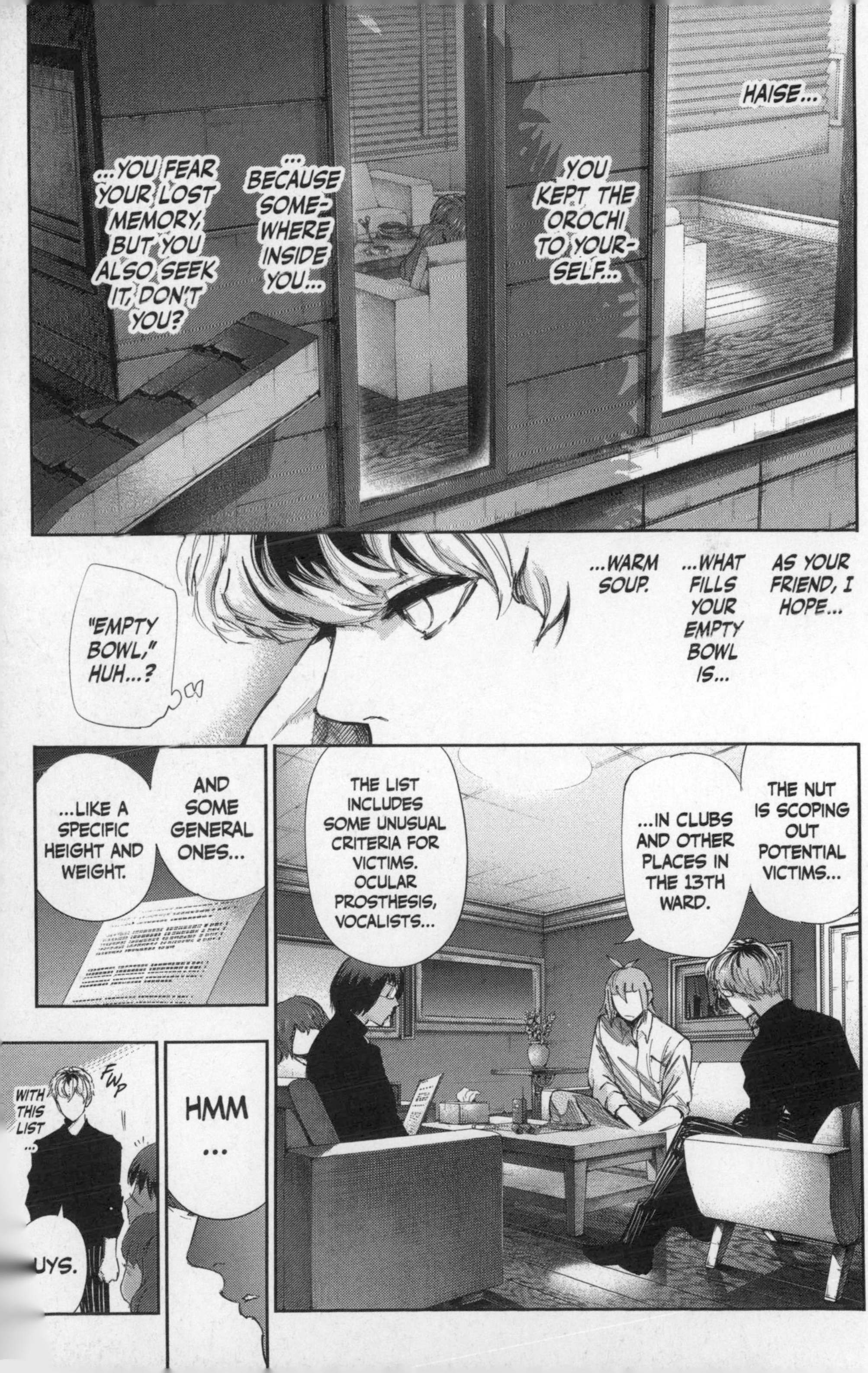
HAISE...
YOU KEPT THE OROCHI TO YOUR-SELF...
...BECAUSE SOME-WHERE INSIDE YOU...
...YOU FEAR YOUR LOST MEMORY, BUT YOU ALSO SEEK IT, DON'T YOU?
AS YOUR FRIEND, I HOPE...
...WHAT FILLS YOUR EMPTY BOWL IS...
...WARM SOUP.
"EMPTY BOWL," HUH...?
THE NUT IS SCOPING OUT POTENTIAL VICTIMS...
...IN CLUBS AND OTHER PLACES IN THE 13TH WARD.
THE LIST INCLUDES SOME UNUSUAL CRITERIA FOR VICTIMS. OCULAR PROSTHESIS, VOCALISTS...
AND SOME GENERAL ONES...
...LIKE A SPECIFIC HEIGHT AND WEIGHT.
HMM ...
FWP
WITH THIS LIST ...
UYS.

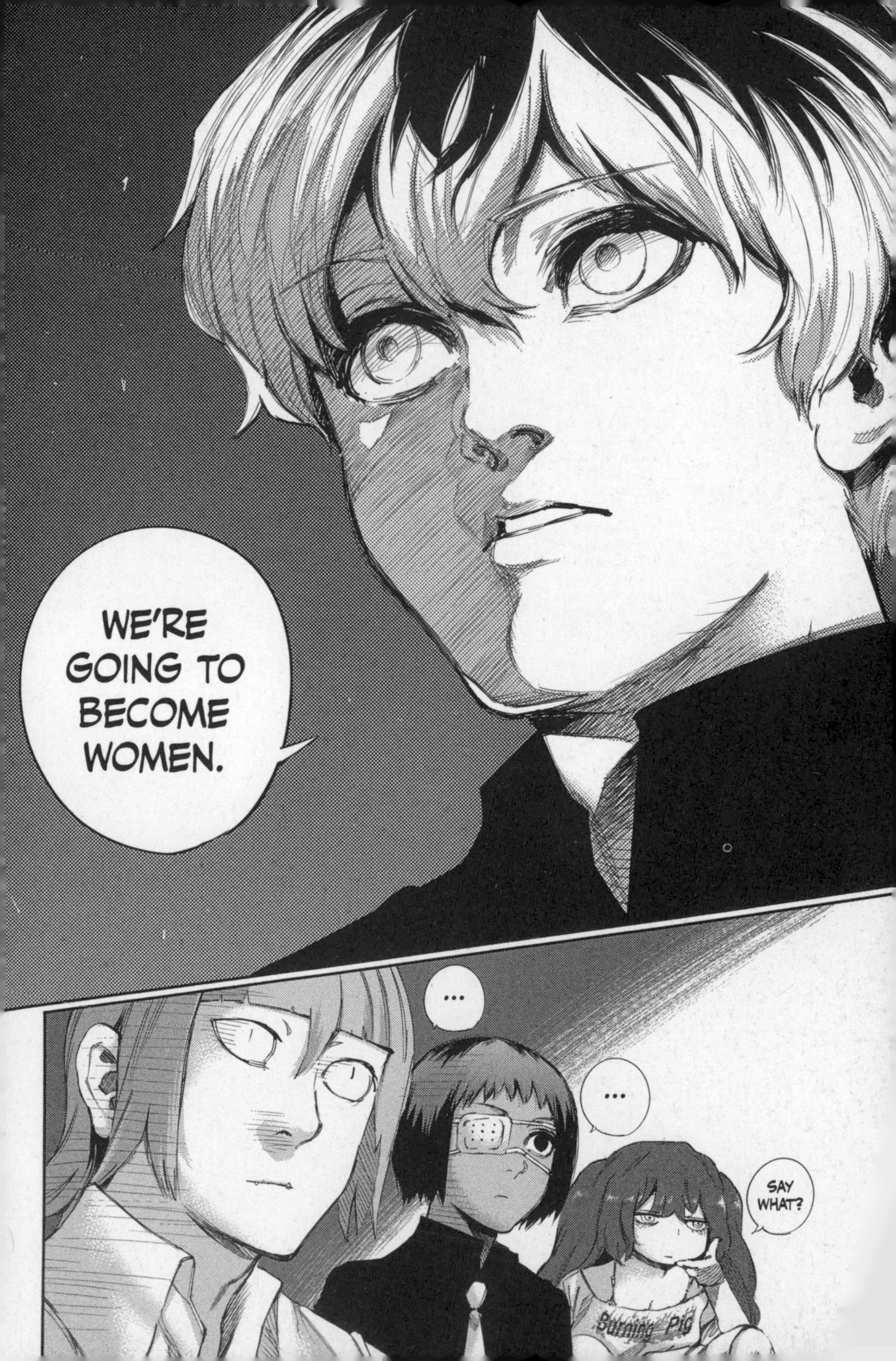
WE'RE GOING TO BECOME WOMEN.
...
...
SAY WHAT?
Burning Pig

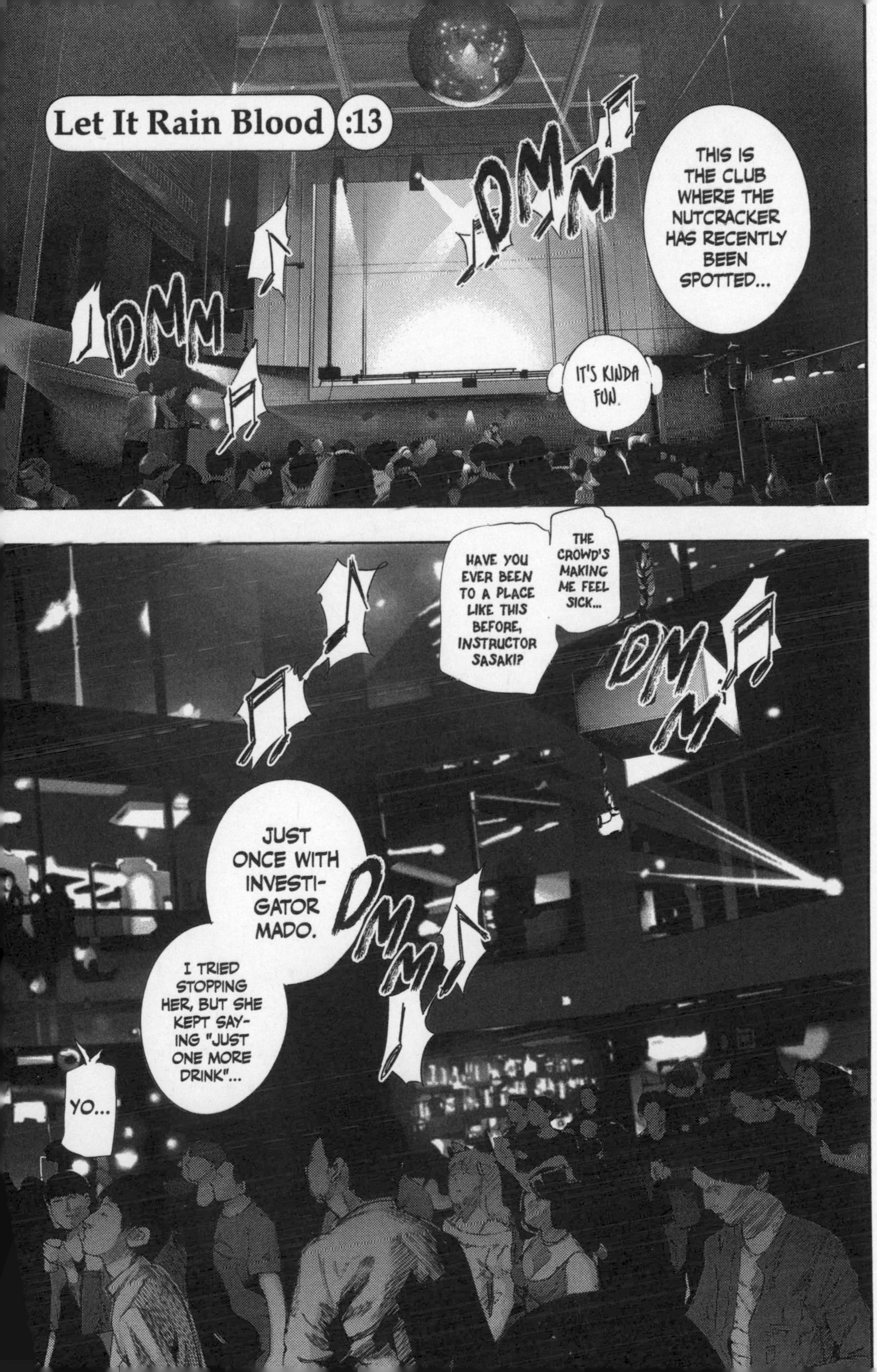
Let It Rain Blood :13
DMM
THIS IS THE CLUB WHERE THE NUTCRACKER HAS RECENTLY BEEN SPOTTED...
DMM
IT'S KINDA FUN.
THE CROWD'S MAKING ME FEEL SICK...
HAVE YOU EVER BEEN TO A PLACE LIKE THIS BEFORE, INSTRUCTOR SASAKI?
DMM
JUST ONCE WITH INVESTI-GATOR MADO.
DMM
I TRIED STOPPING HER, BUT SHE KEPT SAY-ING "JUST ONE MORE DRINK"...
YO...

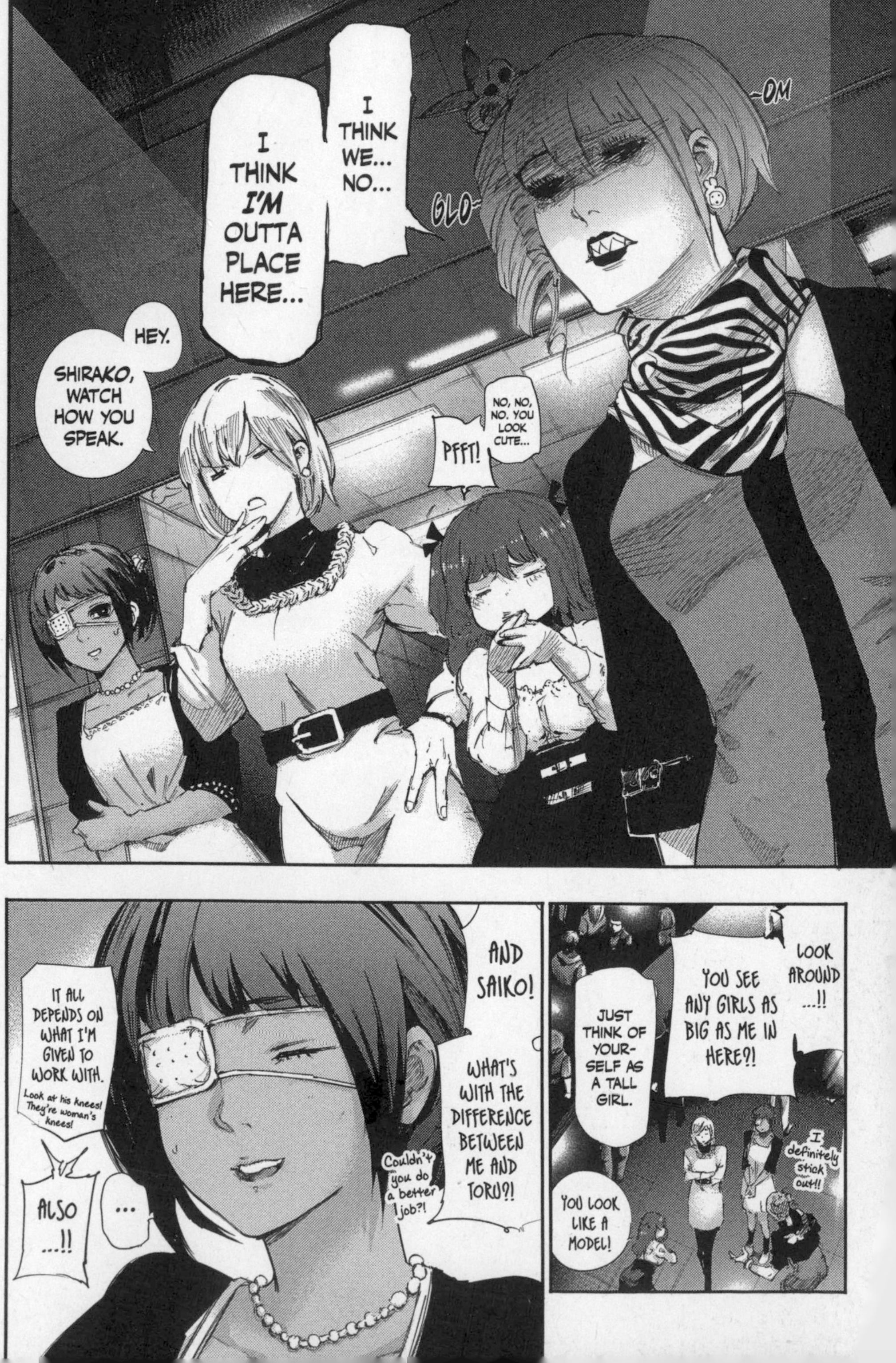
GLO-OM
I THINK WE... NO...
I THINK I'M OUTTA PLACE HERE...
NO, NO, NO. YOU LOOK CUTE...
PFFT!
HEY. SHIRAKO, WATCH HOW YOU SPEAK.
LOOK AROUND ...!!
YOU SEE ANY GIRLS AS BIG AS ME IN HERE?!
JUST THINK OF YOURSELF AS A TALL GIRL.
I definitely stick out!!
YOU LOOK LIKE A MODEL!
AND SAIKO!
WHAT'S WITH THE DIFFERENCE BETWEEN ME AND TORU?!
Couldn't you do a better job?!
IT ALL DEPENDS ON WHAT I'M GIVEN TO WORK WITH.
Look at his knees! They're woman's knees!
...
ALSO ...!!

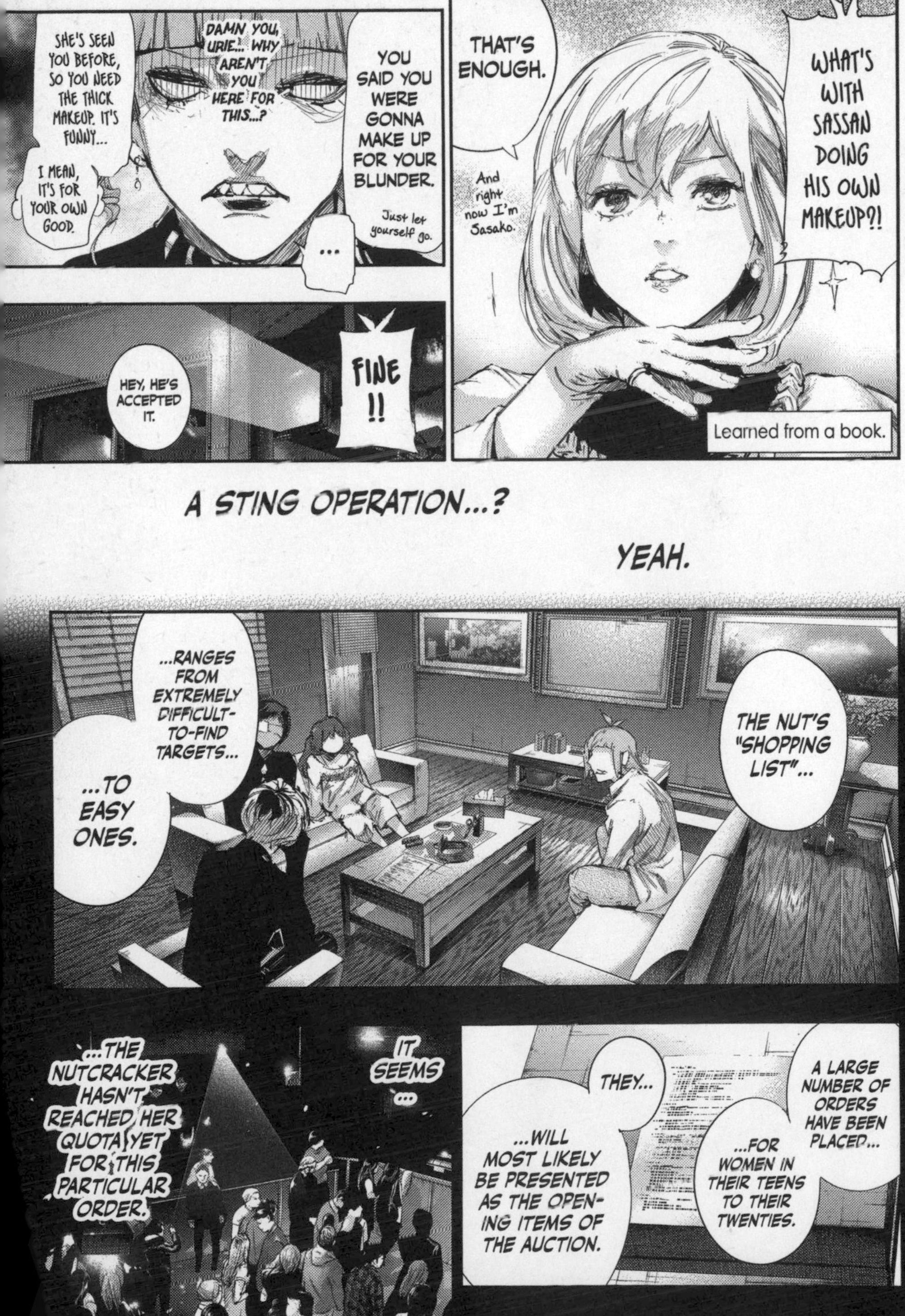
WHAT'S WITH SASSAN DOING HIS OWN MAKEUP?!
THAT'S ENOUGH.
And right now I'm Sasako.
Learned from a book.
YOU SAID YOU WERE GONNA MAKE UP FOR YOUR BLUNDER.
Just let yourself go.
DAMN YOU, URIE... WHY AREN'T YOU HERE FOR THIS...?
SHE'S SEEN YOU BEFORE, SO YOU NEED THE THICK MAKEUP. IT'S FUNNY...
I MEAN, IT'S FOR YOUR OWN GOOD.
...
FINE!!
HEY, HE'S ACCEPTED IT.
A STING OPERATION...?
YEAH.
THE NUT'S "SHOPPING LIST"...
...RANGES FROM EXTREMELY DIFFICULT-TO-FIND TARGETS...
...TO EASY ONES.
A LARGE NUMBER OF ORDERS HAVE BEEN PLACED...
...FOR WOMEN IN THEIR TEENS TO THEIR TWENTIES.
THEY...
...WILL MOST LIKELY BE PRESENTED AS THE OPEN-ING ITEMS OF THE AUCTION.
IT SEEMS...
...THE NUTCRACKER HASN'T REACHED HER QUOTA YET FOR THIS PARTICULAR ORDER.

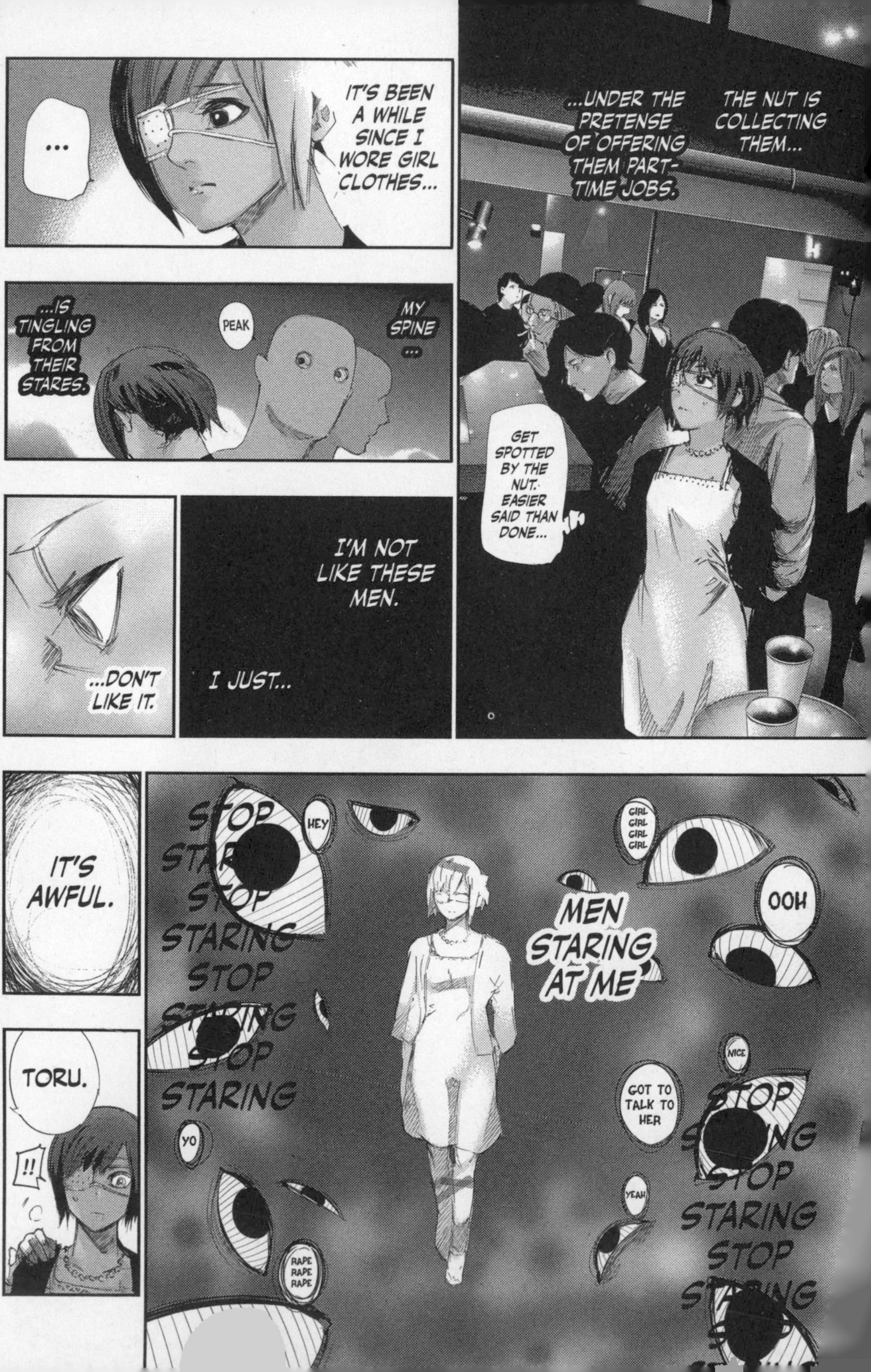
THE NUT IS COLLECTING THEM...
...UNDER THE PRETENSE OF OFFERING THEM PART-TIME JOBS.
GET SPOTTED BY THE NUT. EASIER SAID THAN DONE...
IT'S BEEN A WHILE SINCE I WORE GIRL CLOTHES...
...
MY SPINE...
PEAK
...IS TINGLING FROM THEIR STARES.
I'M NOT LIKE THESE MEN.
I JUST...
...DON'T LIKE IT.
GIRL GIRL GIRL GIRL
OOH
MEN STARING AT ME
HEY
STOP STARING STOP STARING STOP STARING STOP STARING
NICE
GOT TO TALK TO HER
STOP STARING STOP STARING STOP STARING
YEAH
YO
RAPE RAPE RAPE
IT'S AWFUL.
TORU.
!!

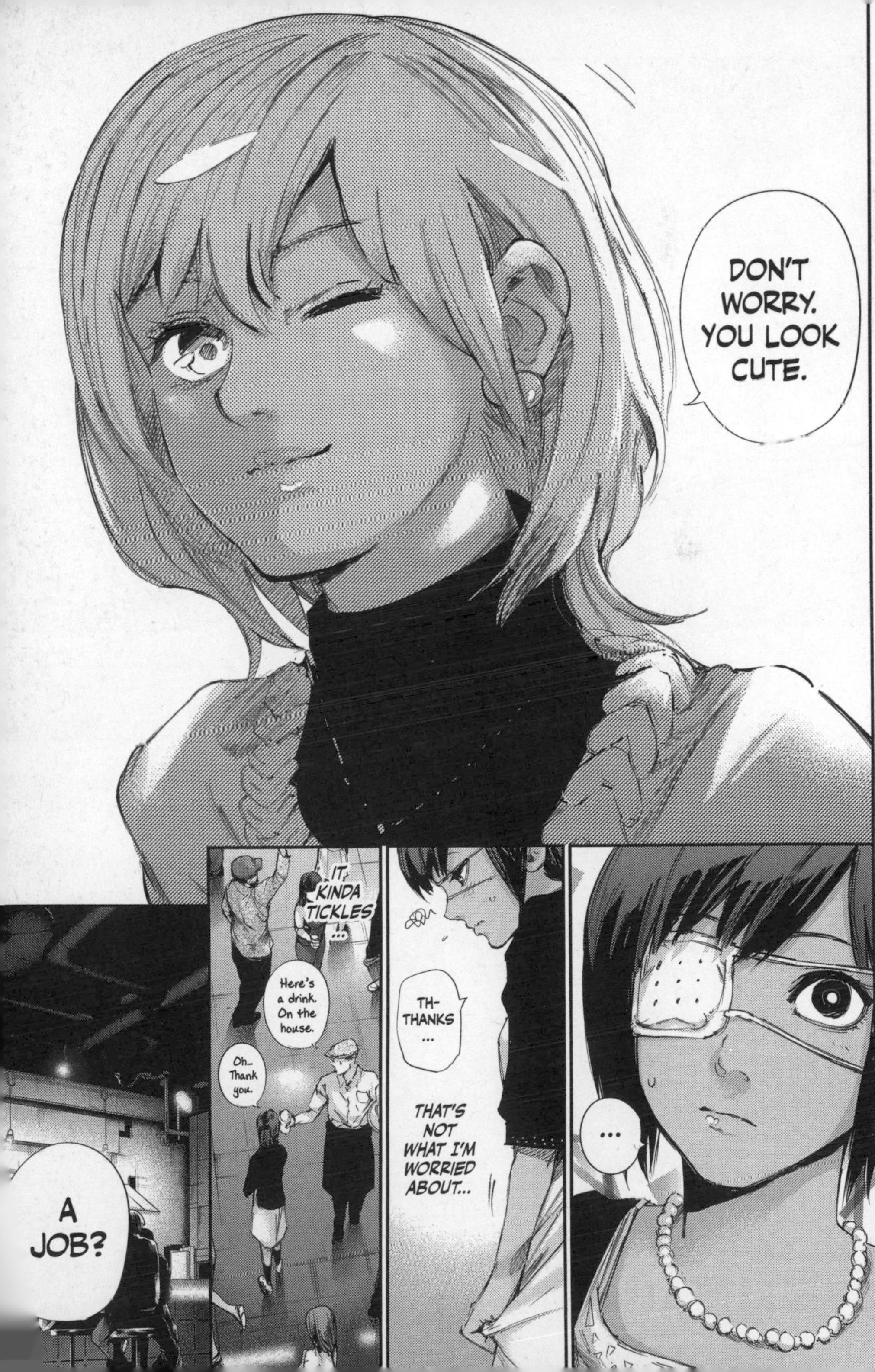
DON'T WORRY. YOU LOOK CUTE.
...
TH-THANKS...
THAT'S NOT WHAT I'M WORRIED ABOUT...
IT KINDA TICKLES...
Here's a drink. On the house.
Oh... Thank you.
A JOB?

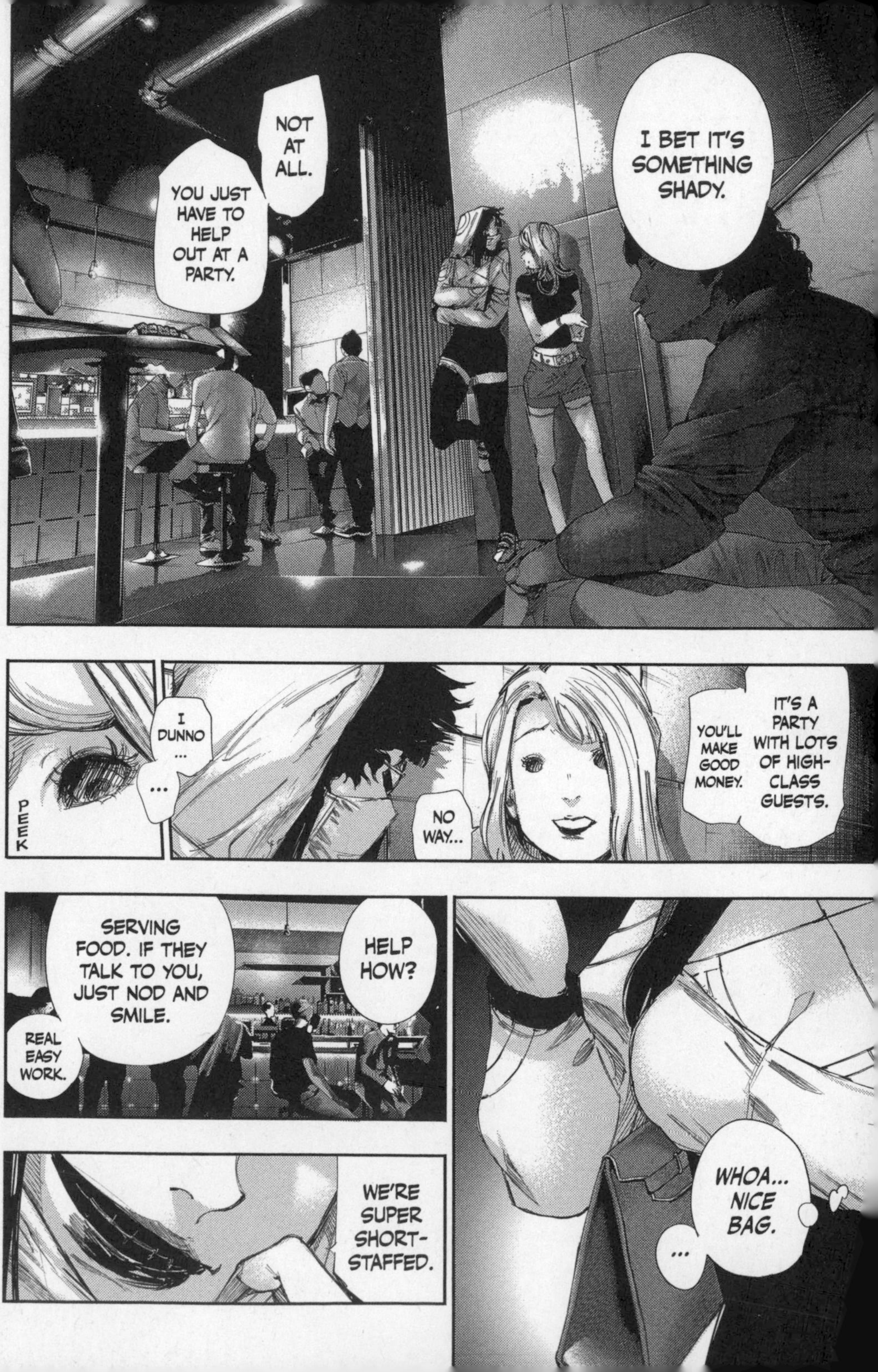
I BET IT'S SOMETHING SHADY.
NOT AT ALL.
YOU JUST HAVE TO HELP OUT AT A PARTY.
IT'S A PARTY WITH LOTS OF HIGH-CLASS GUESTS.
YOU'LL MAKE GOOD MONEY.
NO WAY...
I DUNNO ...
...
PEEK
WHOA... NICE BAG.
...
HELP HOW?
SERVING FOOD. IF THEY TALK TO YOU, JUST NOD AND SMILE.
REAL EASY WORK.
WE'RE SUPER SHORT-STAFFED.

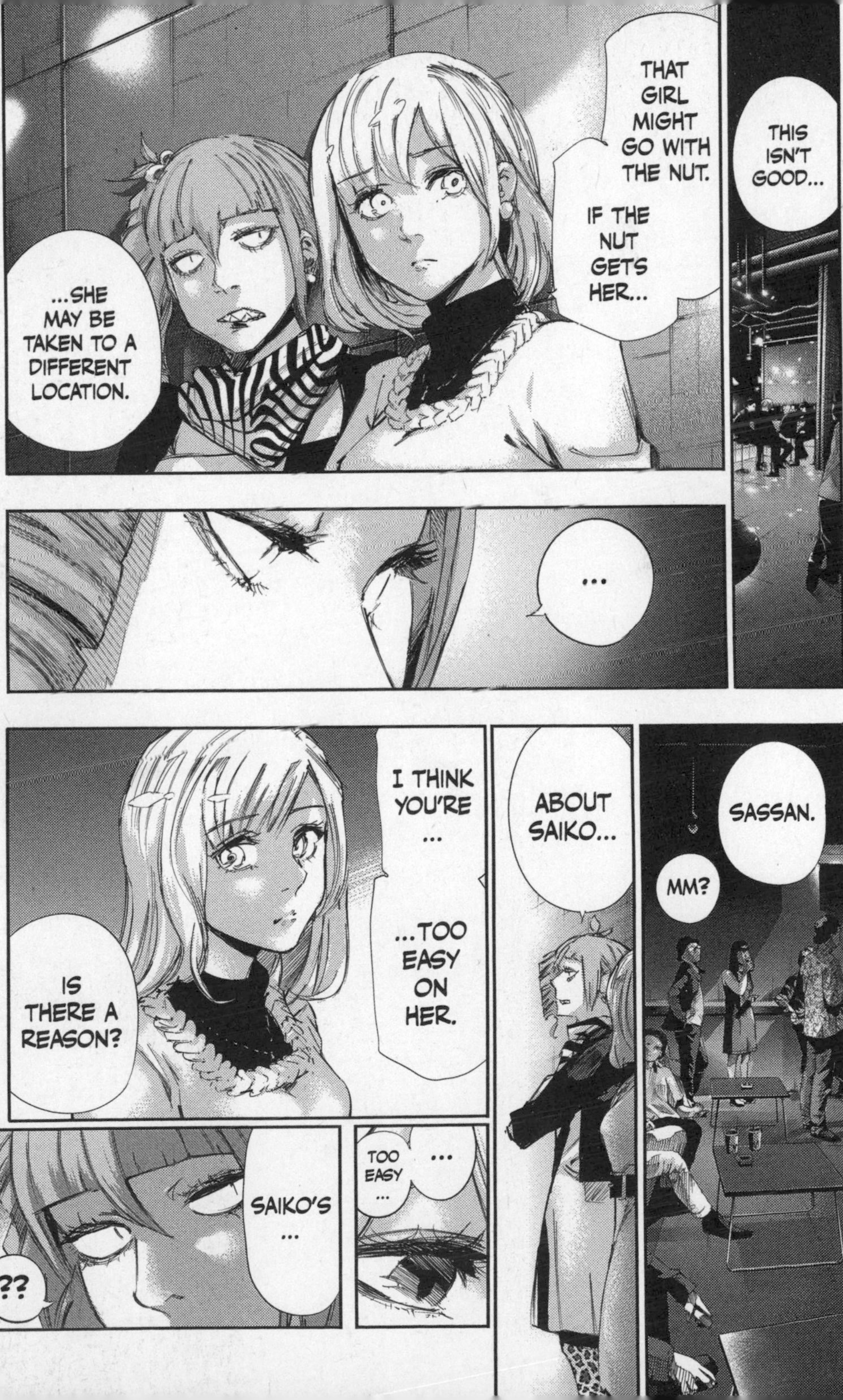
THIS ISN'T GOOD...
THAT GIRL MIGHT GO WITH THE NUT.
IF THE NUT GETS HER...
...SHE MAY BE TAKEN TO A DIFFERENT LOCATION.
...
SASSAN.
MM?
ABOUT SAIKO...
I THINK YOU'RE ...
...TOO EASY ON HER.
IS THERE A REASON?
...
TOO EASY ...
SAIKO'S ...
??

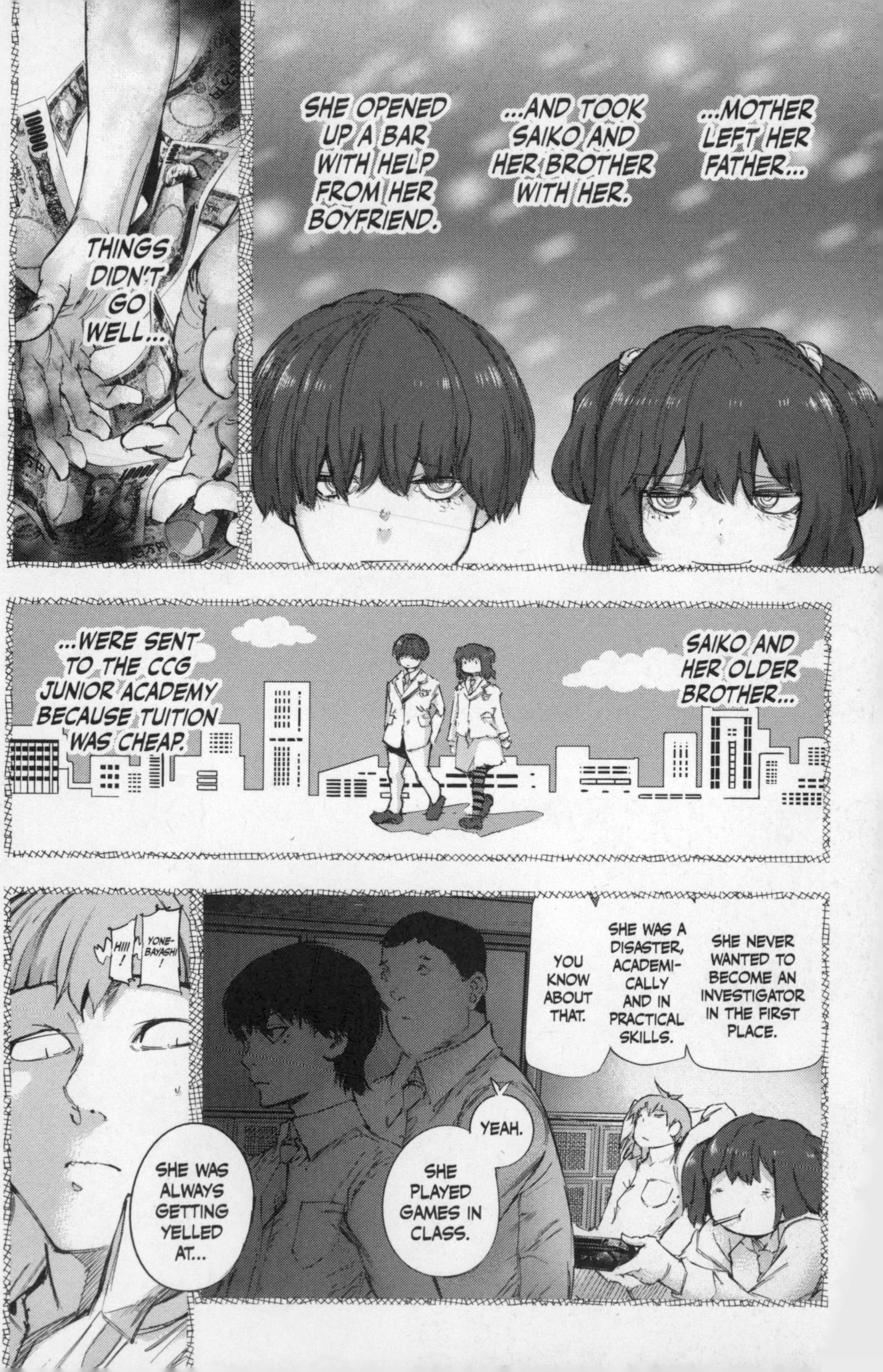
...MOTHER LEFT HER FATHER...
...AND TOOK SAIKO AND HER BROTHER WITH HER.
SHE OPENED UP A BAR WITH HELP FROM HER BOYFRIEND.
THINGS DIDN'T GO WELL...
SAIKO AND HER OLDER BROTHER...
...WERE SENT TO THE CCG JUNIOR ACADEMY BECAUSE TUITION WAS CHEAP.
SHE NEVER WANTED TO BECOME AN INVESTIGATOR IN THE FIRST PLACE.
SHE WAS A DISASTER, ACADEMICALLY AND IN PRACTICAL SKILLS.
YOU KNOW ABOUT THAT.
YEAH.
SHE PLAYED GAMES IN CLASS.
SHE WAS ALWAYS GETTING YELLED AT...
YONE-BAYASHI!
HIII!

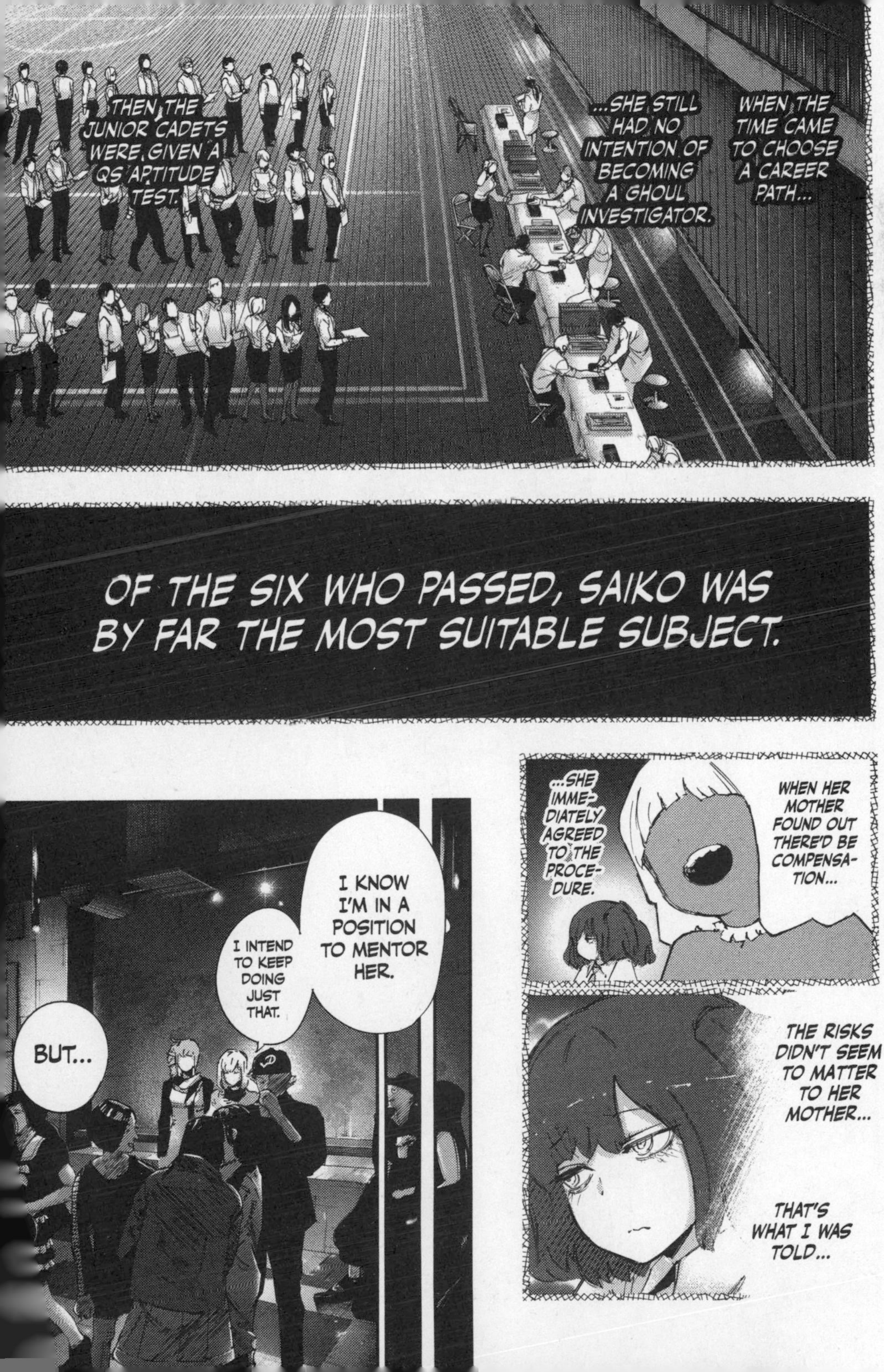
WHEN THE TIME CAME TO CHOOSE A CAREER PATH...
...SHE STILL HAD NO INTENTION OF BECOMING A GHOUL INVESTIGATOR.
THEN THE JUNIOR CADETS WERE GIVEN A QS APTITUDE TEST.
OF THE SIX WHO PASSED, SAIKO WAS BY FAR THE MOST SUITABLE SUBJECT.
WHEN HER MOTHER FOUND OUT THERE'D BE COMPENSATION...
...SHE IMMEDIATELY AGREED TO THE PROCEDURE.
THE RISKS DIDN'T SEEM TO MATTER TO HER MOTHER...
THAT'S WHAT I WAS TOLD...
I KNOW I'M IN A POSITION TO MENTOR HER.
I INTEND TO KEEP DOING JUST THAT.
BUT...

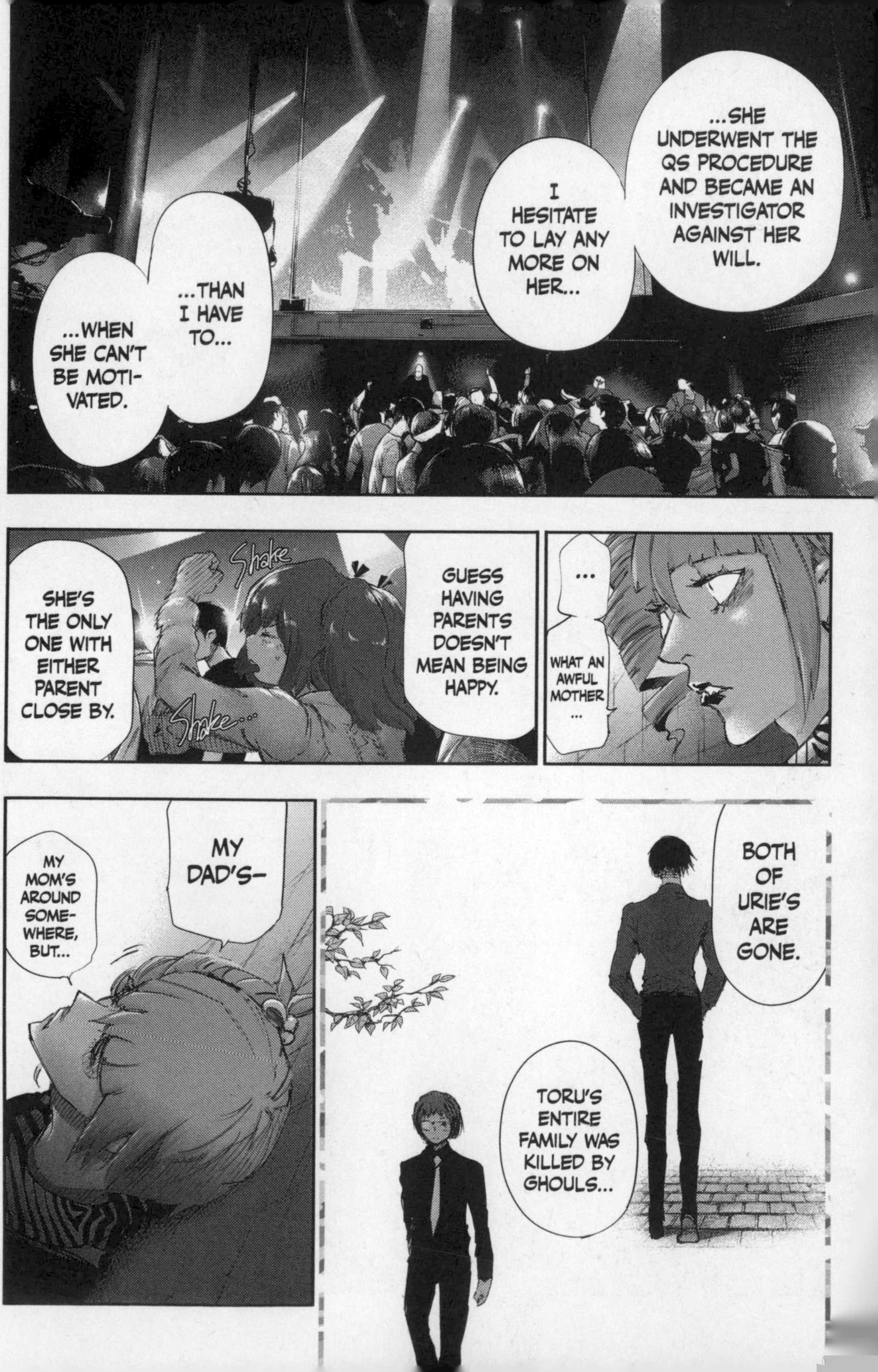
...SHE UNDERWENT THE QS PROCEDURE AND BECAME AN INVESTIGATOR AGAINST HER WILL.
I HESITATE TO LAY ANY MORE ON HER...
...THAN I HAVE TO...
...WHEN SHE CAN'T BE MOTI-VATED.
...
WHAT AN AWFUL MOTHER...
GUESS HAVING PARENTS DOESN'T MEAN BEING HAPPY.
Shake
SHE'S THE ONLY ONE WITH EITHER PARENT CLOSE BY.
Shake...
BOTH OF URIE'S ARE GONE.
TORU'S ENTIRE FAMILY WAS KILLED BY GHOULS...
MY DAD'S-
MY MOM'S AROUND SOME-WHERE, BUT...

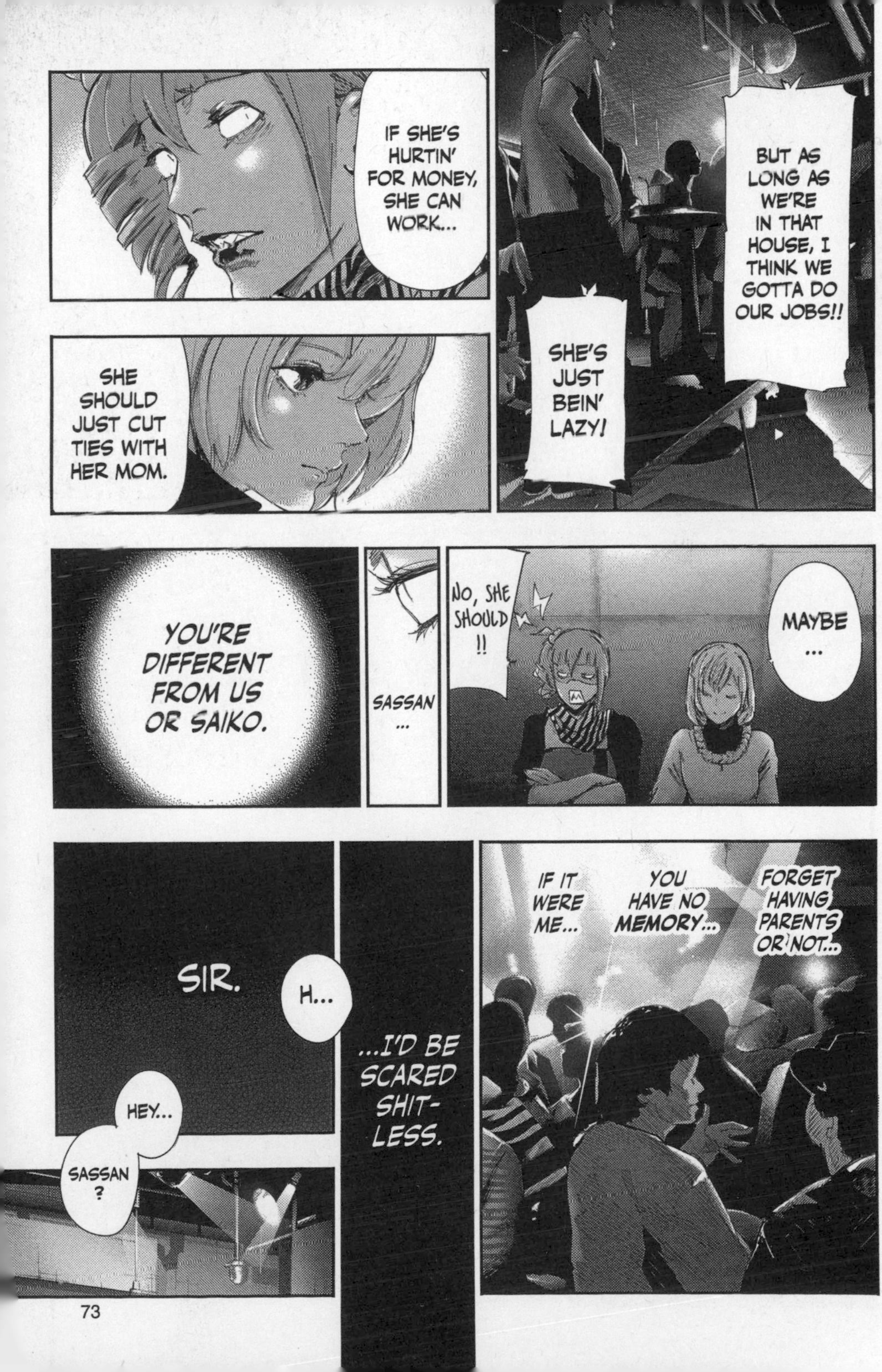
BUT AS LONG AS WE'RE IN THAT HOUSE, I THINK WE GOTTA DO OUR JOBS!!
SHE'S JUST BEIN' LAZY!
IF SHE'S HURTIN' FOR MONEY, SHE CAN WORK...
SHE SHOULD JUST CUT TIES WITH HER MOM.
MAYBE...
NO, SHE SHOULD!!
SASSAN...
YOU'RE DIFFERENT FROM US OR SAIKO.
FORGET HAVING PARENTS OR NOT...
YOU HAVE NO MEMORY...
IF IT WERE ME...
...I'D BE SCARED SHIT-LESS.
SIR.
H...
HEY...
SASSAN?

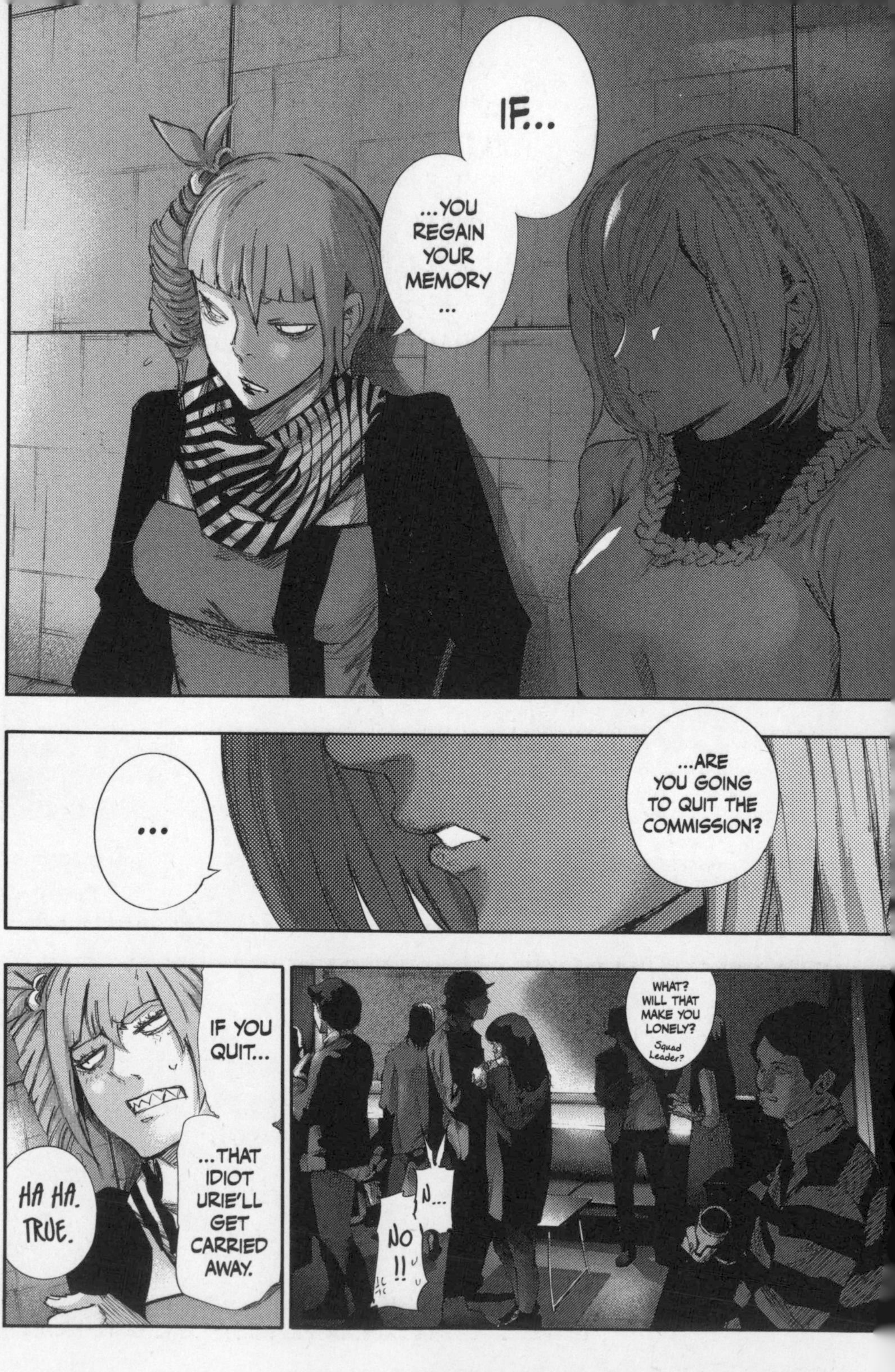
IF...
...YOU REGAIN YOUR MEMORY ...
...ARE YOU GOING TO QUIT THE COMMISSION?
...
WHAT? WILL THAT MAKE YOU LONELY? Squad Leader?
N...
NO !!
IF YOU QUIT...
...THAT IDIOT URIE'LL GET CARRIED AWAY.
HA HA. TRUE.

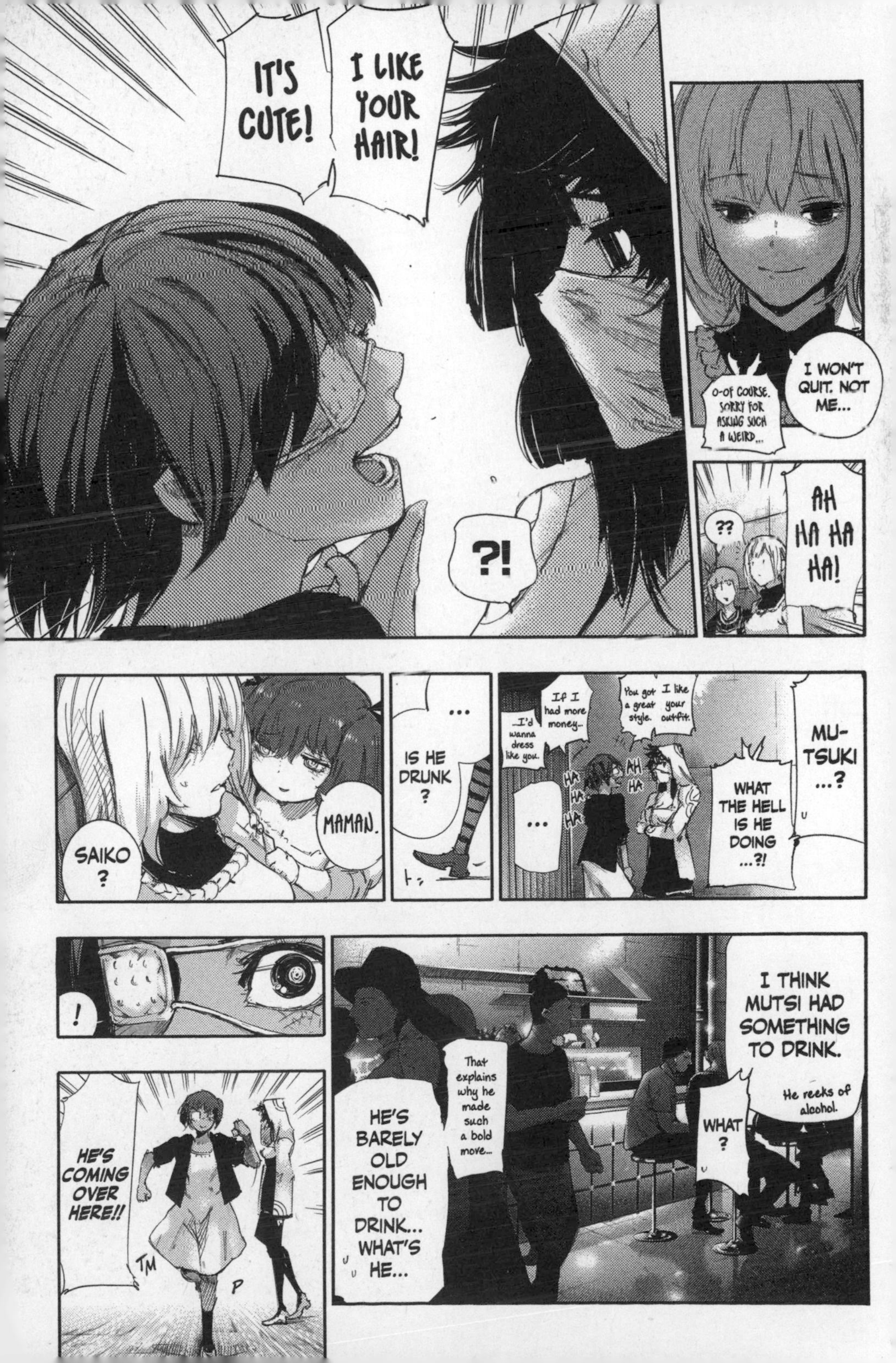
I WON'T QUIT. NOT ME...
O-OF COURSE. SORRY FOR ASKING SUCH A WEIRD...
AH HA HA HA!
??
I LIKE YOUR HAIR!
IT'S CUTE!
?!
MU-TSUKI ...?
WHAT THE HELL IS HE DOING ...?!
I like your outfit.
You got a great style.
If I had more money...
...I'd wanna dress like you.
AH HA
HA HA HA
...
...
IS HE DRUNK?
MAMAN.
SAIKO?
I THINK MUTSI HAD SOMETHING TO DRINK.
He reeks of alcohol.
WHAT?
That explains why he made such a bold move...
HE'S BARELY OLD ENOUGH TO DRINK... WHAT'S HE...
!
HE'S COMING OVER HERE!!
TM
P

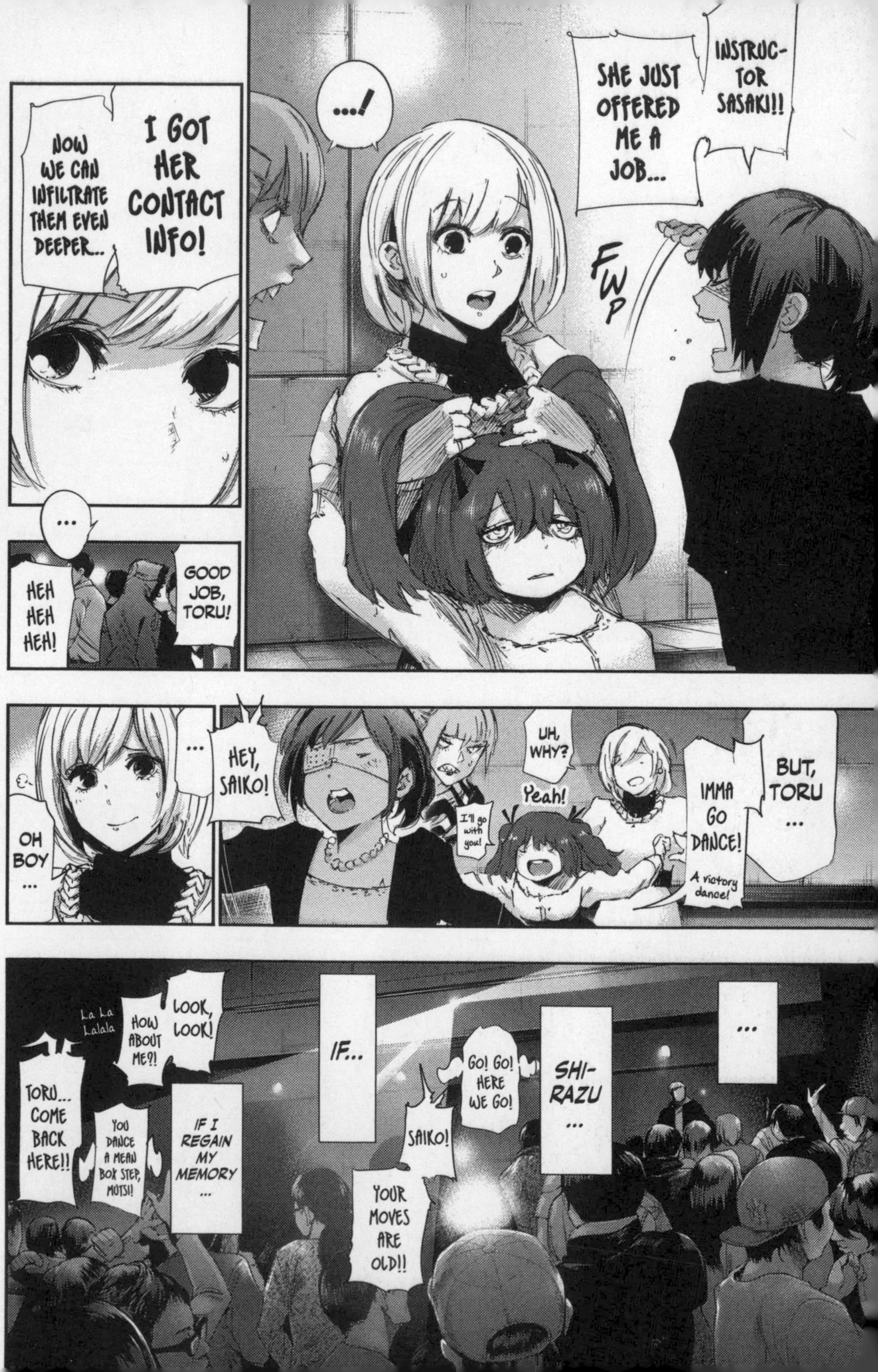
INSTRUCTOR SASAKI!!
SHE JUST OFFERED ME A JOB...
FWP
...!
I GOT HER CONTACT INFO!
NOW WE CAN INFILTRATE THEM EVEN DEEPER...
...
GOOD JOB, TORU!
HEH HEH HEH!
BUT, TORU...
IMMA GO DANCE!
A victory dance!
UH, WHY?
Yeah!
I'll go with you!
HEY, SAIKO!
...
OH BOY...
...
SHIRAZU...
IF...
GO! GO! HERE WE GO!
SAIKO!
YOUR MOVES ARE OLD!!
IF I REGAIN MY MEMORY...
LOOK, LOOK!
HOW ABOUT ME?!
La La Lalala
YOU DANCE A MEAN BOX STEP, MUTSI!
TORU... COME BACK HERE!!

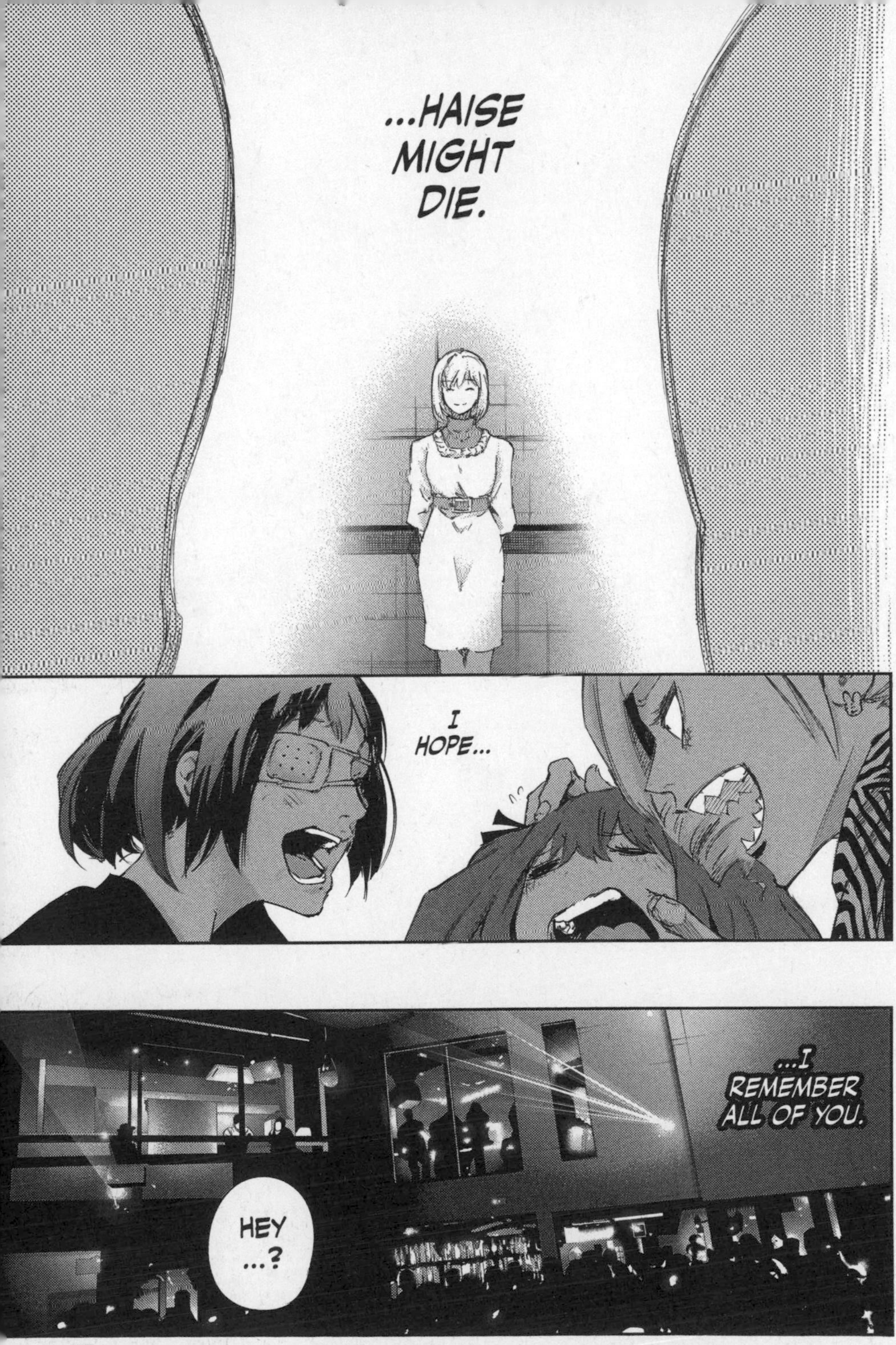
...HAISE MIGHT DIE.
I HOPE...
...I REMEMBER ALL OF YOU.
HEY ...?

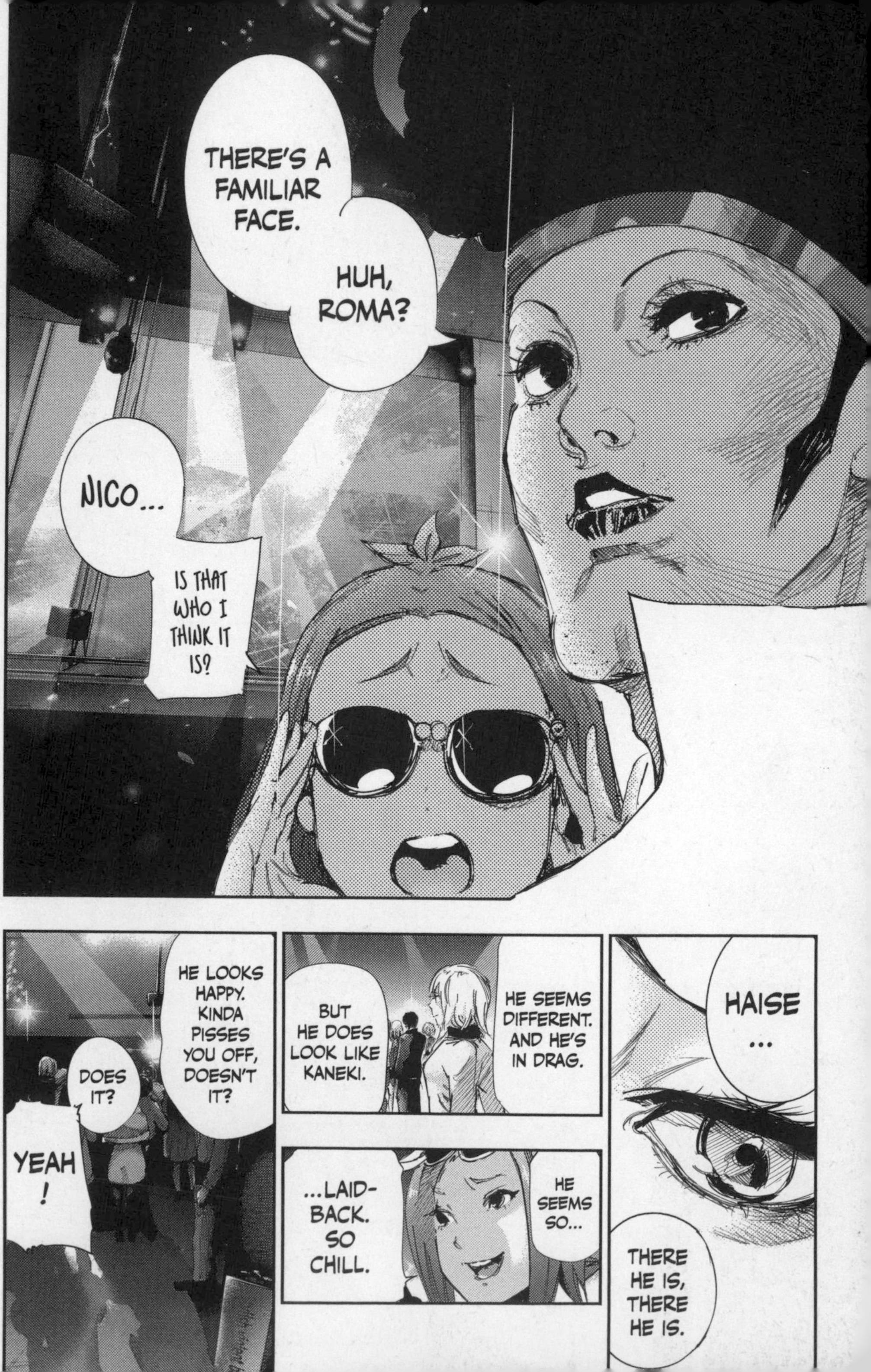
THERE'S A FAMILIAR FACE.
HUH, ROMA?
NICO...
IS THAT WHO I THINK IT IS?
HAISE ...
THERE HE IS, THERE HE IS.
HE SEEMS DIFFERENT. AND HE'S IN DRAG.
BUT HE DOES LOOK LIKE KANEKI.
HE SEEMS SO...
...LAID-BACK. SO CHILL.
HE LOOKS HAPPY. KINDA PISSES YOU OFF, DOESN'T IT?
DOES IT?
YEAH!

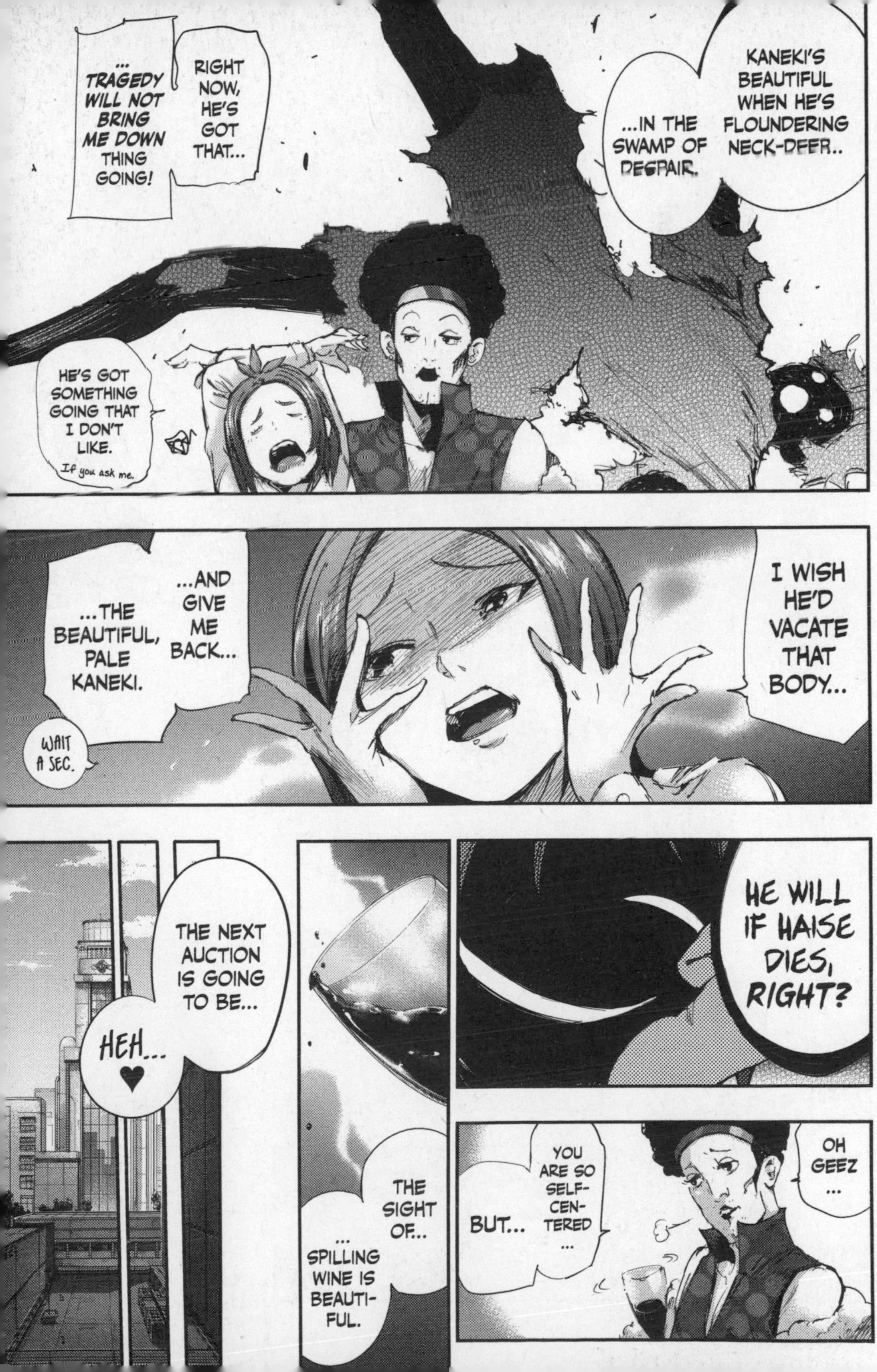
KANEKI'S BEAUTIFUL WHEN HE'S FLOUNDERING NECK-DEEP..
...IN THE SWAMP OF DESPAIR.
RIGHT NOW, HE'S GOT THAT...
...TRAGEDY WILL NOT BRING ME DOWN THING GOING!
HE'S GOT SOMETHING GOING THAT I DON'T LIKE.
If you ask me.
I WISH HE'D VACATE THAT BODY...
...AND GIVE ME BACK...
...THE BEAUTIFUL, PALE KANEKI.
WAIT A SEC.
HE WILL IF HAISE DIES, RIGHT?
OH GEEZ...
YOU ARE SO SELF-CENTERED...
BUT...
THE SIGHT OF...
...SPILLING WINE IS BEAUTIFUL.
THE NEXT AUCTION IS GOING TO BE...
HEH...♥

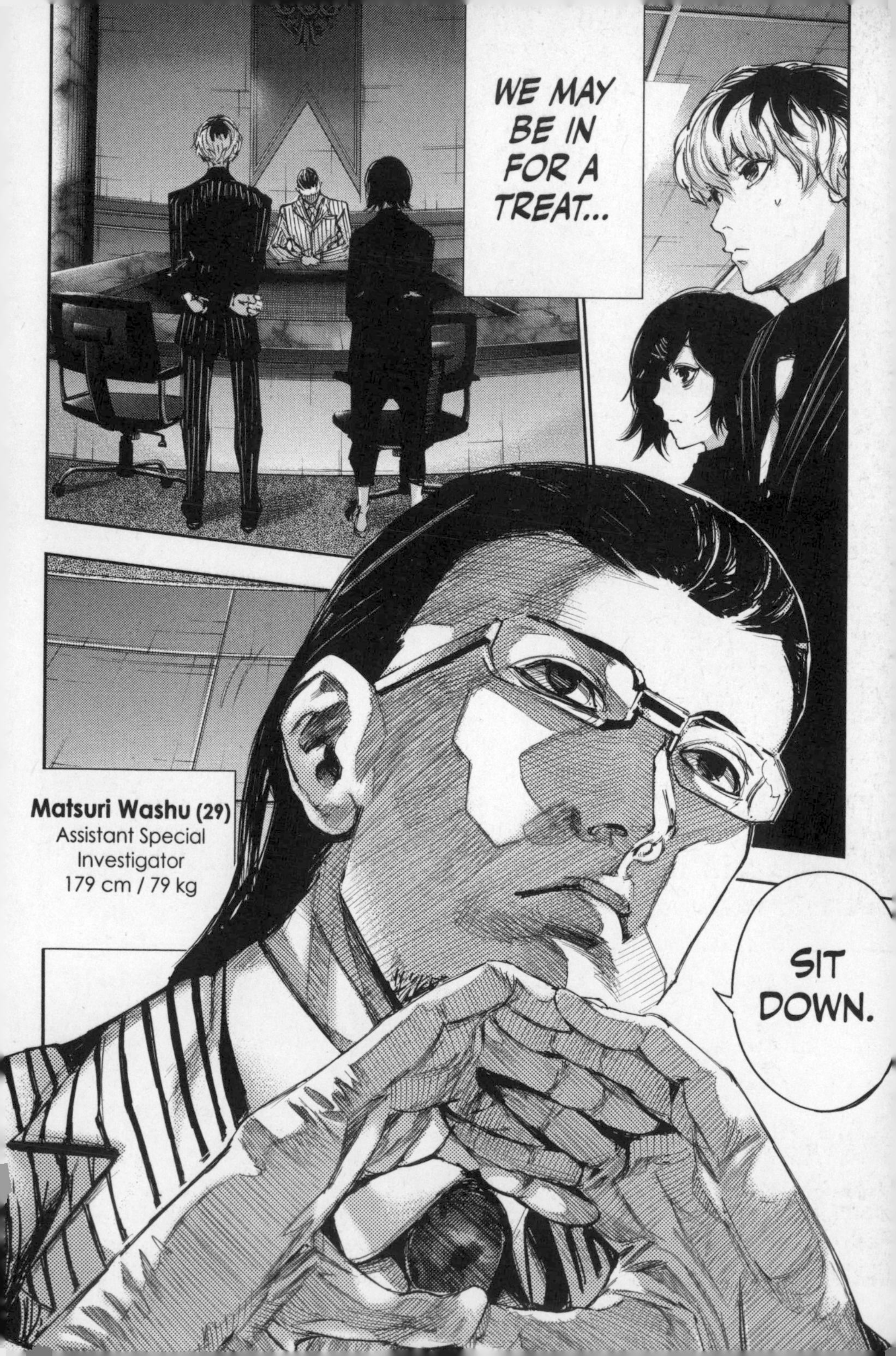
WE MAY BE IN FOR A TREAT...
Matsuri Washu (29)
Assistant Special Investigator
179 cm / 79 kg
SIT DOWN.

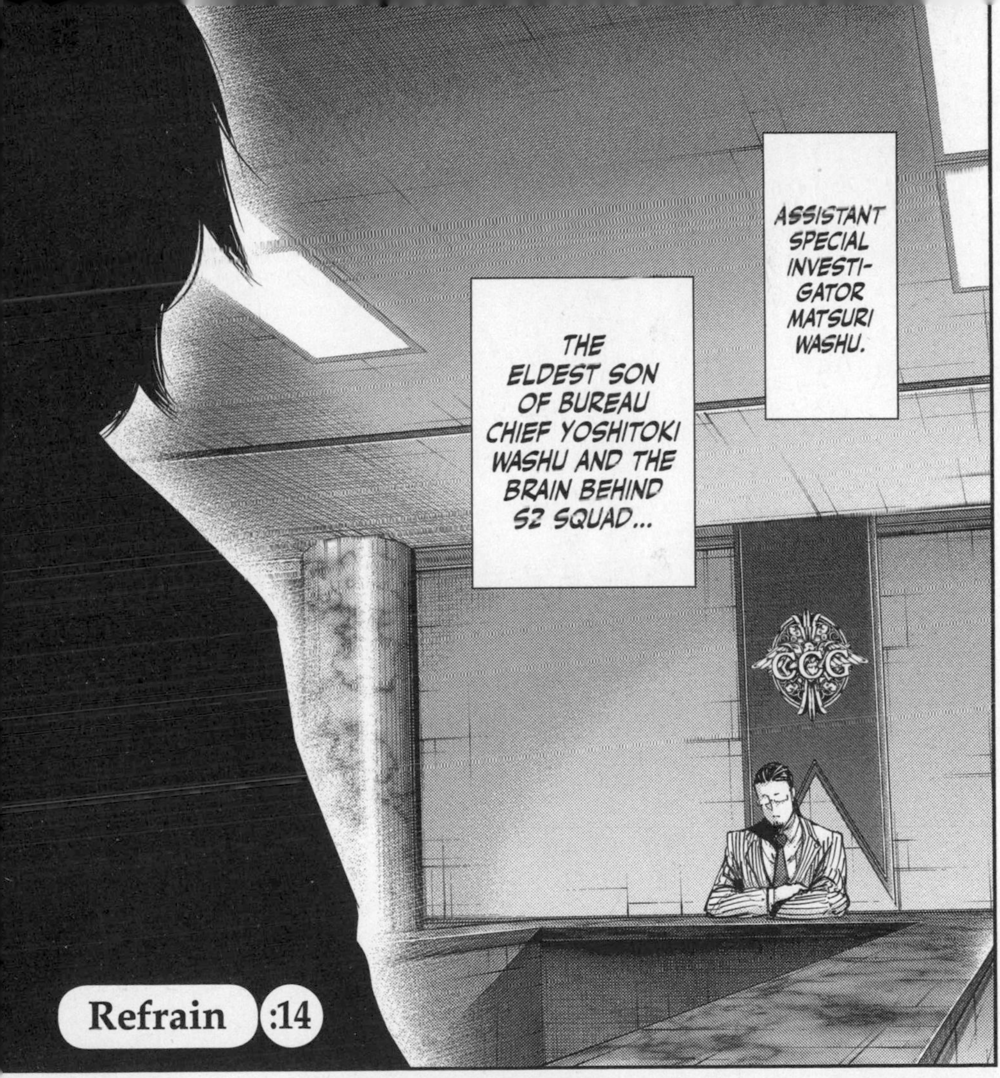
ASSISTANT SPECIAL INVESTIGATOR MATSURI WASHU.
THE ELDEST SON OF BUREAU CHIEF YOSHITOKI WASHU AND THE BRAIN BEHIND S2 SQUAD...
Refrain :14

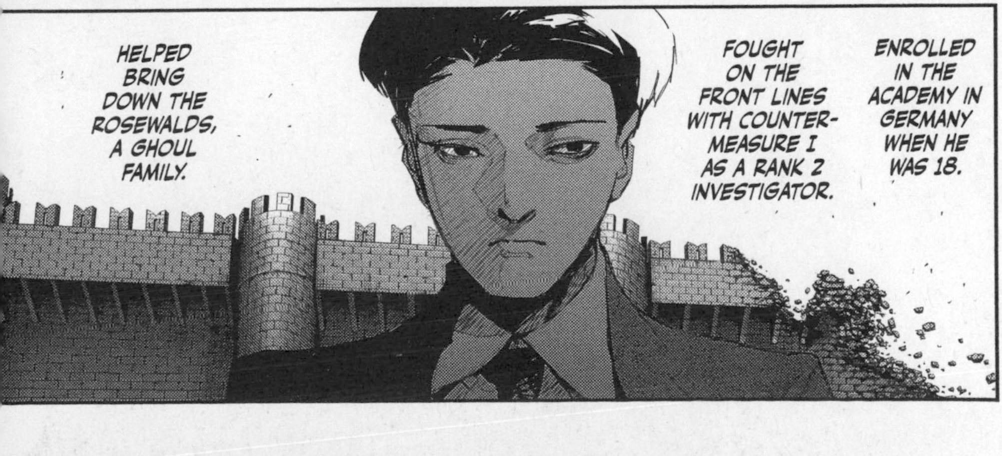
ENROLLED IN THE ACADEMY IN GERMANY WHEN HE WAS 18.
FOUGHT ON THE FRONT LINES WITH COUNTER-MEASURE I AS A RANK 2 INVESTIGATOR.
HELPED BRING DOWN THE ROSEWALDS, A GHOUL FAMILY.

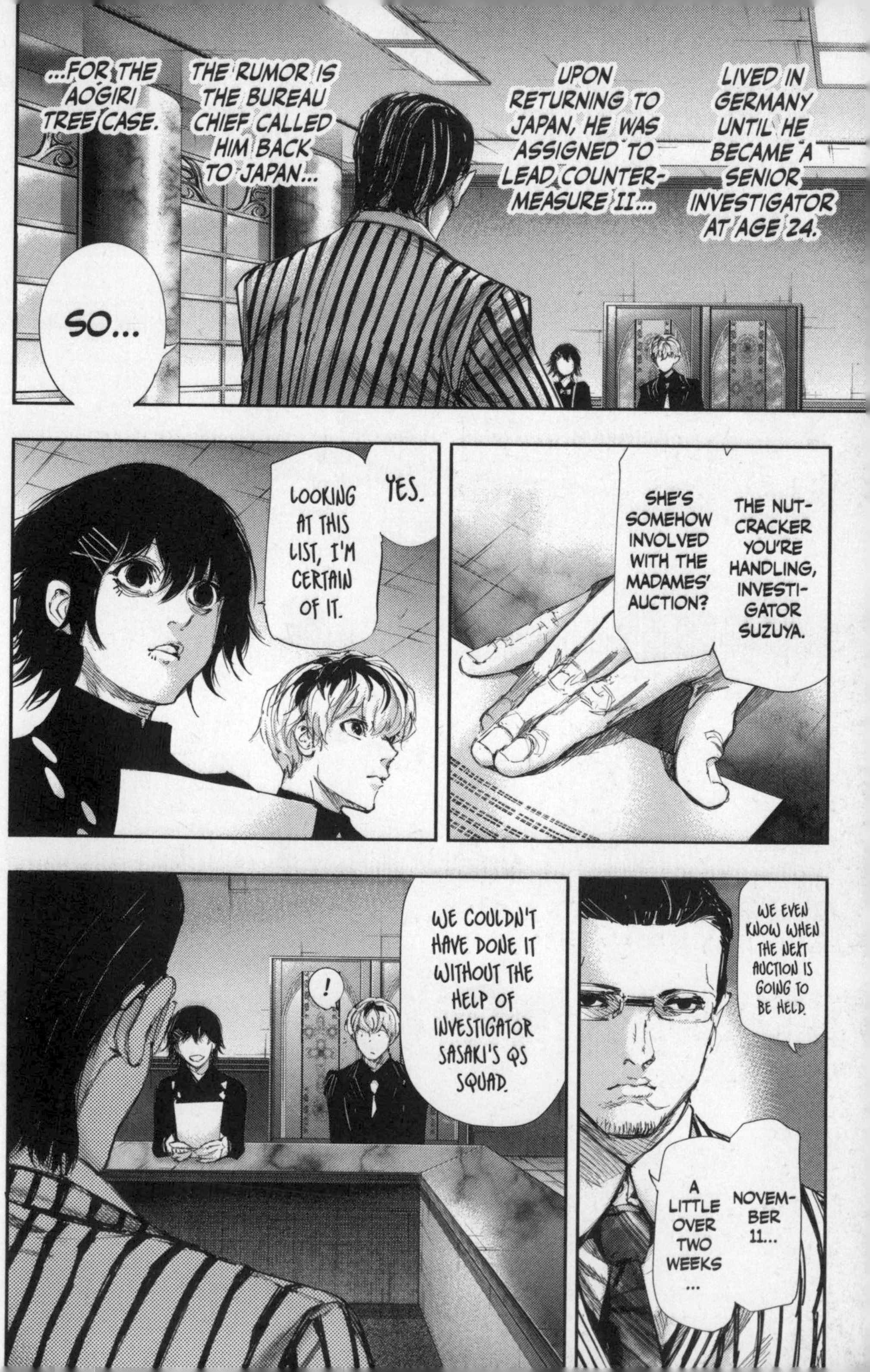
LIVED IN GERMANY UNTIL HE BECAME A SENIOR INVESTIGATOR AT AGE 24.
UPON RETURNING TO JAPAN, HE WAS ASSIGNED TO LEAD COUNTER-MEASURE II...
THE RUMOR IS THE BUREAU CHIEF CALLED HIM BACK TO JAPAN...
...FOR THE AOGIRI TREE CASE.
SO...
THE NUT-CRACKER YOU'RE HANDLING, INVESTI-GATOR SUZUYA.
SHE'S SOMEHOW INVOLVED WITH THE MADAMES' AUCTION?
YES.
LOOKING AT THIS LIST, I'M CERTAIN OF IT.
WE EVEN KNOW WHEN THE NEXT AUCTION IS GOING TO BE HELD.
NOVEM-BER 11...
A LITTLE OVER TWO WEEKS...
WE COULDN'T HAVE DONE IT WITHOUT THE HELP OF INVESTIGATOR SASAKI'S QS SQUAD.
!

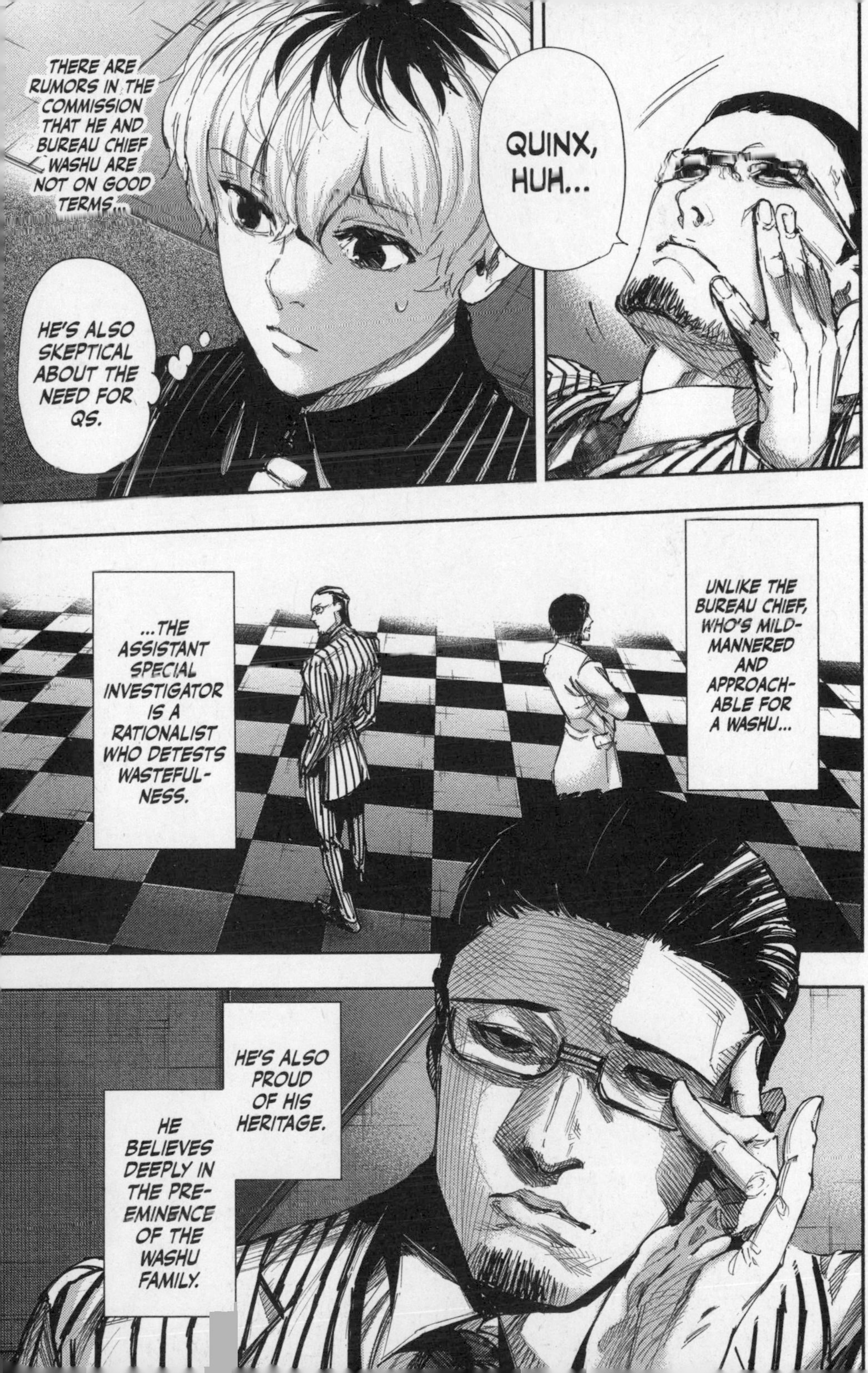
QUINX, HUH...
THERE ARE RUMORS IN THE COMMISSION THAT HE AND BUREAU CHIEF WASHU ARE NOT ON GOOD TERMS...
HE'S ALSO SKEPTICAL ABOUT THE NEED FOR QS.
UNLIKE THE BUREAU CHIEF, WHO'S MILD-MANNERED AND APPROACH-ABLE FOR A WASHU...
...THE ASSISTANT SPECIAL INVESTIGATOR IS A RATIONALIST WHO DETESTS WASTEFUL-NESS.
HE'S ALSO PROUD OF HIS HERITAGE.
HE BELIEVES DEEPLY IN THE PRE-EMINENCE OF THE WASHU FAMILY.

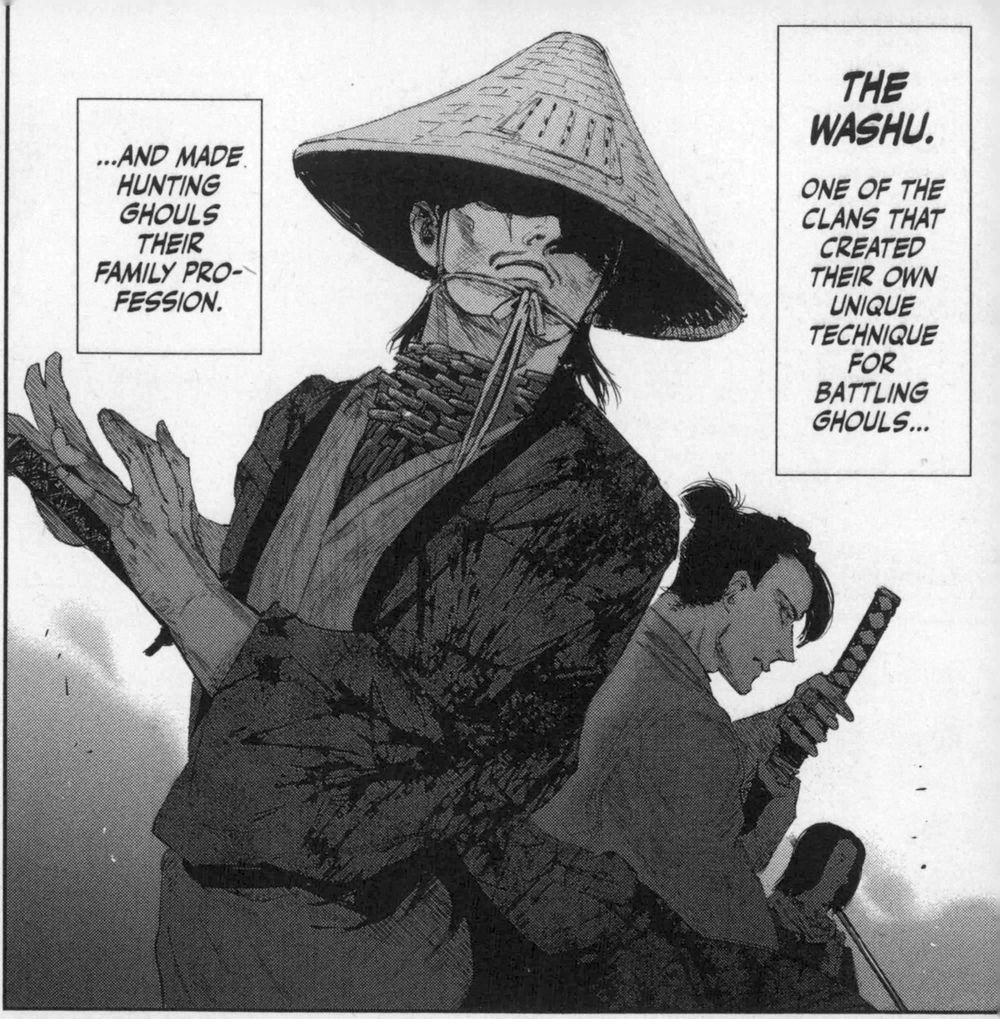
THE WASHU.
ONE OF THE CLANS THAT CREATED THEIR OWN UNIQUE TECHNIQUE FOR BATTLING GHOULS...
...AND MADE HUNTING GHOULS THEIR FAMILY PRO-FESSION.

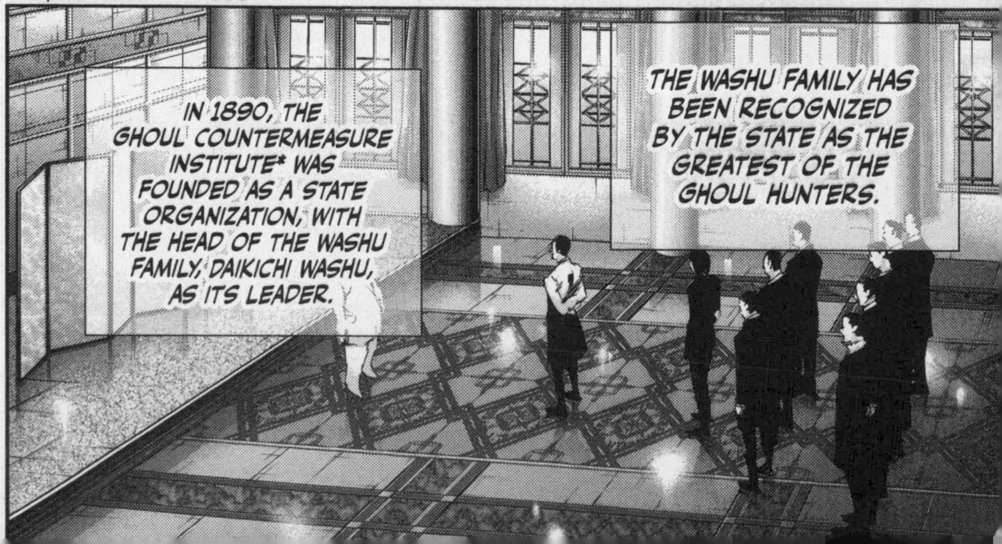
THE WASHU FAMILY HAS BEEN RECOGNIZED BY THE STATE AS THE GREATEST OF THE GHOUL HUNTERS.
IN 1890, THE GHOUL COUNTERMEASURE INSTITUTE* WAS FOUNDED AS A STATE ORGANIZATION, WITH THE HEAD OF THE WASHU FAMILY, DAIKICHI WASHU, AS ITS LEADER.

*The predecessor to the CCG

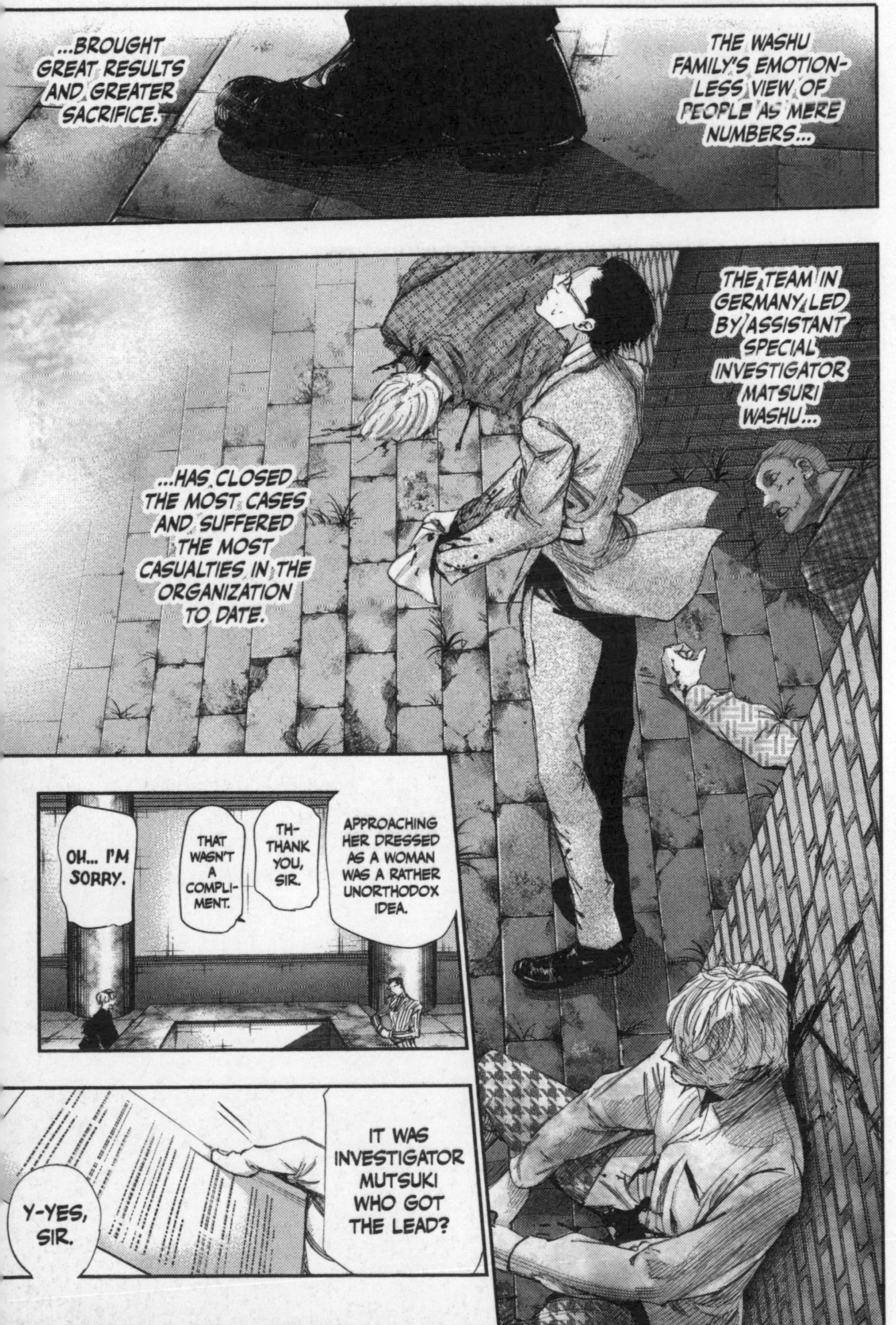
THE WASHU FAMILY'S EMOTION-LESS VIEW OF PEOPLE AS MERE NUMBERS...
...BROUGHT GREAT RESULTS AND GREATER SACRIFICE.
THE TEAM IN GERMANY LED BY ASSISTANT SPECIAL INVESTIGATOR MATSURI WASHU...
...HAS CLOSED THE MOST CASES AND SUFFERED THE MOST CASUALTIES IN THE ORGANIZATION TO DATE.
APPROACHING HER DRESSED AS A WOMAN WAS A RATHER UNORTHODOX IDEA.
TH-THANK YOU, SIR.
THAT WASN'T A COMPLI-MENT.
OH... I'M SORRY.
IT WAS INVESTIGATOR MUTSUKI WHO GOT THE LEAD?
Y-YES, SIR.

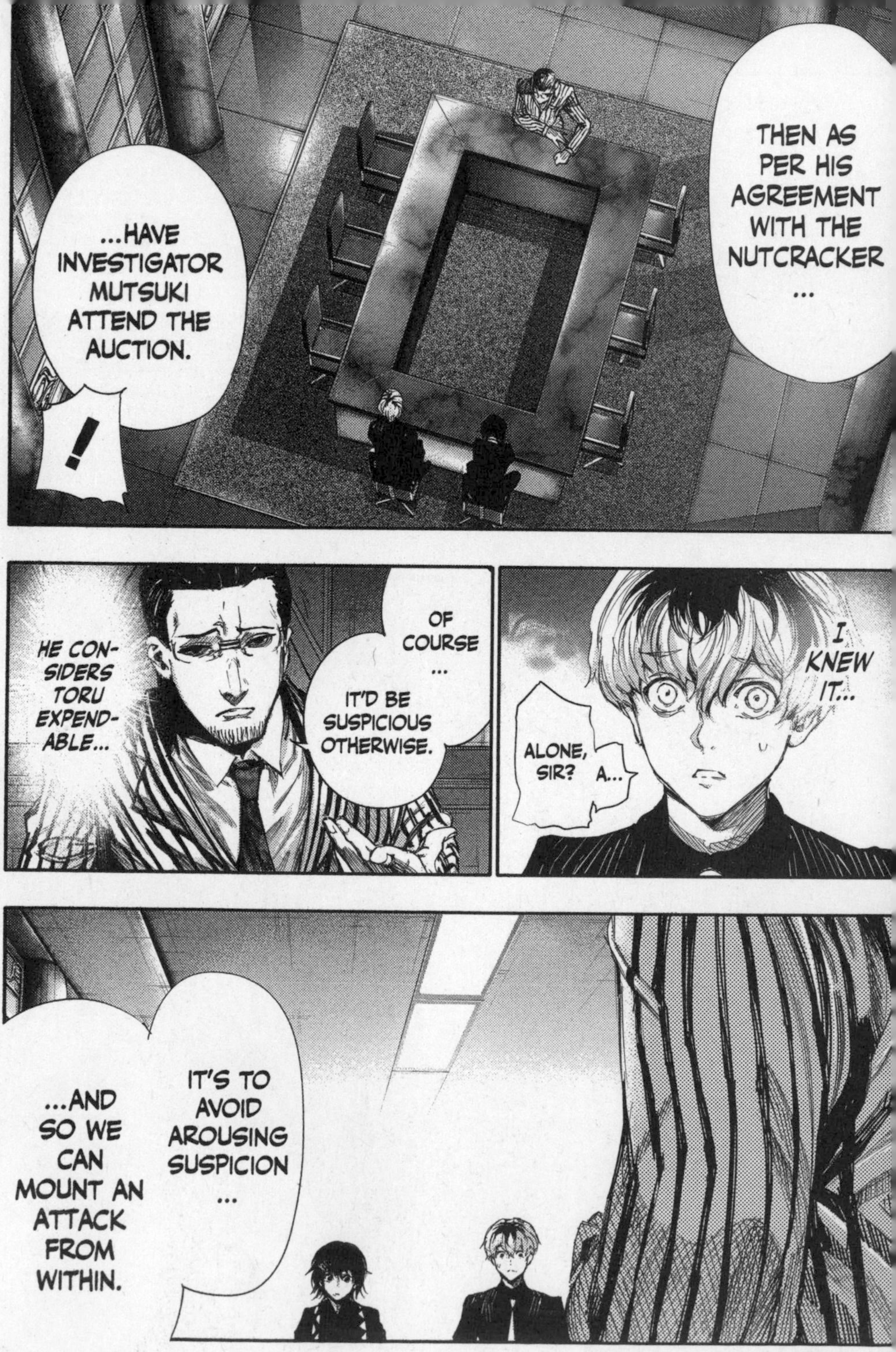
THEN AS PER HIS AGREEMENT WITH THE NUTCRACKER ...
...HAVE INVESTIGATOR MUTSUKI ATTEND THE AUCTION.
!
I KNEW IT...
A...
ALONE, SIR?
OF COURSE ...
IT'D BE SUSPICIOUS OTHERWISE.
HE CONSIDERS TORU EXPENDABLE...
IT'S TO AVOID AROUSING SUSPICION ...
...AND SO WE CAN MOUNT AN ATTACK FROM WITHIN.

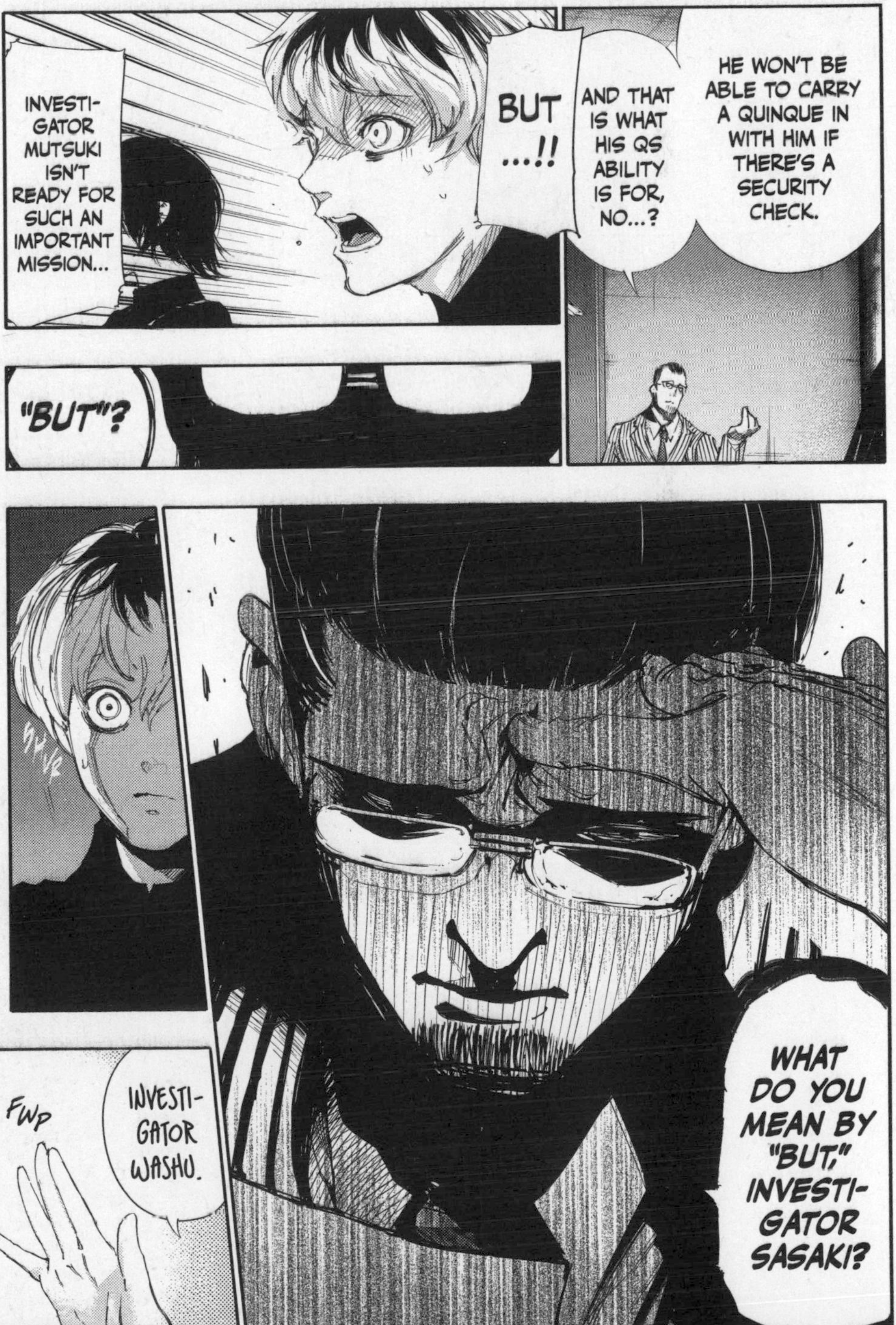
HE WON'T BE ABLE TO CARRY A QUINQUE IN WITH HIM IF THERE'S A SECURITY CHECK.
AND THAT IS WHAT HIS QS ABILITY IS FOR, NO...?
BUT ...!!
INVESTI-GATOR MUTSUKI ISN'T READY FOR SUCH AN IMPORTANT MISSION...
"BUT"?
WHAT DO YOU MEAN BY "BUT," INVESTI-GATOR SASAKI?
INVESTI-GATOR WASHU.
FWP

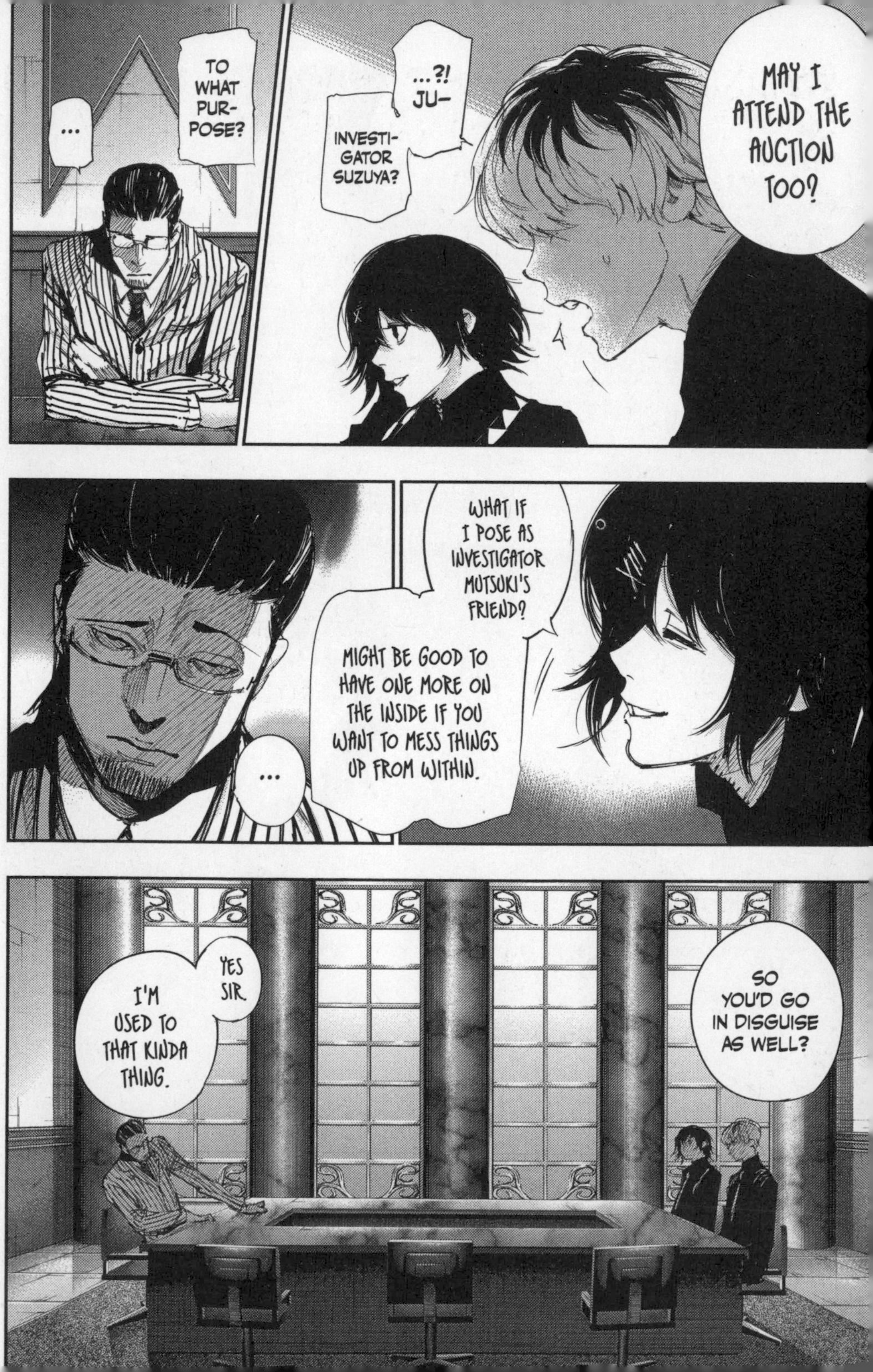
MAY I ATTEND THE AUCTION TOO?
...?! JU-
INVESTIGATOR SUZUYA?
TO WHAT PURPOSE?
...
WHAT IF I POSE AS INVESTIGATOR MUTSUKI'S FRIEND?
MIGHT BE GOOD TO HAVE ONE MORE ON THE INSIDE IF YOU WANT TO MESS THINGS UP FROM WITHIN.
...
SO YOU'D GO IN DISGUISE AS WELL?
YES SIR.
I'M USED TO THAT KINDA THING.

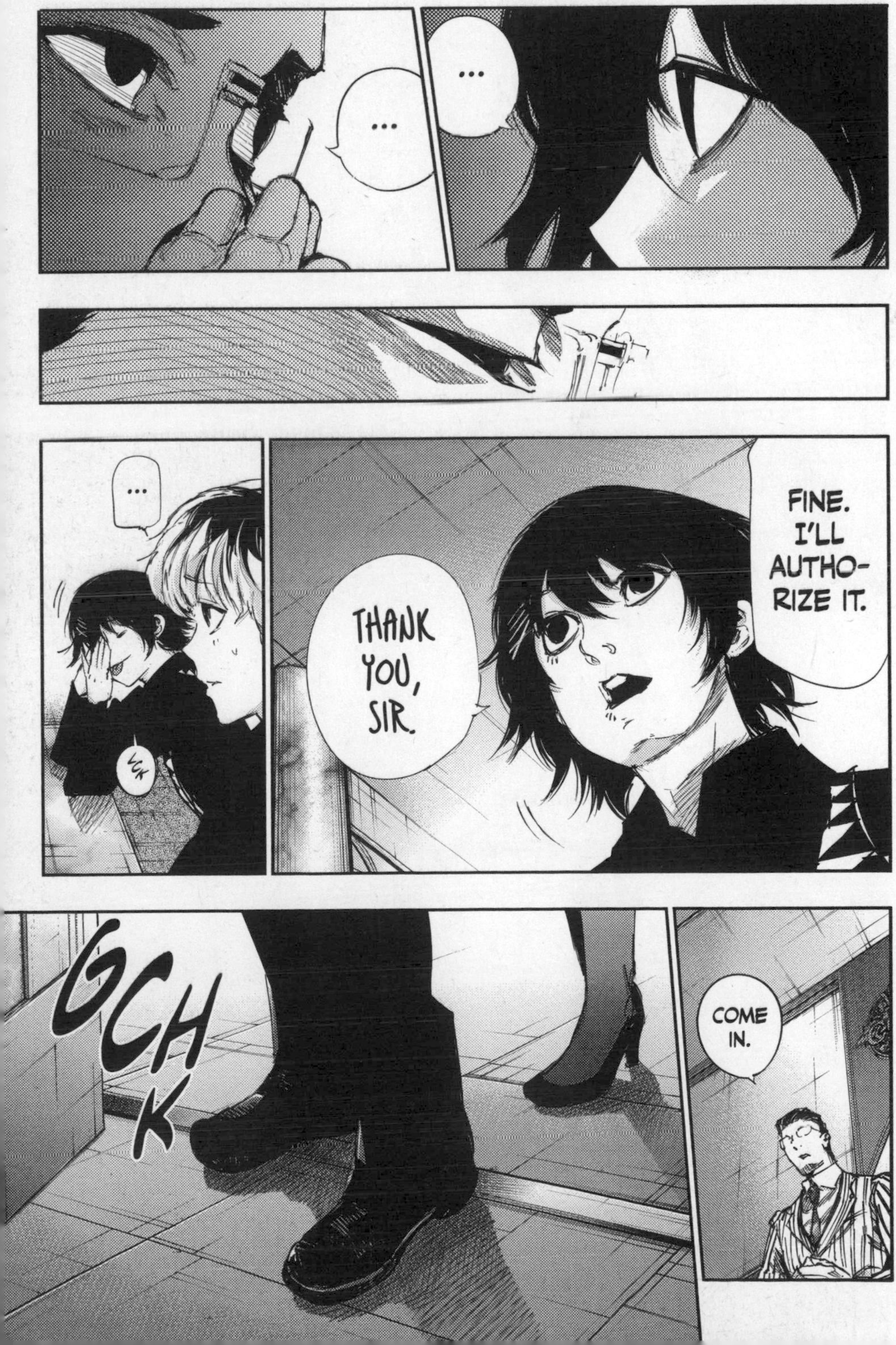
...
...
FINE. I'LL AUTHORIZE IT.
THANK YOU, SIR.
...
UCK
COME IN.
GCHK

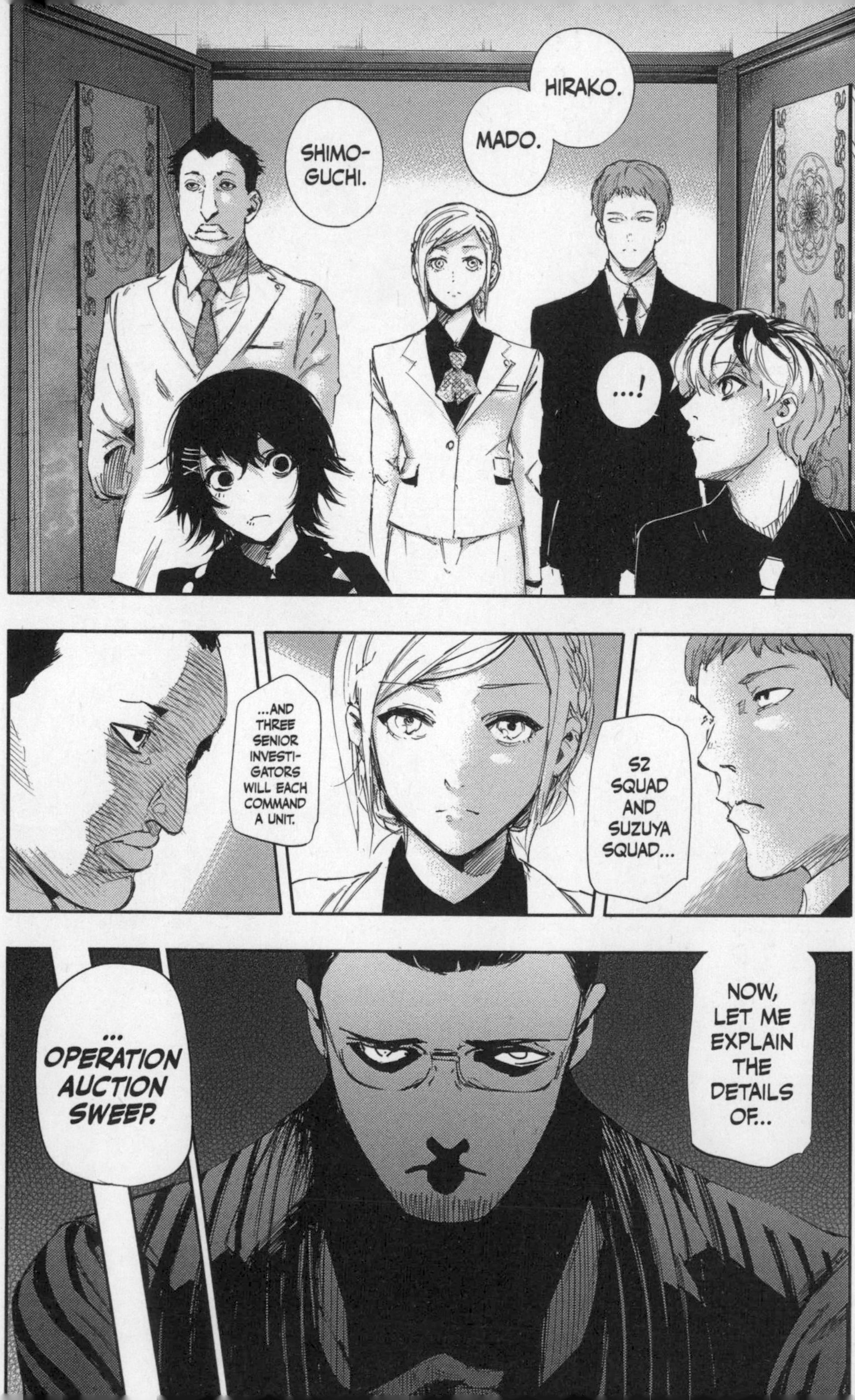
HIRAKO.
MADO.
SHIMO-GUCHI.
...!
S2 SQUAD AND SUZUYA SQUAD...
...AND THREE SENIOR INVESTI-GATORS WILL EACH COMMAND A UNIT.
NOW, LET ME EXPLAIN THE DETAILS OF...
...OPERATION AUCTION SWEEP.

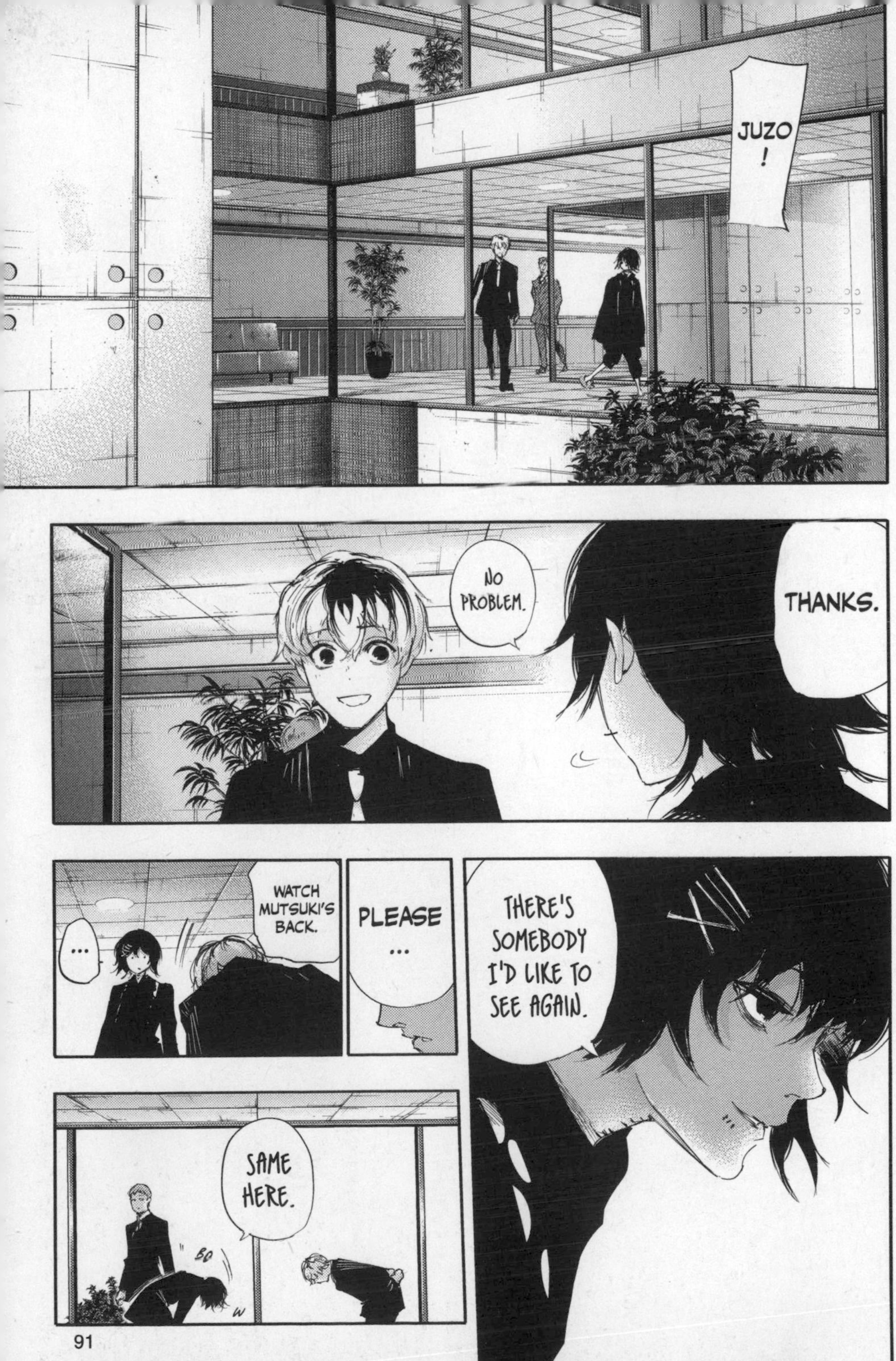

JUZO !
THANKS.
NO PROBLEM.
THERE'S SOMEBODY I'D LIKE TO SEE AGAIN.
PLEASE ...
WATCH MUTSUKI'S BACK.
...
SAME HERE.
BOW

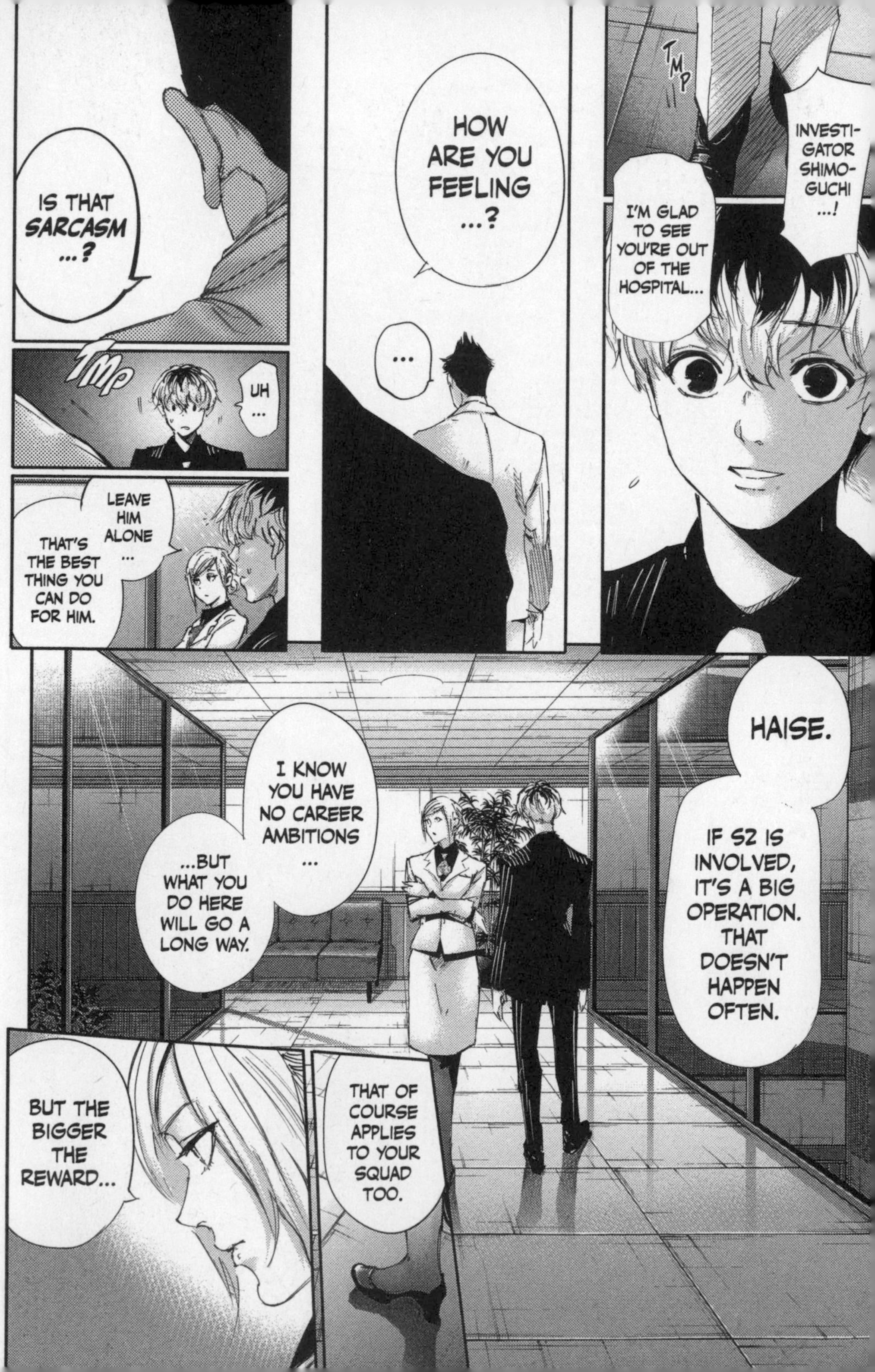
TMP
INVESTIGATOR SHIMOGUCHI ...!
I'M GLAD TO SEE YOU'RE OUT OF THE HOSPITAL...
HOW ARE YOU FEELING ...?
...
IS THAT SARCASM ...?
TMP
UH ...
LEAVE HIM ALONE ...
THAT'S THE BEST THING YOU CAN DO FOR HIM.
HAISE.
IF S2 IS INVOLVED, IT'S A BIG OPERATION. THAT DOESN'T HAPPEN OFTEN.
I KNOW YOU HAVE NO CAREER AMBITIONS ...
...BUT WHAT YOU DO HERE WILL GO A LONG WAY.
THAT OF COURSE APPLIES TO YOUR SQUAD TOO.
BUT THE BIGGER THE REWARD...

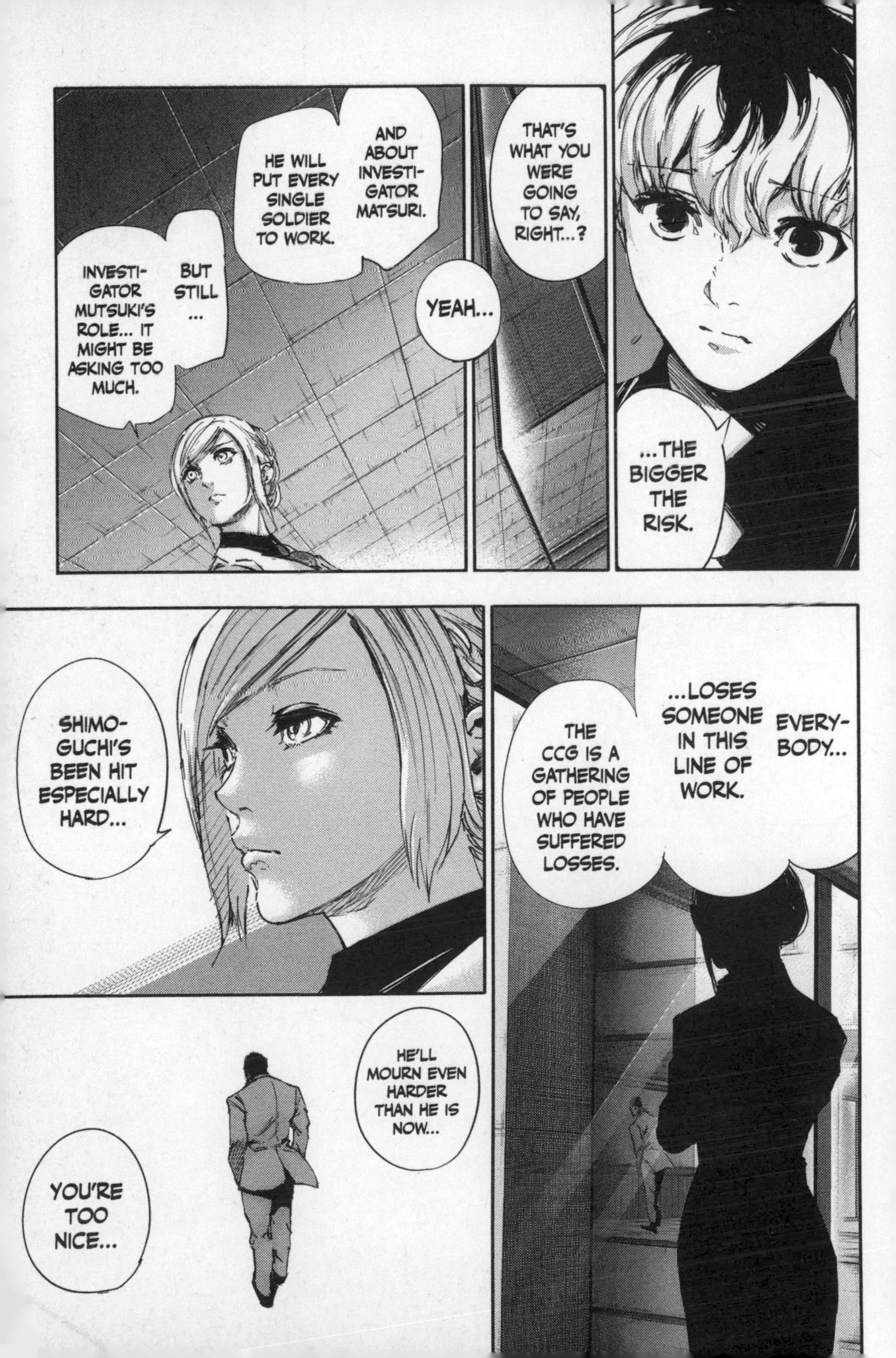
...THE BIGGER THE RISK.
THAT'S WHAT YOU WERE GOING TO SAY, RIGHT...?
YEAH...
AND ABOUT INVESTIGATOR MATSURI.
HE WILL PUT EVERY SINGLE SOLDIER TO WORK.
BUT STILL...
INVESTIGATOR MUTSUKI'S ROLE... IT MIGHT BE ASKING TOO MUCH.
EVERYBODY...
...LOSES SOMEONE IN THIS LINE OF WORK.
THE CCG IS A GATHERING OF PEOPLE WHO HAVE SUFFERED LOSSES.
SHIMOGUCHI'S BEEN HIT ESPECIALLY HARD...
HE'LL MOURN EVEN HARDER THAN HE IS NOW...
YOU'RE TOO NICE...

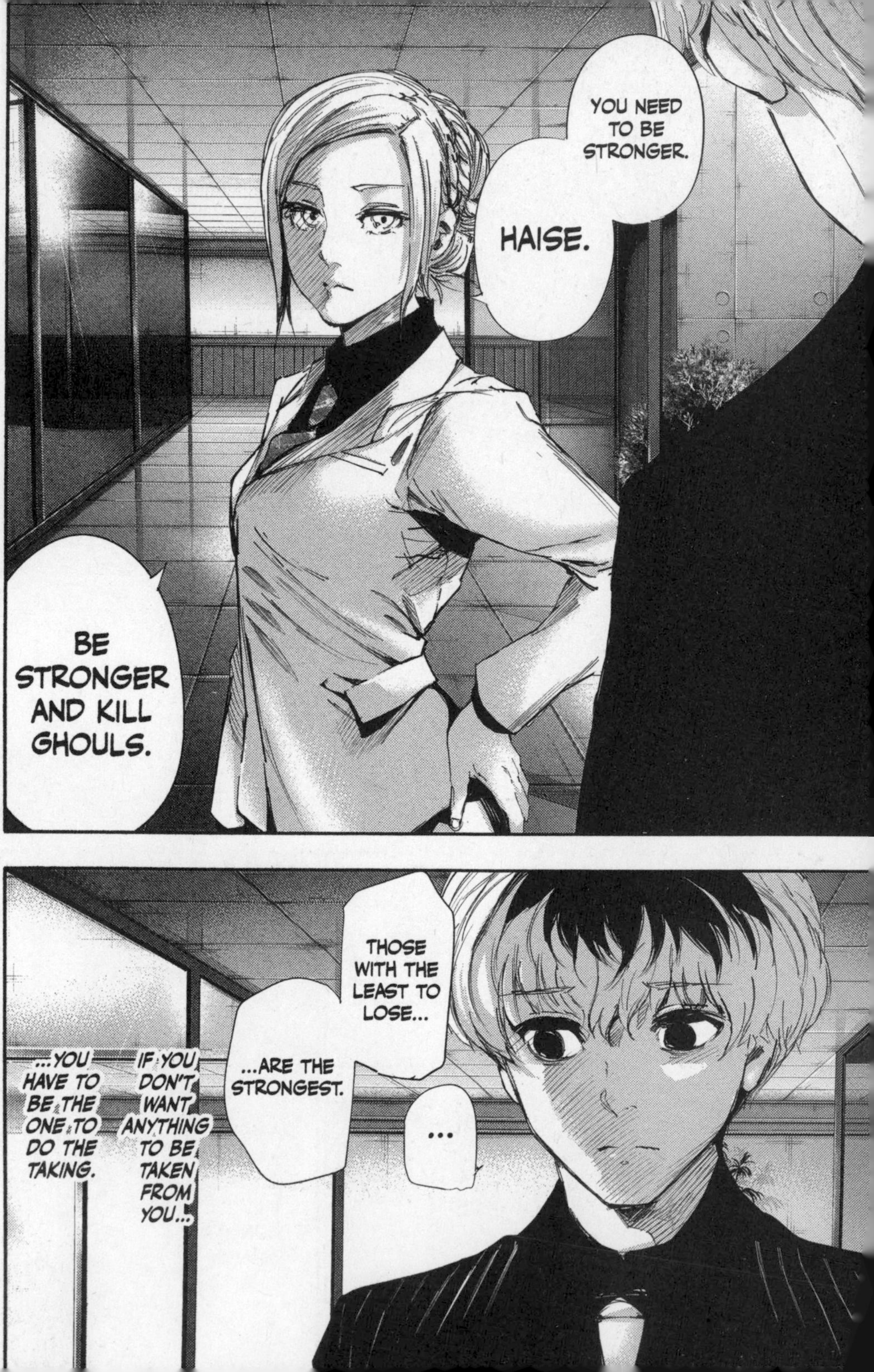
YOU NEED TO BE STRONGER.
HAISE.
BE STRONGER AND KILL GHOULS.
THOSE WITH THE LEAST TO LOSE...
...ARE THE STRONGEST.
...
IF YOU DON'T WANT ANYTHING TO BE TAKEN FROM YOU...
...YOU HAVE TO BE THE ONE TO DO THE TAKING.

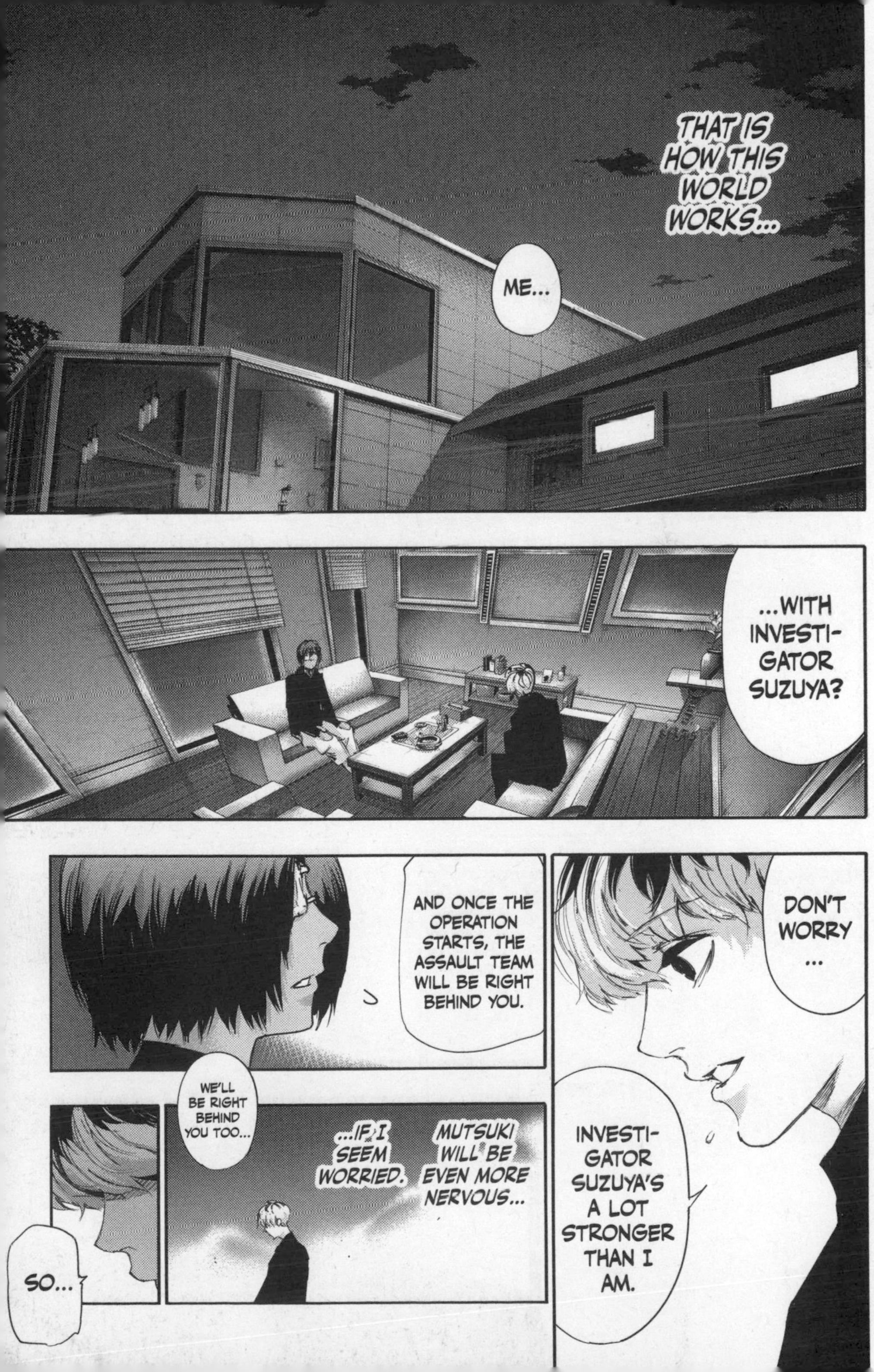
THAT IS HOW THIS WORLD WORKS...
ME...
...WITH INVESTI-GATOR SUZUYA?
DON'T WORRY ...
INVESTI-GATOR SUZUYA'S A LOT STRONGER THAN I AM.
AND ONCE THE OPERATION STARTS, THE ASSAULT TEAM WILL BE RIGHT BEHIND YOU.
WE'LL BE RIGHT BEHIND YOU TOO...
MUTSUKI WILL BE EVEN MORE NERVOUS...
...IF I SEEM WORRIED.
SO...

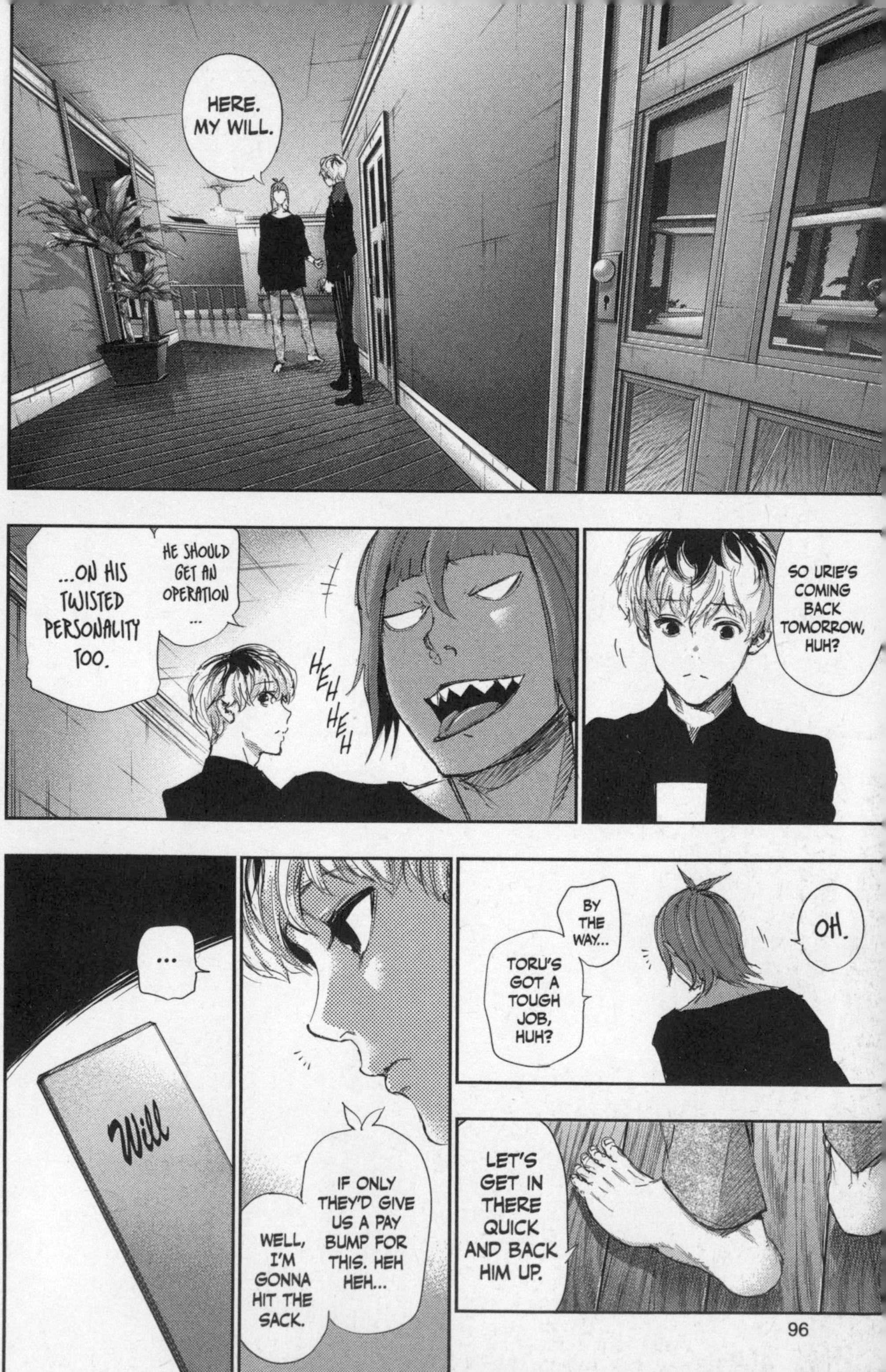
HERE. MY WILL.
SO URIE'S COMING BACK TOMORROW, HUH?
HE SHOULD GET AN OPERATION ...
...ON HIS TWISTED PERSONALITY TOO.
HEH HEH HEH
OH.
BY THE WAY...
TORU'S GOT A TOUGH JOB, HUH?
LET'S GET IN THERE QUICK AND BACK HIM UP.
IF ONLY THEY'D GIVE US A PAY BUMP FOR THIS. HEH HEH...
WELL, I'M GONNA HIT THE SACK.
...
Will

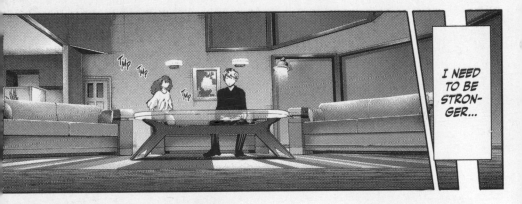

I NEED
TO BE
STRON-
GER...

...clean
my
ears?

Can you...

I HAVE
TO BE
STRONG
...

FLUFF...

SURE,
SURE.

...SO
I CAN
PROTECT
EVERY-
ONE.

...

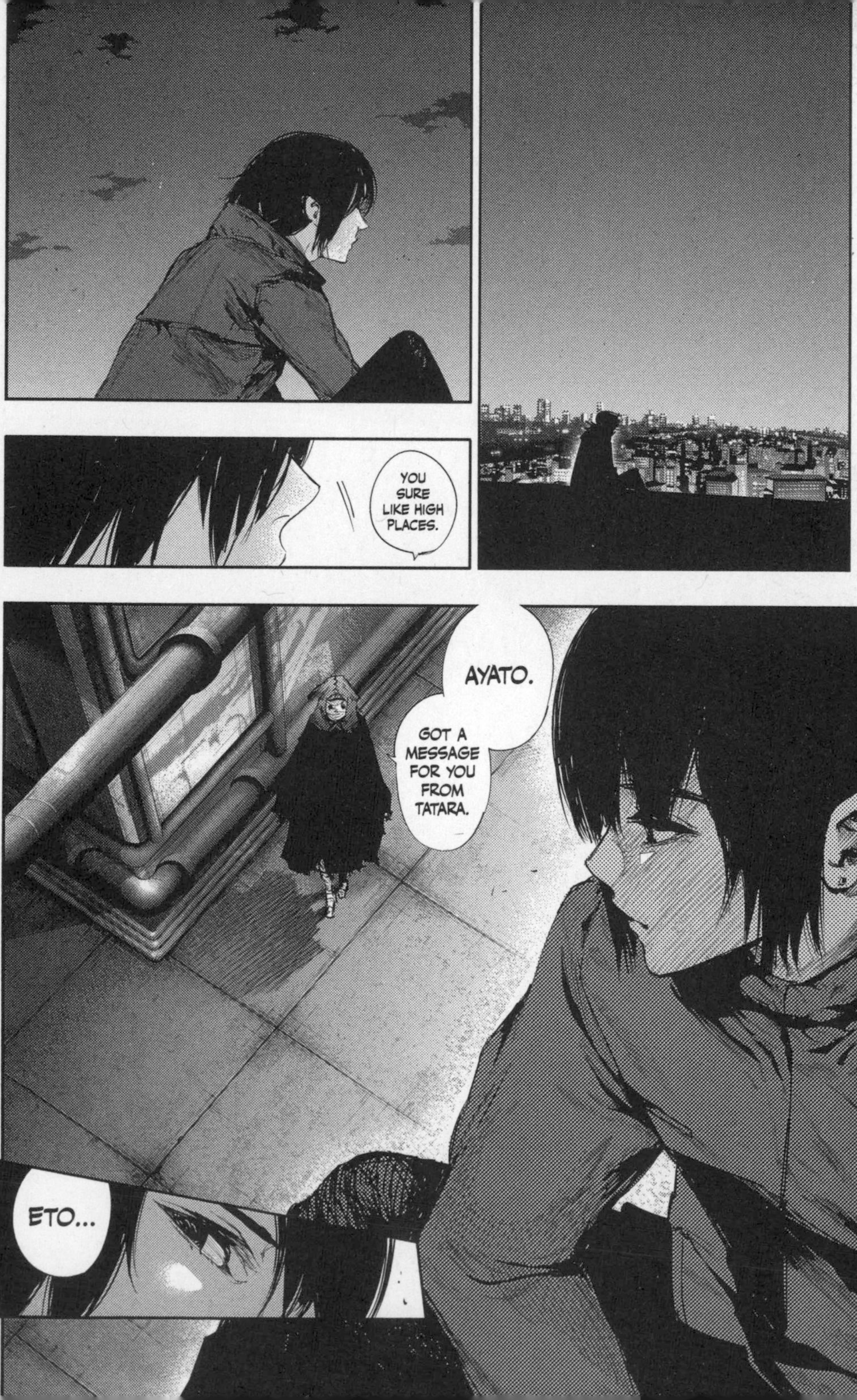
YOU SURE LIKE HIGH PLACES.
AYATO.
GOT A MESSAGE FOR YOU FROM TATARA.
ETO...

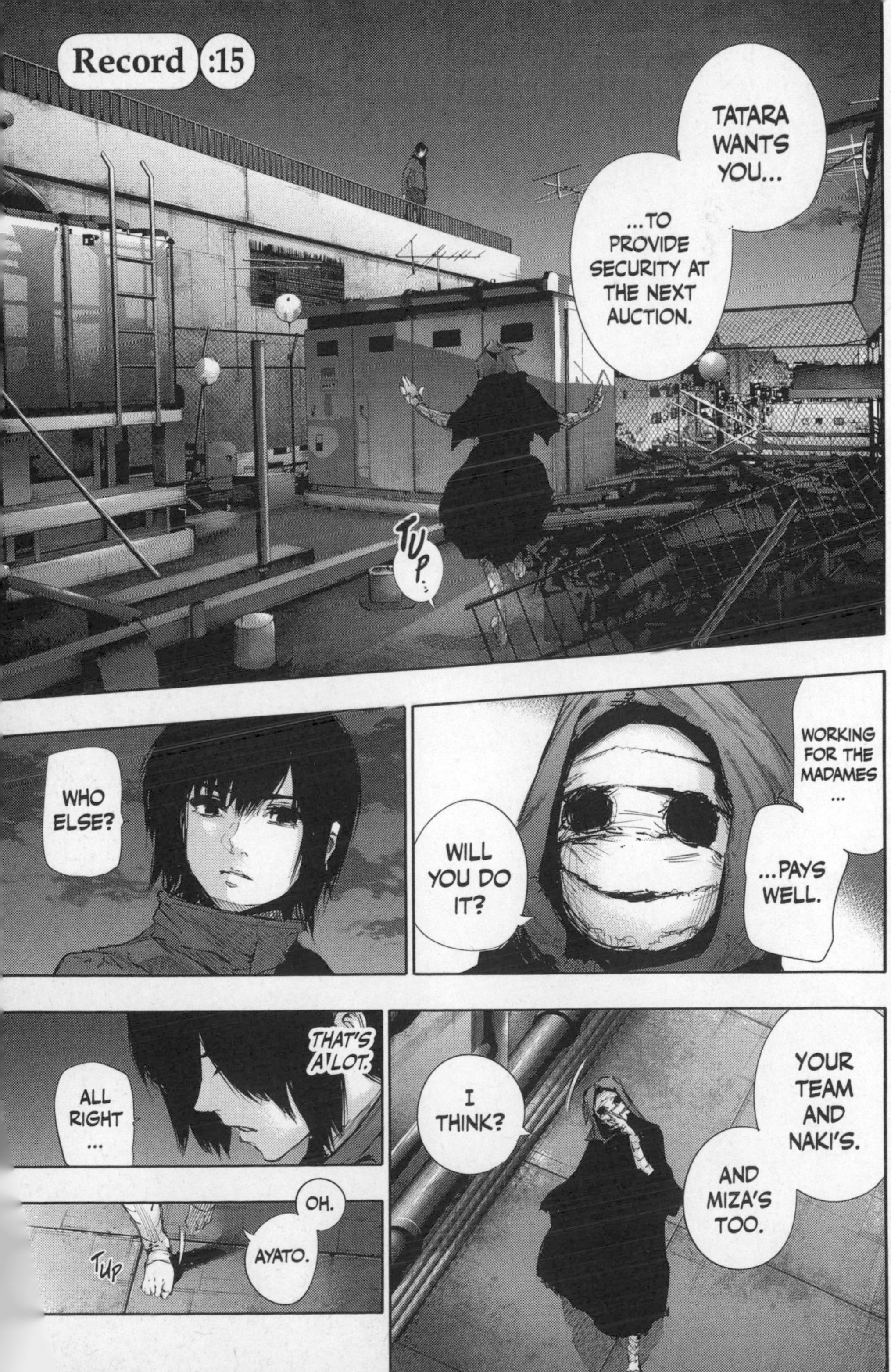
Record :15
TATARA WANTS YOU...
...TO PROVIDE SECURITY AT THE NEXT AUCTION.
TUP...
WORKING FOR THE MADAMES ...
...PAYS WELL.
WILL YOU DO IT?
WHO ELSE?
YOUR TEAM AND NAKI'S.
AND MIZA'S TOO.
I THINK?
THAT'S A LOT.
ALL RIGHT ...
OH.
AYATO.
TUP

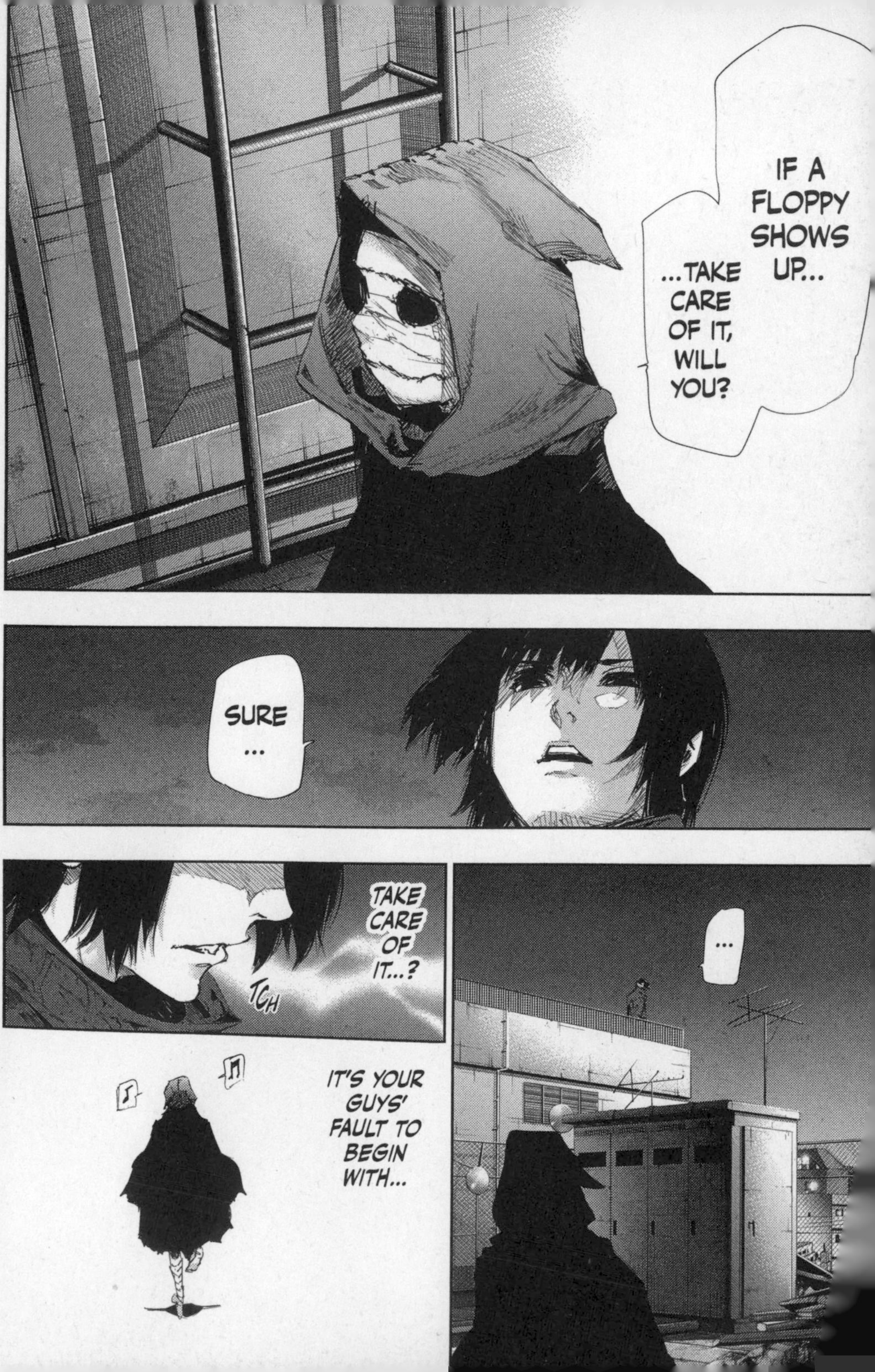

IF A FLOPPY SHOWS UP...
...TAKE CARE OF IT, WILL YOU?
SURE ...
...
TAKE CARE OF IT...?
TCH
IT'S YOUR GUYS' FAULT TO BEGIN WITH...

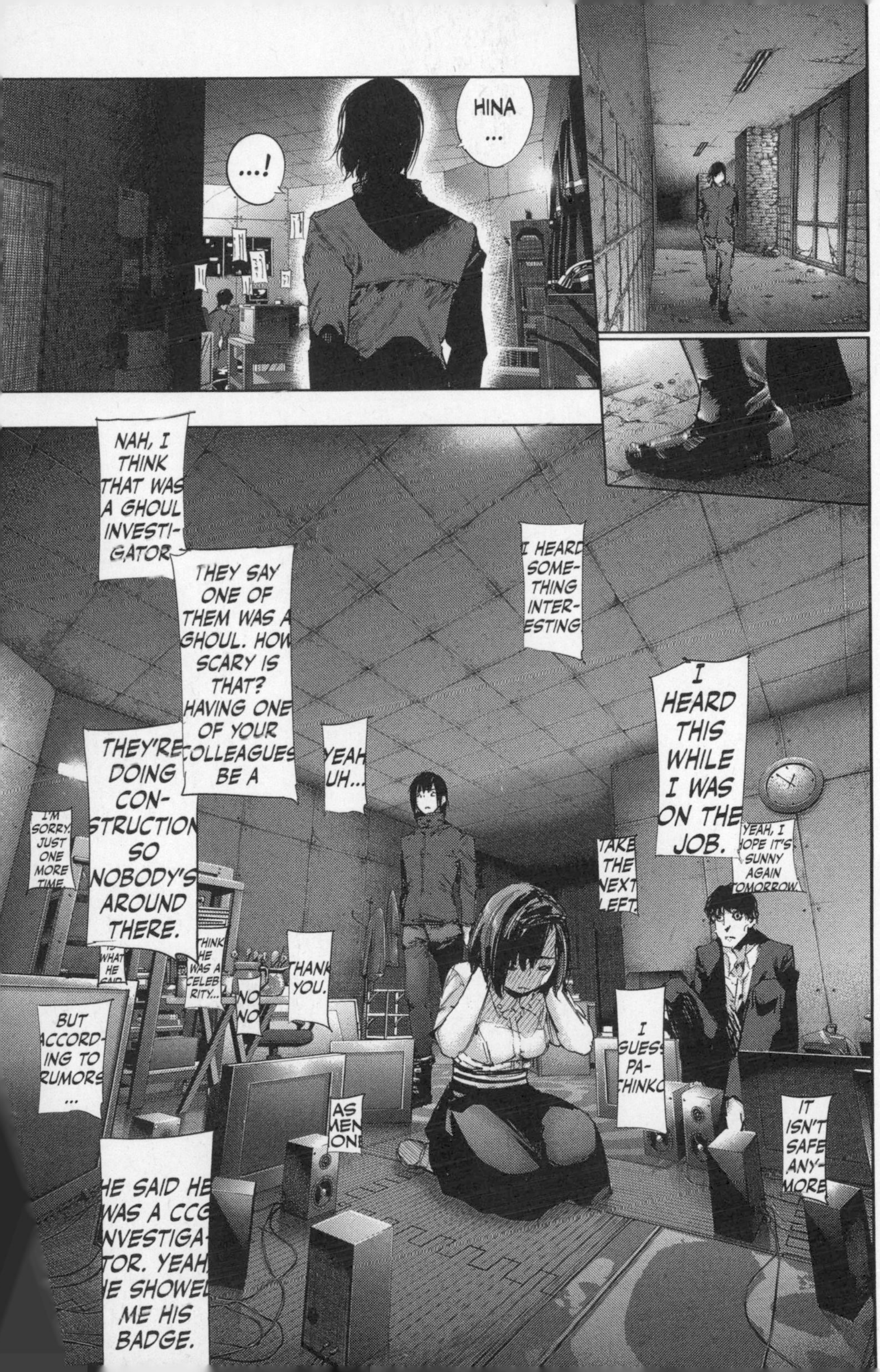
HINA...
...!
I HEARD SOMETHING INTERESTING
NAH, I THINK THAT WAS A GHOUL INVESTIGATOR
THEY SAY ONE OF THEM WAS A GHOUL. HOW SCARY IS THAT? HAVING ONE OF YOUR COLLEAGUES BE A
I HEARD THIS WHILE I WAS ON THE JOB.
YEAH, I HOPE IT'S SUNNY AGAIN TOMORROW.
TAKE THE NEXT LEFT.
YEAH UH...
THEY'RE DOING CONSTRUCTION SO NOBODY'S AROUND THERE.
I'M SORRY, JUST ONE MORE TIME.
THINK HE WAS A CELEBRITY...
WHAT HE SAID
THANK YOU.
NO NO
I GUESS PA-
IT ISN'T SAFE ANYMORE
BUT ACCORDING TO RUMORS...
HE SAID HE WAS A CCG INVESTIGATOR. YEAH, HE SHOWED ME HIS BADGE.

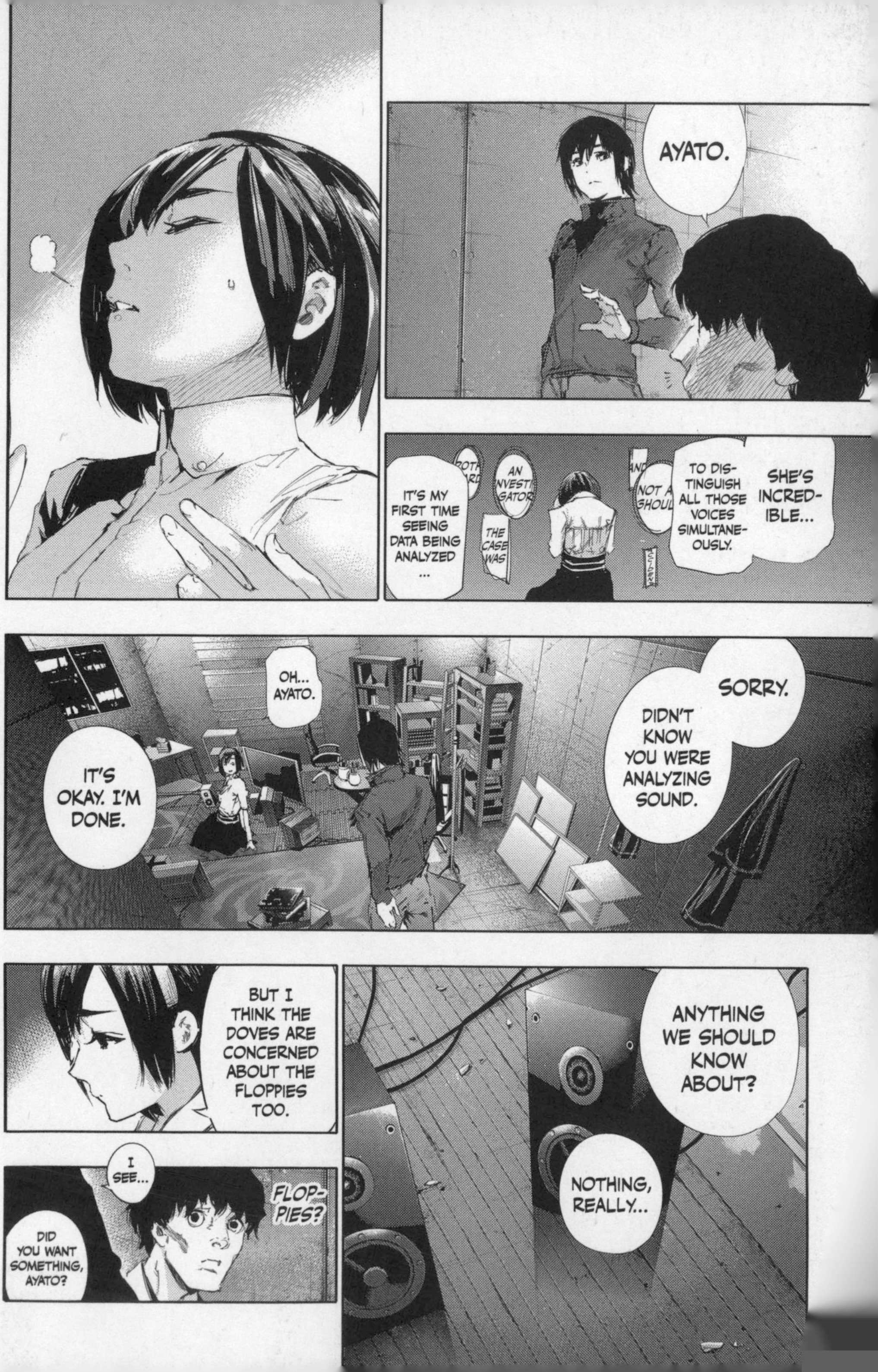
AYATO.
SHE'S INCREDIBLE...
TO DISTINGUISH ALL THOSE VOICES SIMULTANEOUSLY.
THE CASE WAS
IT'S MY FIRST TIME SEEING DATA BEING ANALYZED...
SORRY.
DIDN'T KNOW YOU WERE ANALYZING SOUND.
OH... AYATO.
IT'S OKAY. I'M DONE.
ANYTHING WE SHOULD KNOW ABOUT?
NOTHING, REALLY...
BUT I THINK THE DOVES ARE CONCERNED ABOUT THE FLOPPIES TOO.
I SEE...
FLOP-PIES?
DID YOU WANT SOMETHING, AYATO?

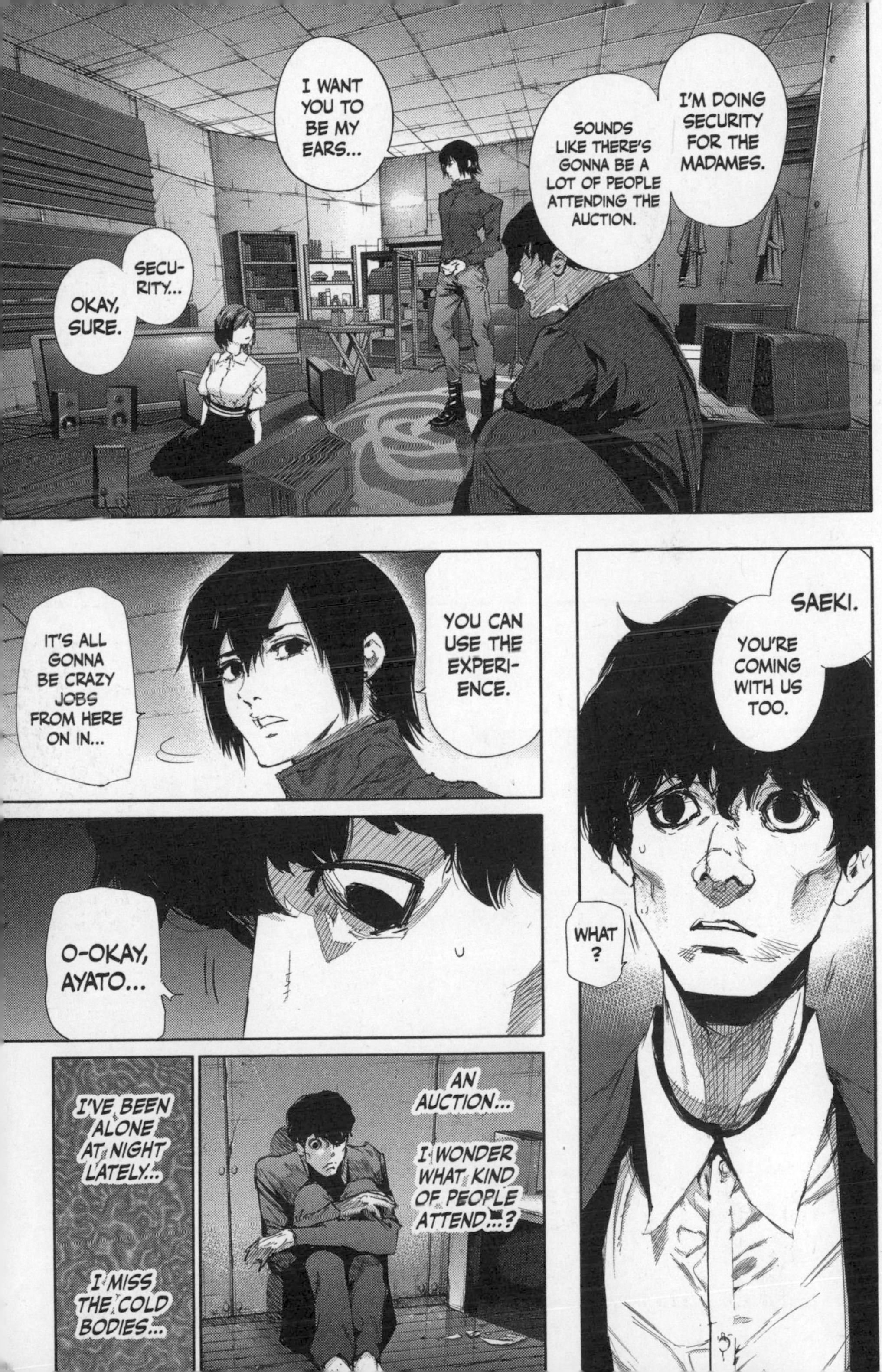
I'M DOING SECURITY FOR THE MADAMES.
SOUNDS LIKE THERE'S GONNA BE A LOT OF PEOPLE ATTENDING THE AUCTION.
I WANT YOU TO BE MY EARS...
SECURITY...
OKAY, SURE.
SAEKI.
YOU'RE COMING WITH US TOO.
WHAT?
YOU CAN USE THE EXPERIENCE.
IT'S ALL GONNA BE CRAZY JOBS FROM HERE ON IN...
O-OKAY, AYATO...
AN AUCTION...
I WONDER WHAT KIND OF PEOPLE ATTEND...?
I'VE BEEN ALONE AT NIGHT LATELY...
I MISS THE COLD BODIES...

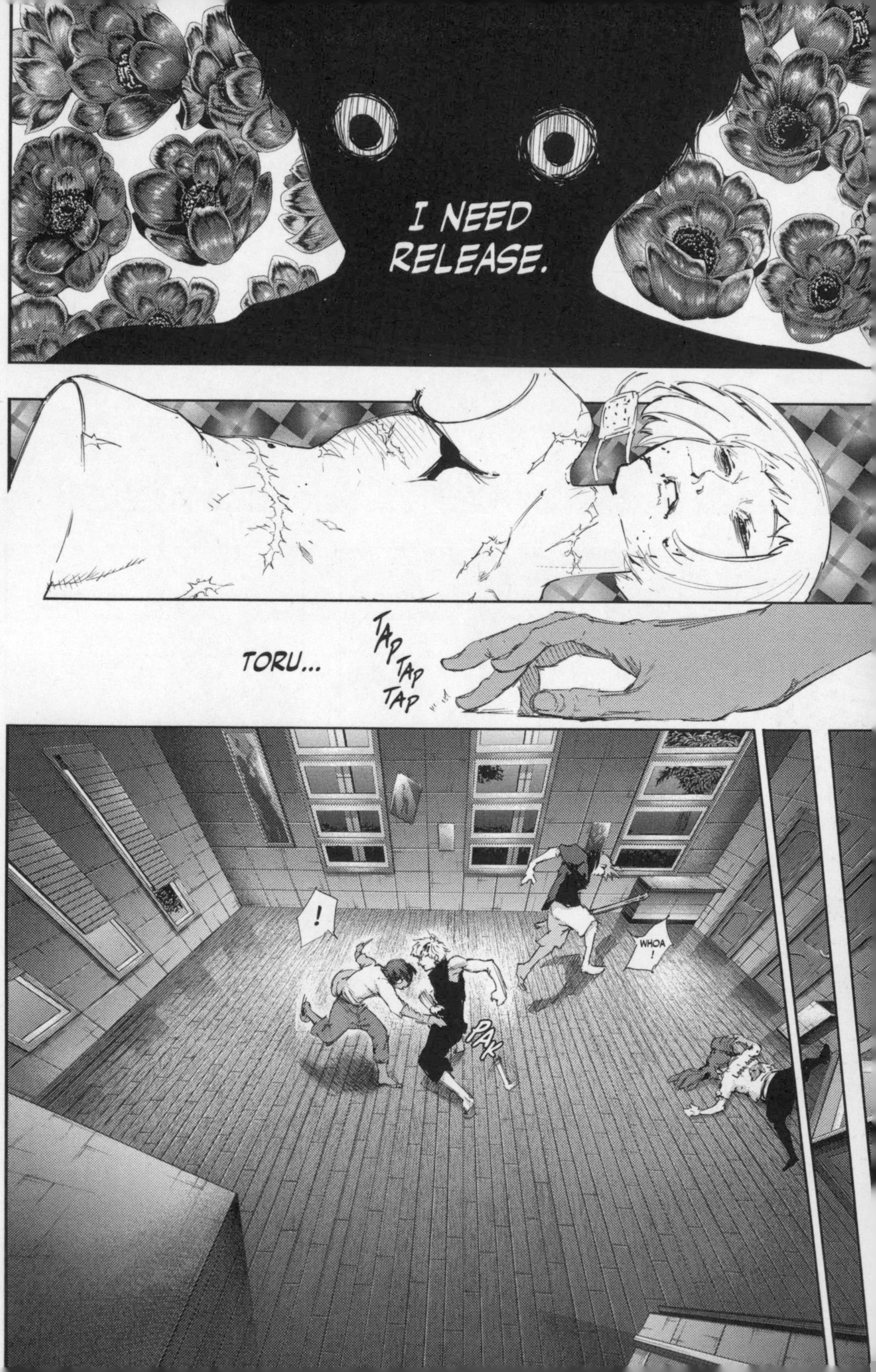
I NEED RELEASE.
TAP TAP TAP TAP
TORU...
WHOA!
PAK
!

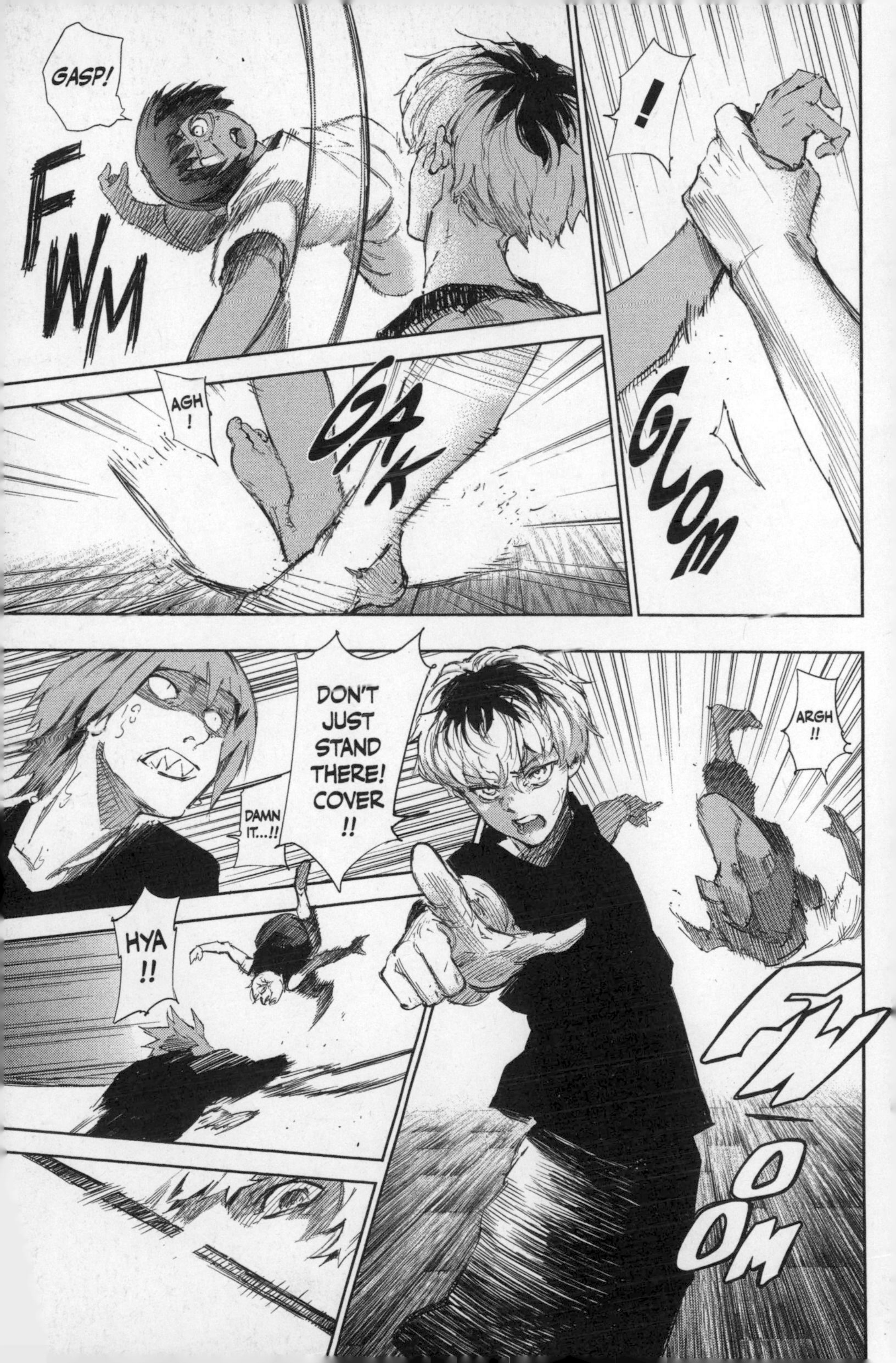
!
GLOM
GASP!
FWM
AGH!
GAK
ARGH!!
DON'T JUST STAND THERE! COVER!!
FWOOM
DAMN IT...!!
HYA!!

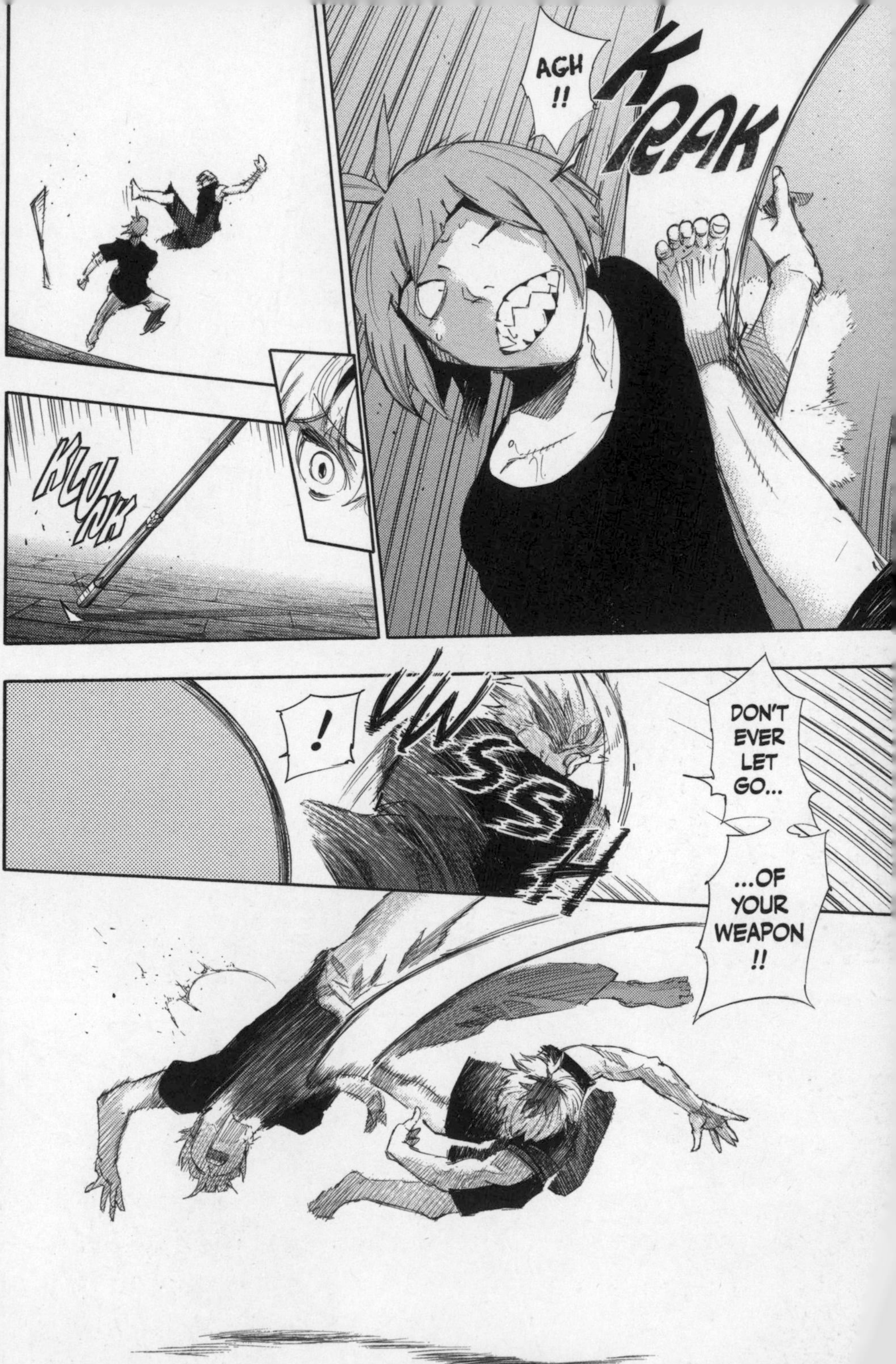
AGH !!
KRAK
KLUNK
DON'T EVER LET GO...
...OF YOUR WEAPON !!
VWSSH
!

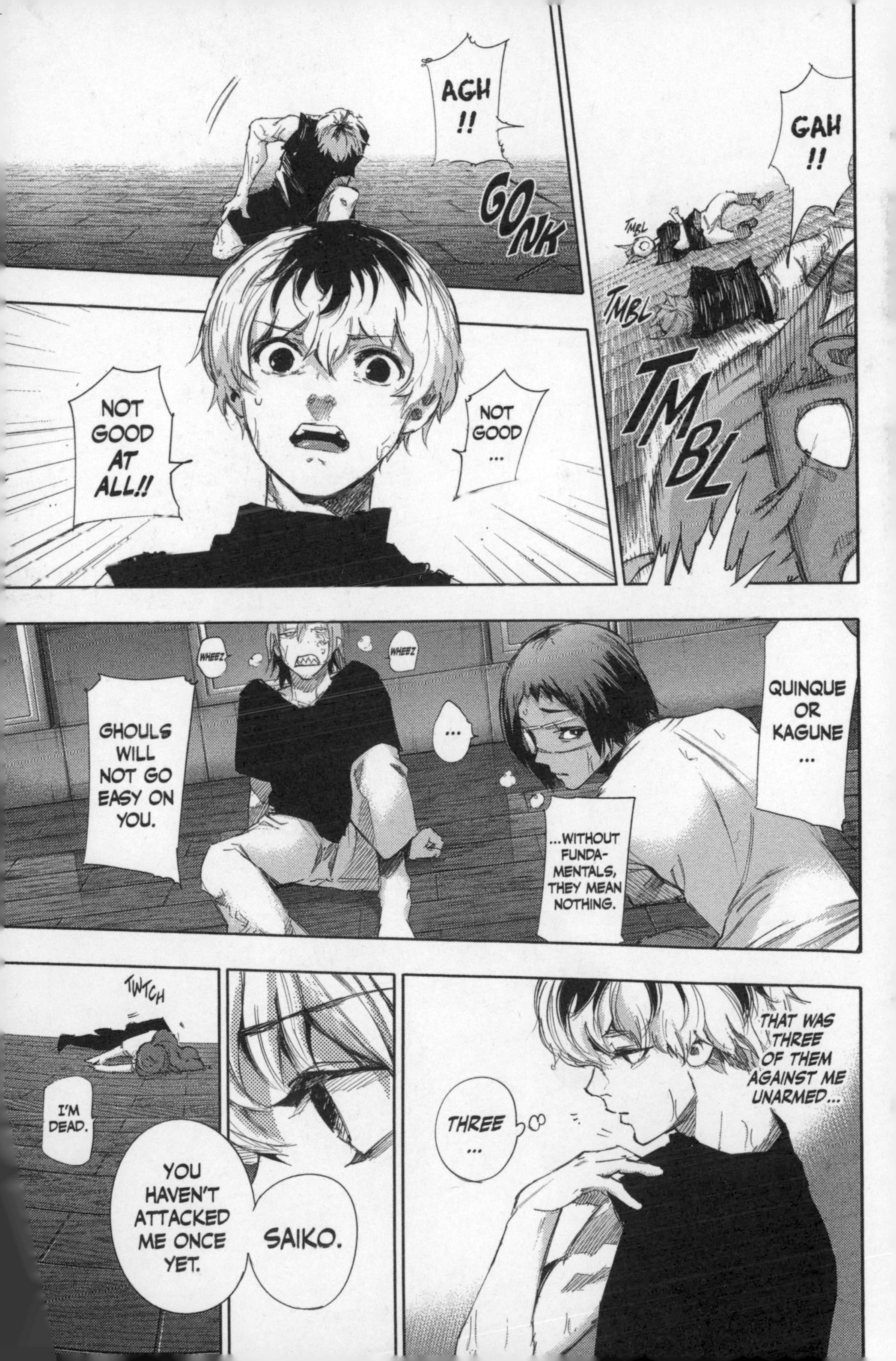
GAH !!
TMBL
TMBL
TMBL
AGH !!
GONK
NOT GOOD ...
NOT GOOD AT ALL!!
QUINQUE OR KAGUNE ...
...WITHOUT FUNDA-MENTALS, THEY MEAN NOTHING.
WHEEZ
...
WHEEZ
GHOULS WILL NOT GO EASY ON YOU.
THAT WAS THREE OF THEM AGAINST ME UNARMED...
THREE ...
SAIKO.
YOU HAVEN'T ATTACKED ME ONCE YET.
TWITCH
I'M DEAD.

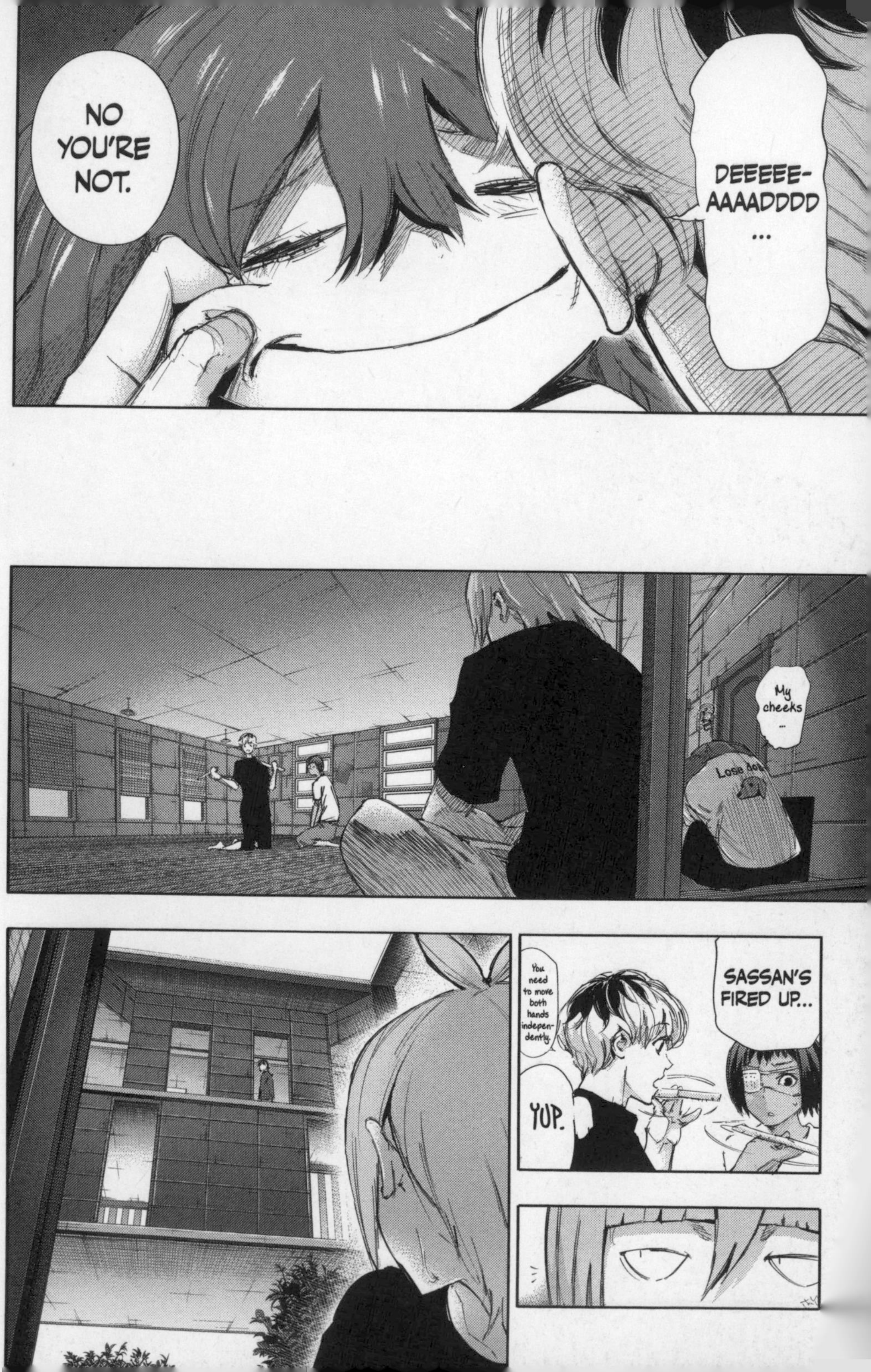
DEEEEE-AAAADDDD ...
NO YOU'RE NOT.
My cheeks ...
SASSAN'S FIRED UP...
You need to move both hands indepen-dently.
YUP.

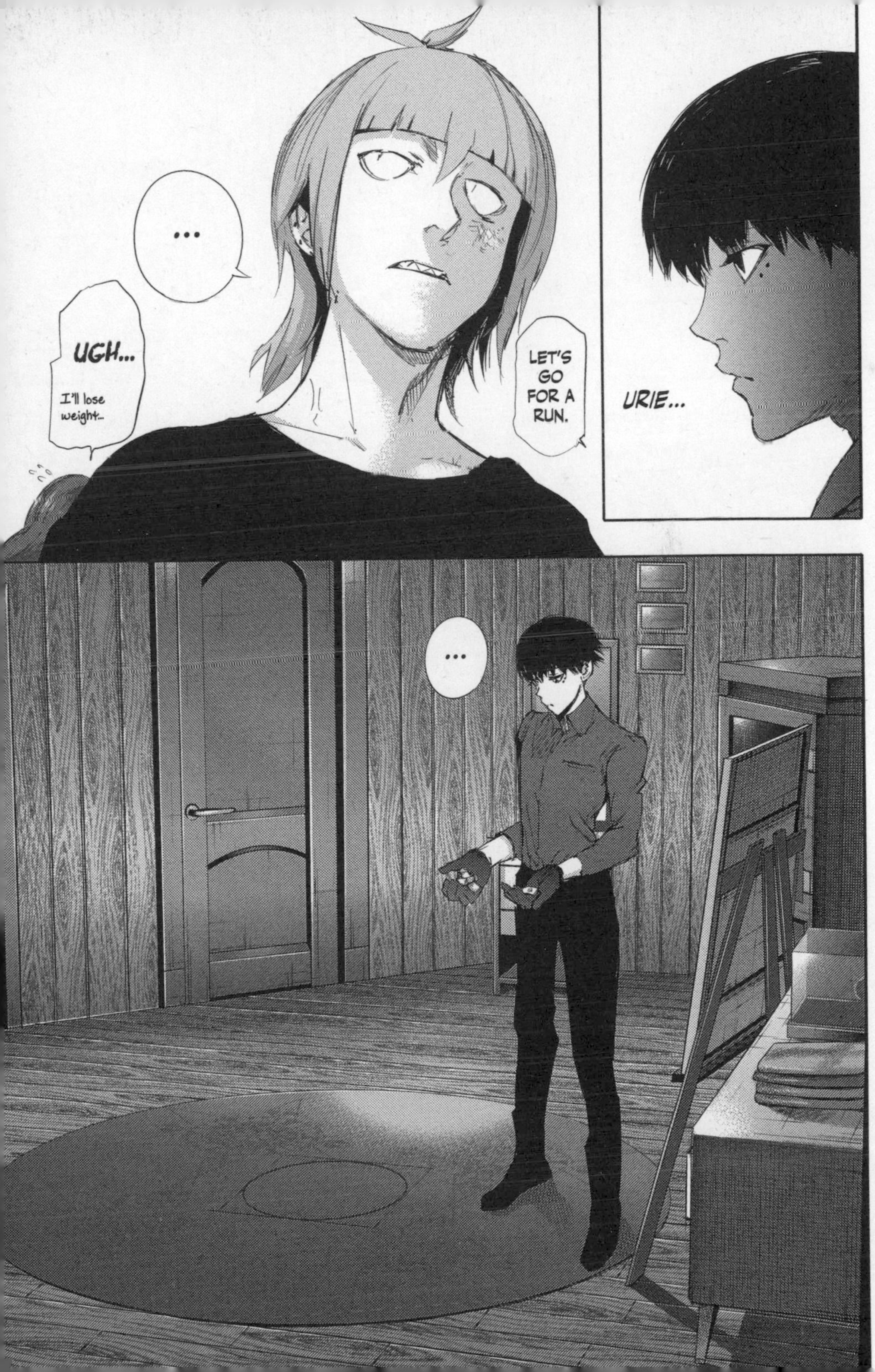
URIE...
...
LET'S GO FOR A RUN.
UGH...
I'll lose weight...
...

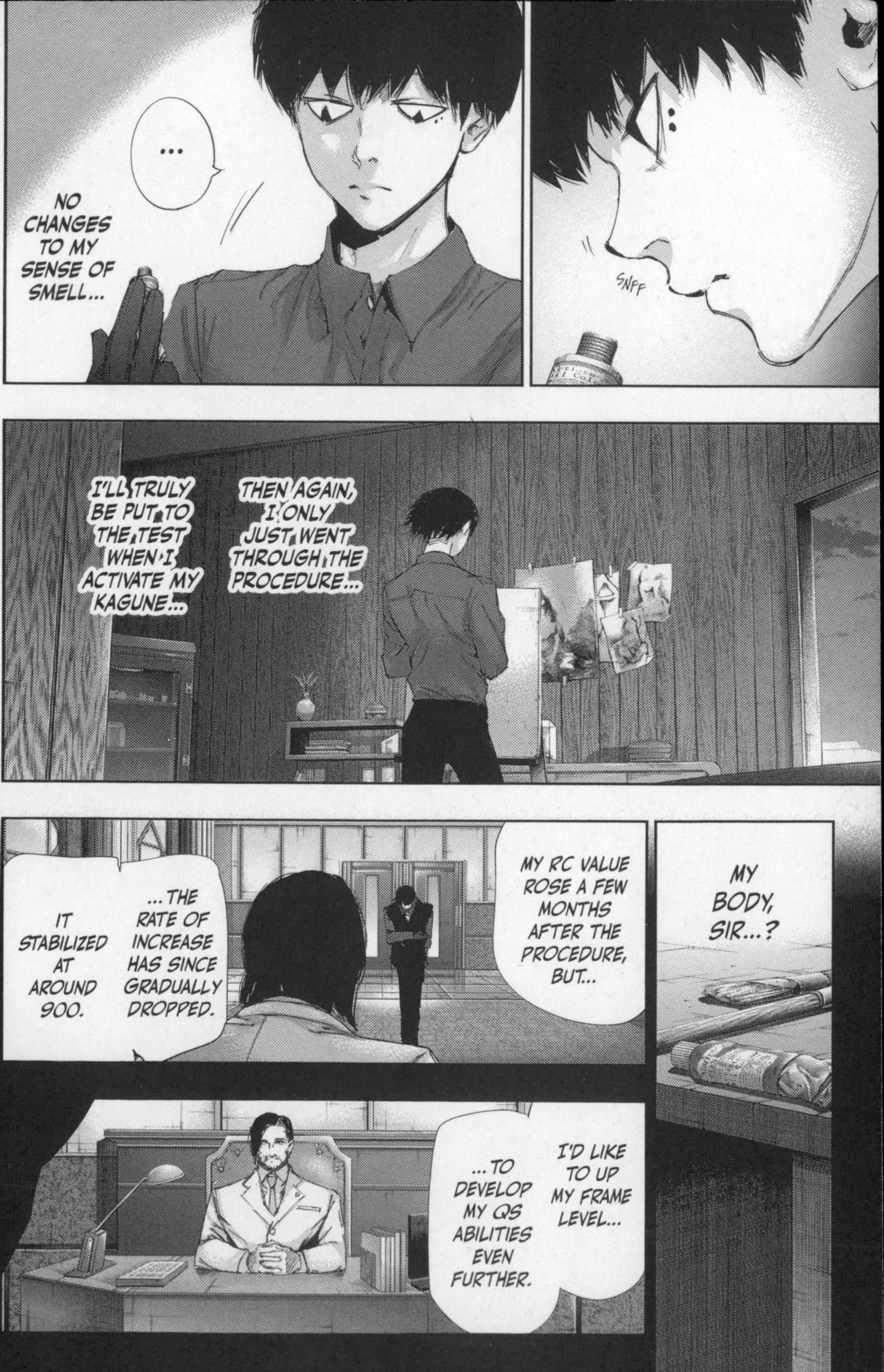
SNFF
...
NO CHANGES TO MY SENSE OF SMELL...
THEN AGAIN, I ONLY JUST WENT THROUGH THE PROCEDURE...
I'LL TRULY BE PUT TO THE TEST WHEN I ACTIVATE MY KAGUNE...
MY BODY, SIR...?
MY RC VALUE ROSE A FEW MONTHS AFTER THE PROCEDURE, BUT...
...THE RATE OF INCREASE HAS SINCE GRADUALLY DROPPED.
IT STABILIZED AT AROUND 900.
I'D LIKE TO UP MY FRAME LEVEL...
...TO DEVELOP MY QS ABILITIES EVEN FURTHER.

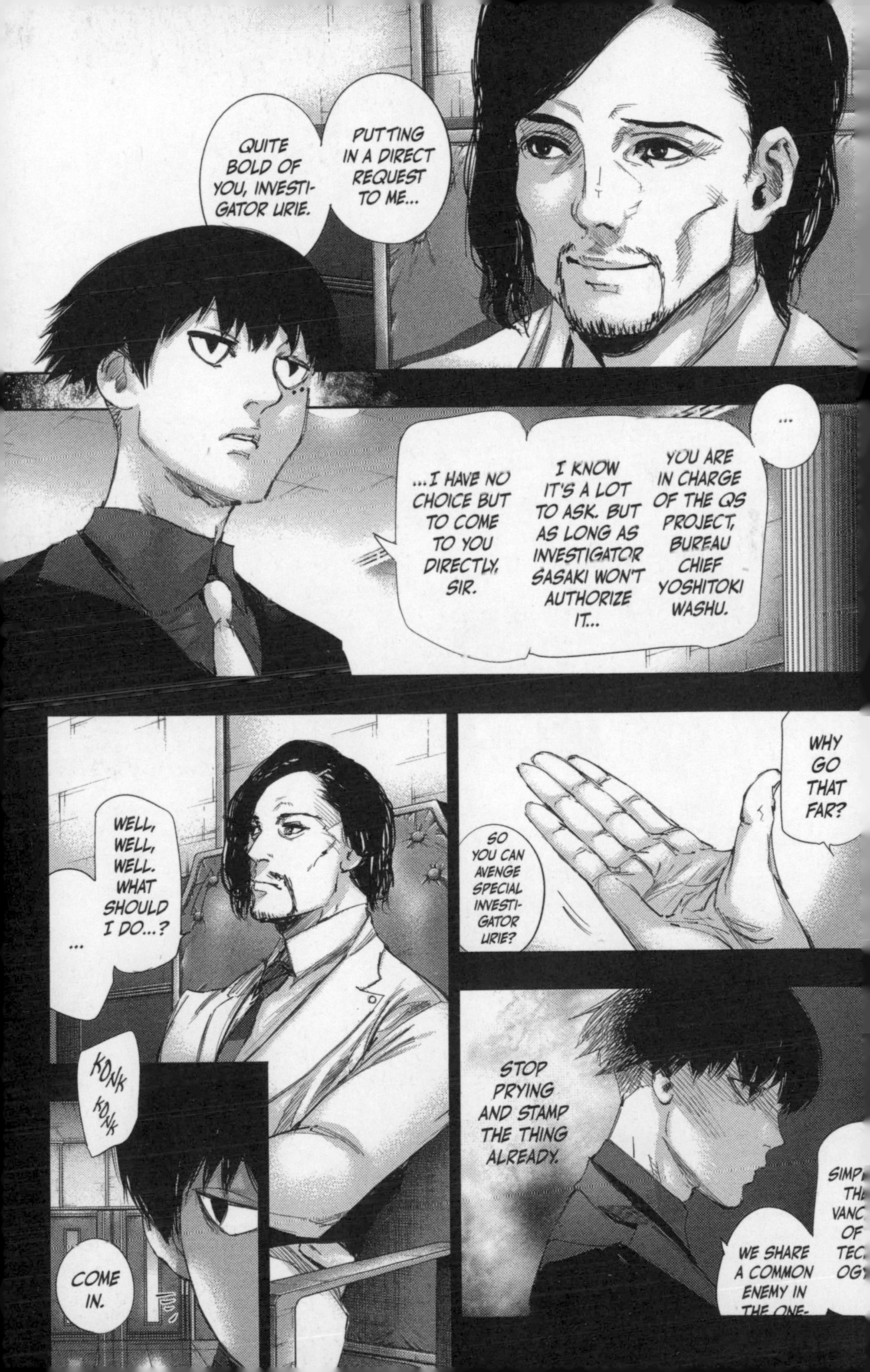

PUTTING IN A DIRECT REQUEST TO ME...
QUITE BOLD OF YOU, INVESTIGATOR URIE.
...
YOU ARE IN CHARGE OF THE QS PROJECT, BUREAU CHIEF YOSHITOKI WASHU.
I KNOW IT'S A LOT TO ASK. BUT AS LONG AS INVESTIGATOR SASAKI WON'T AUTHORIZE IT...
...I HAVE NO CHOICE BUT TO COME TO YOU DIRECTLY, SIR.
WHY GO THAT FAR?
SO YOU CAN AVENGE SPECIAL INVESTIGATOR URIE?
WE SHARE A COMMON ENEMY IN THE ONE-
STOP PRYING AND STAMP THE THING ALREADY.
WELL, WELL, WELL. WHAT SHOULD I DO...?
...
KONK KONK
COME IN.

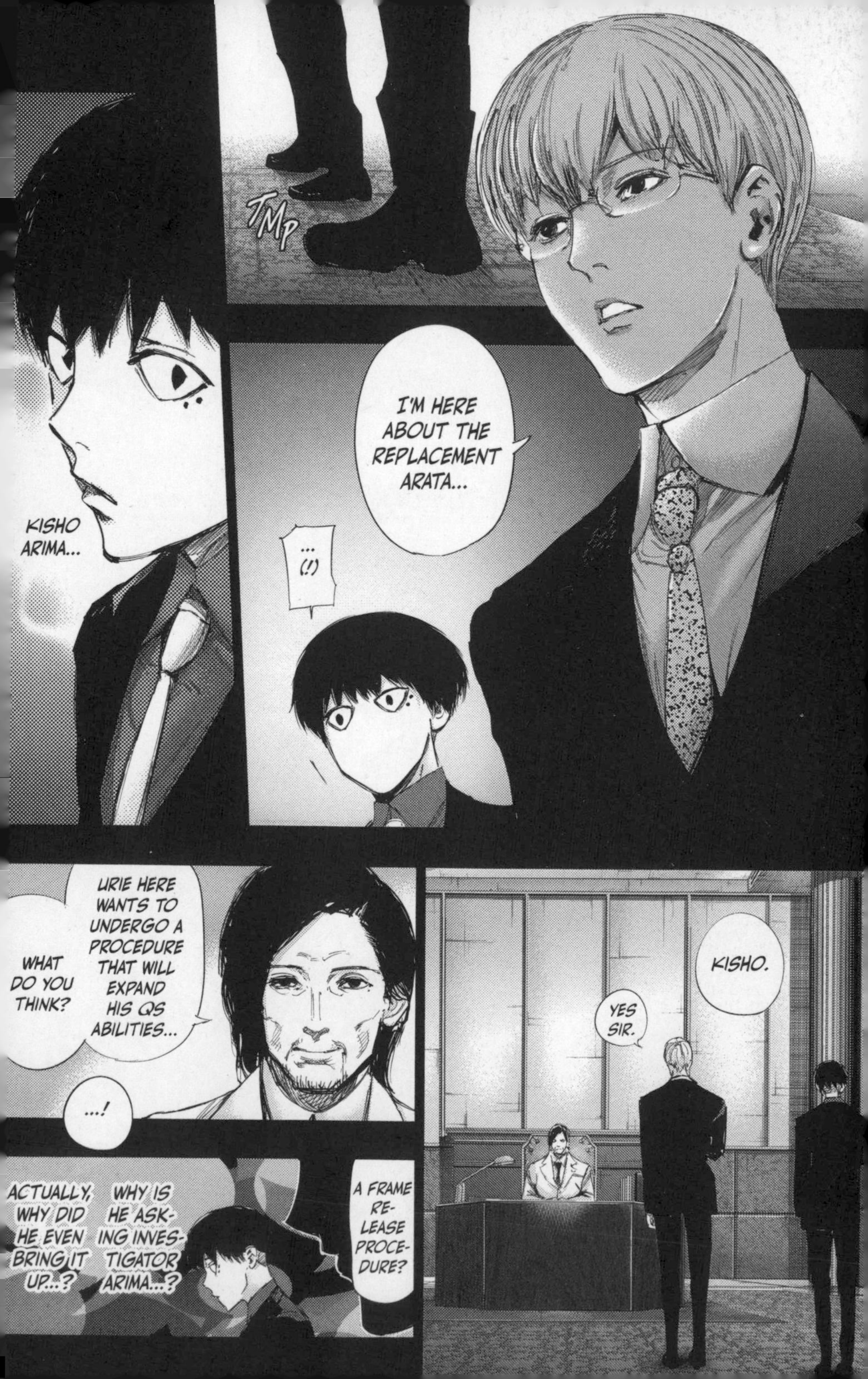
TMP
I'M HERE ABOUT THE REPLACEMENT ARATA...
...(!)
KISHO ARIMA...
KISHO.
YES SIR.
URIE HERE WANTS TO UNDERGO A PROCEDURE THAT WILL EXPAND HIS QS ABILITIES...
WHAT DO YOU THINK?
...!
A FRAME RE-LEASE PROCE-DURE?
WHY IS HE ASK-ING INVES-TIGATOR ARIMA...?
ACTUALLY, WHY DID HE EVEN BRING IT UP...?

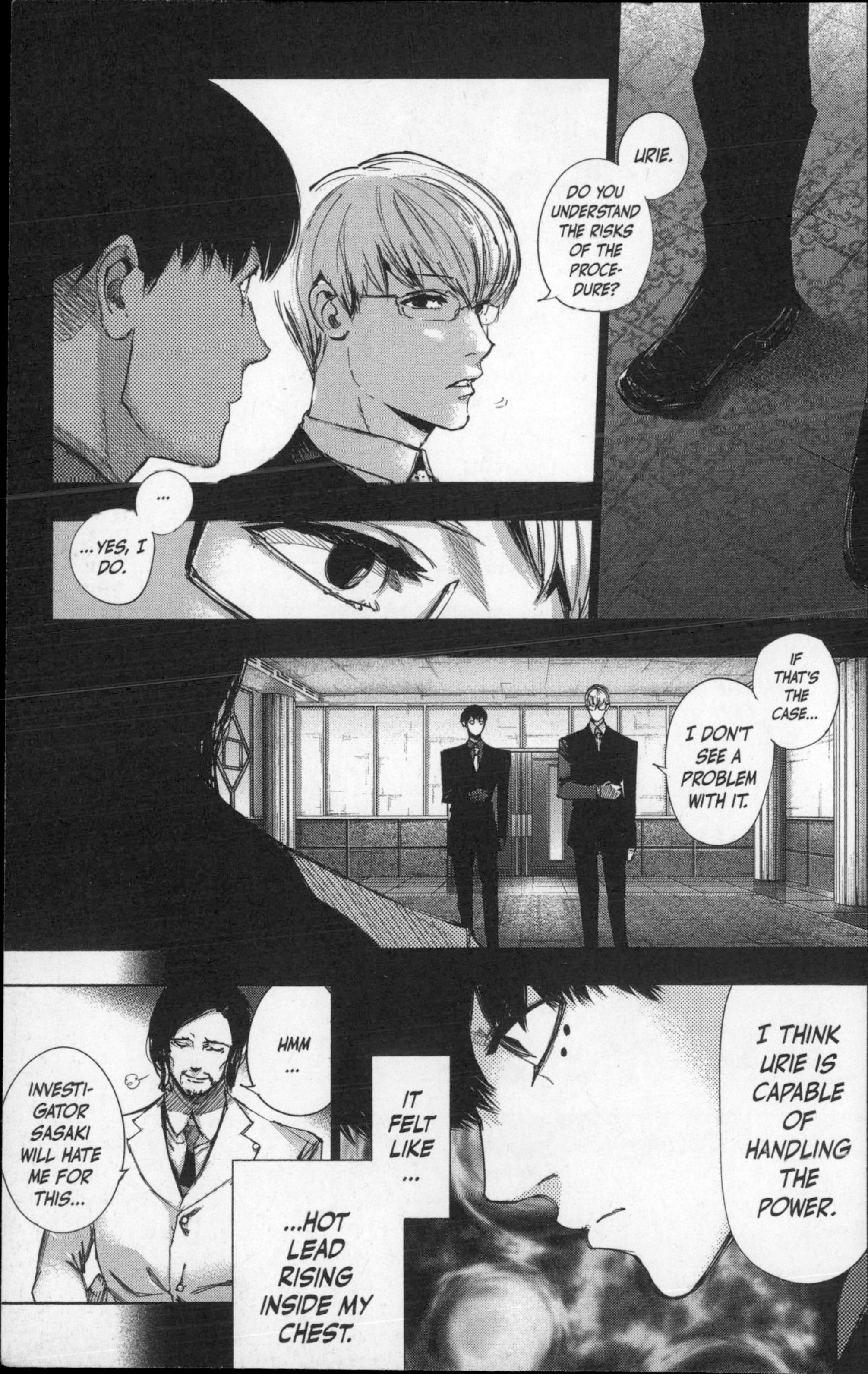
URIE.
DO YOU UNDERSTAND THE RISKS OF THE PROCEDURE?
...
...YES, I DO.
IF THAT'S THE CASE...
I DON'T SEE A PROBLEM WITH IT.
I THINK URIE IS CAPABLE OF HANDLING THE POWER.
IT FELT LIKE...
...HOT LEAD RISING INSIDE MY CHEST.
HMM...
INVESTIGATOR SASAKI WILL HATE ME FOR THIS...

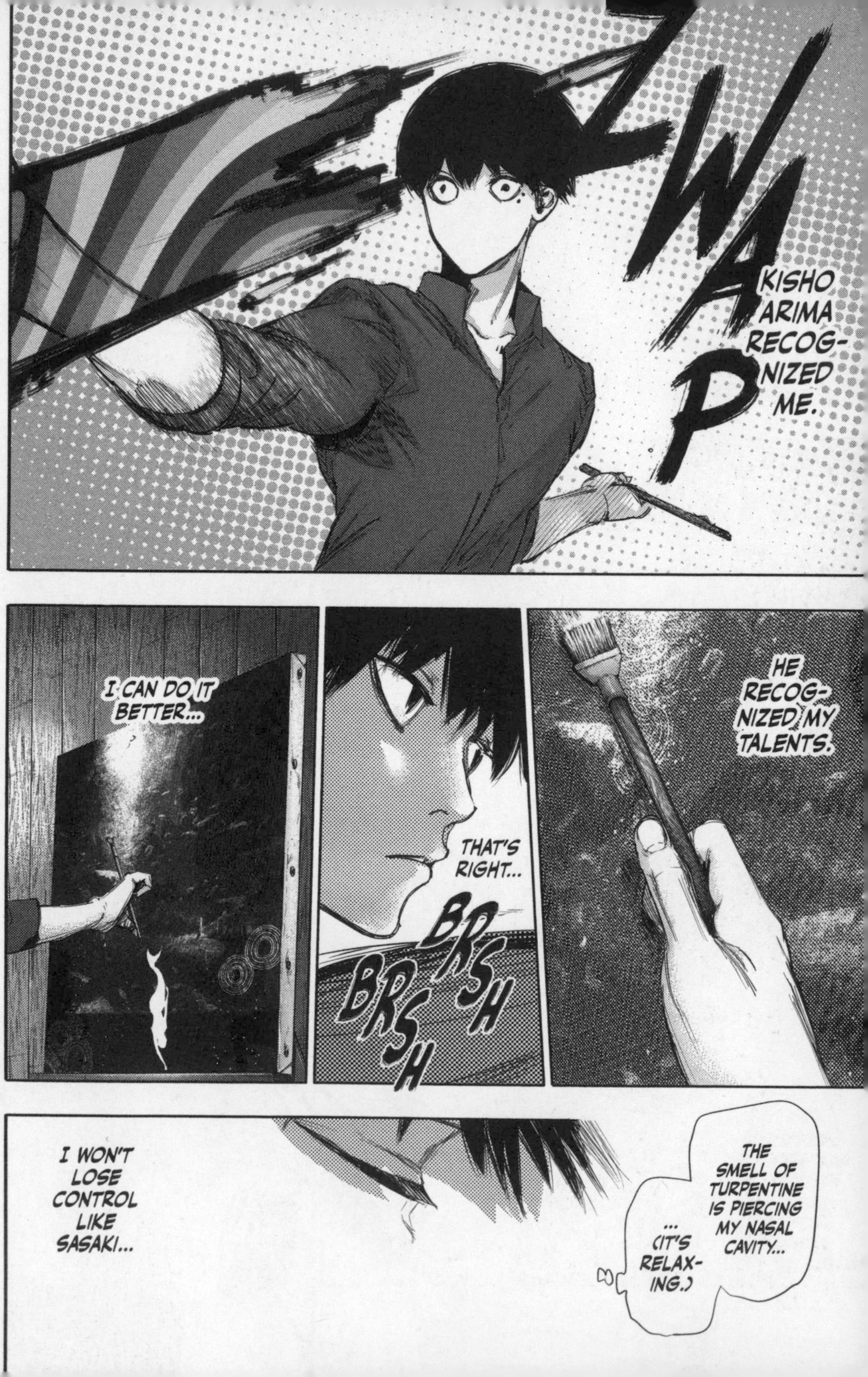
ZWAP
KISHO ARIMA RECOGNIZED ME.
HE RECOGNIZED MY TALENTS.
THAT'S RIGHT...
BRSH BRSH
I CAN DO IT BETTER...
THE SMELL OF TURPENTINE IS PIERCING MY NASAL CAVITY...
... (IT'S RELAXING.)
I WON'T LOSE CONTROL LIKE SASAKI...

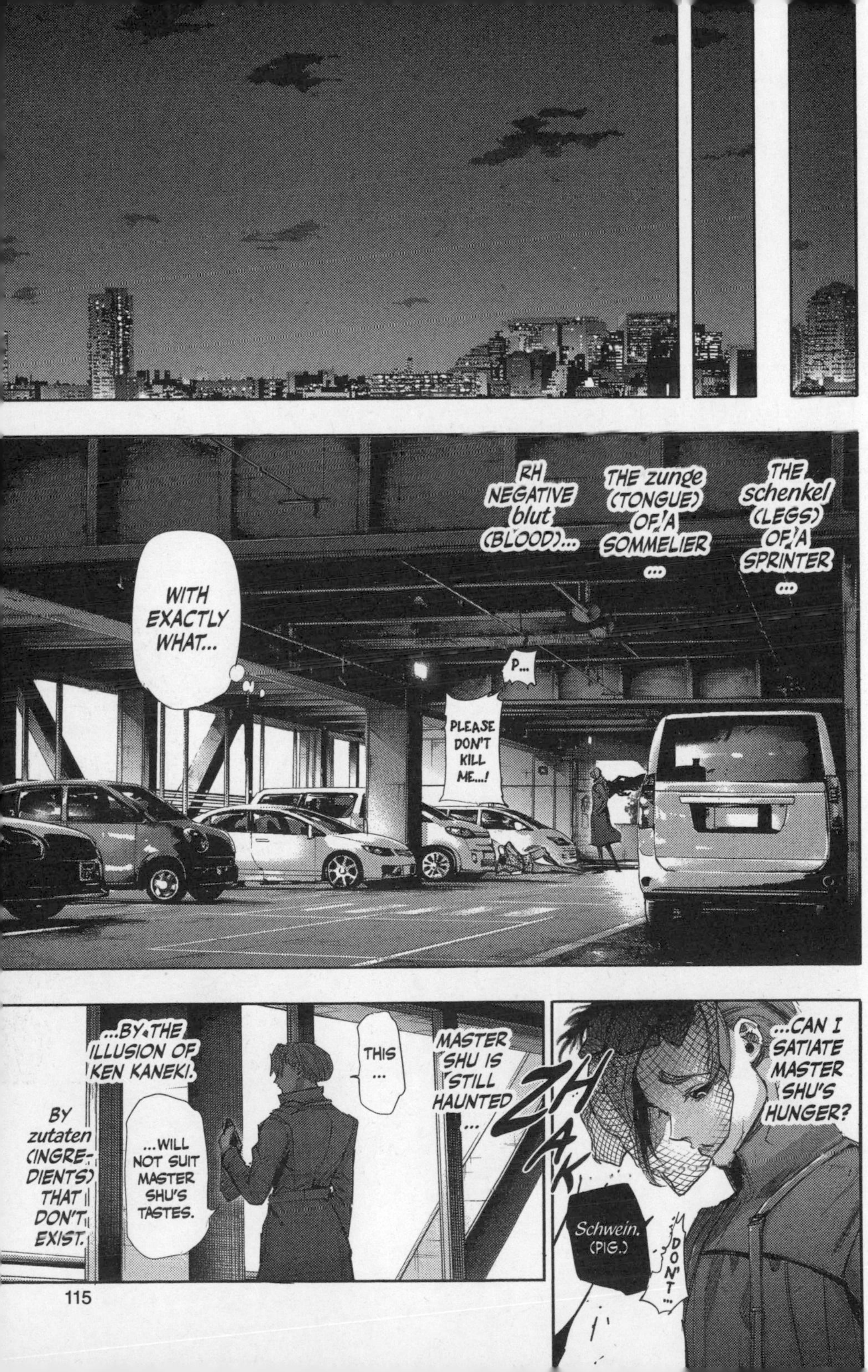
THE schenkel (LEGS) OF A SPRINTER ...
THE zunge (TONGUE) OF A SOMMELIER ...
RH NEGATIVE blut (BLOOD)...
P...
PLEASE DON'T KILL ME...!
WITH EXACTLY WHAT...
...CAN I SATIATE MASTER SHU'S HUNGER?
ZHAK
Schwein. (PIG.)
DON'T...
MASTER SHU IS STILL HAUNTED ...
THIS ...
...BY THE ILLUSION OF KEN KANEKI.
...WILL NOT SUIT MASTER SHU'S TASTES.
BY zutaten (INGREDIENTS) THAT DON'T EXIST.

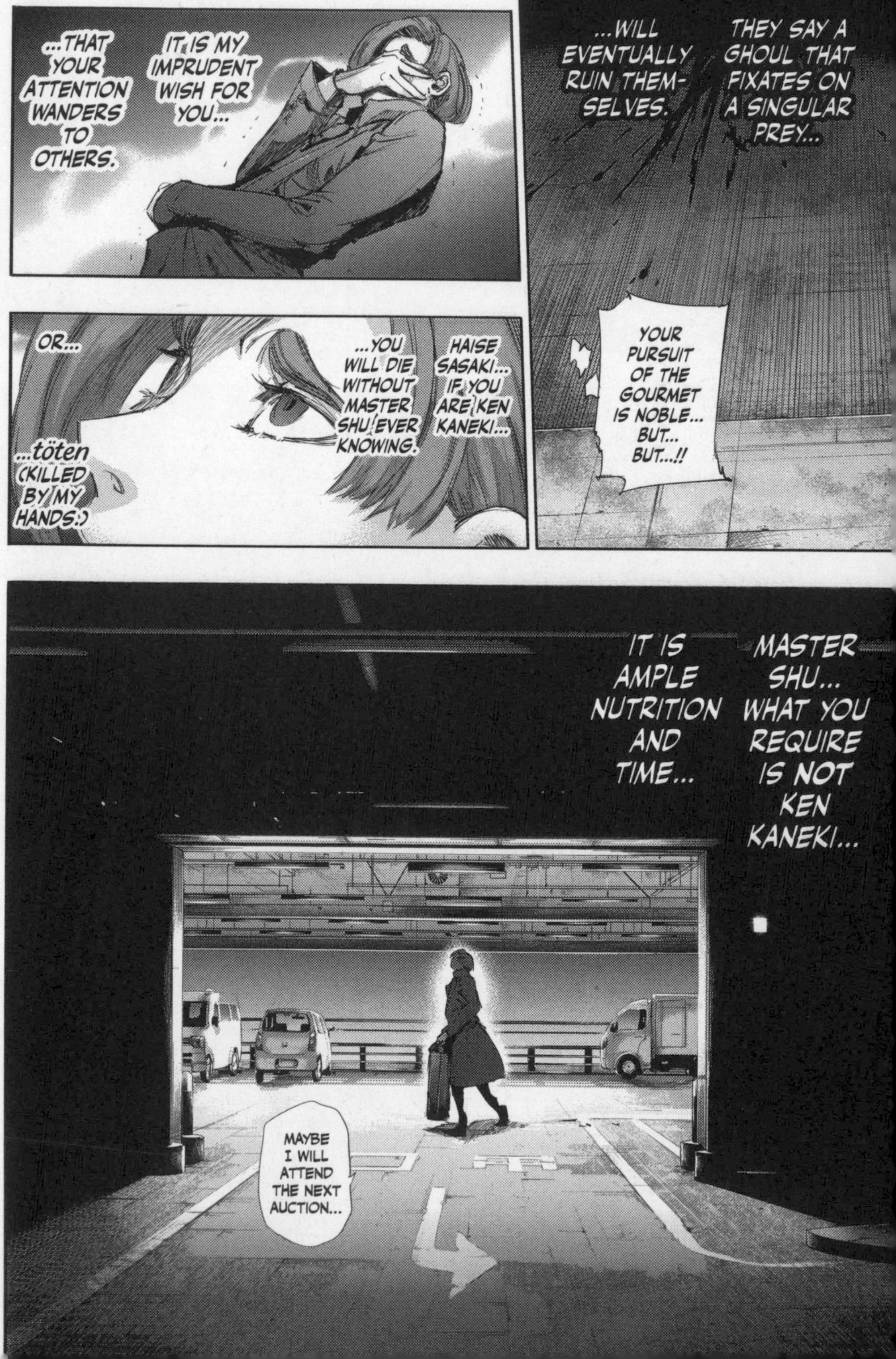
THEY SAY A GHOUL THAT FIXATES ON A SINGULAR PREY...
...WILL EVENTUALLY RUIN THEMSELVES.
YOUR PURSUIT OF THE GOURMET IS NOBLE... BUT... BUT...!!
IT IS MY IMPRUDENT WISH FOR YOU...
...THAT YOUR ATTENTION WANDERS TO OTHERS.
HAISE SASAKI... IF YOU ARE KEN KANEKI...
...YOU WILL DIE WITHOUT MASTER SHU EVER KNOWING.
OR...
...töten (KILLED BY MY HANDS.)
MASTER SHU... WHAT YOU REQUIRE IS NOT KEN KANEKI...
IT IS AMPLE NUTRITION AND TIME...
MAYBE I WILL ATTEND THE NEXT AUCTION...

Right :16

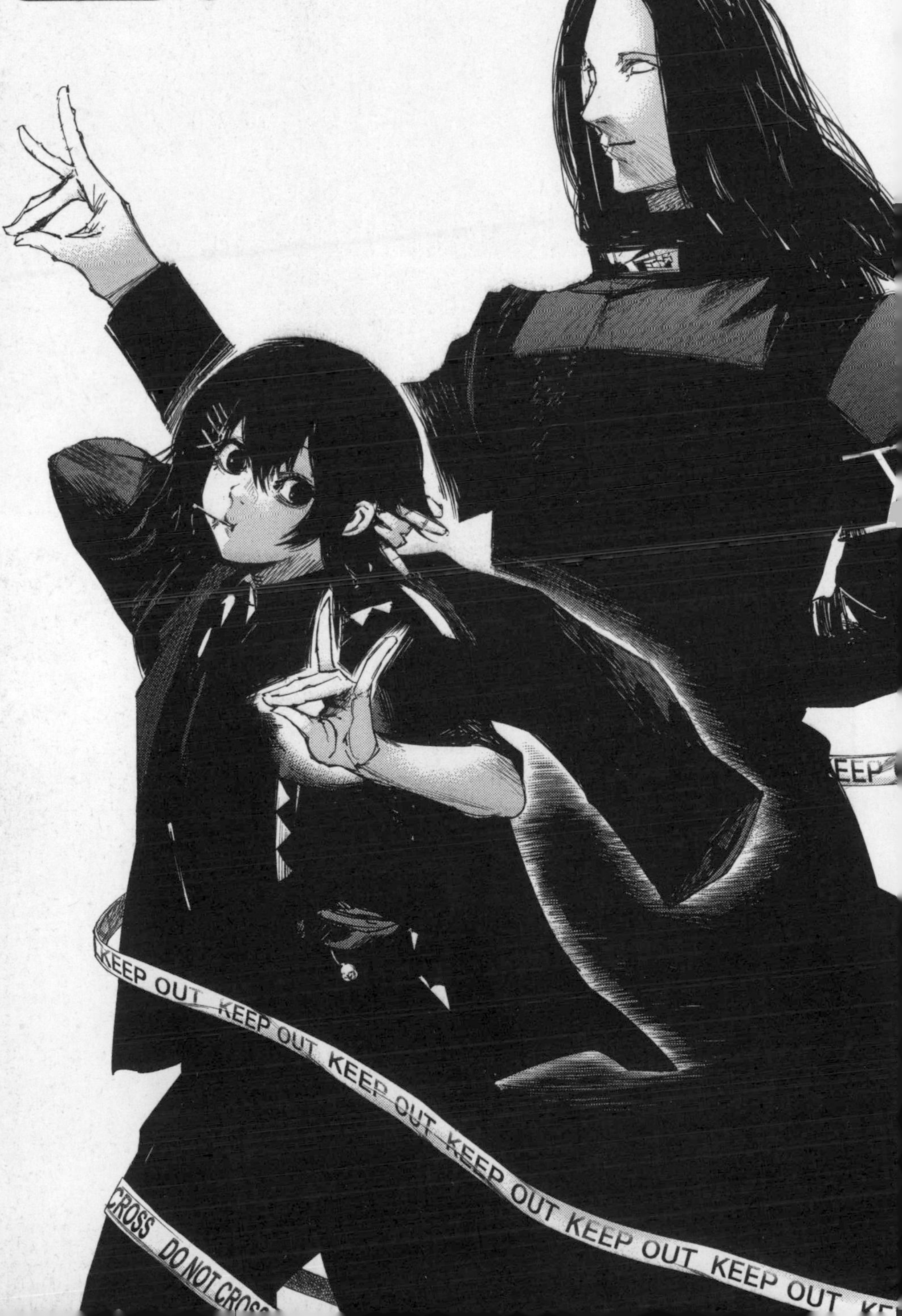

KEEP OUT KEEP OUT KEEP OUT KEEP OUT KEEP OUT KEEP OUT
KEEP
CROSS DO NOT CROSS

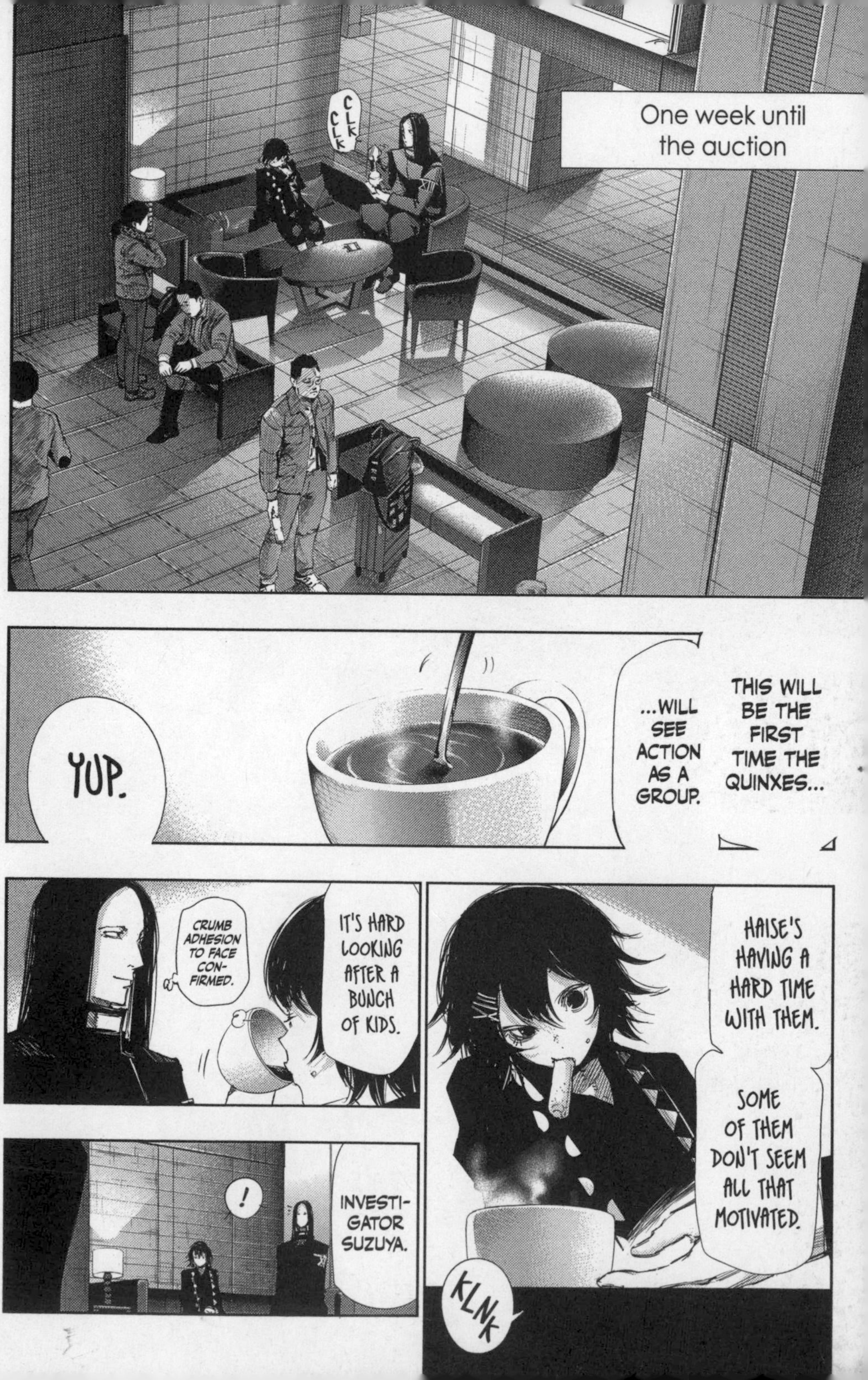
One week until the auction
CLK CLK
THIS WILL BE THE FIRST TIME THE QUINXES...
...WILL SEE ACTION AS A GROUP.
YUP.
HAISE'S HAVING A HARD TIME WITH THEM.
SOME OF THEM DON'T SEEM ALL THAT MOTIVATED.
KLNK
IT'S HARD LOOKING AFTER A BUNCH OF KIDS.
CRUMB ADHESION TO FACE CON-FIRMED.
!
INVESTI-GATOR SUZUYA.

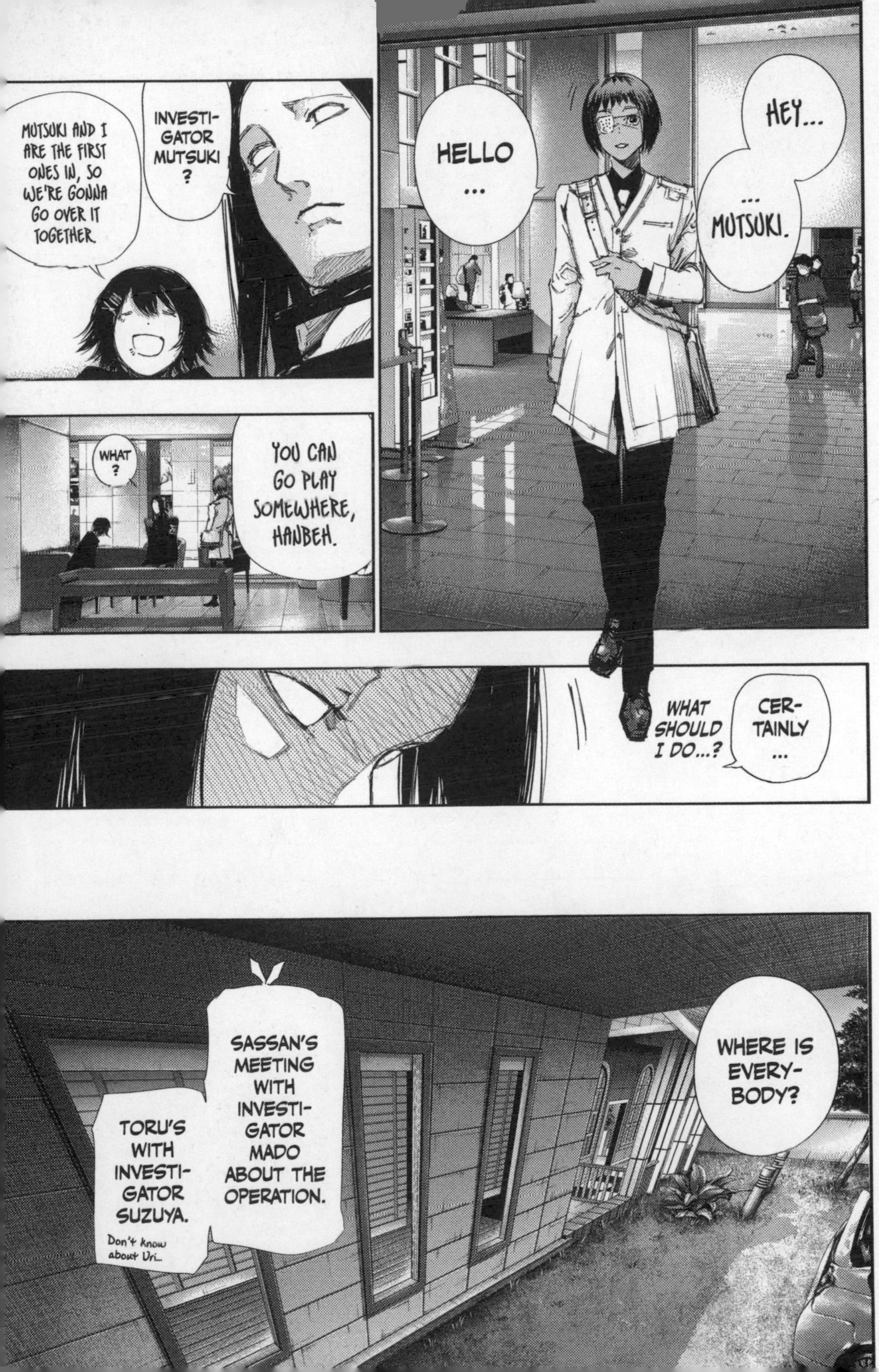
HEY...
... MUTSUKI.
HELLO ...
INVESTIGATOR MUTSUKI?
MUTSUKI AND I ARE THE FIRST ONES IN, SO WE'RE GONNA GO OVER IT TOGETHER.
YOU CAN GO PLAY SOMEWHERE, HANBEH.
WHAT?
CERTAINLY ...
WHAT SHOULD I DO...?
WHERE IS EVERYBODY?
SASSAN'S MEETING WITH INVESTIGATOR MADO ABOUT THE OPERATION.
TORU'S WITH INVESTIGATOR SUZUYA.
Don't know about Uri...

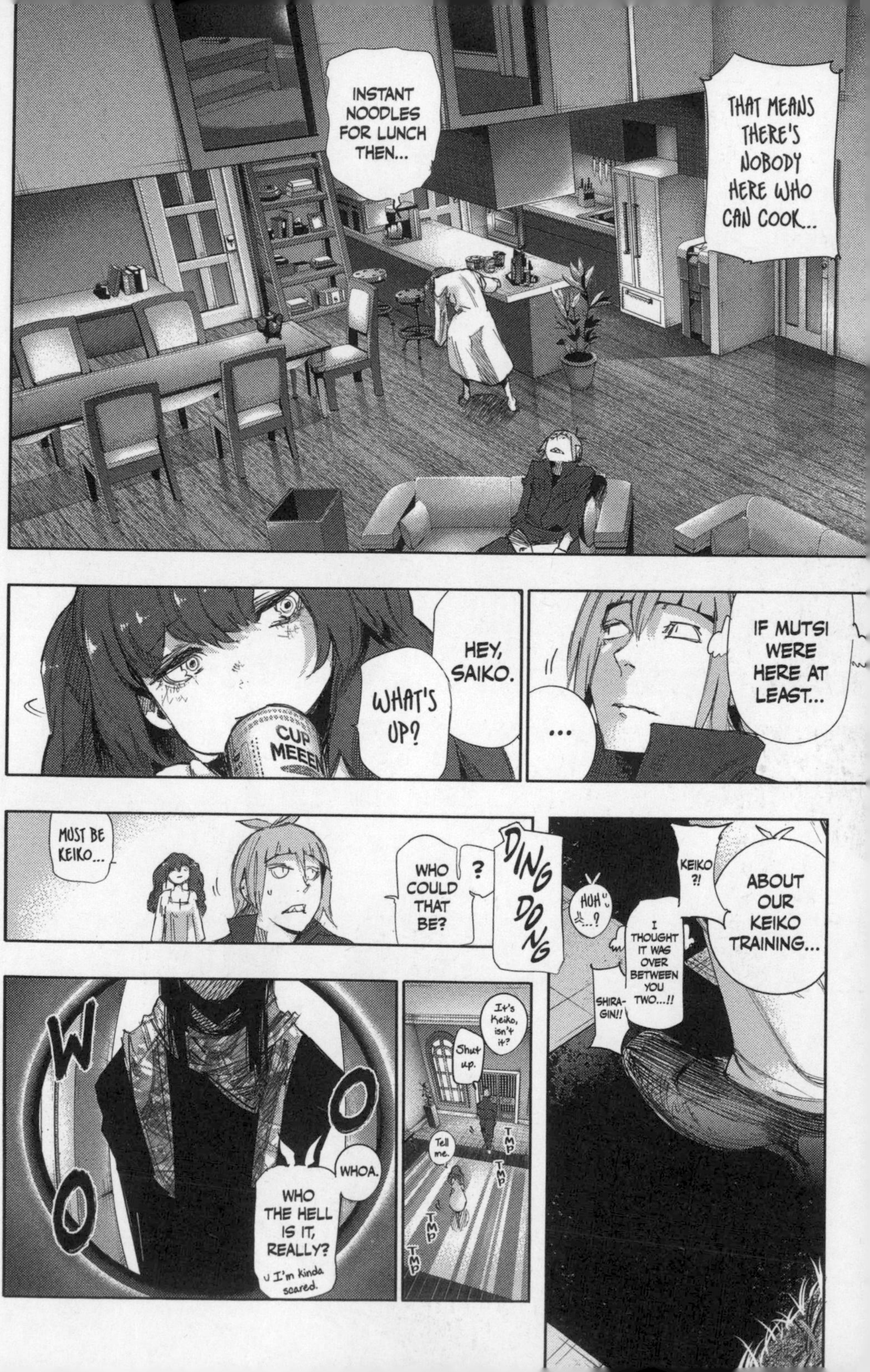
THAT MEANS THERE'S NOBODY HERE WHO CAN COOK...
INSTANT NOODLES FOR LUNCH THEN...
IF MUTSI WERE HERE AT LEAST...
...
HEY, SAIKO.
WHAT'S UP?
CUP MEEEEN
ABOUT OUR KEIKO TRAINING...
KEIKO ?!
HUH ...?
I THOUGHT IT WAS OVER BETWEEN YOU TWO...!!
SHIRA-GIN!!
DING DONG
?
WHO COULD THAT BE?
MUST BE KEIKO...
It's Keiko, isn't it?
Shut up.
Tell me.
TMP TMP TMP TMP
WHOA.
WHO THE HELL IS IT, REALLY?
I'm kinda scared.
WOO

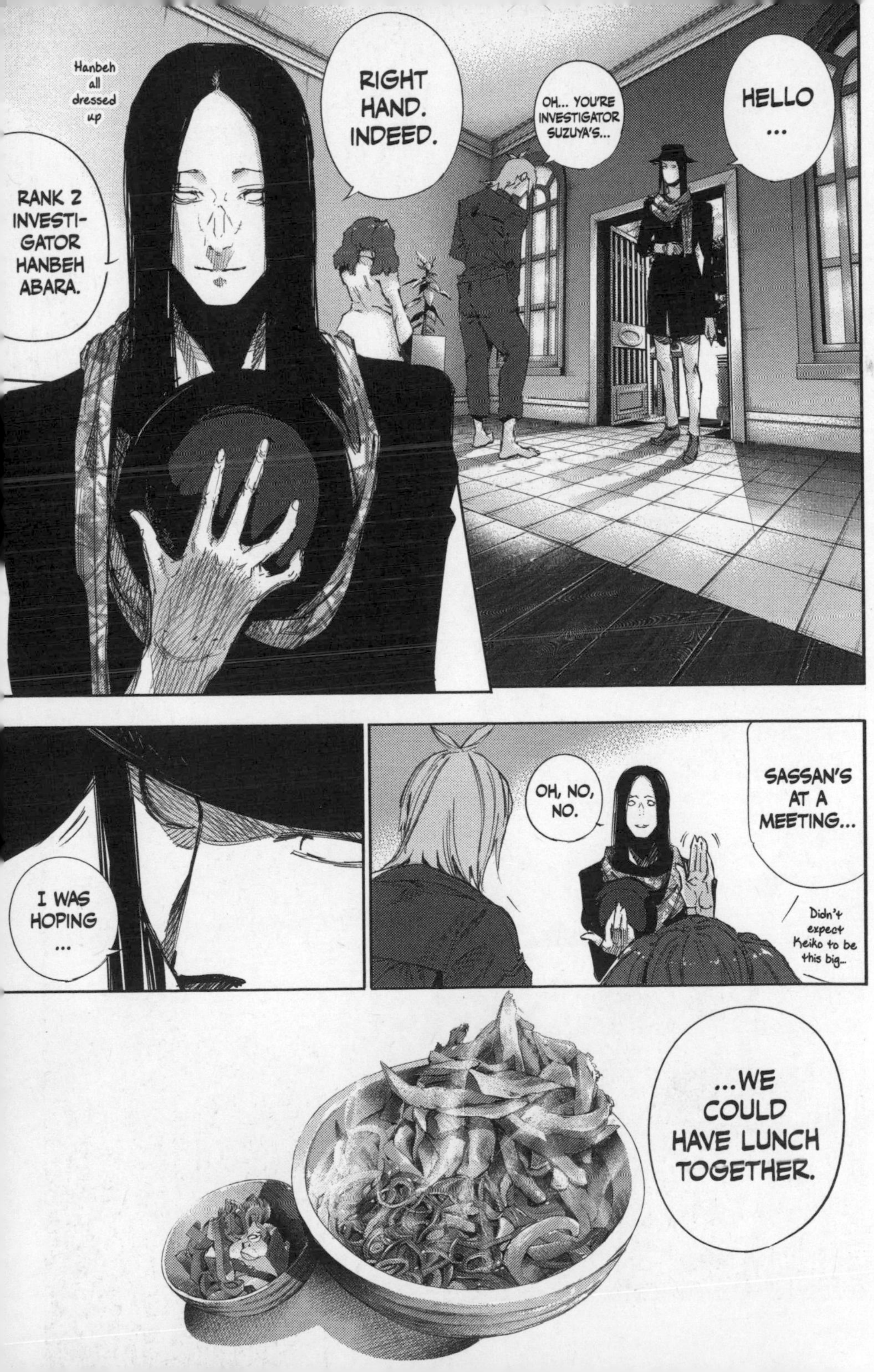
HELLO ...
OH... YOU'RE INVESTIGATOR SUZUYA'S...
RIGHT HAND. INDEED.
Hanbeh all dressed up
RANK 2 INVESTI-GATOR HANBEH ABARA.
SASSAN'S AT A MEETING...
OH, NO, NO.
Didn't expect Keiko to be this big...
I WAS HOPING ...
...WE COULD HAVE LUNCH TOGETHER.

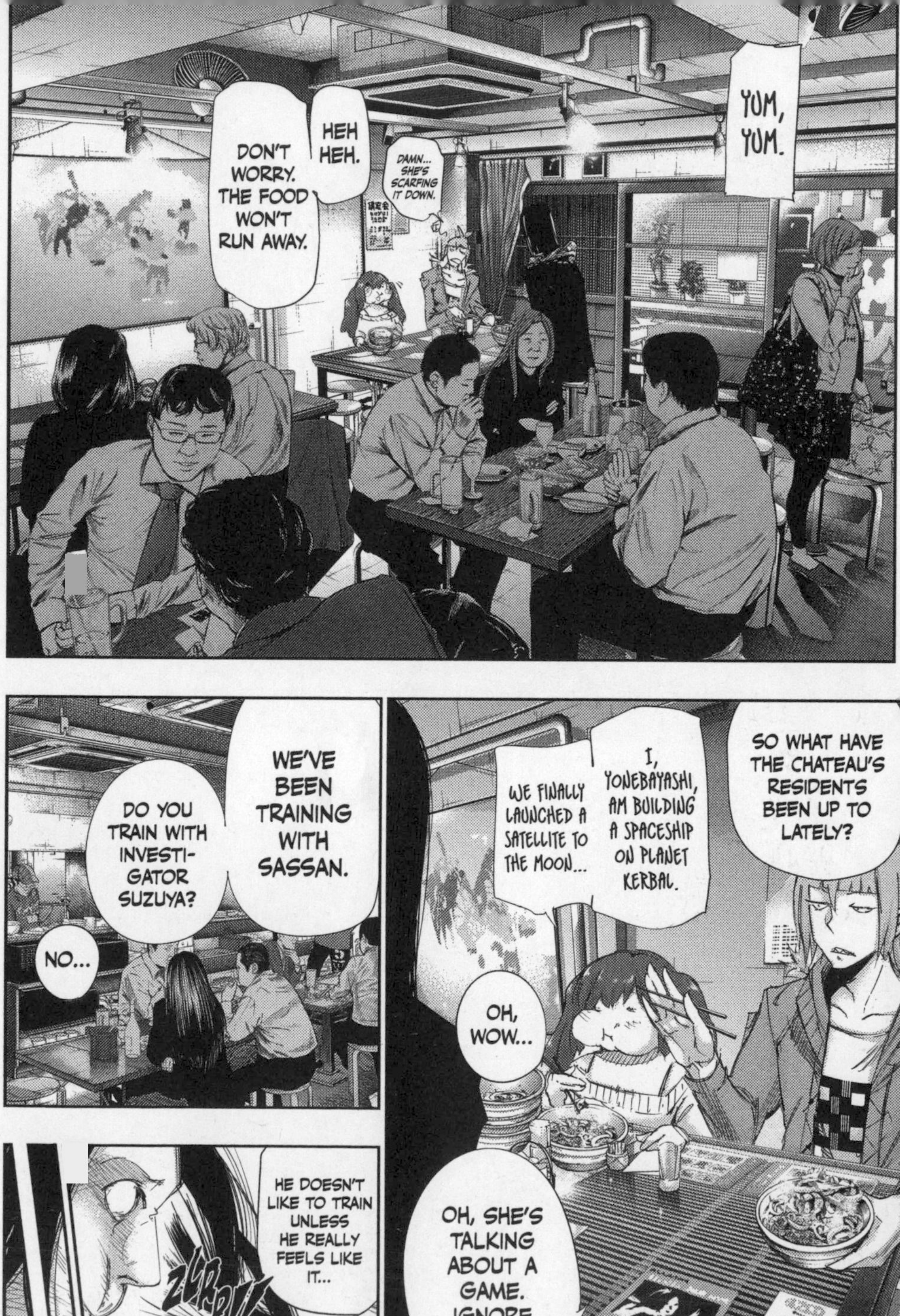
YUM, YUM.
DAMN... SHE'S SCARFING IT DOWN.
HEH HEH.
DON'T WORRY. THE FOOD WON'T RUN AWAY.
SO WHAT HAVE THE CHATEAU'S RESIDENTS BEEN UP TO LATELY?
I, YONEBAYASHI, AM BUILDING A SPACESHIP ON PLANET KERBAL.
WE FINALLY LAUNCHED A SATELLITE TO THE MOON...
OH, WOW...
OH, SHE'S TALKING ABOUT A GAME. IGNORE HER.
WE'VE BEEN TRAINING WITH SASSAN.
DO YOU TRAIN WITH INVESTIGATOR SUZUYA?
NO...
HE DOESN'T LIKE TO TRAIN UNLESS HE REALLY FEELS LIKE IT...
ZURP!!

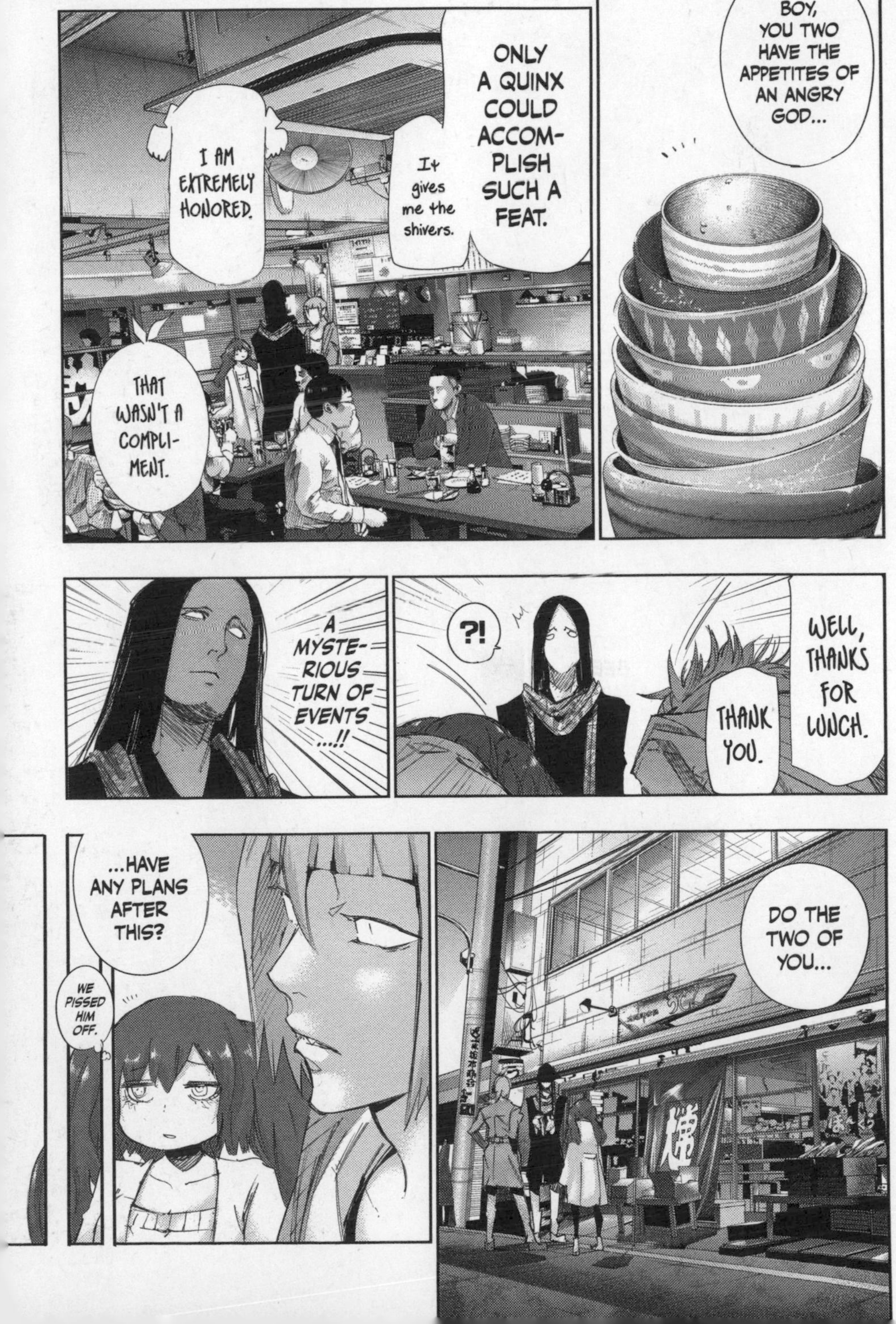
BOY, YOU TWO HAVE THE APPETITES OF AN ANGRY GOD...
ONLY A QUINX COULD ACCOMPLISH SUCH A FEAT.
It gives me the shivers.
I AM EXTREMELY HONORED.
THAT WASN'T A COMPLIMENT.
WELL, THANKS FOR LUNCH.
THANK YOU.
?!
A MYSTERIOUS TURN OF EVENTS ...!!
DO THE TWO OF YOU...
...HAVE ANY PLANS AFTER THIS?
WE PISSED HIM OFF.

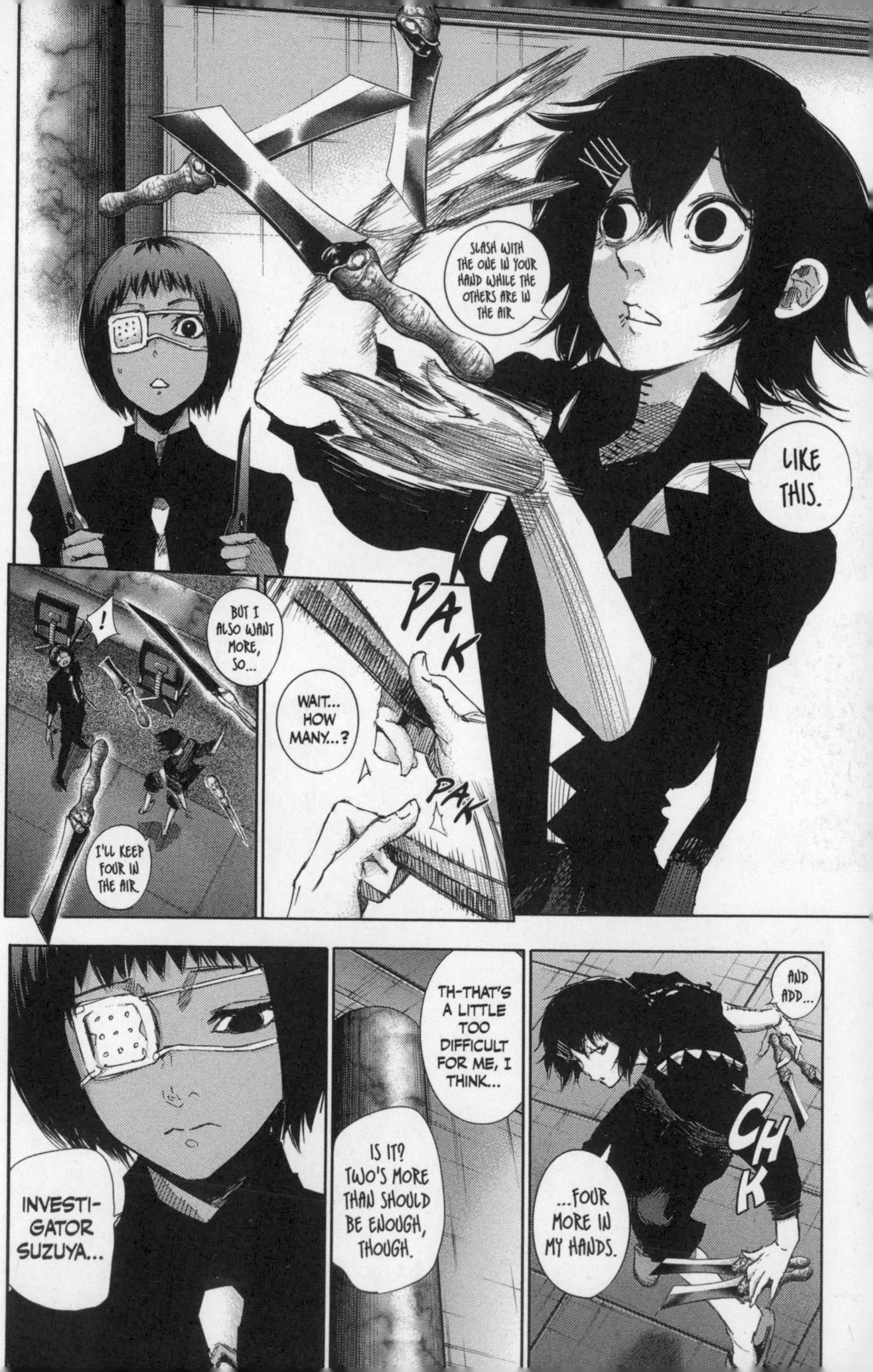
SLASH WITH THE ONE IN YOUR HAND WHILE THE OTHERS ARE IN THE AIR
LIKE THIS.
PAK
WAIT... HOW MANY...?
PAK
BUT I ALSO WANT MORE, SO...
!
I'LL KEEP FOUR IN THE AIR.
AND ADD...
CHK
...FOUR MORE IN MY HANDS.
TH-THAT'S A LITTLE TOO DIFFICULT FOR ME, I THINK...
IS IT? TWO'S MORE THAN SHOULD BE ENOUGH, THOUGH.
INVESTI-GATOR SUZUYA...

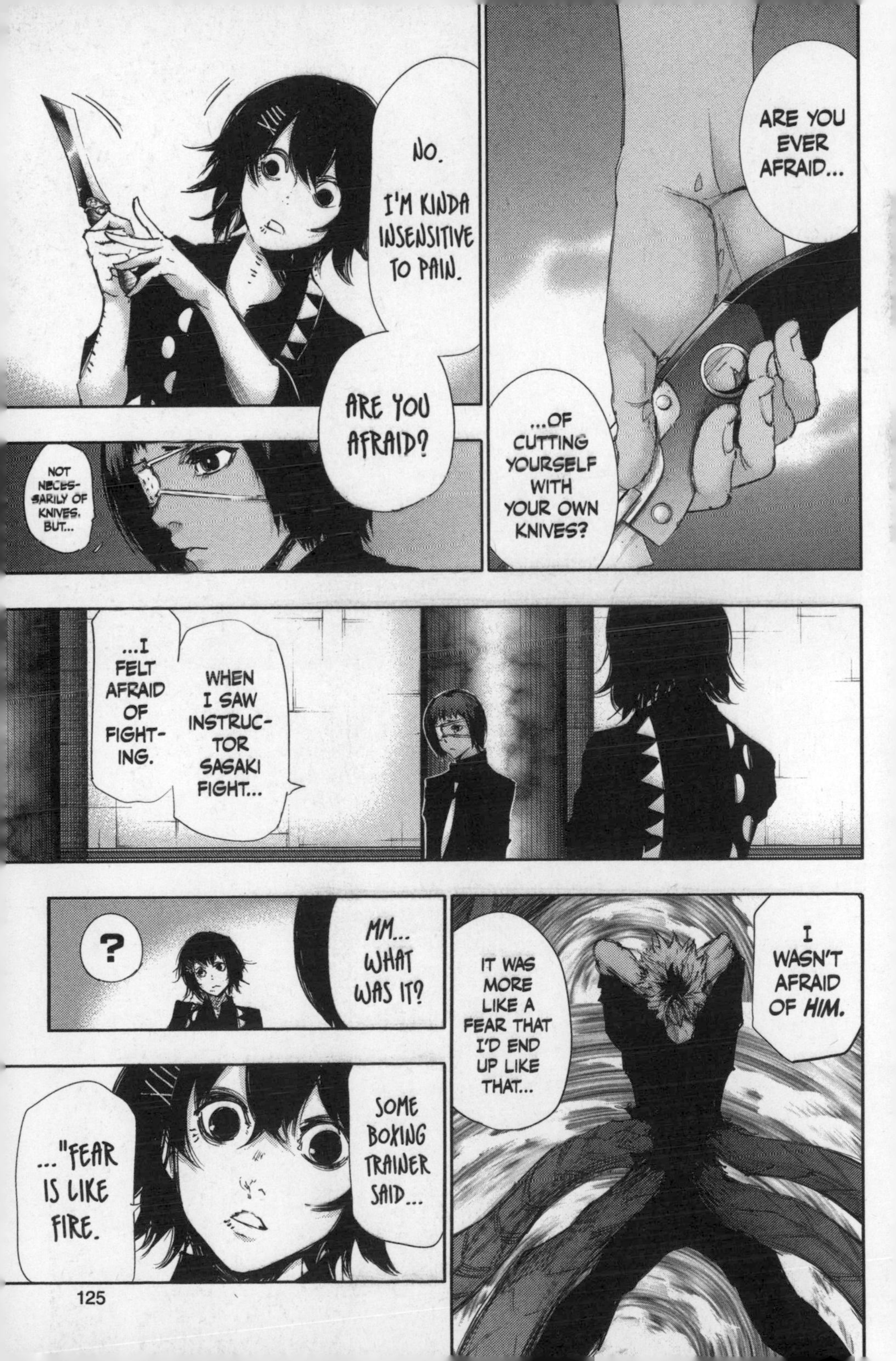
ARE YOU EVER AFRAID...
...OF CUTTING YOURSELF WITH YOUR OWN KNIVES?
NO.
I'M KINDA INSENSITIVE TO PAIN.
ARE YOU AFRAID?
NOT NECES-SARILY OF KNIVES, BUT...
WHEN I SAW INSTRUC-TOR SASAKI FIGHT...
...I FELT AFRAID OF FIGHT-ING.
I WASN'T AFRAID OF *HIM*.
IT WAS MORE LIKE A FEAR THAT I'D END UP LIKE THAT...
MM... WHAT WAS IT?
?
SOME BOXING TRAINER SAID...
..."FEAR IS LIKE FIRE.

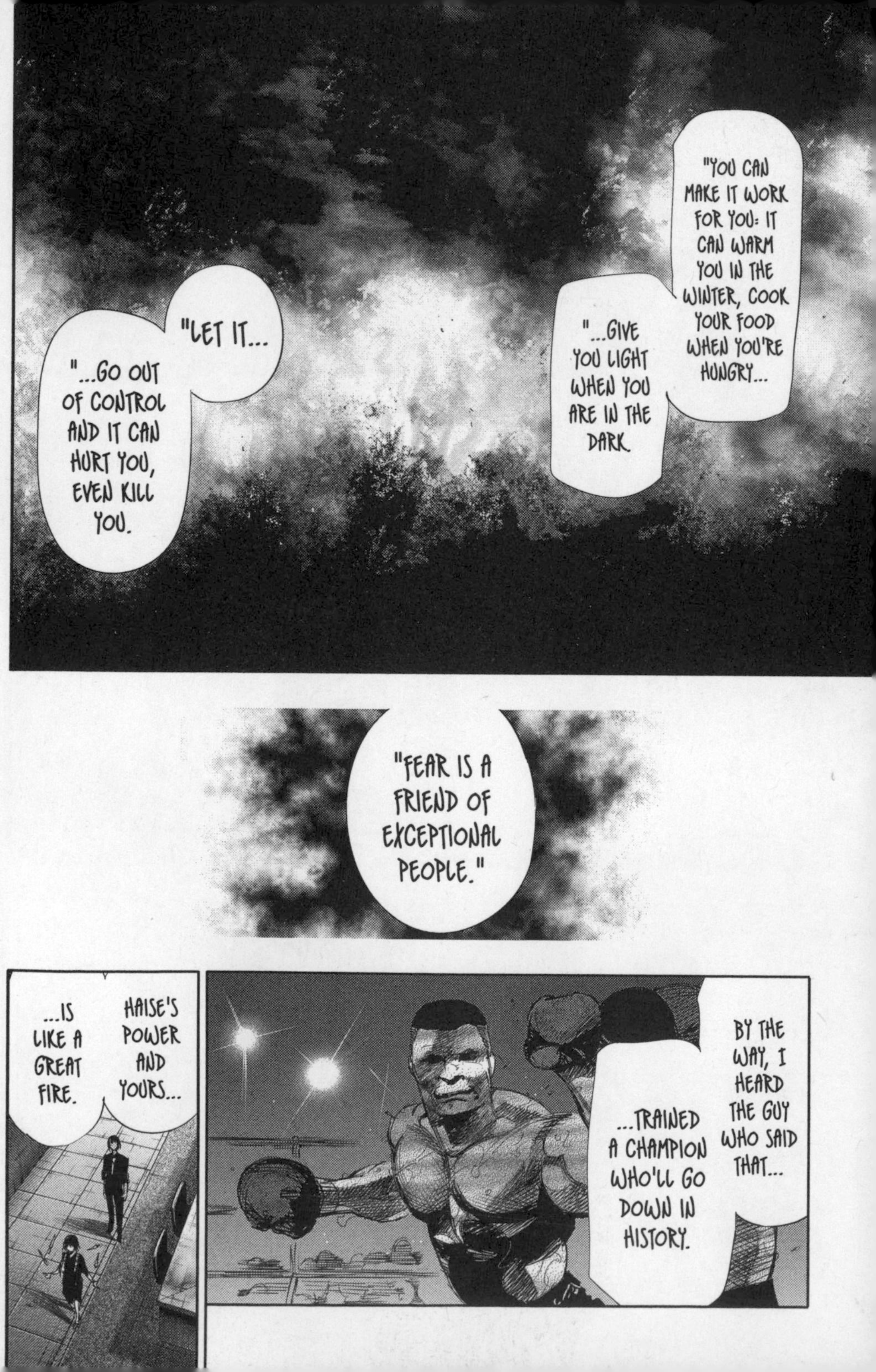
"YOU CAN MAKE IT WORK FOR YOU: IT CAN WARM YOU IN THE WINTER, COOK YOUR FOOD WHEN YOU'RE HUNGRY...
"...GIVE YOU LIGHT WHEN YOU ARE IN THE DARK.
"LET IT...
"...GO OUT OF CONTROL AND IT CAN HURT YOU, EVEN KILL YOU.
"FEAR IS A FRIEND OF EXCEPTIONAL PEOPLE."
BY THE WAY, I HEARD THE GUY WHO SAID THAT...
...TRAINED A CHAMPION WHO'LL GO DOWN IN HISTORY.
HAISE'S POWER AND YOURS...
...IS LIKE A GREAT FIRE.

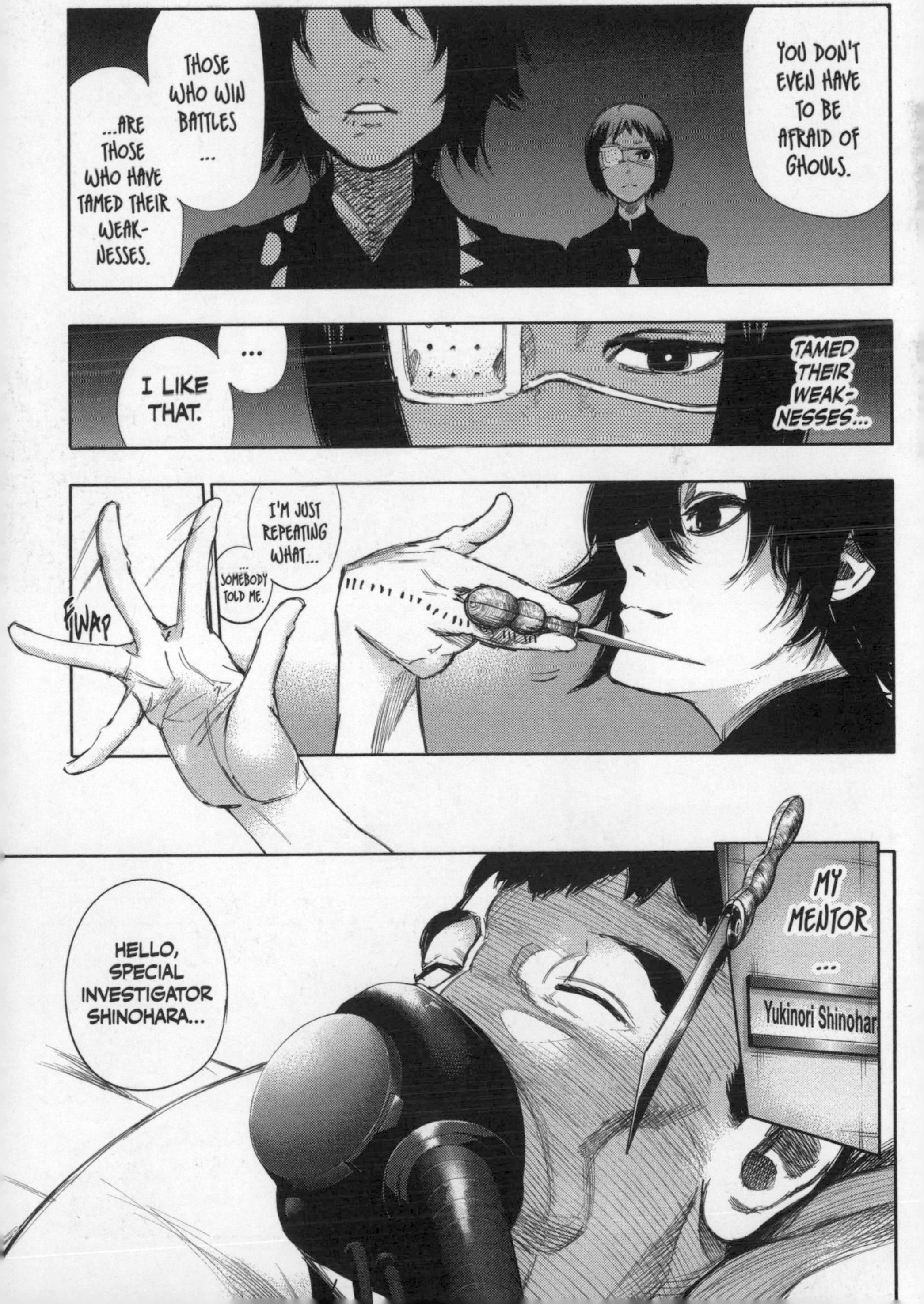
YOU DON'T EVEN HAVE TO BE AFRAID OF GHOULS.
THOSE WHO WIN BATTLES ...
...ARE THOSE WHO HAVE TAMED THEIR WEAK-NESSES.
TAMED THEIR WEAK-NESSES...
...
I LIKE THAT.
I'M JUST REPEATING WHAT...
... SOMEBODY TOLD ME.
FWAP
MY MENTOR ...
Yukinori Shinohar
HELLO, SPECIAL INVESTIGATOR SHINOHARA...

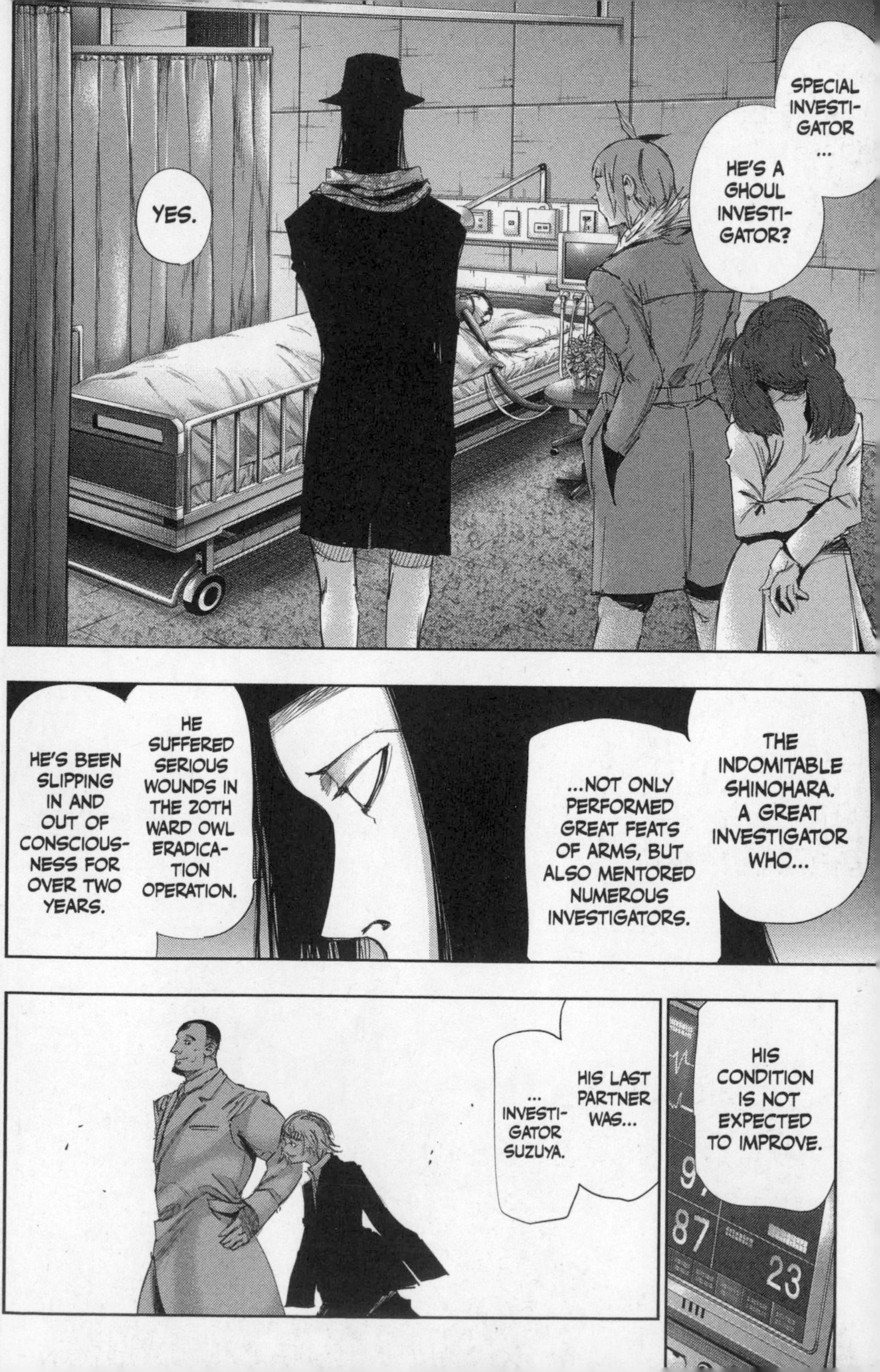
SPECIAL INVESTIGATOR ...
HE'S A GHOUL INVESTIGATOR?
YES.
THE INDOMITABLE SHINOHARA. A GREAT INVESTIGATOR WHO...
...NOT ONLY PERFORMED GREAT FEATS OF ARMS, BUT ALSO MENTORED NUMEROUS INVESTIGATORS.
HE SUFFERED SERIOUS WOUNDS IN THE 20TH WARD OWL ERADICATION OPERATION.
HE'S BEEN SLIPPING IN AND OUT OF CONSCIOUSNESS FOR OVER TWO YEARS.
HIS CONDITION IS NOT EXPECTED TO IMPROVE.
HIS LAST PARTNER WAS...
... INVESTIGATOR SUZUYA.

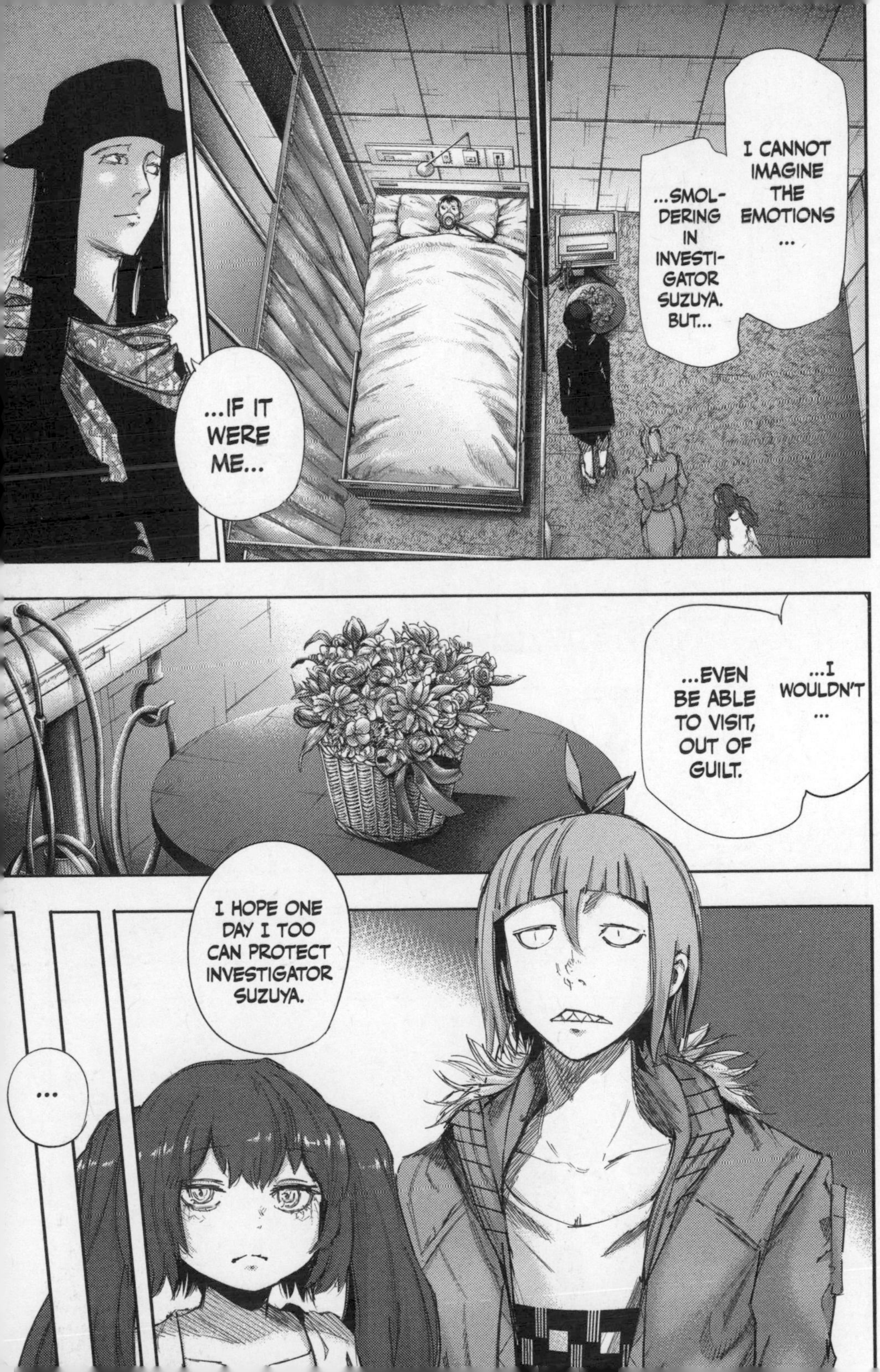
I CANNOT IMAGINE THE EMOTIONS ...
...SMOLDERING IN INVESTIGATOR SUZUYA. BUT...
...IF IT WERE ME...
...I WOULDN'T ...
...EVEN BE ABLE TO VISIT, OUT OF GUILT.
I HOPE ONE DAY I TOO CAN PROTECT INVESTIGATOR SUZUYA.
...

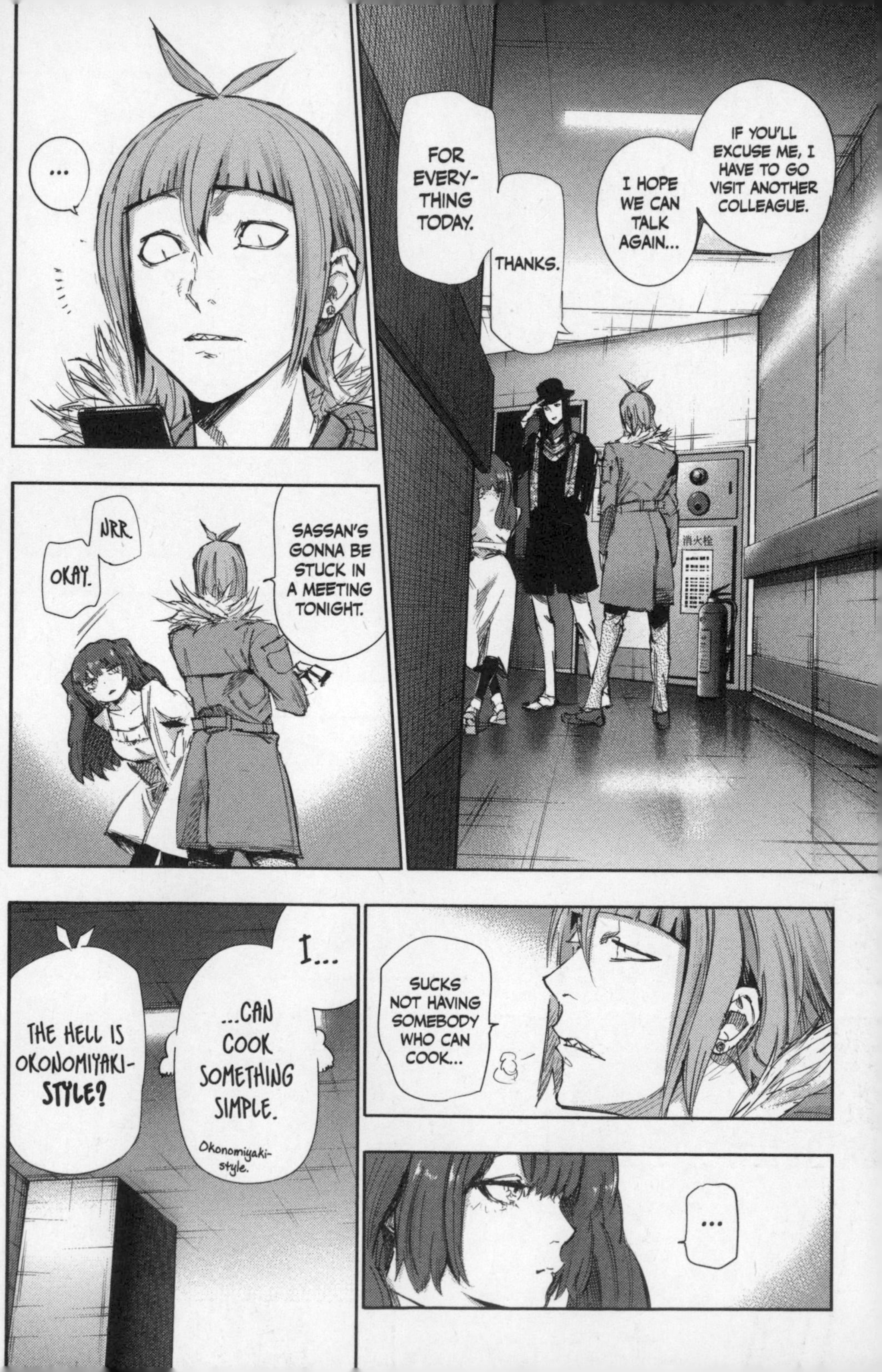
IF YOU'LL EXCUSE ME, I HAVE TO GO VISIT ANOTHER COLLEAGUE.
I HOPE WE CAN TALK AGAIN...
THANKS.
FOR EVERY-THING TODAY.
...
SASSAN'S GONNA BE STUCK IN A MEETING TONIGHT.
NRR.
OKAY.
SUCKS NOT HAVING SOMEBODY WHO CAN COOK...
...
I...
...CAN COOK SOMETHING SIMPLE.
Okonomiyaki-style.
THE HELL IS OKONOMIYAKI-STYLE?

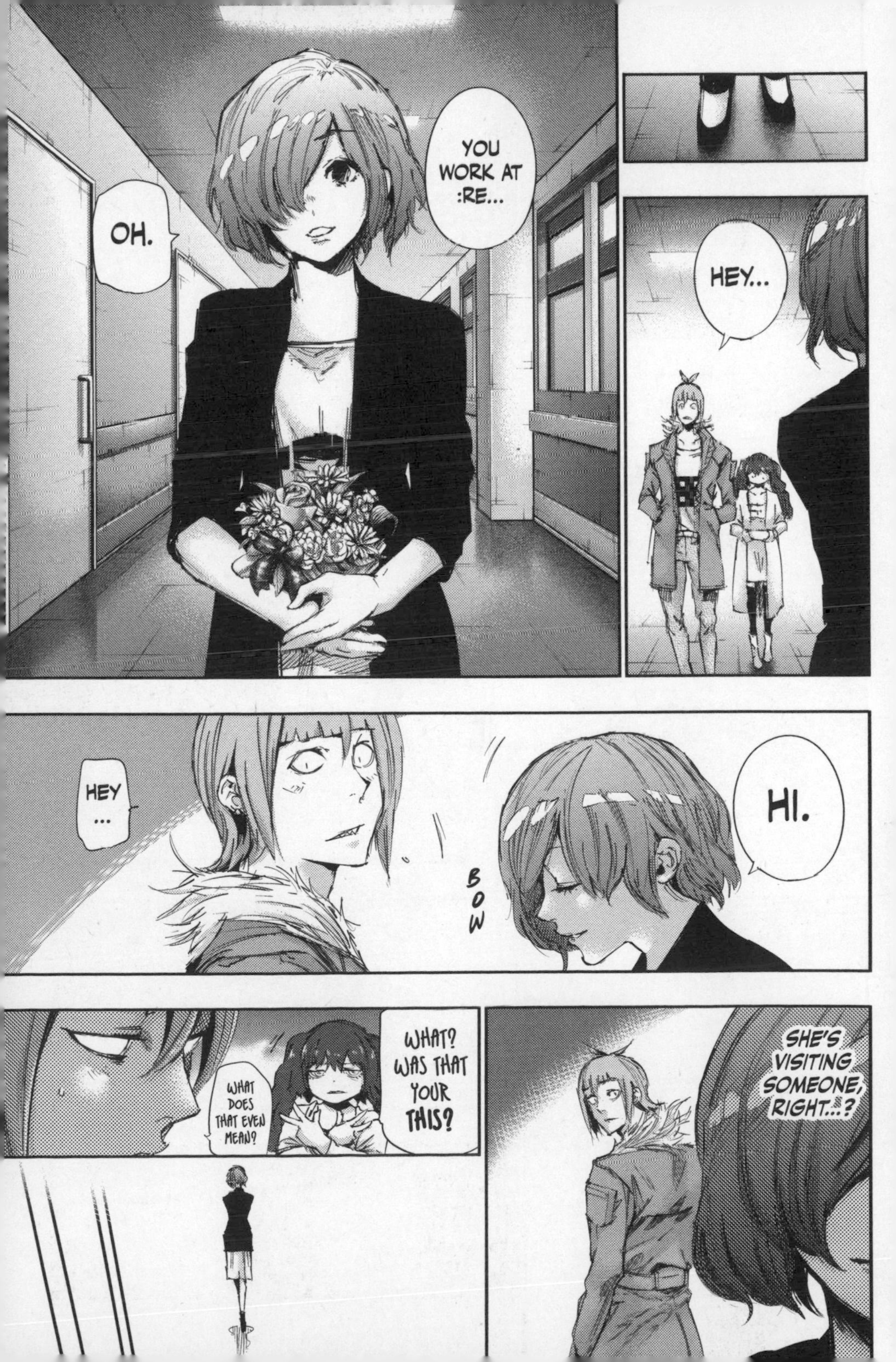
HEY...
YOU WORK AT :RE...
OH.
HI.
BOW
HEY ...
SHE'S VISITING SOMEONE, RIGHT...?
WHAT? WAS THAT YOUR THIS?
WHAT DOES THAT EVEN MEAN?

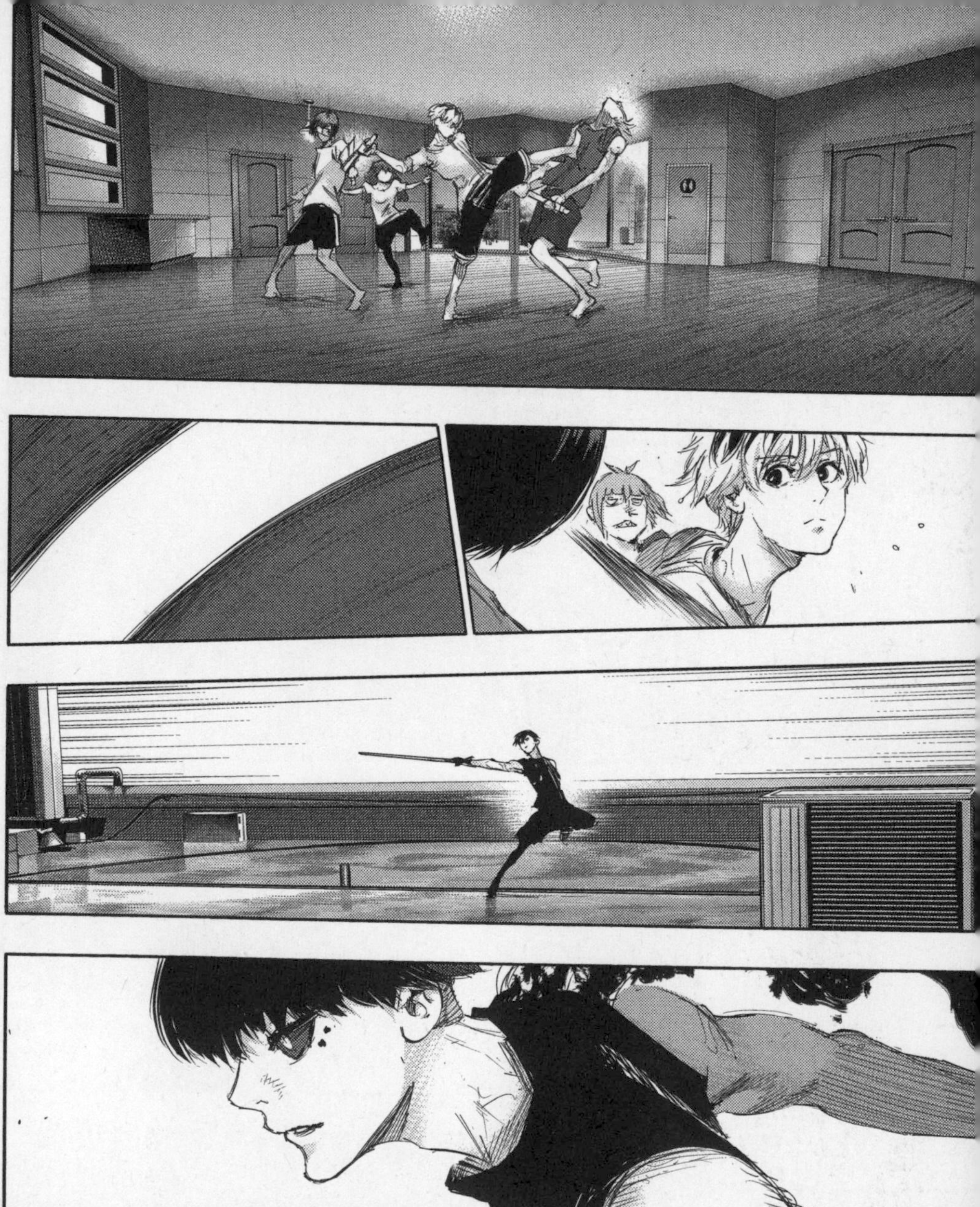

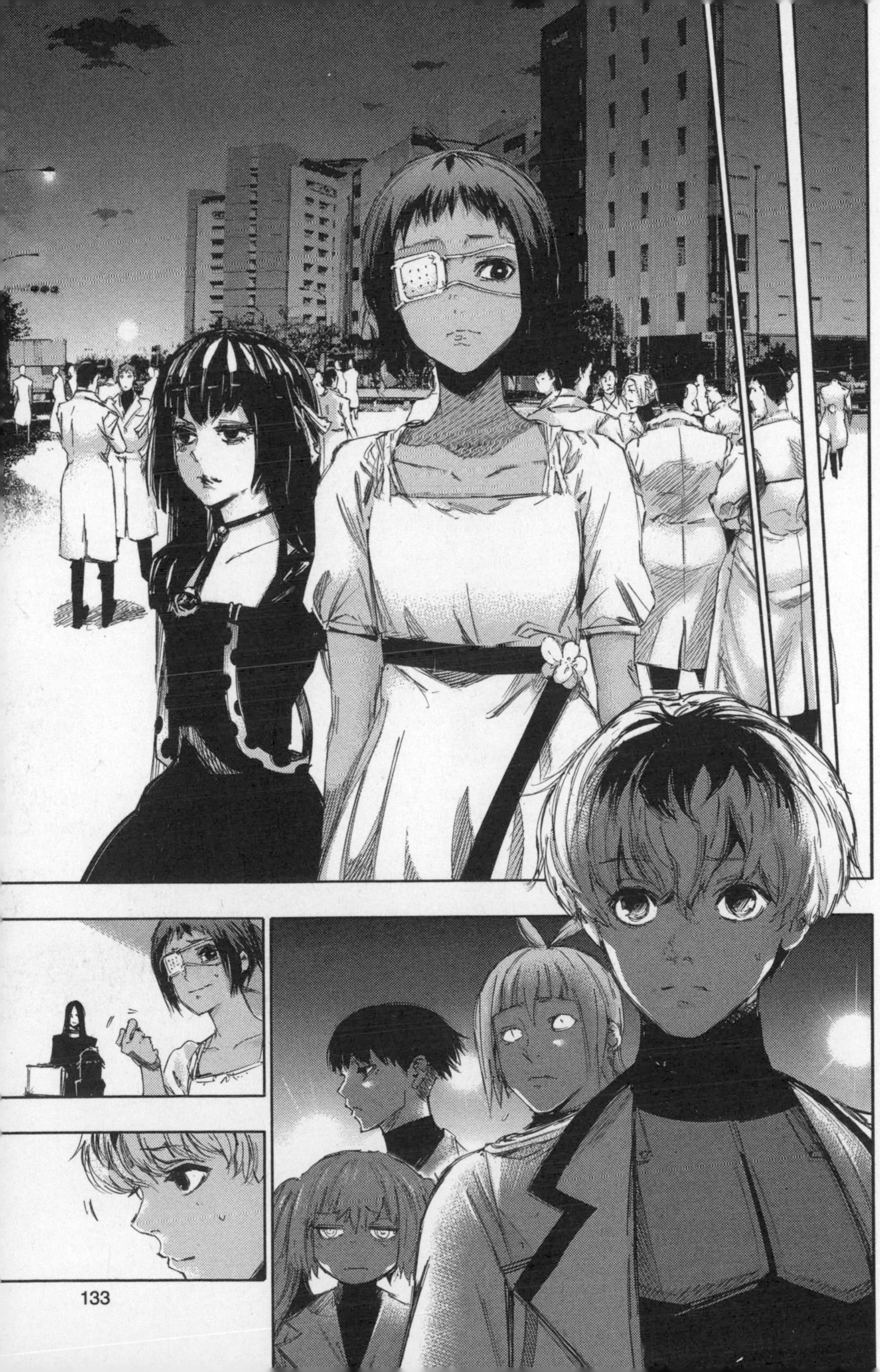
テヘ...

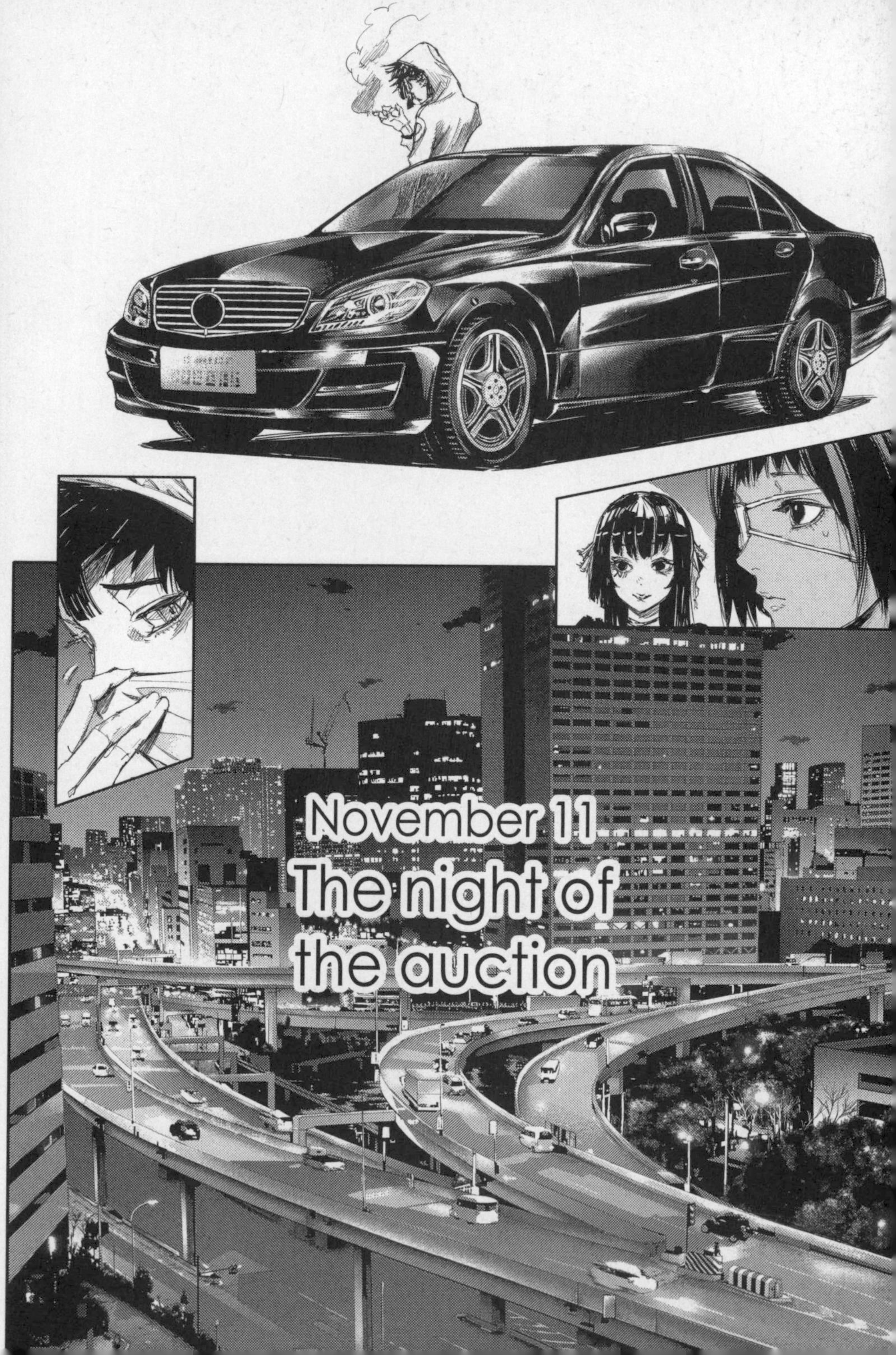
November 11
The night of the auction

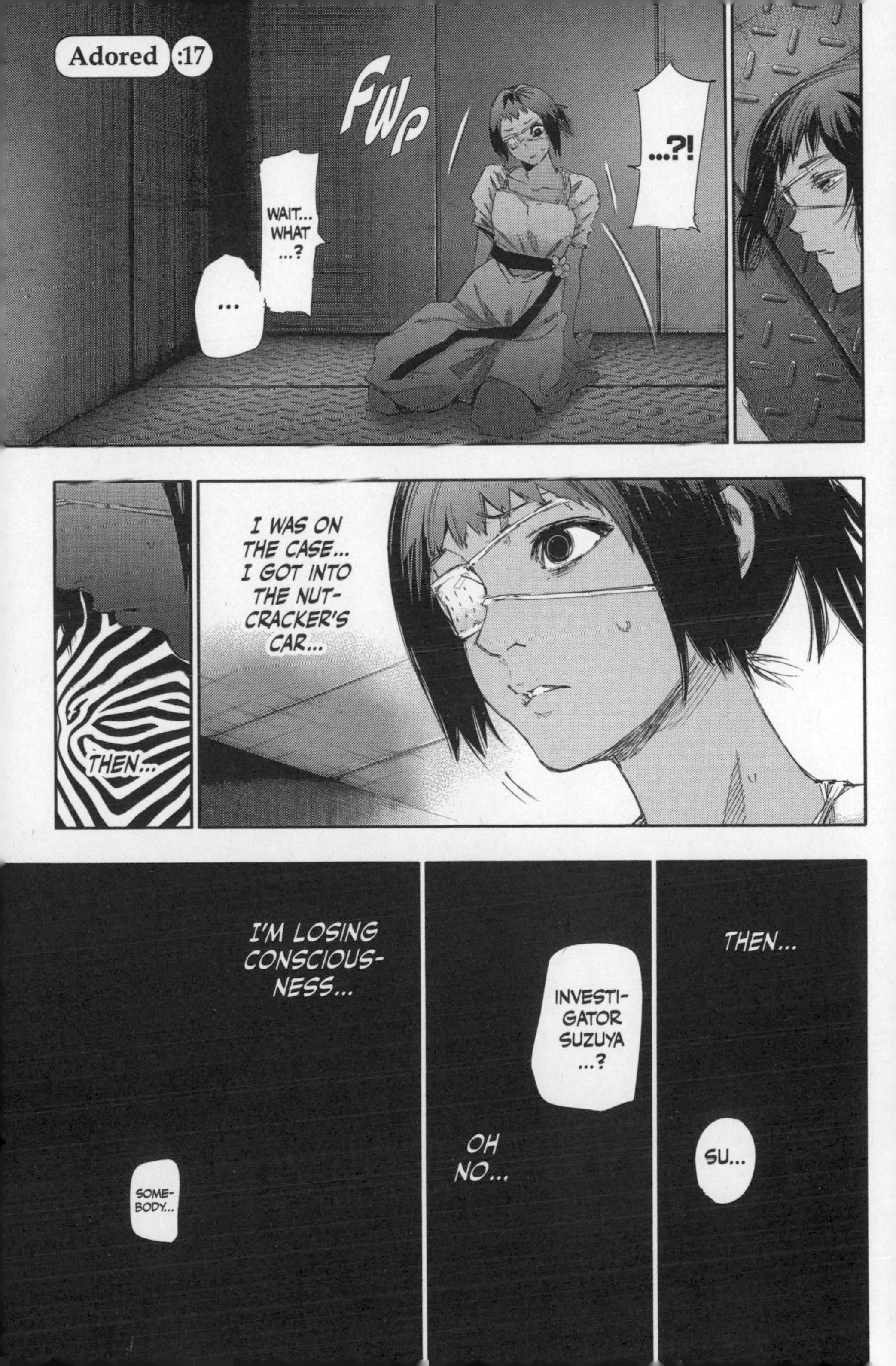
Adored :17
...?!
FWP
WAIT... WHAT ...?
...
I WAS ON THE CASE... I GOT INTO THE NUT-CRACKER'S CAR...
THEN...
THEN...
SU...
INVESTI-GATOR SUZUYA ...?
OH NO...
I'M LOSING CONSCIOUS-NESS...
SOME-BODY...

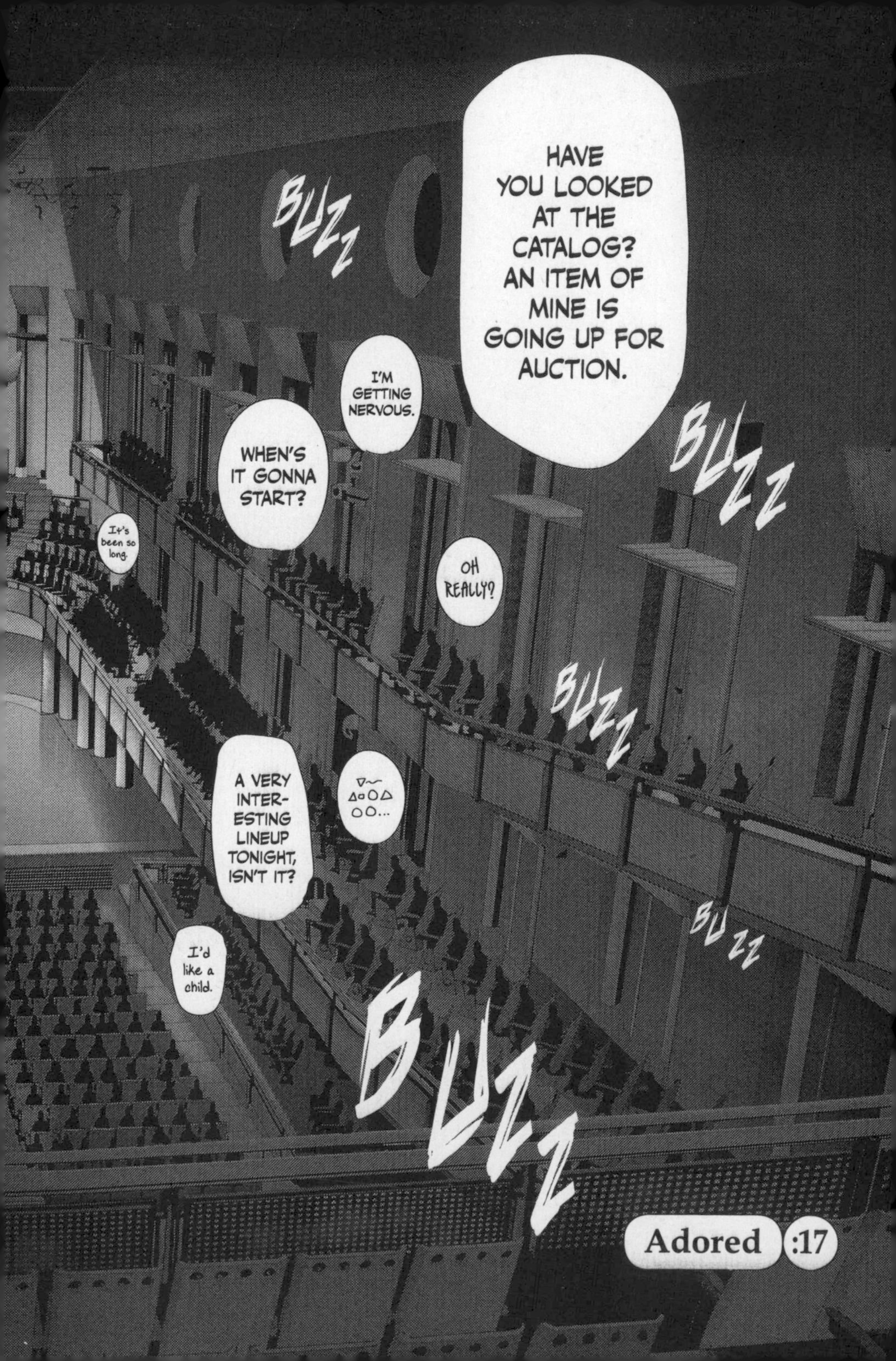
HAVE YOU LOOKED AT THE CATALOG? AN ITEM OF MINE IS GOING UP FOR AUCTION.
BUZZ
BUZZ
I'M GETTING NERVOUS.
WHEN'S IT GONNA START?
OH REALLY?
It's been so long.
BUZZ
A VERY INTER-ESTING LINEUP TONIGHT, ISN'T IT?
BUZZ
I'd like a child.
BUZZ
Adored :17

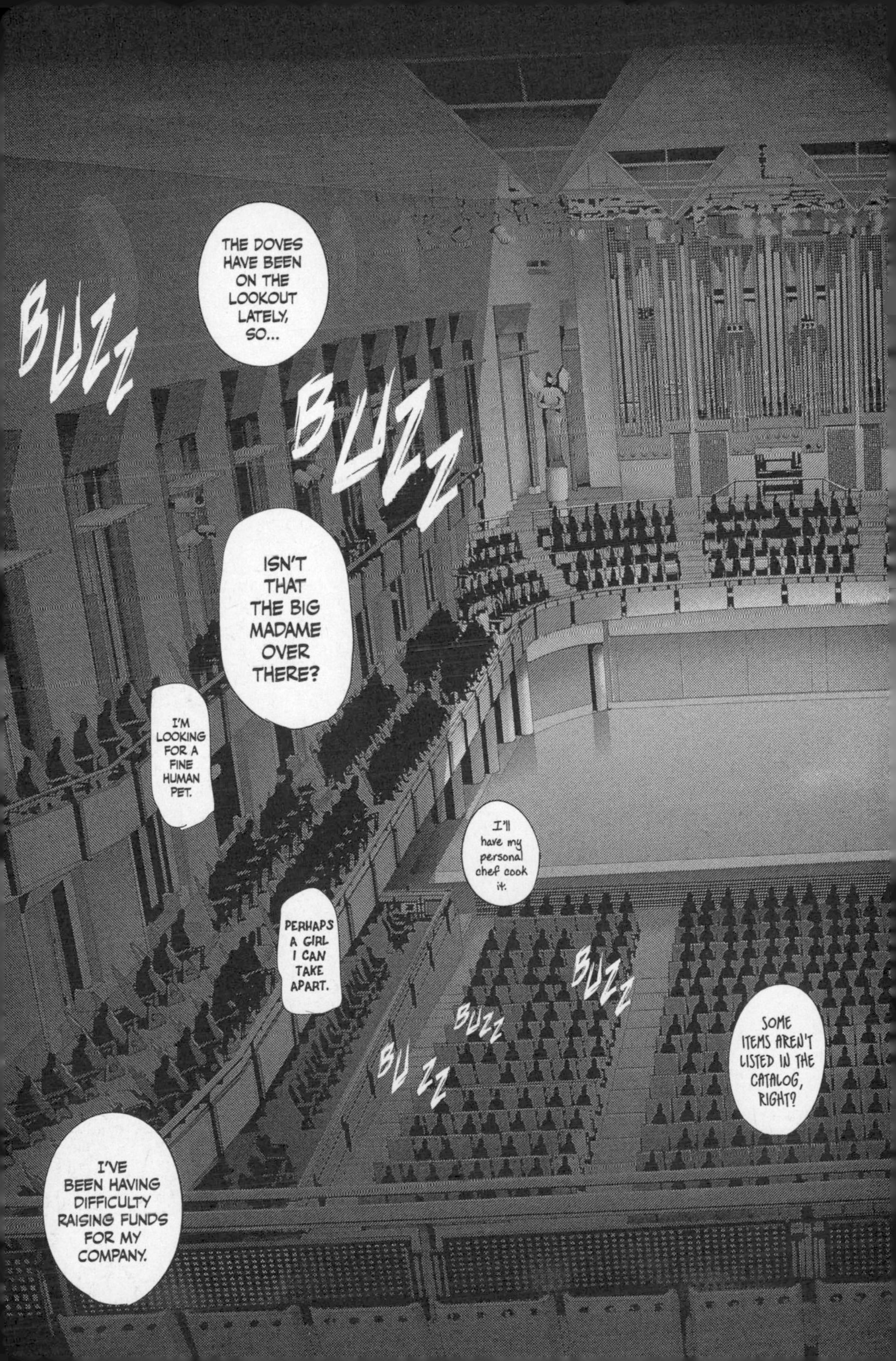
BUZZ
THE DOVES HAVE BEEN ON THE LOOKOUT LATELY, SO...
BUZZ
ISN'T THAT THE BIG MADAME OVER THERE?
I'M LOOKING FOR A FINE HUMAN PET.
I'll have my personal chef cook it.
PERHAPS A GIRL I CAN TAKE APART.
BUZZ
BUZZ
BUZZ
SOME ITEMS AREN'T LISTED IN THE CATALOG, RIGHT?
I'VE BEEN HAVING DIFFICULTY RAISING FUNDS FOR MY COMPANY.

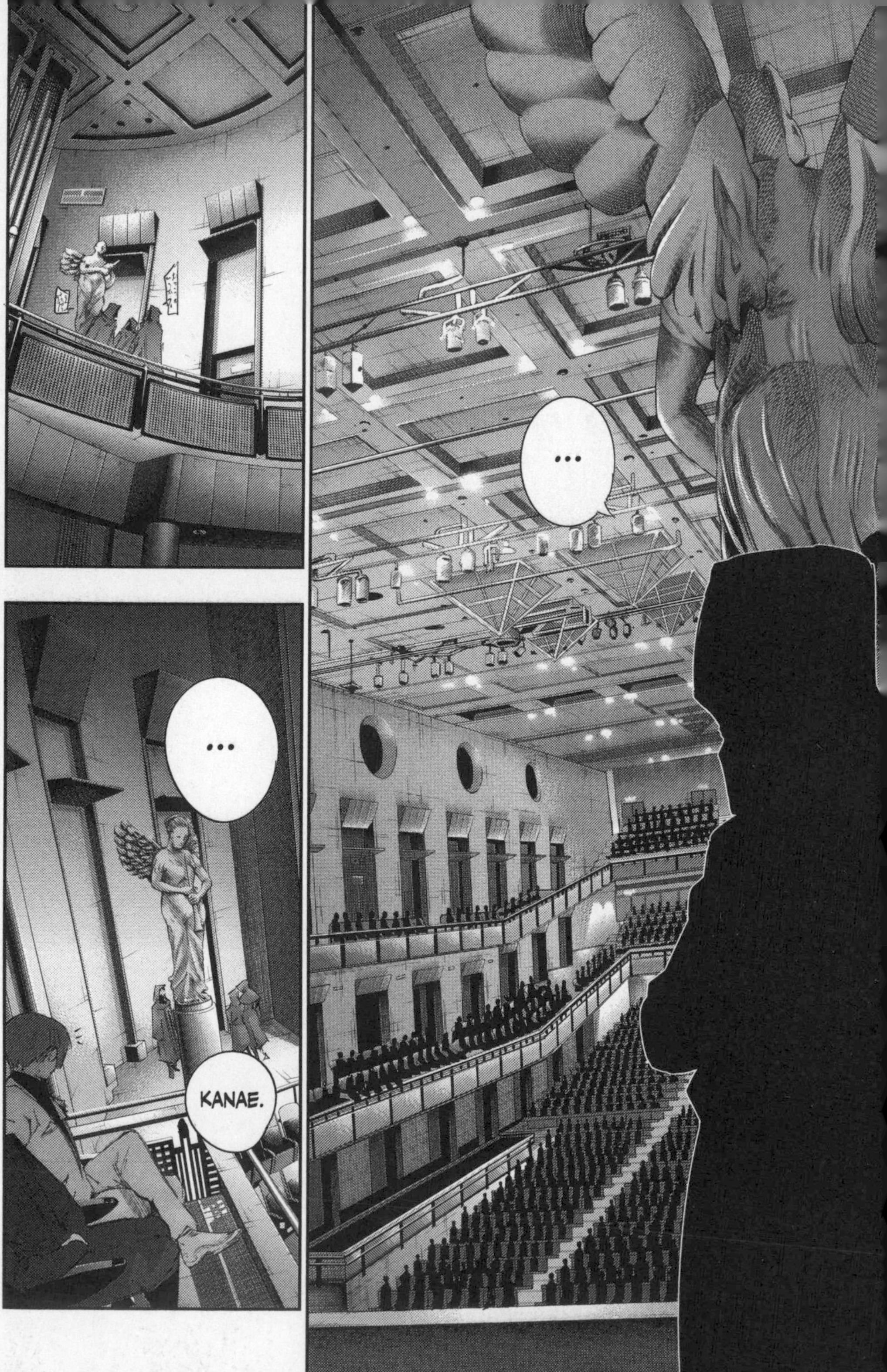
...
...
KANAE.

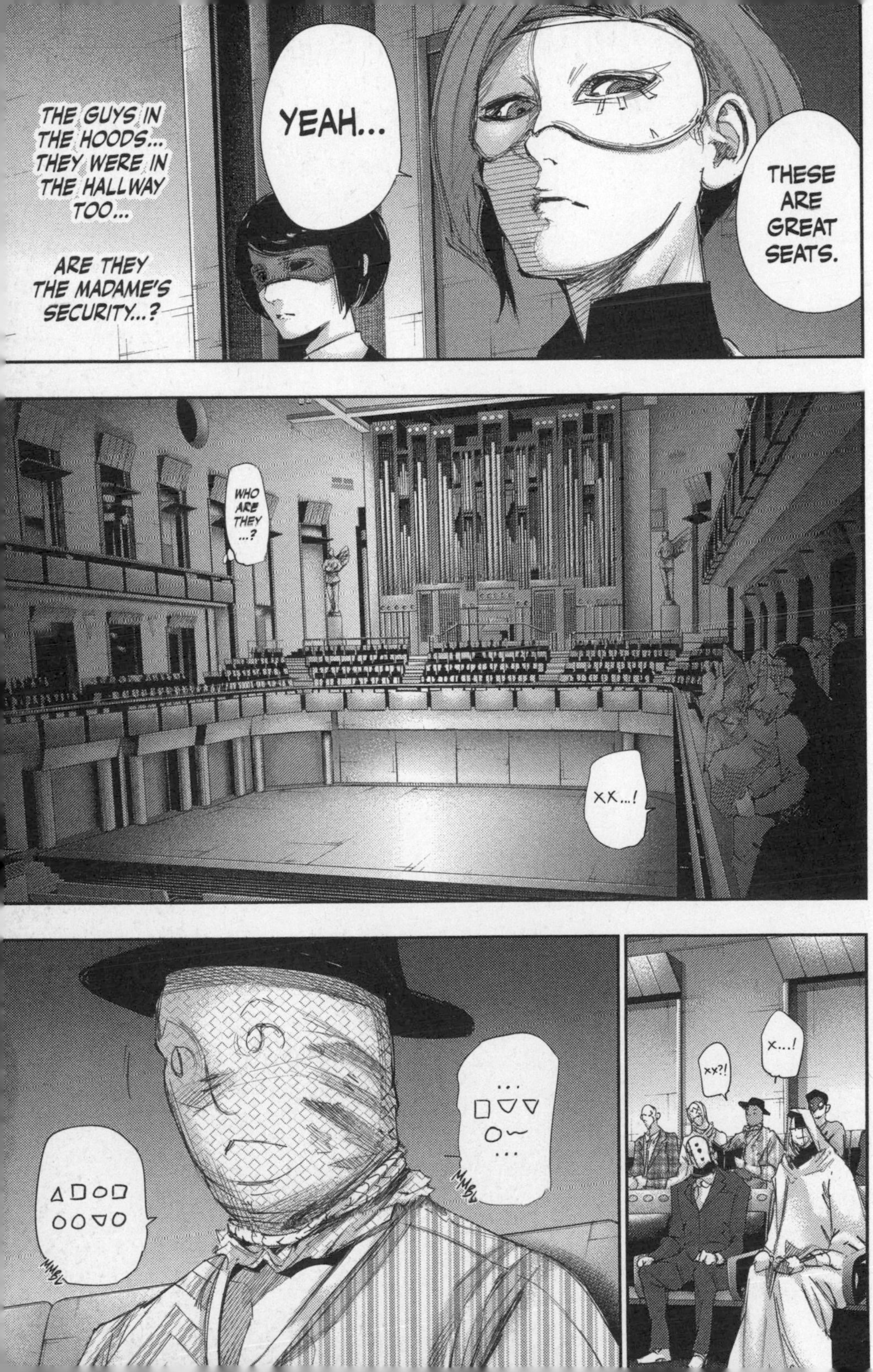
THESE ARE GREAT SEATS.
YEAH...
THE GUYS IN THE HOODS... THEY WERE IN THE HALLWAY TOO...
ARE THEY THE MADAME'S SECURITY...?
WHO ARE THEY ...?
XX...!
X...!
XX?!
... □▽▽ O~ ...
MMBL
△□O□ OO▽O
MMBL

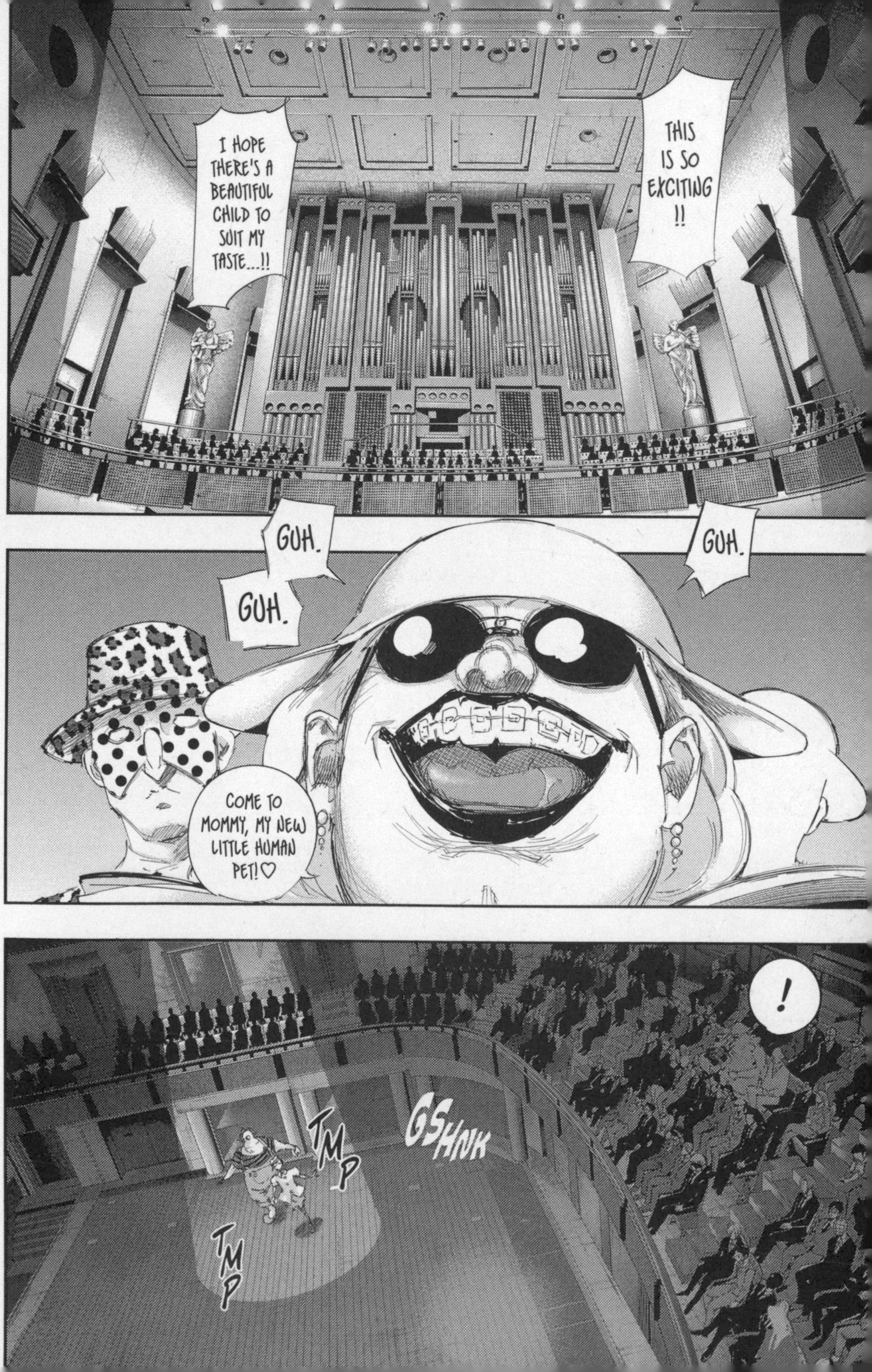
THIS IS SO EXCITING !!
I HOPE THERE'S A BEAUTIFUL CHILD TO SUIT MY TASTE...!!
GUH.
GUH.
GUH.
COME TO MOMMY, MY NEW LITTLE HUMAN PET!♡
!
GSHNK
TMP
TMP

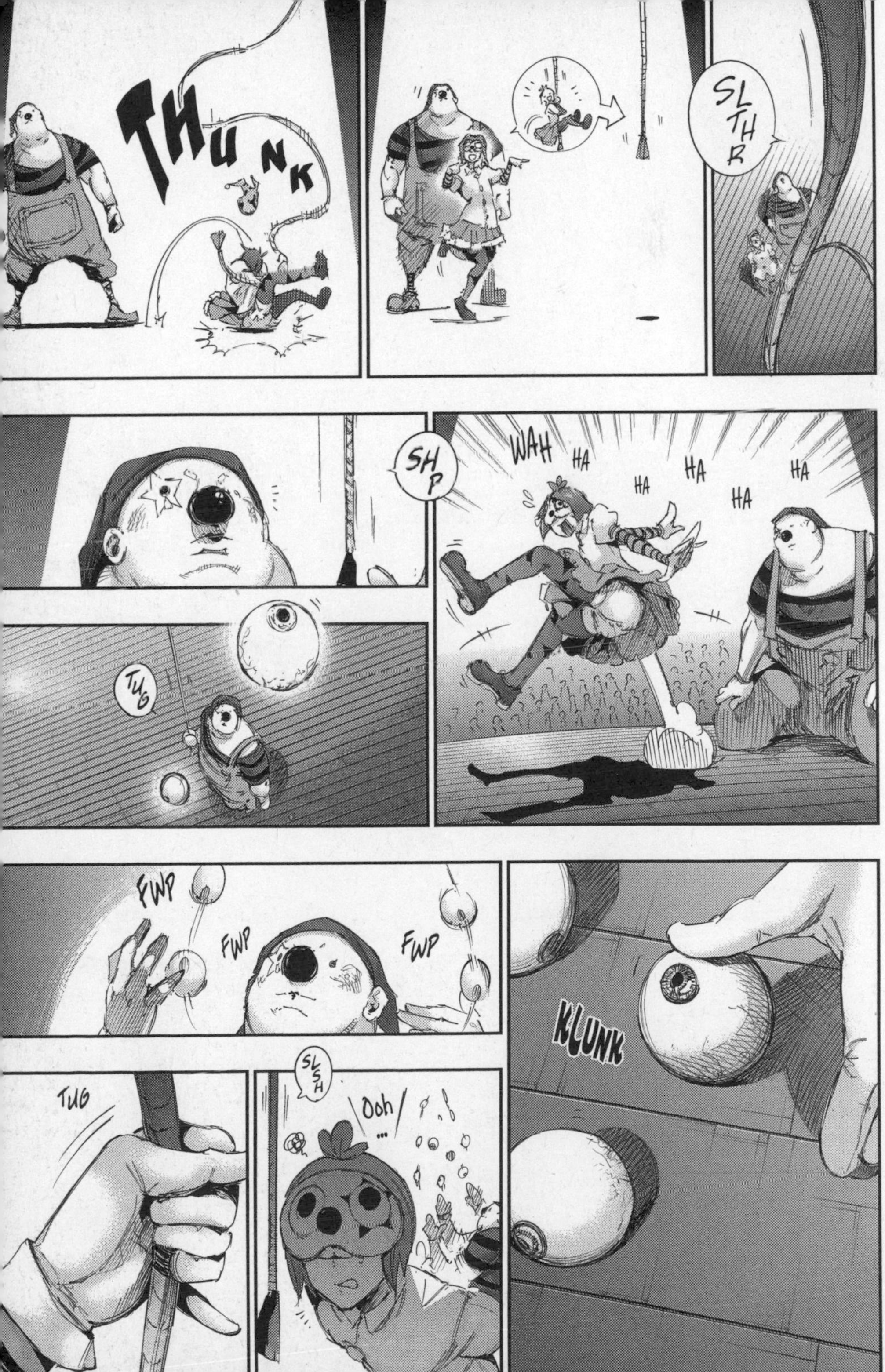
SLTHR
THUNK
SHP
WAH HA HA HA HA HA
TUG
KLUNK
FWP
FWP
FWP
SLSH
\Ooh/ ...
TUG

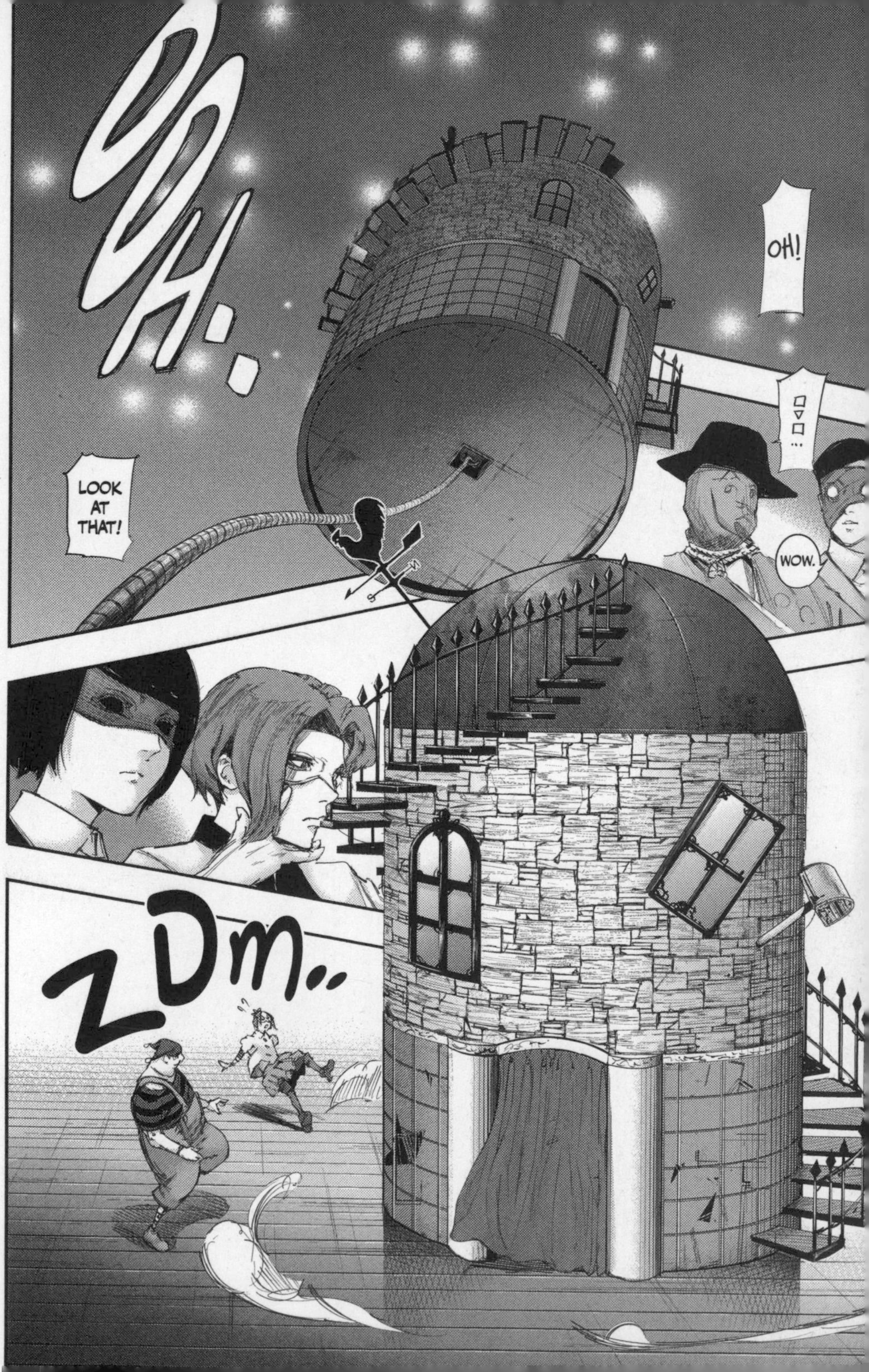
OH!
□▽□..
WOW.
OOH..
LOOK AT THAT!
ZDM..

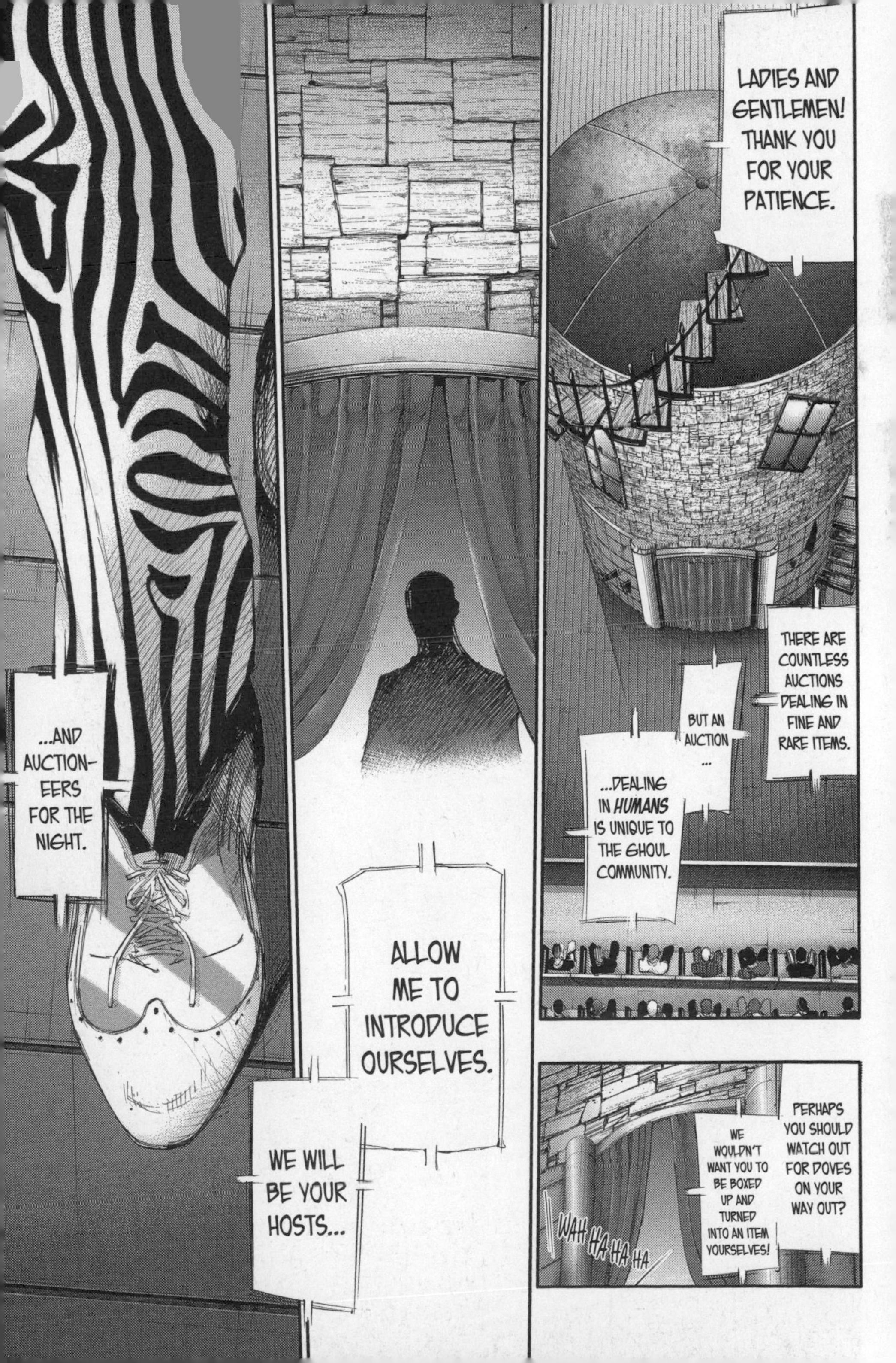
LADIES AND GENTLEMEN! THANK YOU FOR YOUR PATIENCE.
THERE ARE COUNTLESS AUCTIONS DEALING IN FINE AND RARE ITEMS.
BUT AN AUCTION...
...DEALING IN *HUMANS* IS UNIQUE TO THE GHOUL COMMUNITY.
PERHAPS YOU SHOULD WATCH OUT FOR DOVES ON YOUR WAY OUT?
WE WOULDN'T WANT YOU TO BE BOXED UP AND TURNED INTO AN ITEM YOURSELVES!
WAH HA HA HA
ALLOW ME TO INTRODUCE OURSELVES.
WE WILL BE YOUR HOSTS...
...AND AUCTION-EERS FOR THE NIGHT.

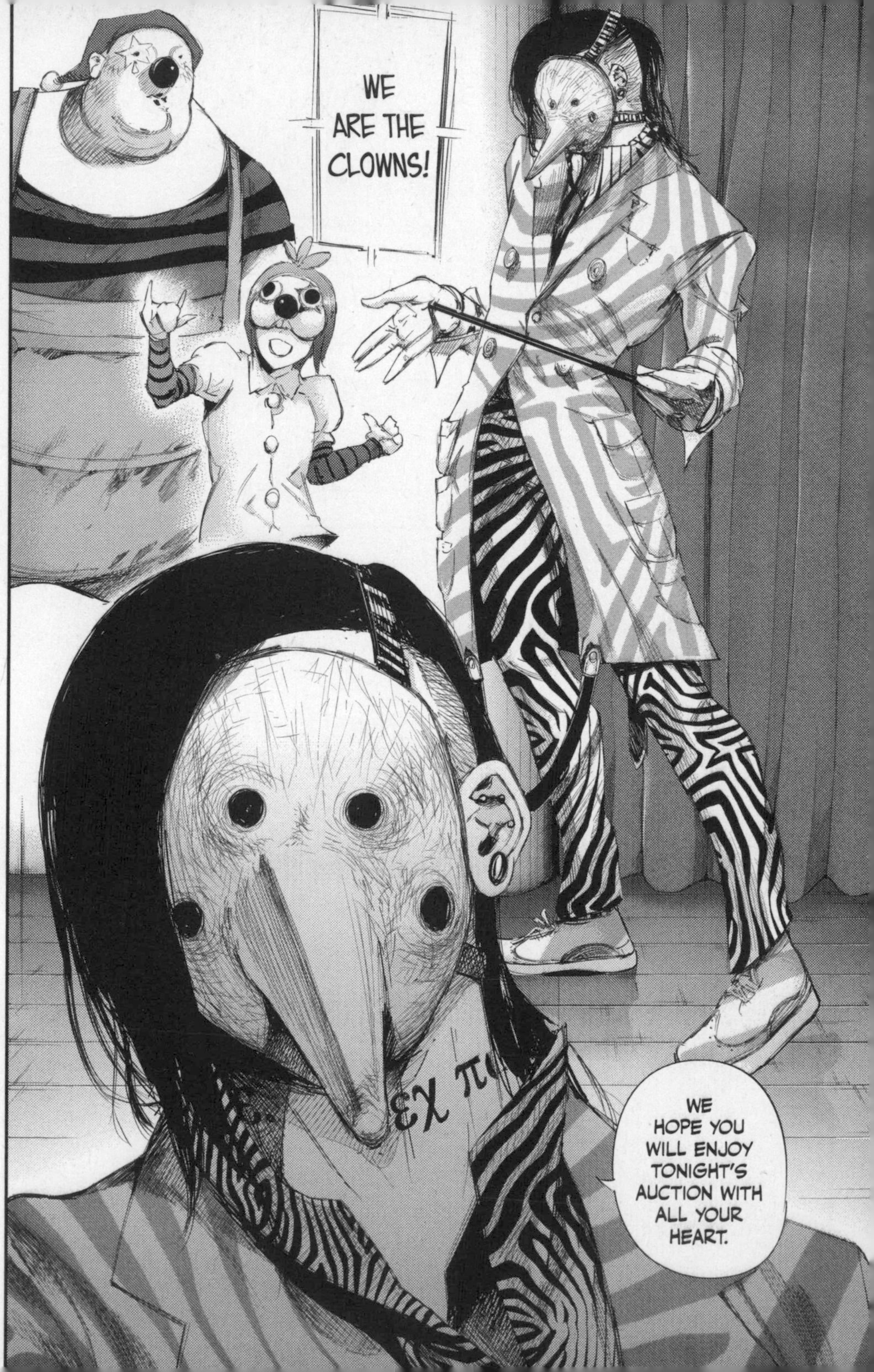
WE ARE THE CLOWNS!
WE HOPE YOU WILL ENJOY TONIGHT'S AUCTION WITH ALL YOUR HEART.

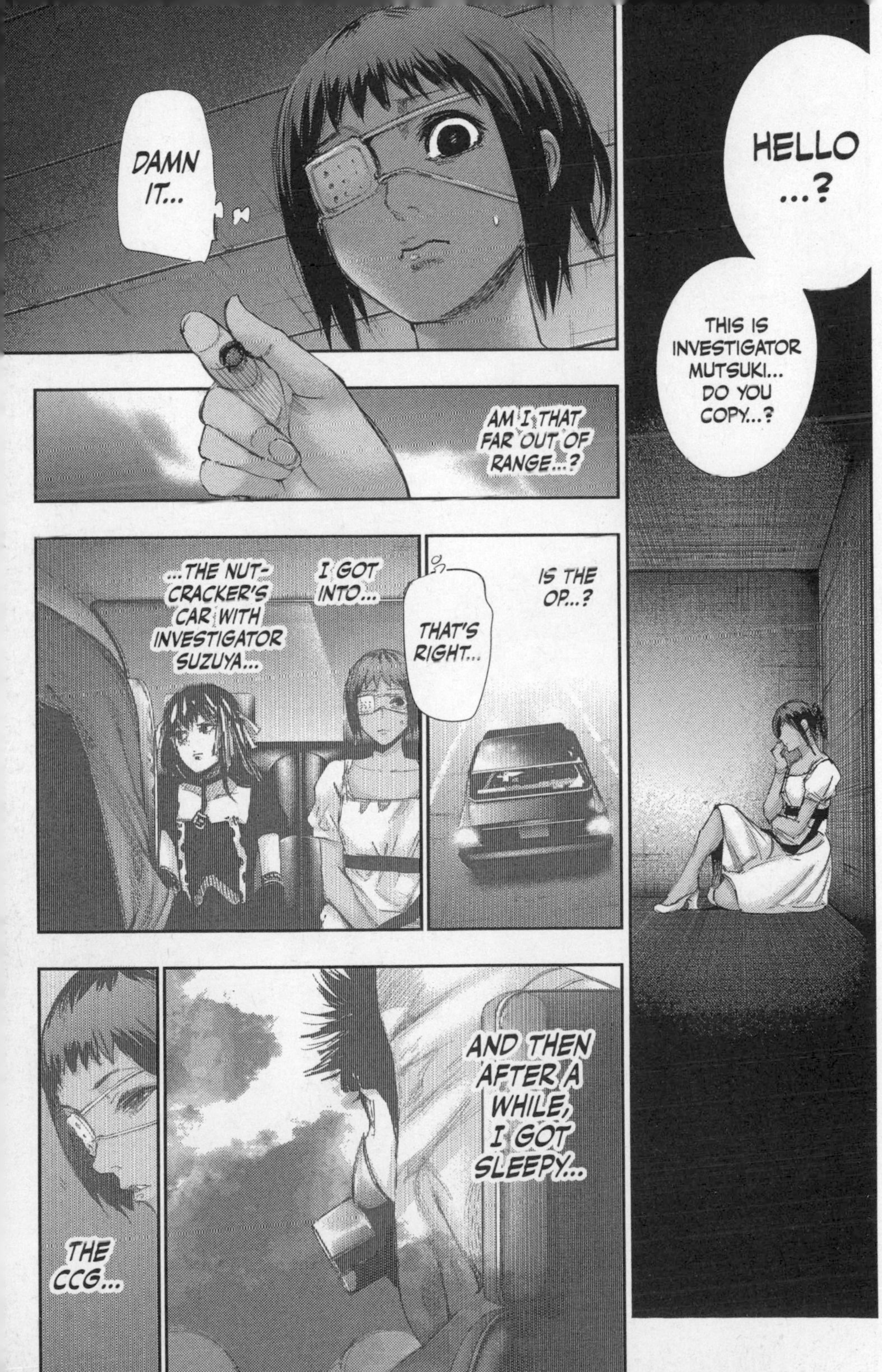
HELLO ...?
THIS IS INVESTIGATOR MUTSUKI... DO YOU COPY...?
DAMN IT...
AM I THAT FAR OUT OF RANGE...?
IS THE OP...?
THAT'S RIGHT...
I GOT INTO...
...THE NUT-CRACKER'S CAR WITH INVESTIGATOR SUZUYA...
AND THEN AFTER A WHILE, I GOT SLEEPY...
THE CCG...

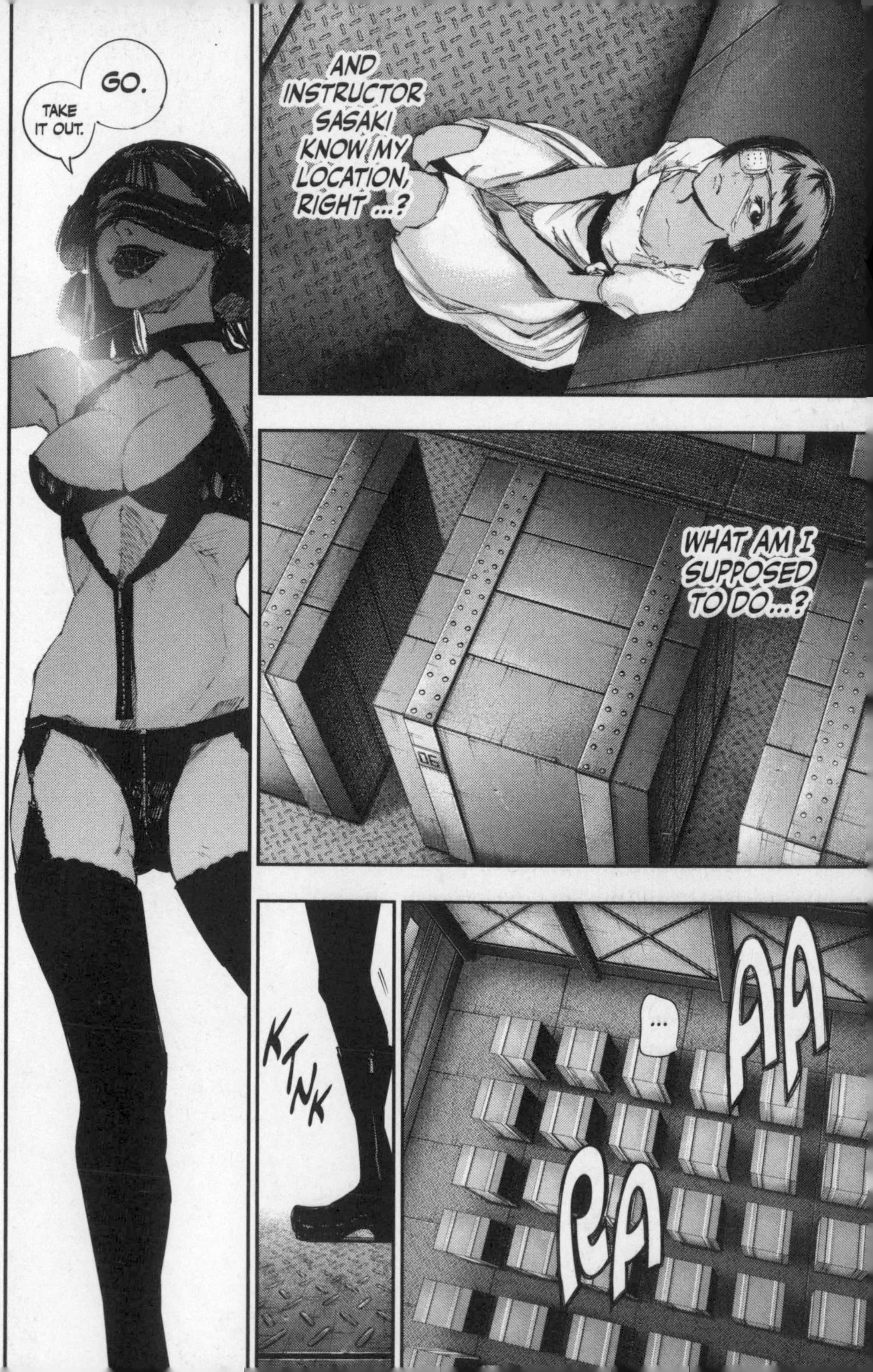
AND INSTRUCTOR SASAKI KNOW MY LOCATION, RIGHT ...?
WHAT AM I SUPPOSED TO DO...?
...
RA
RA
KANK
GO.
TAKE IT OUT.

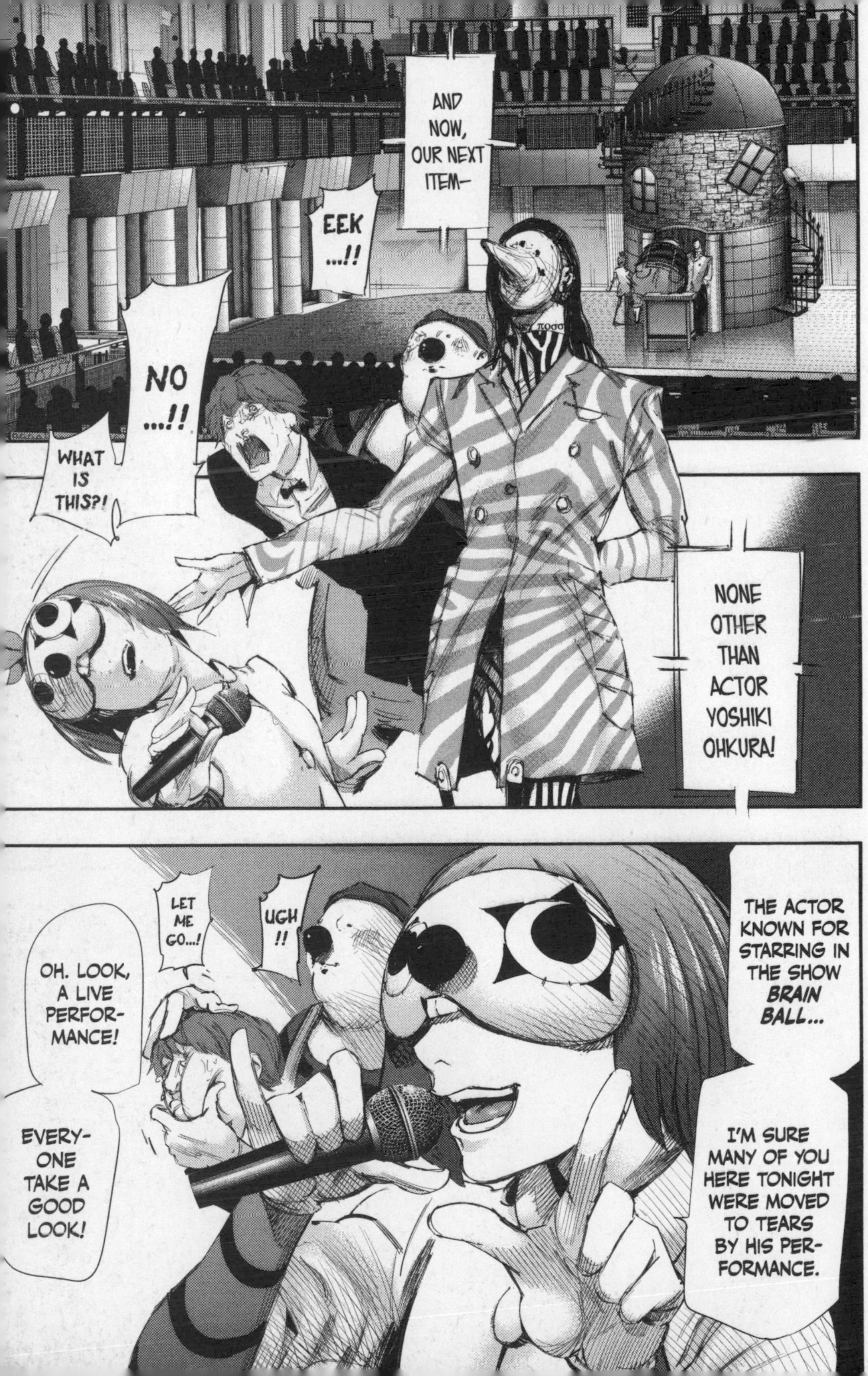
AND NOW, OUR NEXT ITEM—
EEK ...!!
NO ...!!
WHAT IS THIS?!
NONE OTHER THAN ACTOR YOSHIKI OHKURA!
THE ACTOR KNOWN FOR STARRING IN THE SHOW *BRAIN BALL*...
I'M SURE MANY OF YOU HERE TONIGHT WERE MOVED TO TEARS BY HIS PERFORMANCE.
UGH !!
LET ME GO...!
OH. LOOK, A LIVE PERFORMANCE!
EVERYONE TAKE A GOOD LOOK!

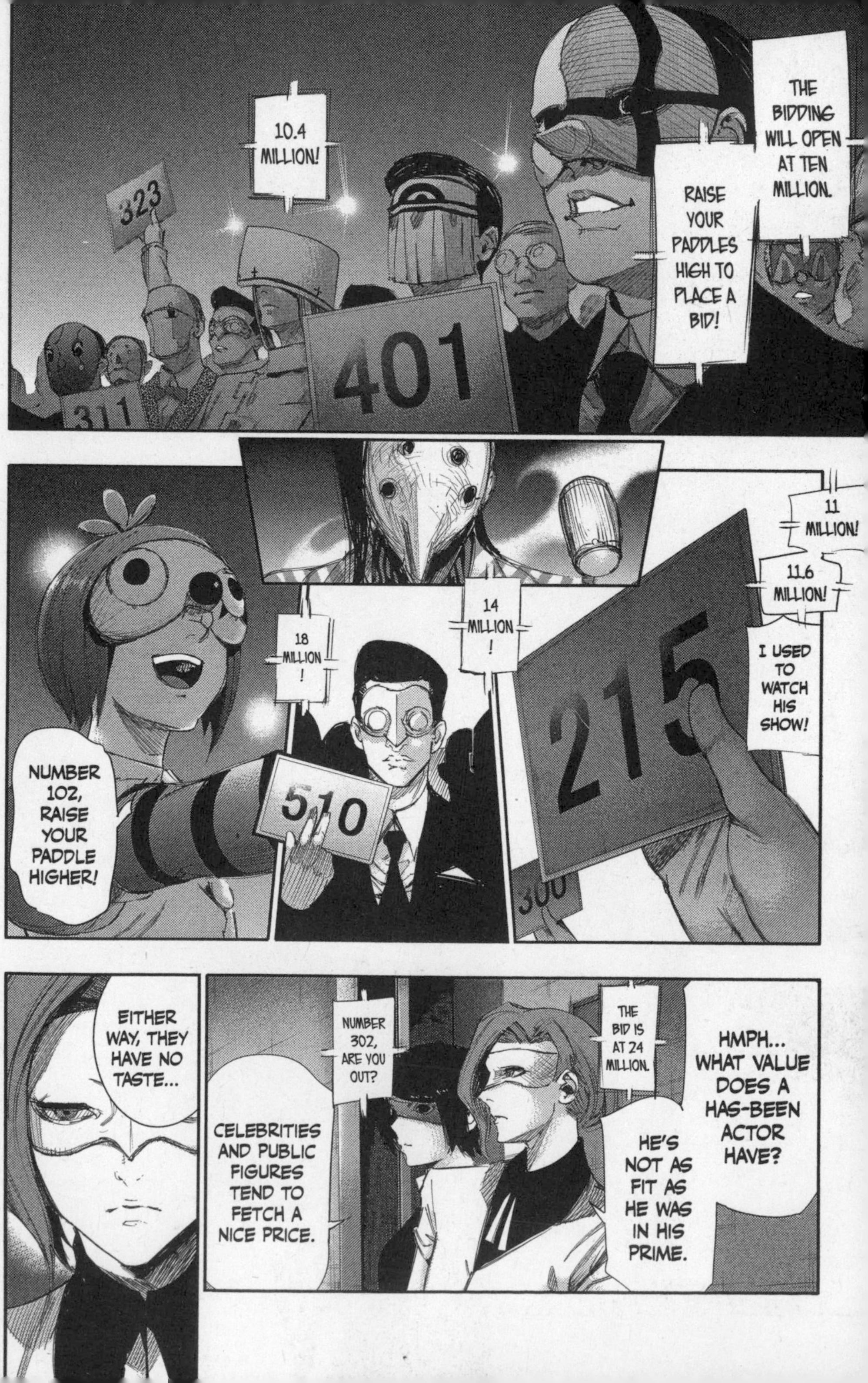
THE BIDDING WILL OPEN AT TEN MILLION.
RAISE YOUR PADDLES HIGH TO PLACE A BID!
401
10.4 MILLION!
323
11 MILLION!
11.6 MILLION!
I USED TO WATCH HIS SHOW!
215
14 MILLION!
18 MILLION!
510
NUMBER 102, RAISE YOUR PADDLE HIGHER!
HMPH... WHAT VALUE DOES A HAS-BEEN ACTOR HAVE?
THE BID IS AT 24 MILLION.
HE'S NOT AS FIT AS HE WAS IN HIS PRIME.
NUMBER 302, ARE YOU OUT?
CELEBRITIES AND PUBLIC FIGURES TEND TO FETCH A NICE PRICE.
EITHER WAY, THEY HAVE NO TASTE...

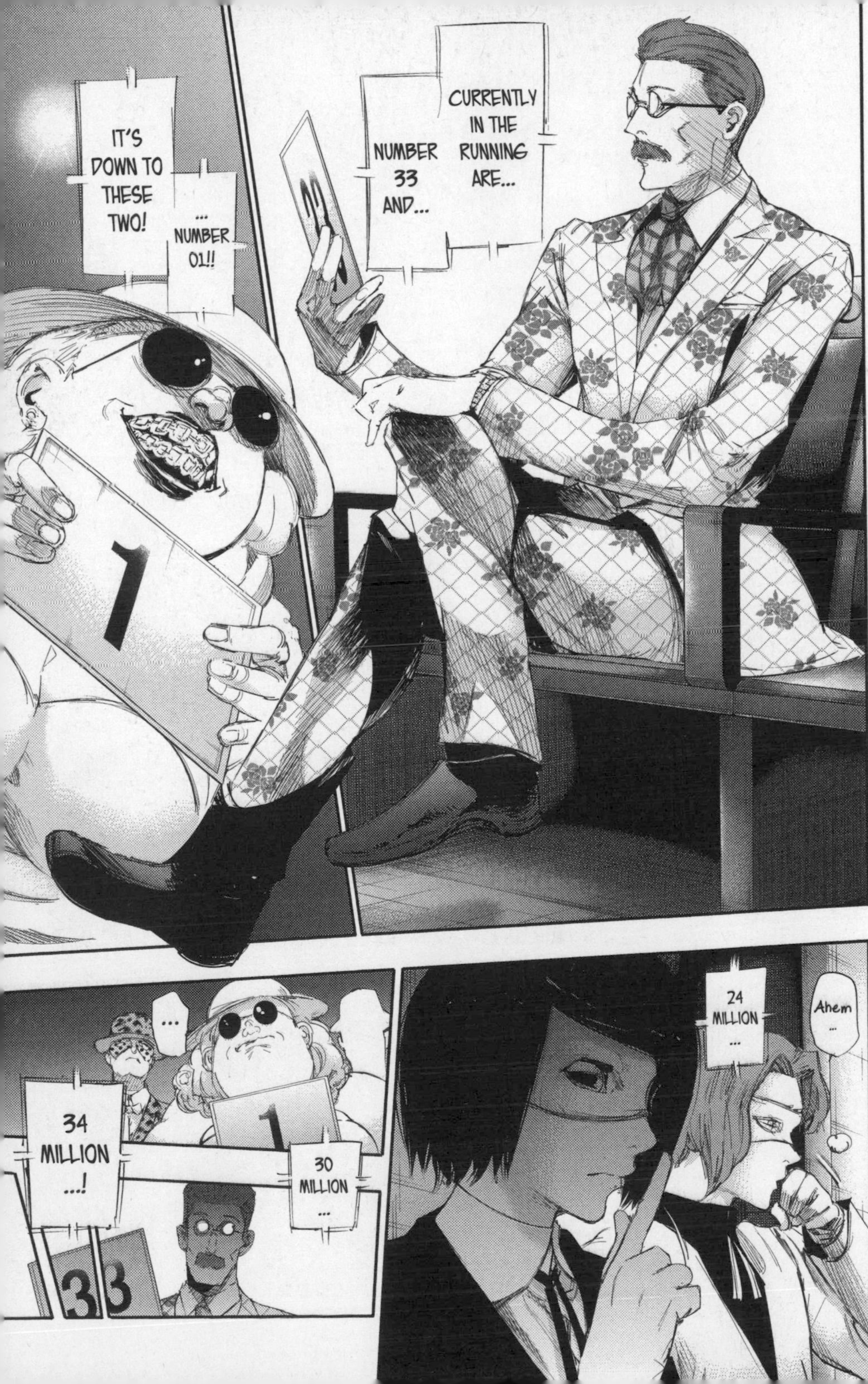
CURRENTLY IN THE RUNNING ARE...
NUMBER 33 AND...
... NUMBER 01!!
IT'S DOWN TO THESE TWO!
Ahem ...
24 MILLION ...
...
34 MILLION ...!
30 MILLION ...

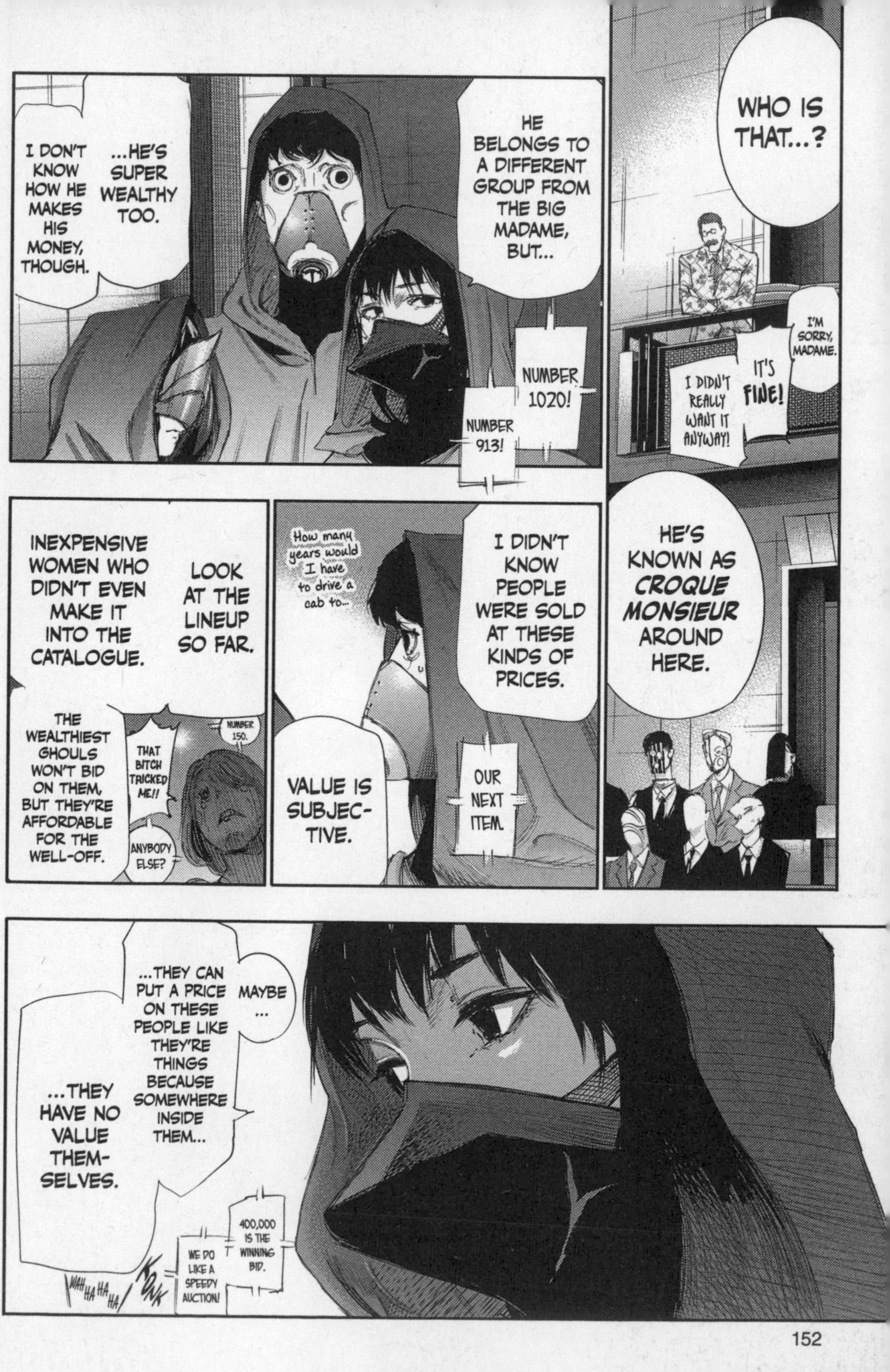
WHO IS THAT...?
I'M SORRY, MADAME.
IT'S FINE!
I DIDN'T REALLY WANT IT ANYWAY!
HE BELONGS TO A DIFFERENT GROUP FROM THE BIG MADAME, BUT...
...HE'S SUPER WEALTHY TOO.
I DON'T KNOW HOW HE MAKES HIS MONEY, THOUGH.
NUMBER 1020!
NUMBER 913!
HE'S KNOWN AS *CROQUE MONSIEUR* AROUND HERE.
I DIDN'T KNOW PEOPLE WERE SOLD AT THESE KINDS OF PRICES.
How many years would I have to drive a cab to...
VALUE IS SUBJEC-TIVE.
OUR NEXT ITEM.
LOOK AT THE LINEUP SO FAR.
INEXPENSIVE WOMEN WHO DIDN'T EVEN MAKE IT INTO THE CATALOGUE.
NUMBER 150.
THAT BITCH TRICKED ME!!
THE WEALTHIEST GHOULS WON'T BID ON THEM, BUT THEY'RE AFFORDABLE FOR THE WELL-OFF.
ANYBODY ELSE?
MAYBE...
...THEY CAN PUT A PRICE ON THESE PEOPLE LIKE THEY'RE THINGS BECAUSE SOMEWHERE INSIDE THEM...
...THEY HAVE NO VALUE THEM-SELVES.
400,000 IS THE WINNING BID.
WE DO LIKE A SPEEDY AUCTION!
KONK
WAH HA HA HA

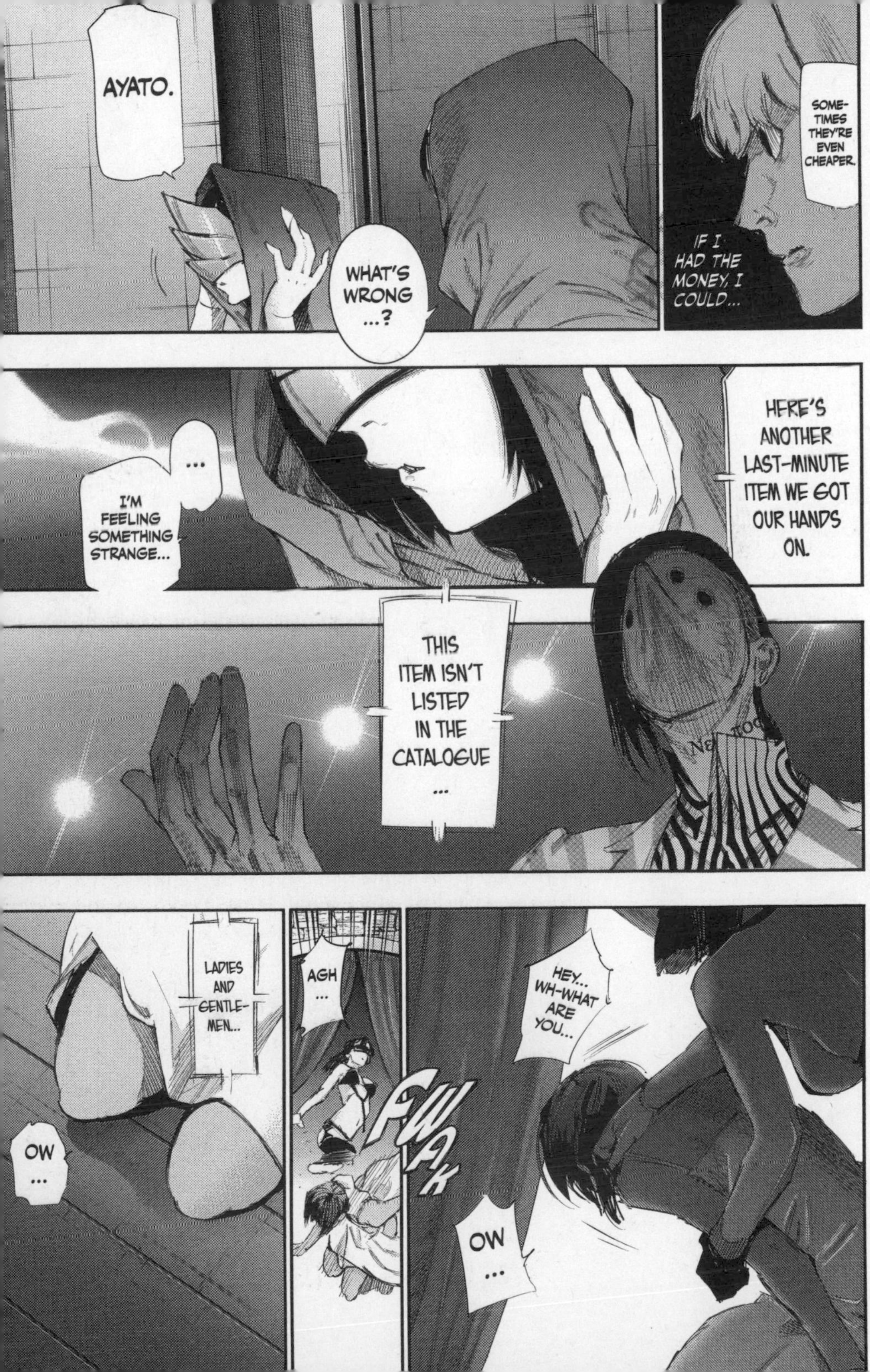
SOME-TIMES THEY'RE EVEN CHEAPER.
IF I HAD THE MONEY, I COULD...
AYATO.
WHAT'S WRONG ...?
HERE'S ANOTHER LAST-MINUTE ITEM WE GOT OUR HANDS ON.
...
I'M FEELING SOMETHING STRANGE...
THIS ITEM ISN'T LISTED IN THE CATALOGUE ...
HEY... WH-WHAT ARE YOU...
OW ...
FWAK
AGH ...
LADIES AND GENTLE-MEN...
OW ...

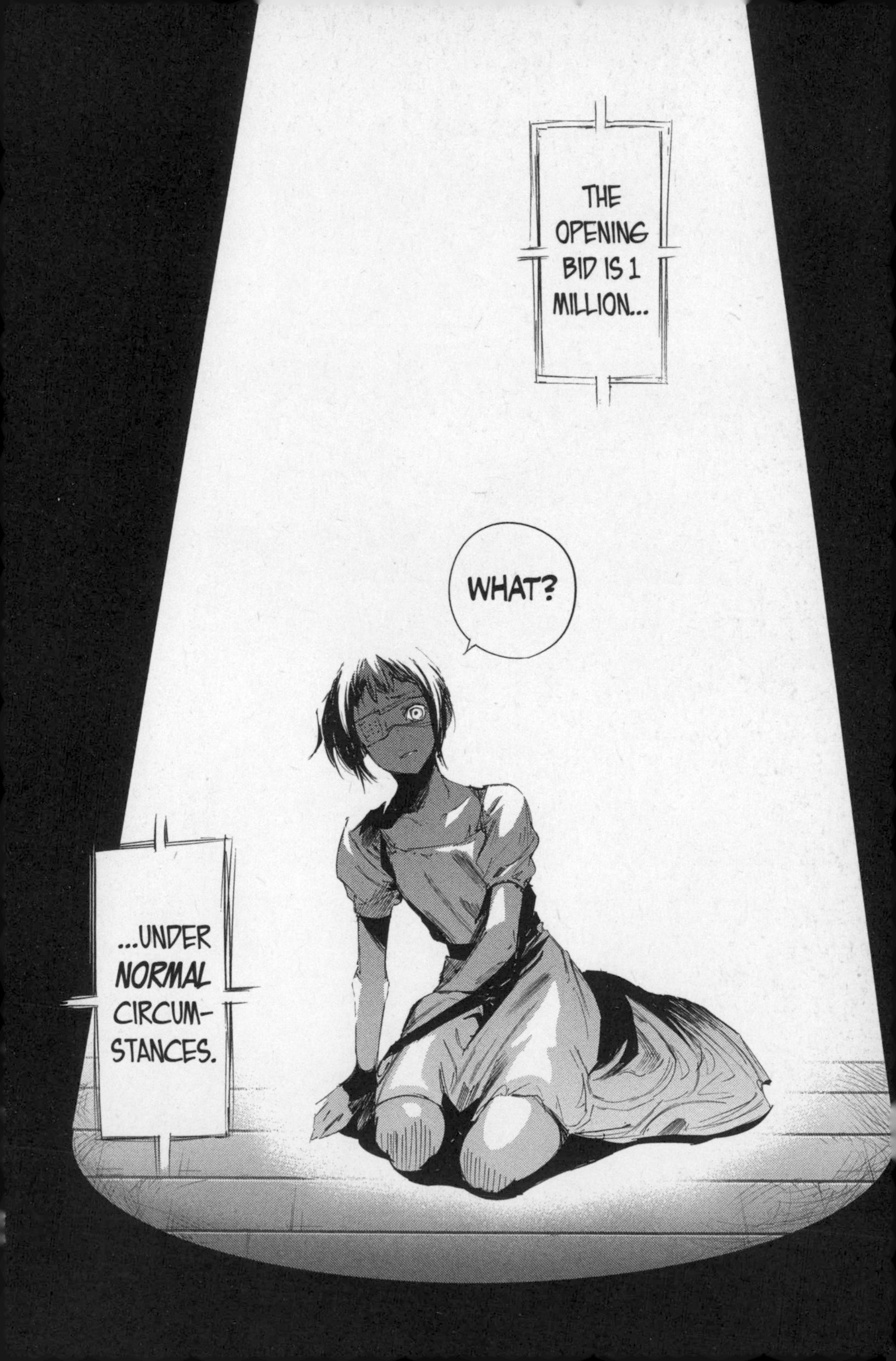
THE OPENING BID IS 1 MILLION...
WHAT?
...UNDER NORMAL CIRCUM-STANCES.

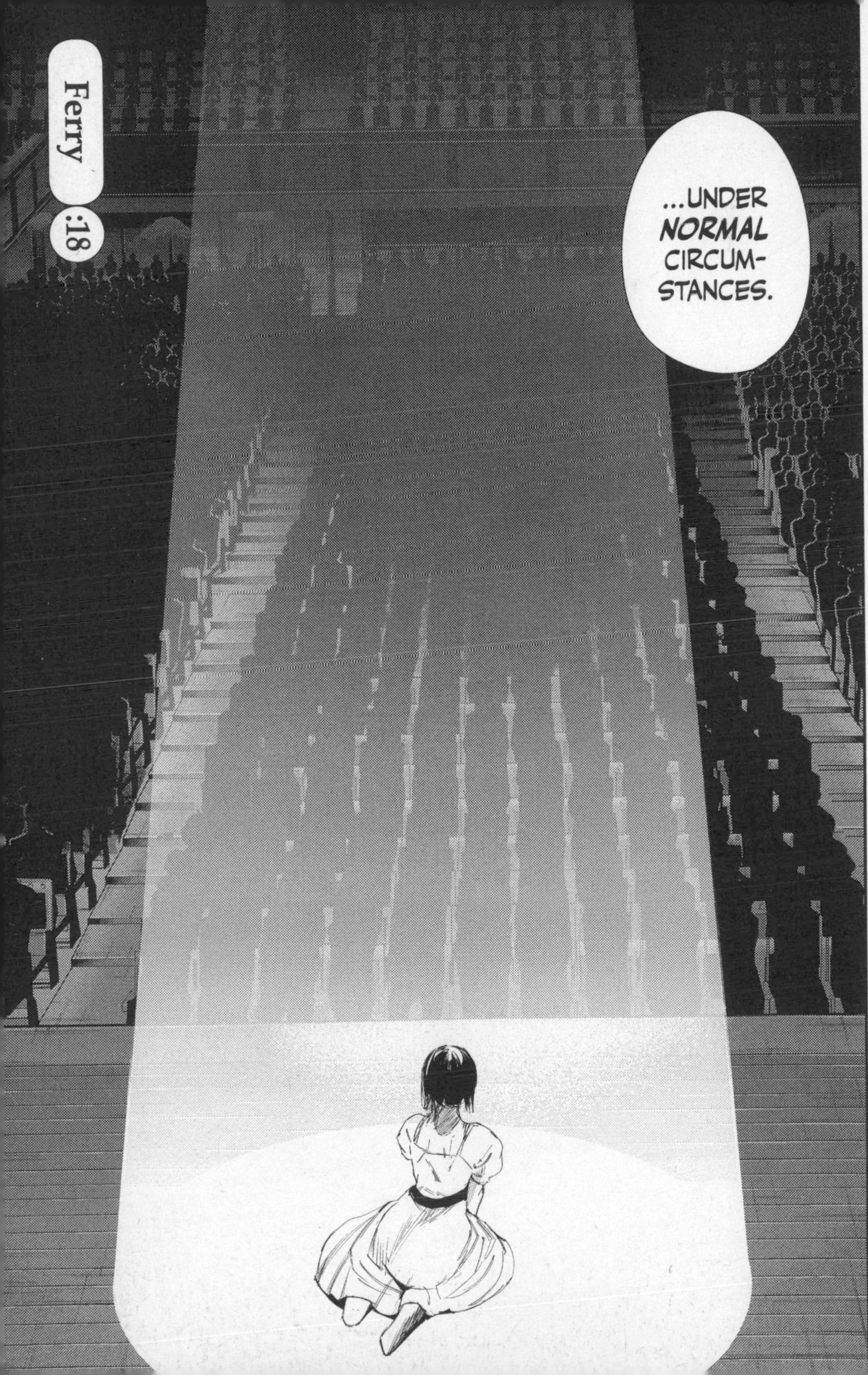

Ferry :18
...UNDER NORMAL CIRCUM-STANCES.

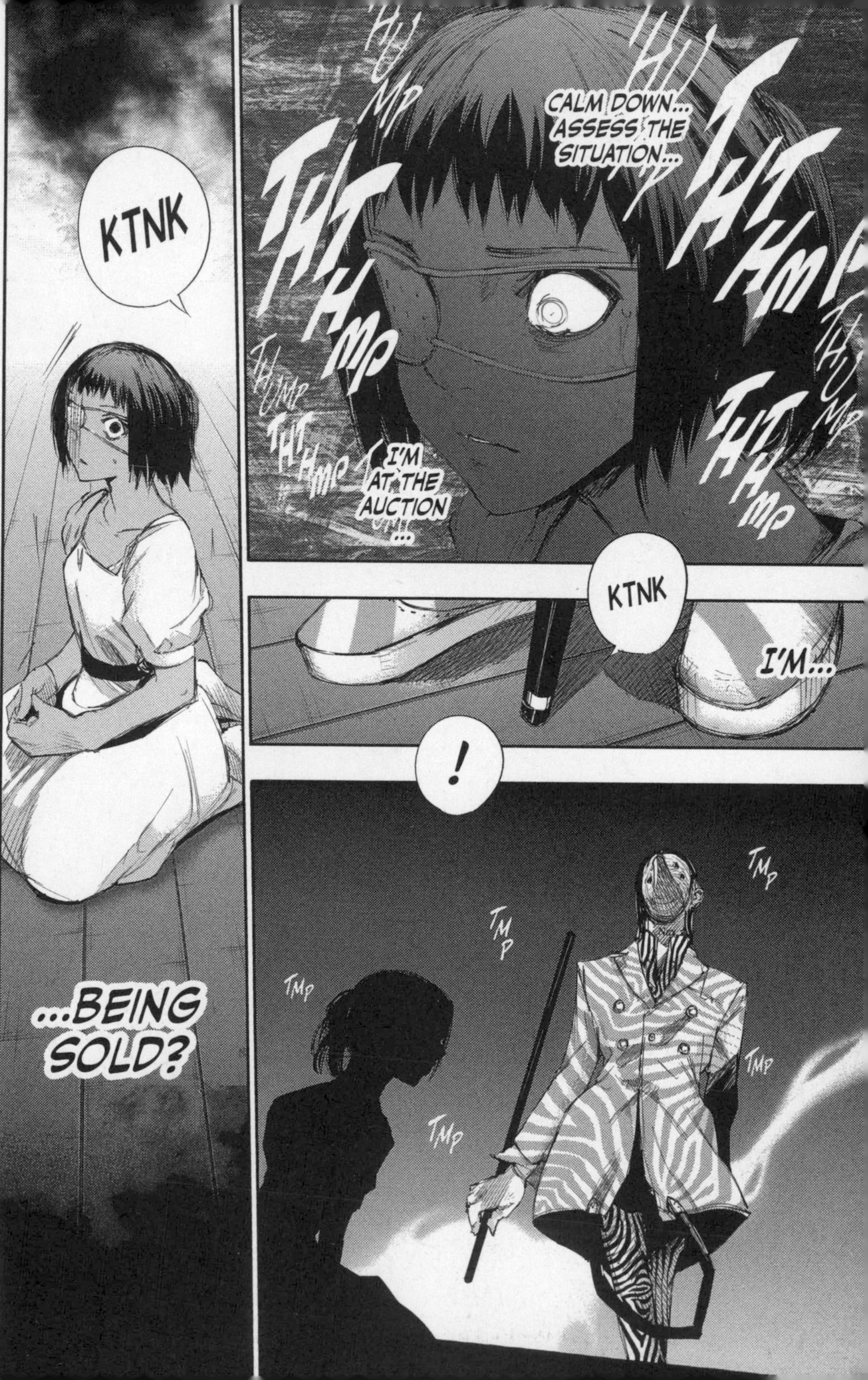
THTHMP
THUMP
CALM DOWN... ASSESS THE SITUATION...
THTHMP
THUMP
THTHMP
THTHMP
I'M AT THE AUCTION...
KTNK
I'M...
!
TMP
TMP
TMP
TMP
KTNK
...BEING SOLD?

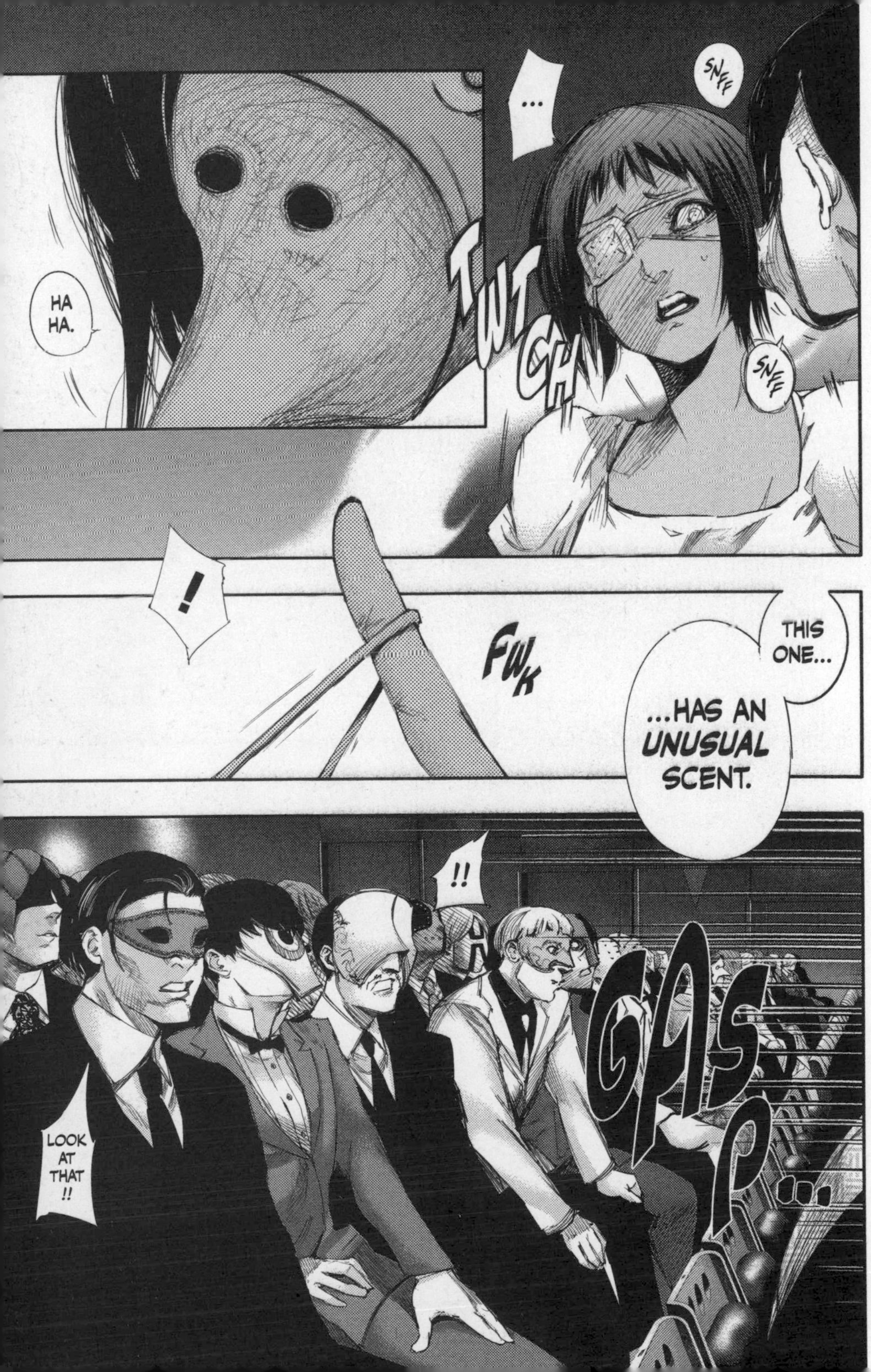
SNFF
...
TWITCH
SNFF
HA HA.
THIS ONE...
...HAS AN **UNUSUAL** SCENT.
FWK
!
!!
GASP...
LOOK AT THAT!!

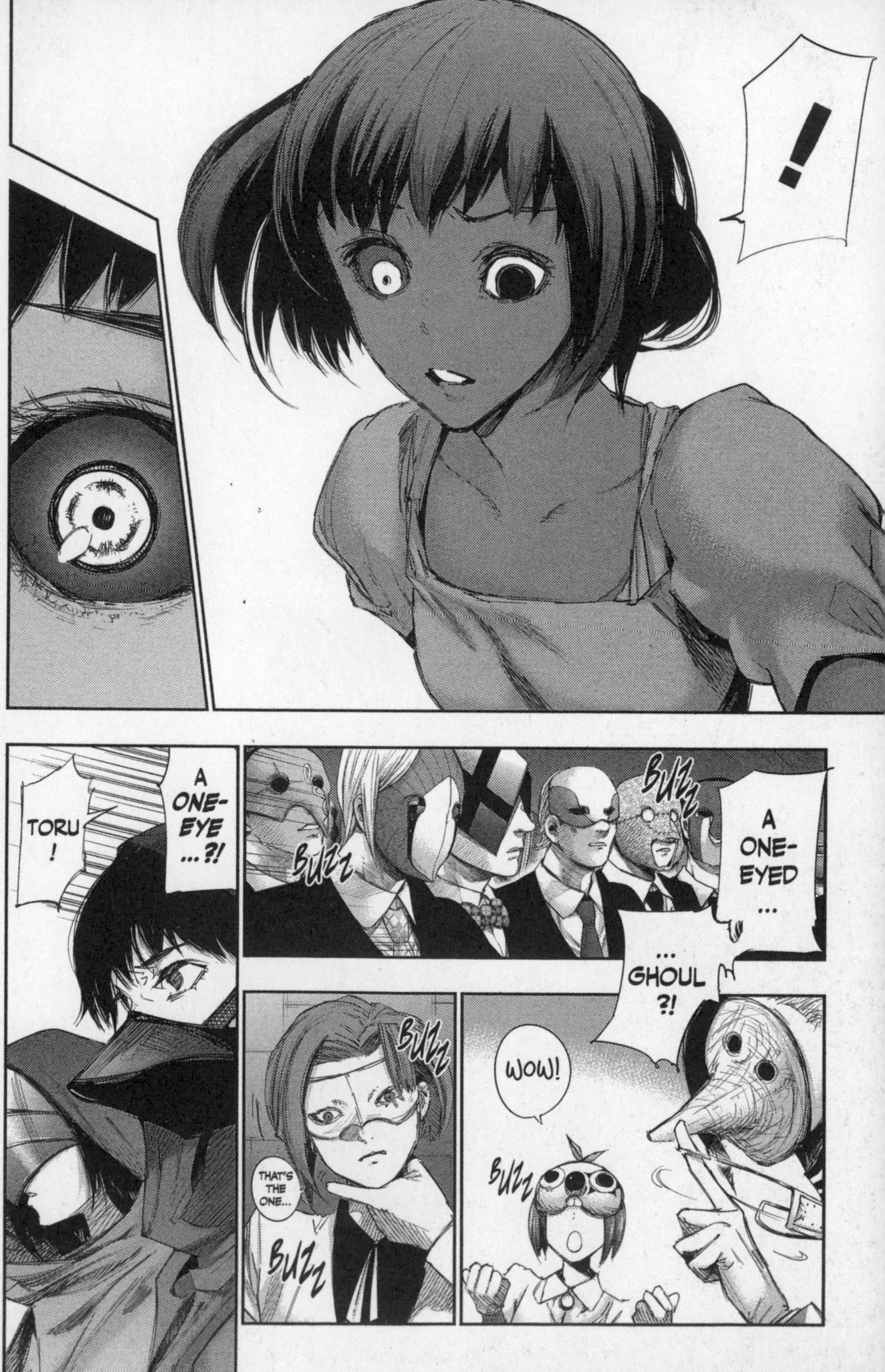
!
BUZZ
BUZZ
A ONE-EYED ...
... GHOUL ?!
WOW!
BUZZ
BUZZ
THAT'S THE ONE...
BUZZ
A ONE-EYE ...?!
TORU!

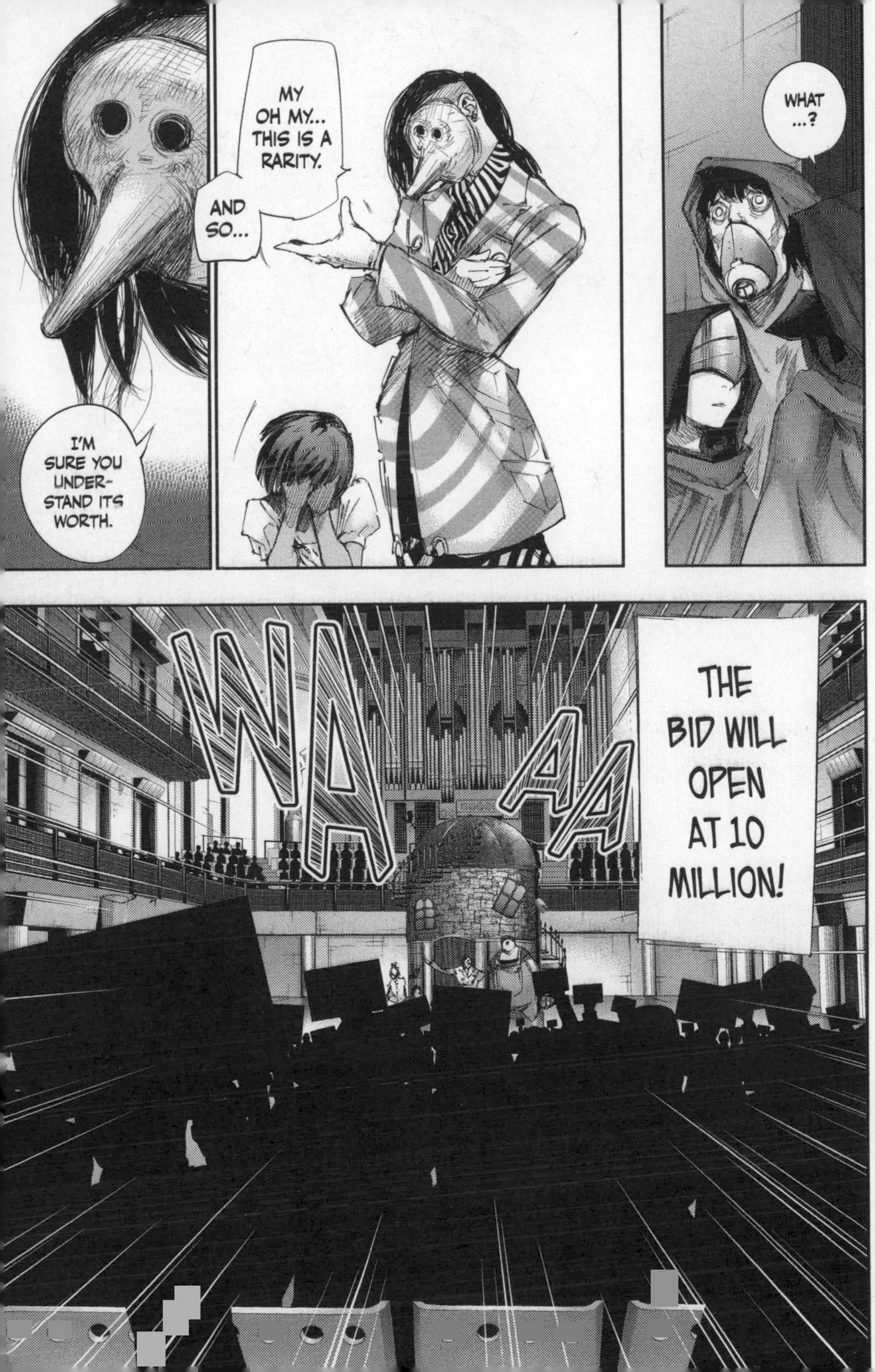
WHAT ...?
MY OH MY... THIS IS A RARITY.
AND SO...
I'M SURE YOU UNDERSTAND ITS WORTH.
THE BID WILL OPEN AT 10 MILLION!
WAAA

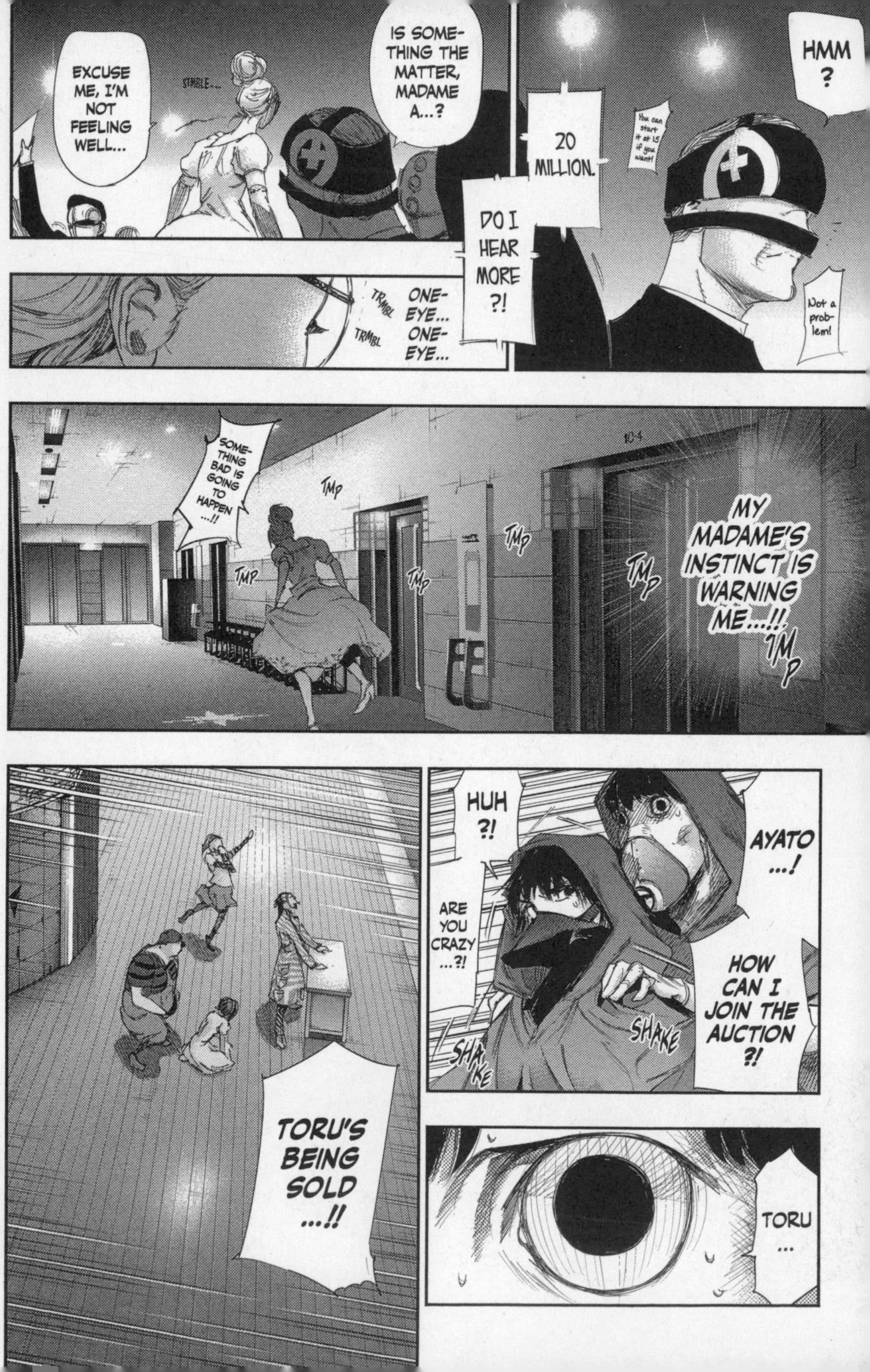
HMM ?
You can start it at 15 if you want!
20 MILLION.
DO I HEAR MORE ?!
Not a problem!
IS SOMETHING THE MATTER, MADAME A...?
STMBLE...
EXCUSE ME, I'M NOT FEELING WELL...
ONE-EYE... ONE-EYE...
TRMBL
TRMBL
MY MADAME'S INSTINCT IS WARNING ME...!!
TMP
TMP
TMP
TMP
TMP
TMP
SOMETHING BAD IS GOING TO HAPPEN ...!!
AYATO ...!
HOW CAN I JOIN THE AUCTION ?!
SHAKE
HUH ?!
ARE YOU CRAZY ...?!
SHAKE
TORU ...
TORU'S BEING SOLD ...!!

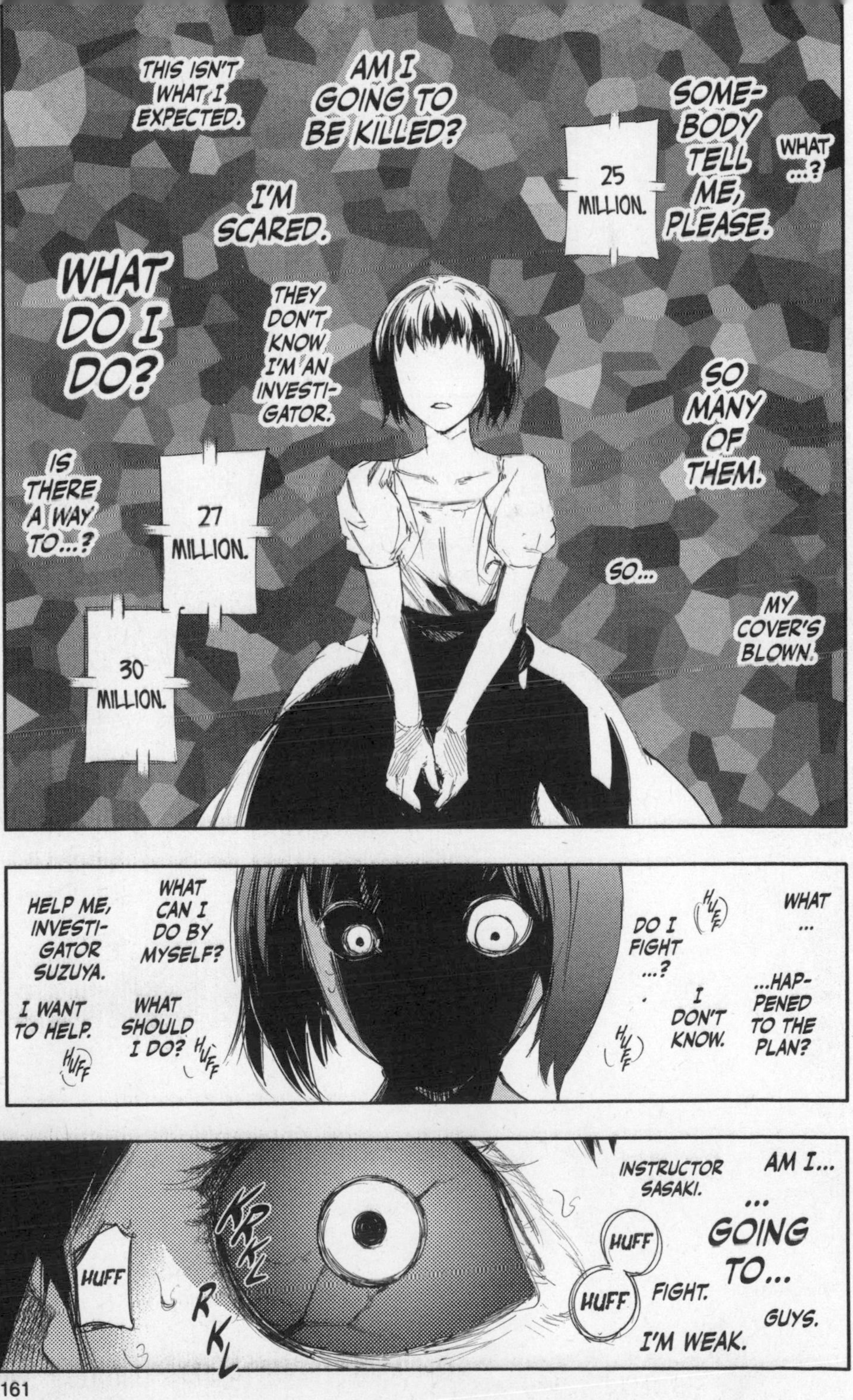
WHAT ...?
SOME-BODY TELL ME, PLEASE.
25 MILLION.
AM I GOING TO BE KILLED?
THIS ISN'T WHAT I EXPECTED.
I'M SCARED.
WHAT DO I DO?
THEY DON'T KNOW I'M AN INVESTI-GATOR.
SO MANY OF THEM.
SO...
MY COVER'S BLOWN.
27 MILLION.
IS THERE A WAY TO...?
30 MILLION.
WHAT ...
...HAP-PENED TO THE PLAN?
HUFF
DO I FIGHT ...?
I DON'T KNOW.
HUFF
WHAT CAN I DO BY MYSELF?
HELP ME, INVESTI-GATOR SUZUYA.
WHAT SHOULD I DO?
HUFF
I WANT TO HELP.
HUFF
AM I... ... GOING TO...
INSTRUCTOR SASAKI.
GUYS.
HUFF
HUFF
FIGHT.
I'M WEAK.
KRKL
RKL
HUFF

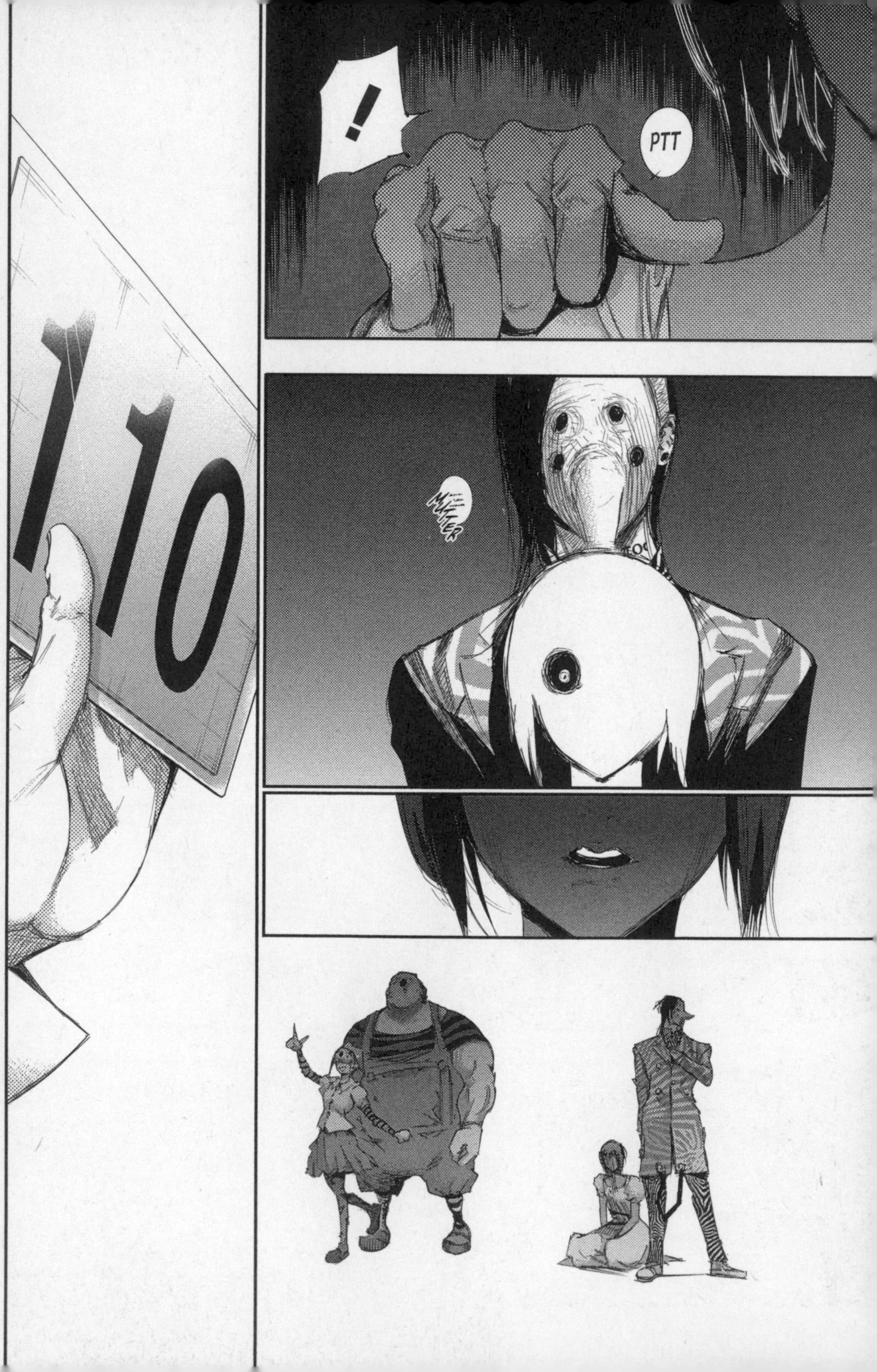
!
PTT
MUTTER
110

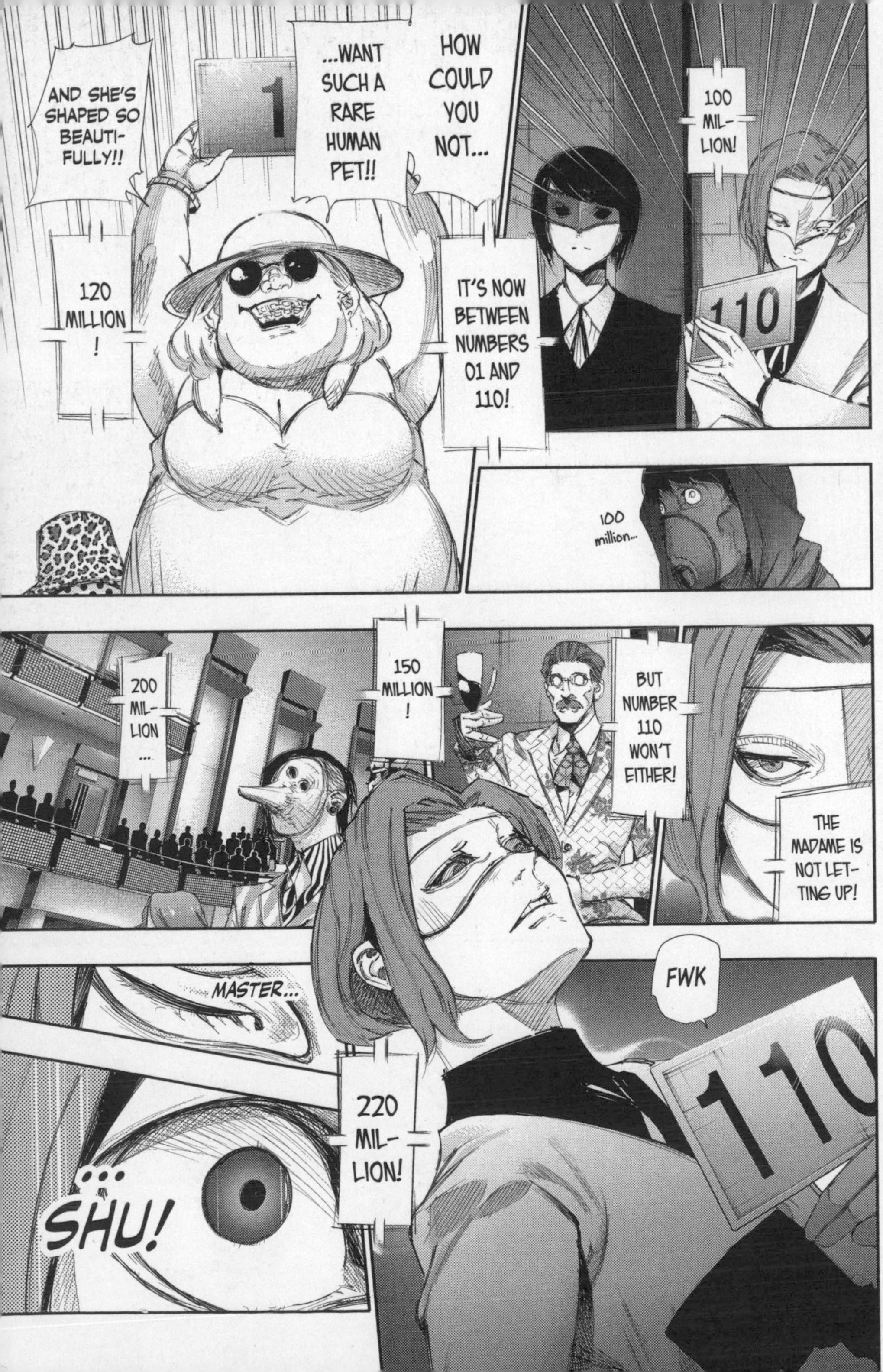
100 MIL-LION!
IT'S NOW BETWEEN NUMBERS 01 AND 110!
110
100 million...
HOW COULD YOU NOT...
...WANT SUCH A RARE HUMAN PET!!
AND SHE'S SHAPED SO BEAUTI-FULLY!!
1
120 MILLION!
THE MADAME IS NOT LET-TING UP!
BUT NUMBER 110 WON'T EITHER!
150 MILLION!
200 MIL-LION...
FWK
110
220 MIL-LION!
MASTER...
...SHU!

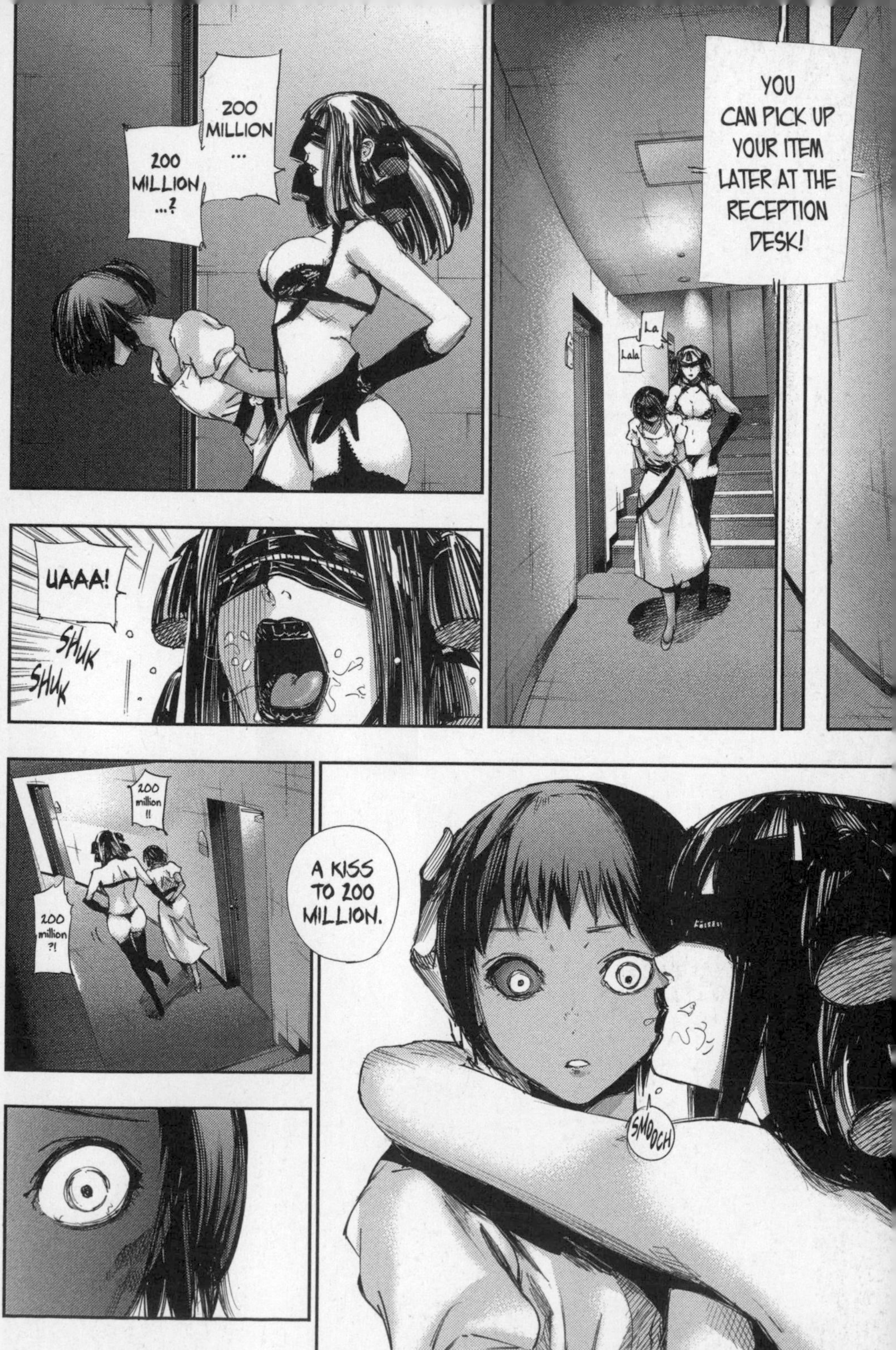
YOU CAN PICK UP YOUR ITEM LATER AT THE RECEPTION DESK!
La
Lala
200 MILLION ...
200 MILLION ...?
UAAA!
SHUK SHUK
A KISS TO 200 MILLION.
SMOOCH
200 million !!
200 million ?!

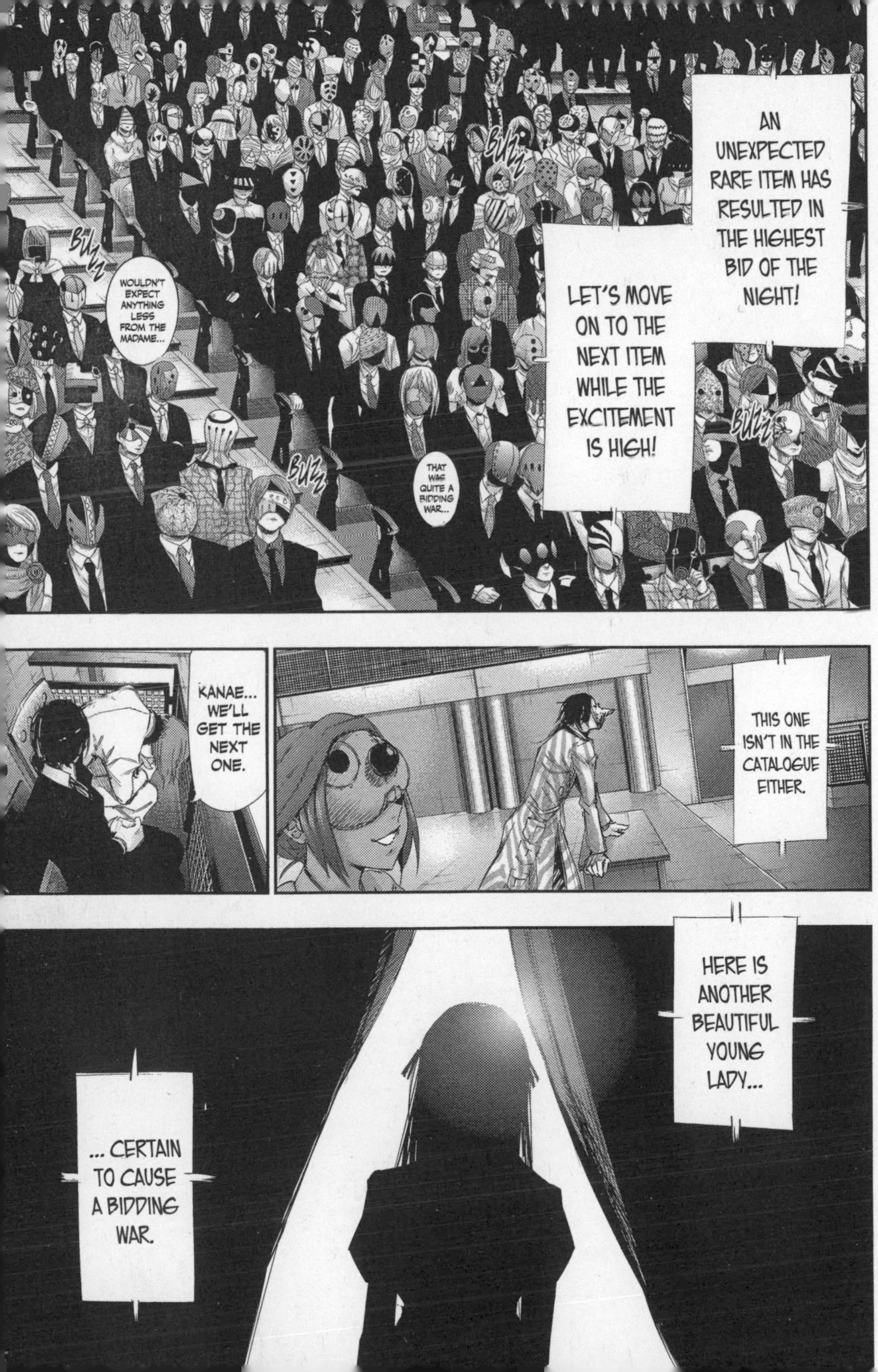
AN UNEXPECTED RARE ITEM HAS RESULTED IN THE HIGHEST BID OF THE NIGHT!
LET'S MOVE ON TO THE NEXT ITEM WHILE THE EXCITEMENT IS HIGH!
BUZZ
BUZZ
BUZZ
THAT WAS QUITE A BIDDING WAR...
BUZZ
WOULDN'T EXPECT ANYTHING LESS FROM THE MADAME...
BUZZ
THIS ONE ISN'T IN THE CATALOGUE EITHER.
KANAE... WE'LL GET THE NEXT ONE.
HERE IS ANOTHER BEAUTIFUL YOUNG LADY...
... CERTAIN TO CAUSE A BIDDING WAR.

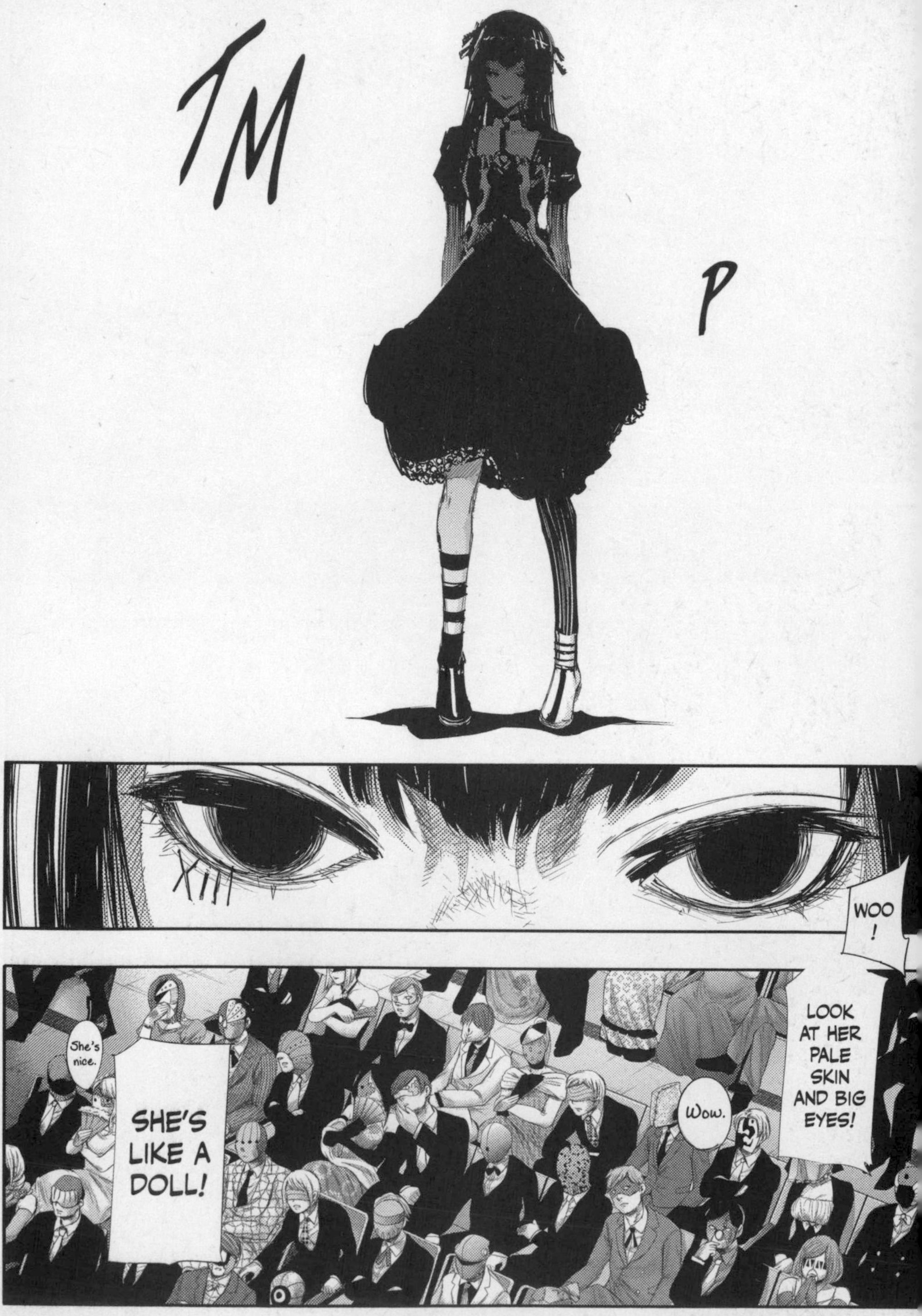
TM
P
WOO!
LOOK AT HER PALE SKIN AND BIG EYES!
Wow.
SHE'S LIKE A DOLL!
She's nice.

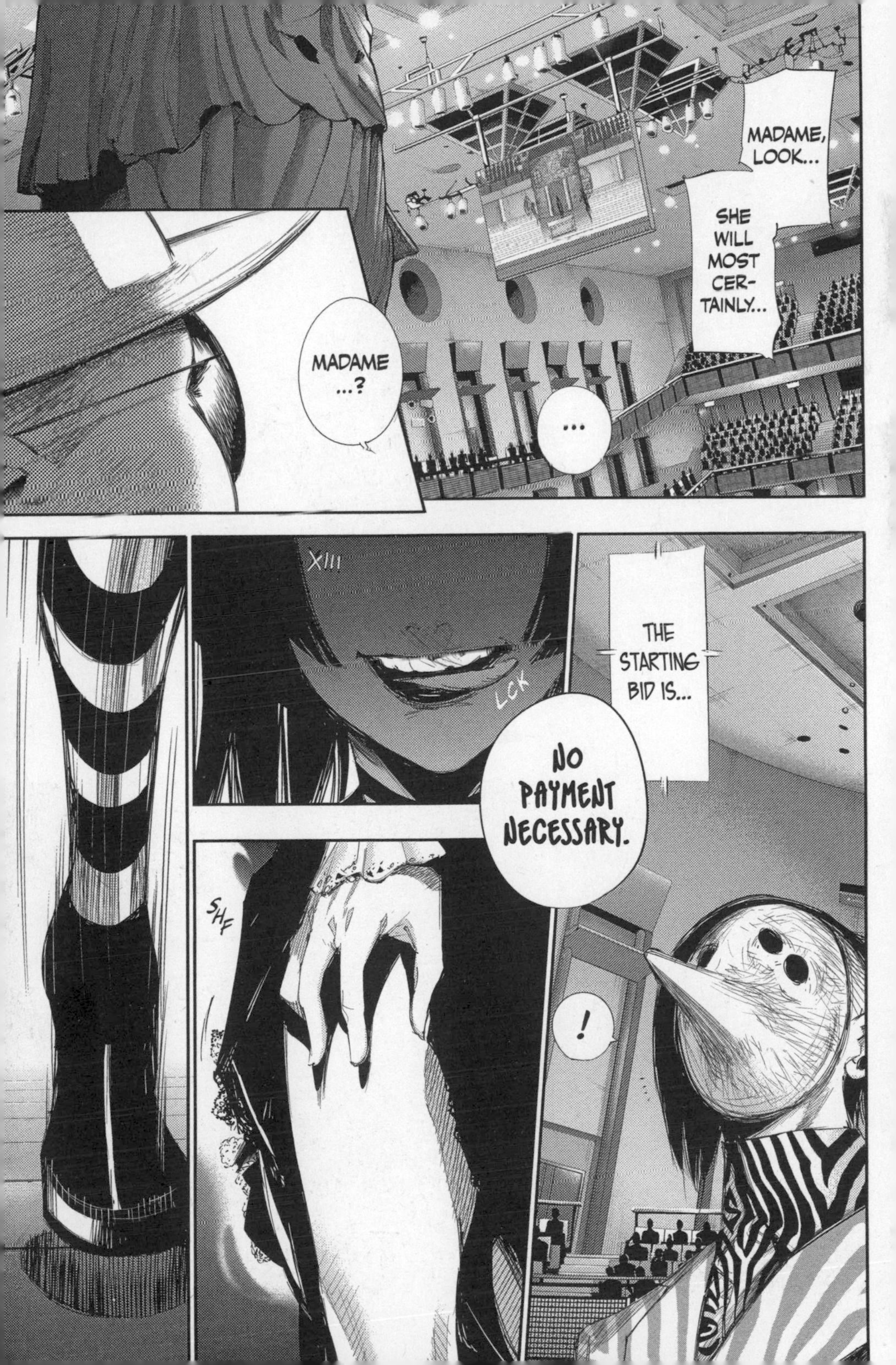
MADAME, LOOK...
SHE WILL MOST CER-TAINLY...
...
MADAME ...?
THE STARTING BID IS...
LCK
NO PAYMENT NECESSARY.
!
SHF

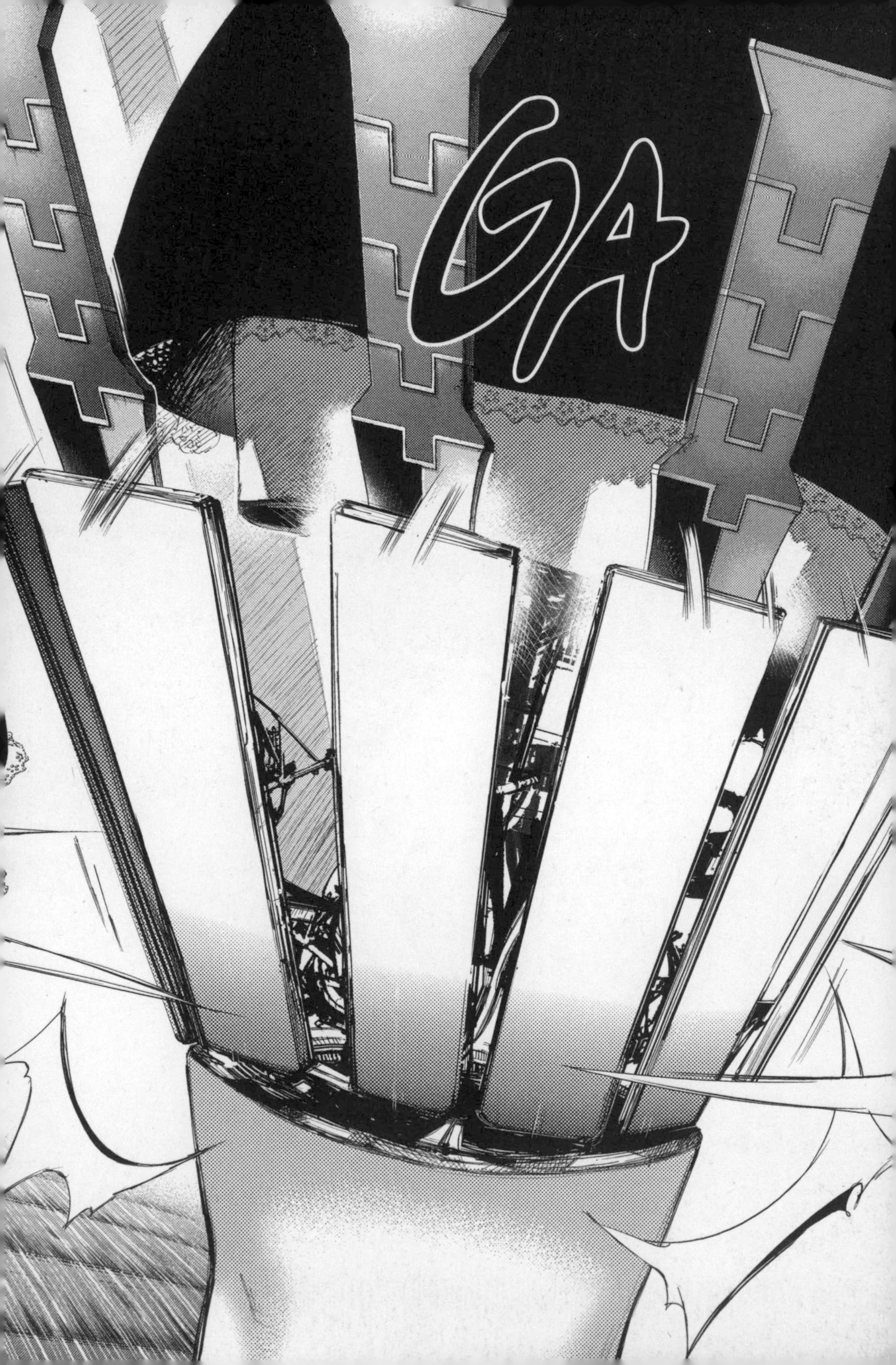
GA

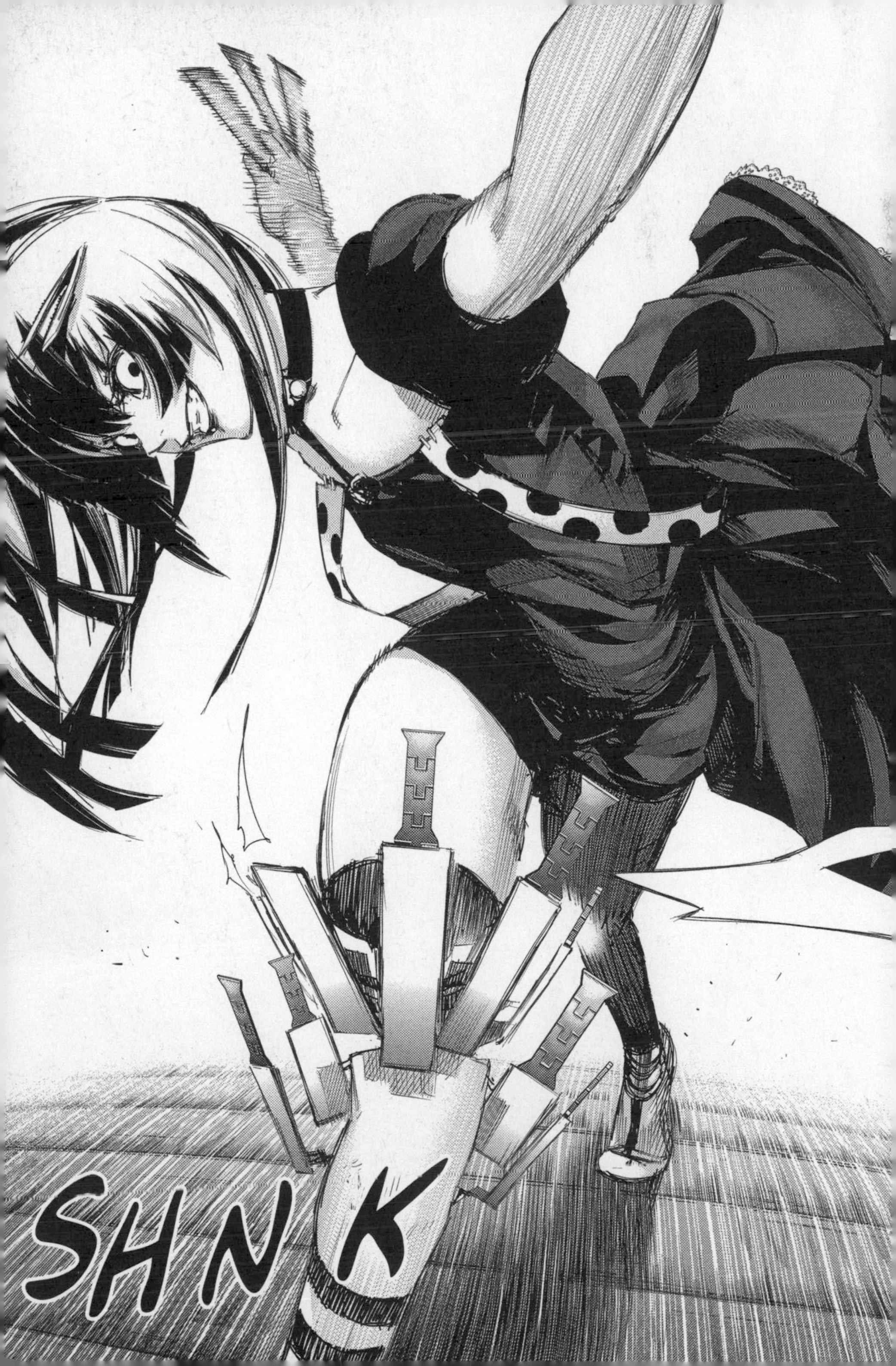
SHNK

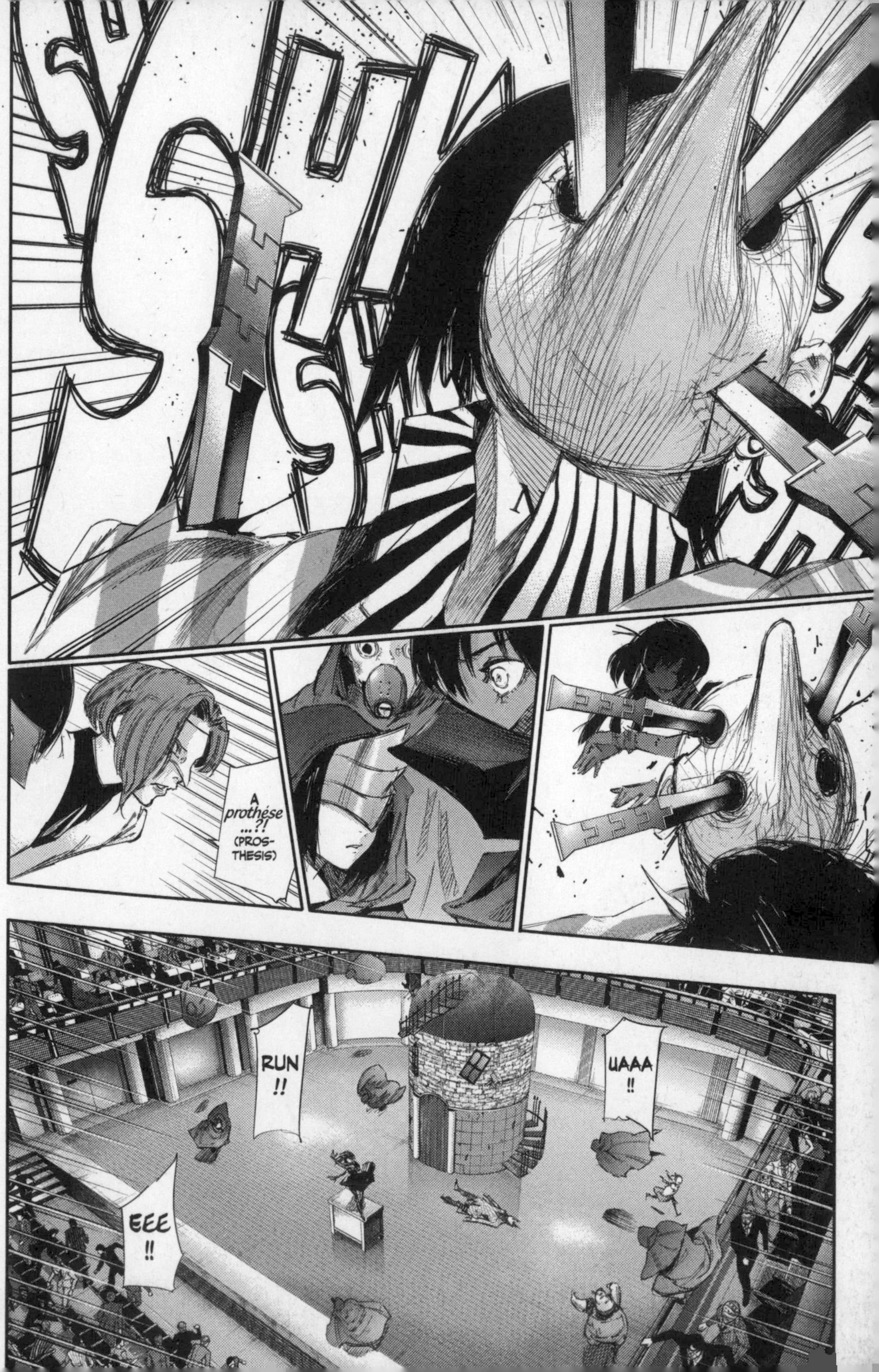
A prothése ...?! (PROSTHESIS)
UAAA !!
RUN !!
EEE !!

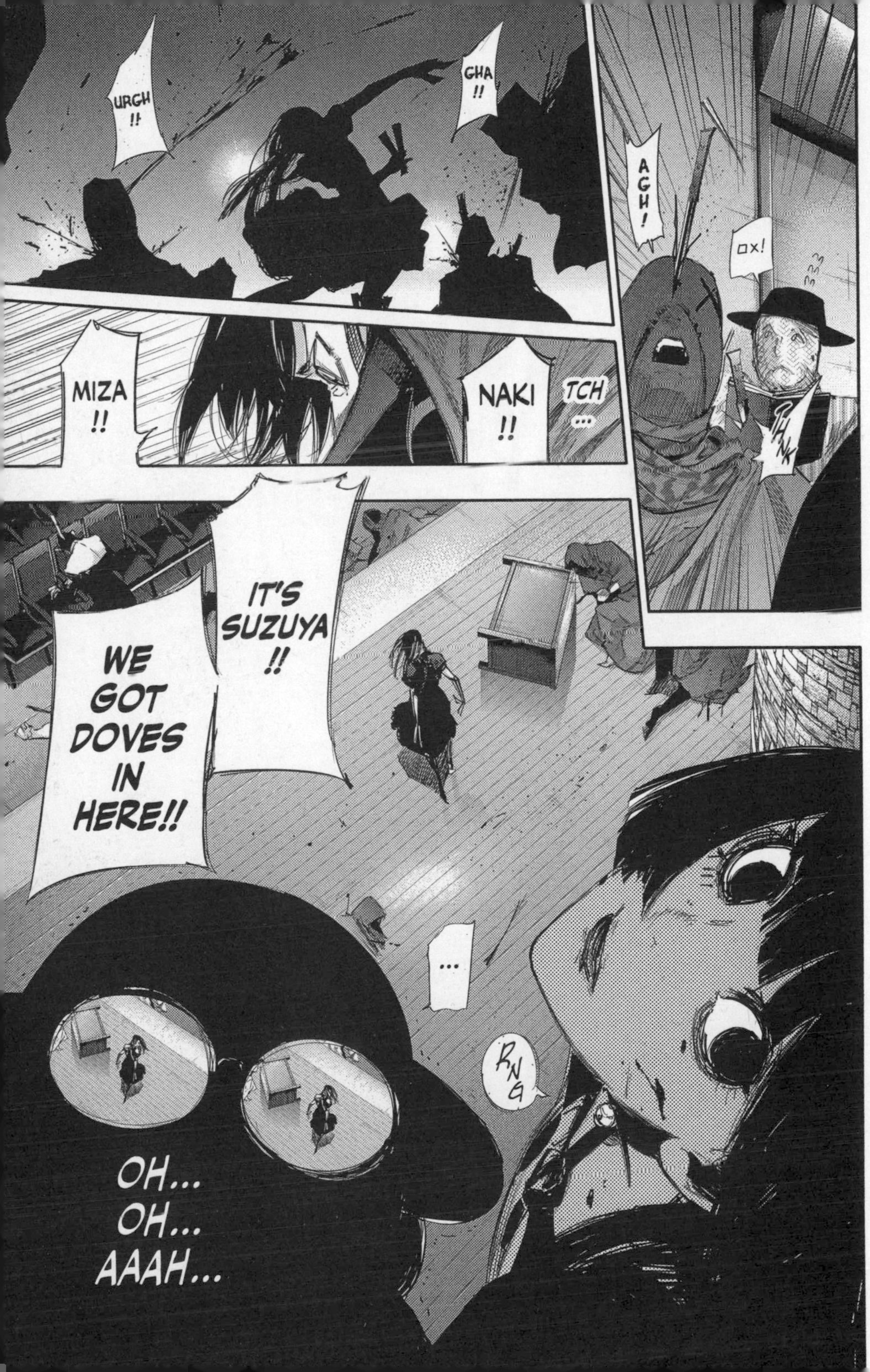
A G H !
OX!
THNK
URGH !!
GHA !!
NAKI !!
TCH ...
MIZA !!
IT'S SUZUYA !!
WE GOT DOVES IN HERE!!
...
RNG
OH... OH... AAAH...

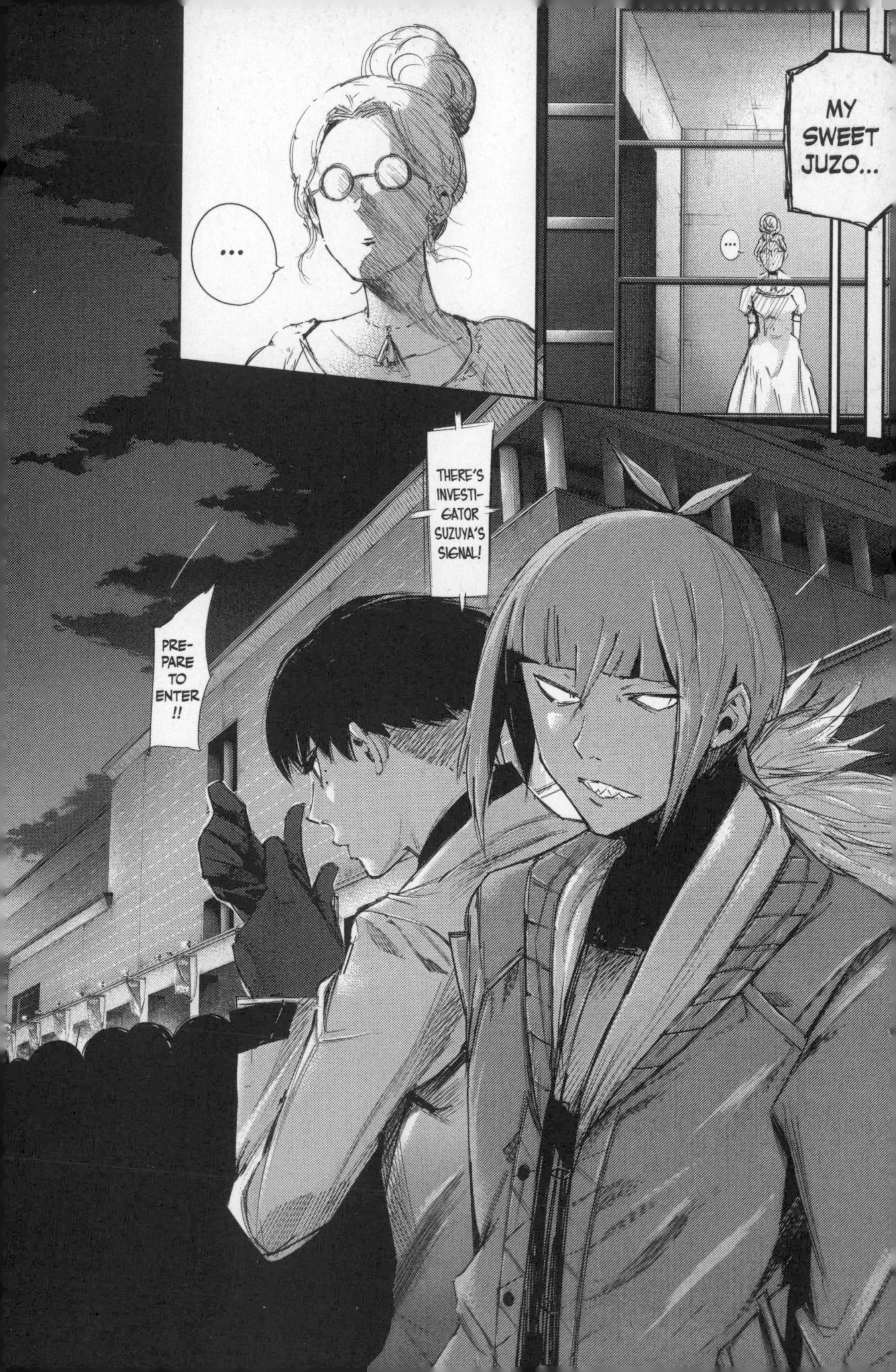
MY SWEET JUZO...
...
...
THERE'S INVESTIGATOR SUZUYA'S SIGNAL!
PREPARE TO ENTER!!

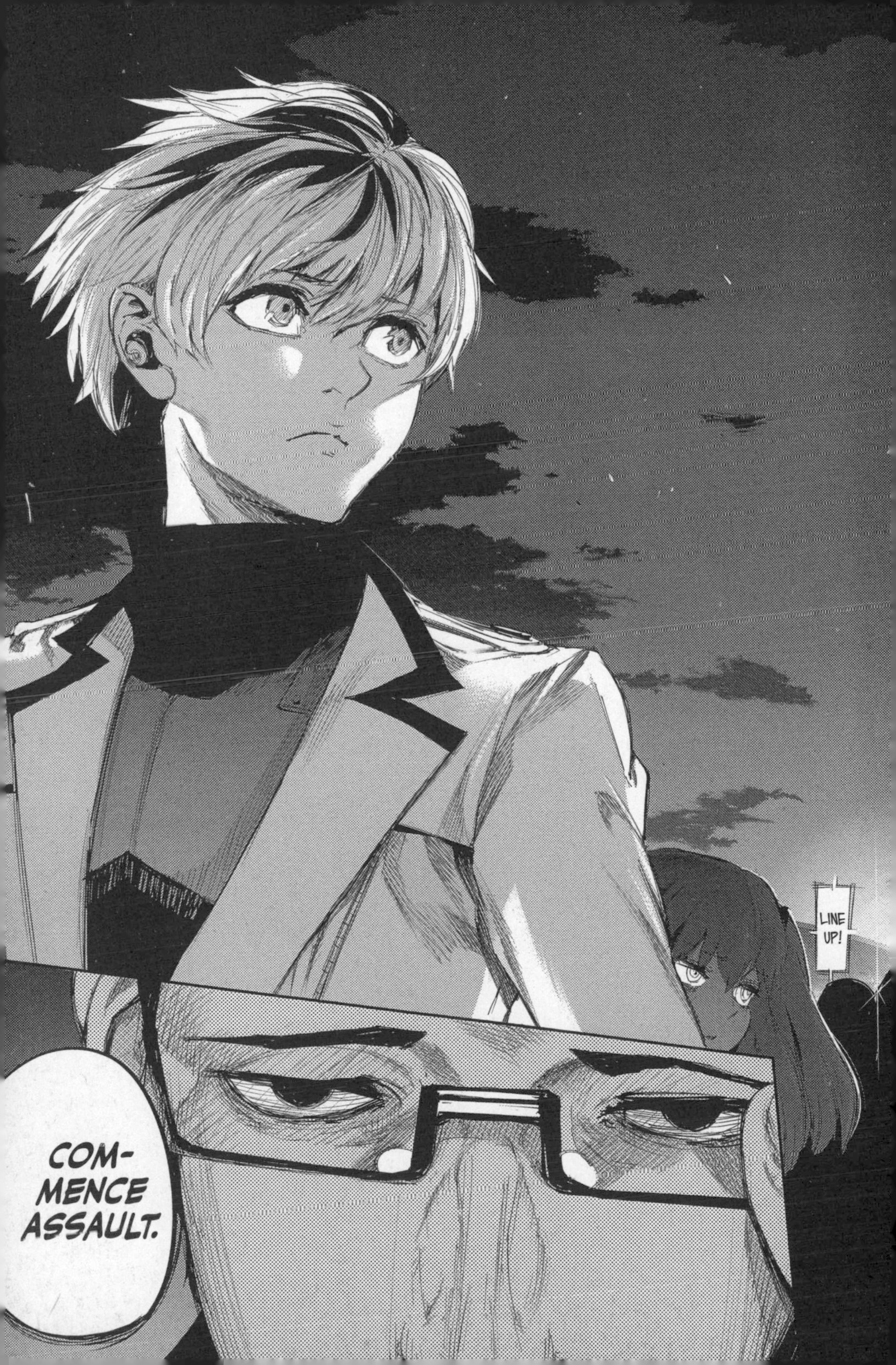
LINE UP!
COM-MENCE ASSAULT.

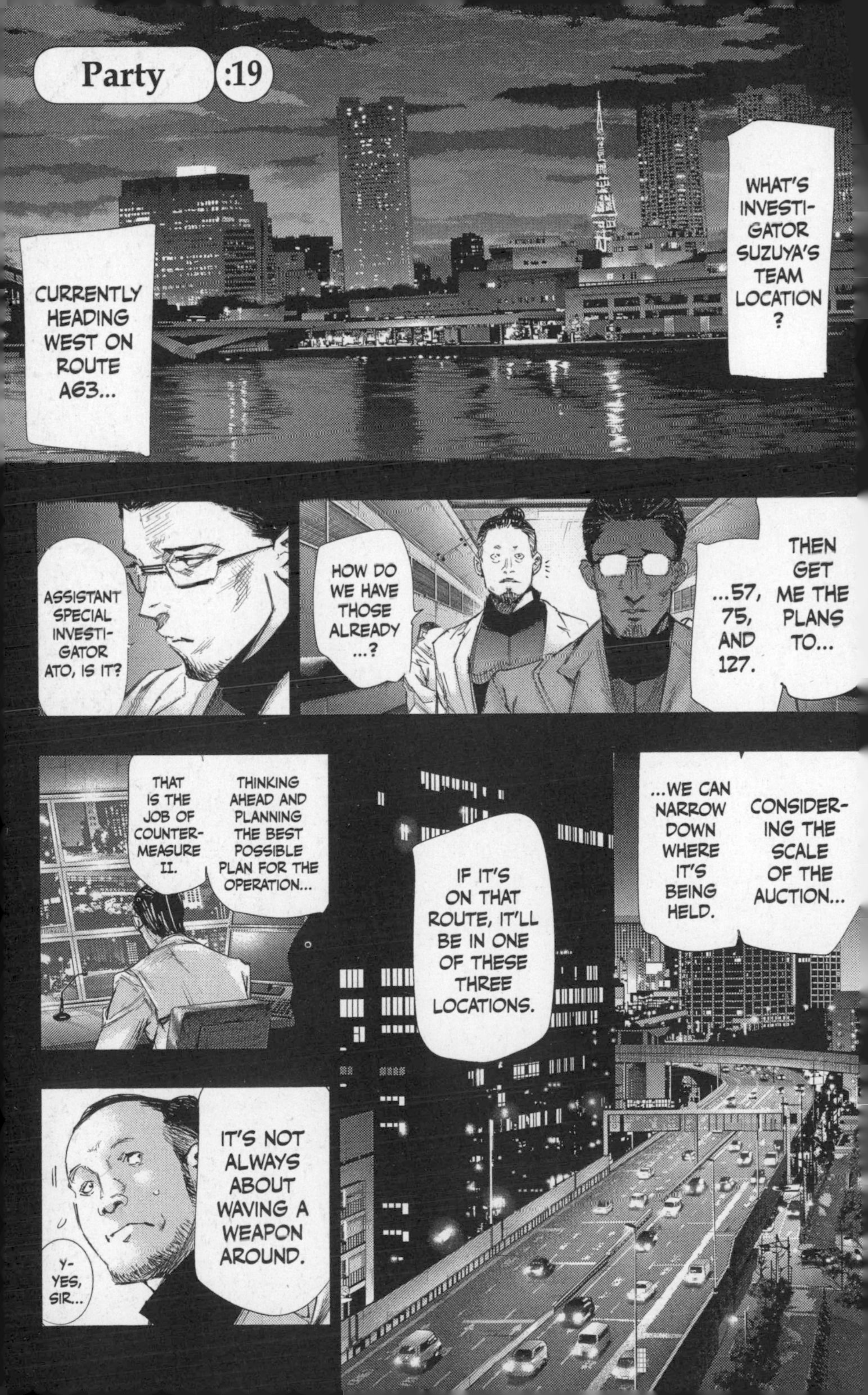
Party :19
WHAT'S INVESTIGATOR SUZUYA'S TEAM LOCATION?
CURRENTLY HEADING WEST ON ROUTE A63...
THEN GET ME THE PLANS TO...
...57, 75, AND 127.
HOW DO WE HAVE THOSE ALREADY...?
ASSISTANT SPECIAL INVESTIGATOR ATO, IS IT?
CONSIDERING THE SCALE OF THE AUCTION...
...WE CAN NARROW DOWN WHERE IT'S BEING HELD.
IF IT'S ON THAT ROUTE, IT'LL BE IN ONE OF THESE THREE LOCATIONS.
THINKING AHEAD AND PLANNING THE BEST POSSIBLE PLAN FOR THE OPERATION...
THAT IS THE JOB OF COUNTERMEASURE II.
IT'S NOT ALWAYS ABOUT WAVING A WEAPON AROUND.
Y-YES, SIR...

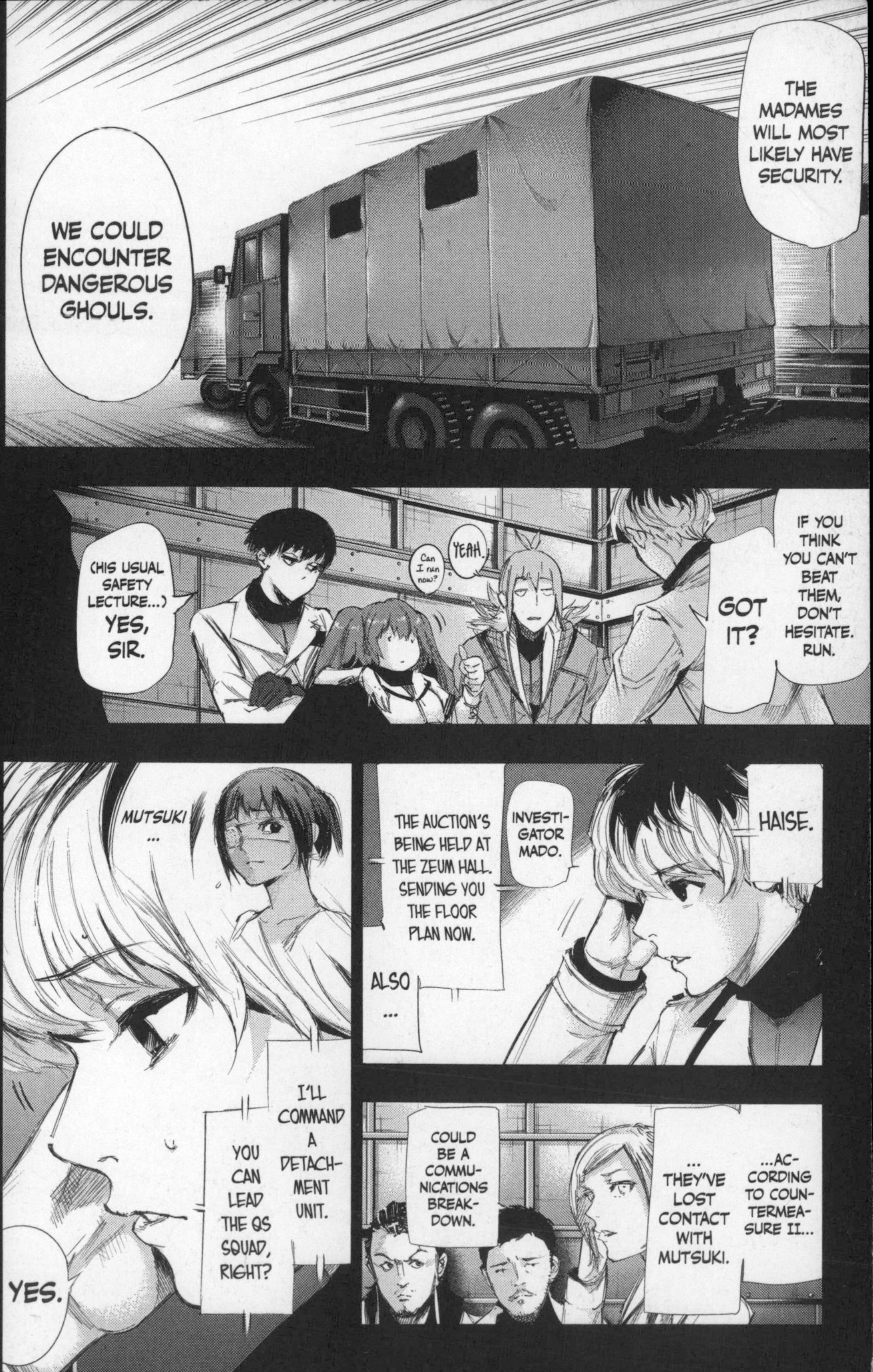
THE MADAMES WILL MOST LIKELY HAVE SECURITY.
WE COULD ENCOUNTER DANGEROUS GHOULS.
IF YOU THINK YOU CAN'T BEAT THEM, DON'T HESITATE. RUN.
GOT IT?
YEAH.
Can I run now?
(HIS USUAL SAFETY LECTURE...) YES, SIR.
HAISE.
INVESTI-GATOR MADO.
THE AUCTION'S BEING HELD AT THE ZEUM HALL. SENDING YOU THE FLOOR PLAN NOW.
ALSO ...
...AC-CORDING TO COUN-TERMEA-SURE II...
... THEY'VE LOST CONTACT WITH MUTSUKI.
COULD BE A COMMU-NICATIONS BREAK-DOWN.
MUTSUKI ...
I'LL COMMAND A DETACH-MENT UNIT.
YOU CAN LEAD THE QS SQUAD, RIGHT?
YES.

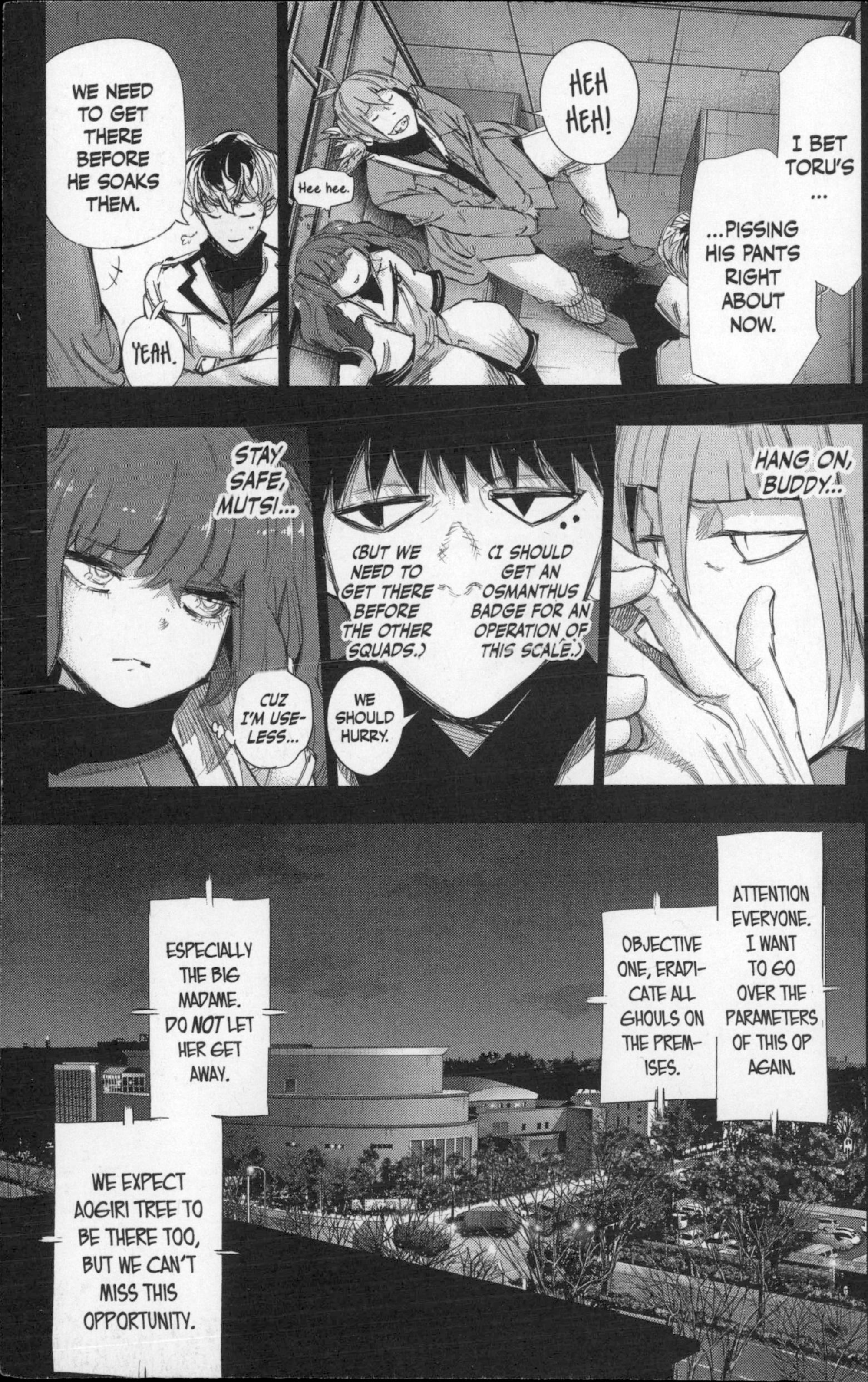
I BET TORU'S ...
...PISSING HIS PANTS RIGHT ABOUT NOW.
HEH HEH!
Hee hee.
WE NEED TO GET THERE BEFORE HE SOAKS THEM.
YEAH.
HANG ON, BUDDY...
(I SHOULD GET AN OSMANTHUS BADGE FOR AN OPERATION OF THIS SCALE.)
(BUT WE NEED TO GET THERE BEFORE THE OTHER SQUADS.)
WE SHOULD HURRY.
STAY SAFE, MUTSI...
CUZ I'M USE-LESS...
ATTENTION EVERYONE. I WANT TO GO OVER THE PARAMETERS OF THIS OP AGAIN.
OBJECTIVE ONE, ERADI-CATE ALL GHOULS ON THE PREM-ISES.
ESPECIALLY THE BIG MADAME. DO **NOT** LET HER GET AWAY.
WE EXPECT AOGIRI TREE TO BE THERE TOO, BUT WE CAN'T MISS THIS OPPORTUNITY.

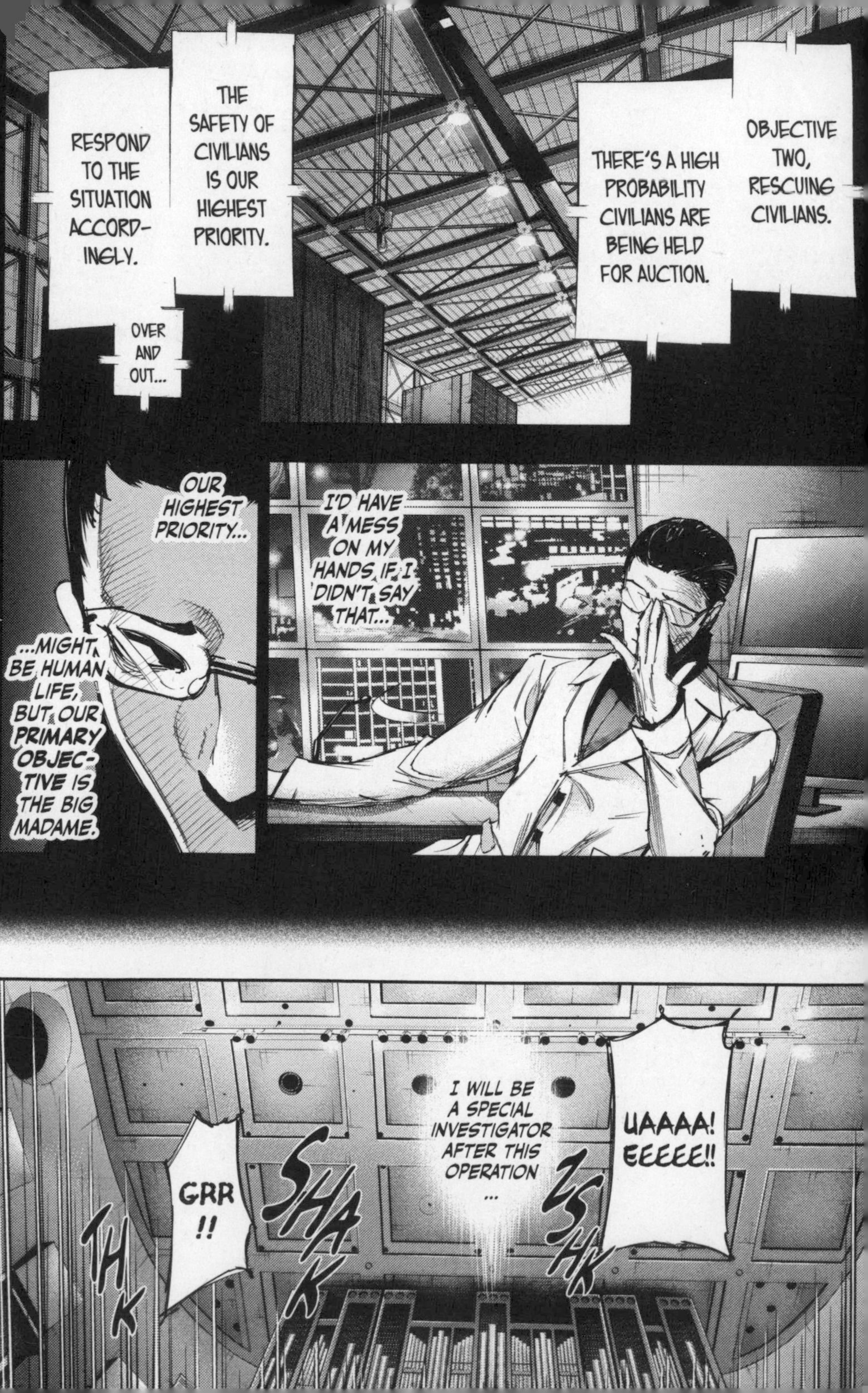
OBJECTIVE TWO, RESCUING CIVILIANS.
THERE'S A HIGH PROBABILITY CIVILIANS ARE BEING HELD FOR AUCTION.
THE SAFETY OF CIVILIANS IS OUR HIGHEST PRIORITY.
RESPOND TO THE SITUATION ACCORDINGLY.
OVER AND OUT...
I'D HAVE A MESS ON MY HANDS IF I DIDN'T SAY THAT...
OUR HIGHEST PRIORITY...
...MIGHT BE HUMAN LIFE, BUT OUR PRIMARY OBJECTIVE IS THE BIG MADAME.
UAAAA! EEEEE!!
ZSHK
I WILL BE A SPECIAL INVESTIGATOR AFTER THIS OPERATION ...
SHAK
GRR !!
THK

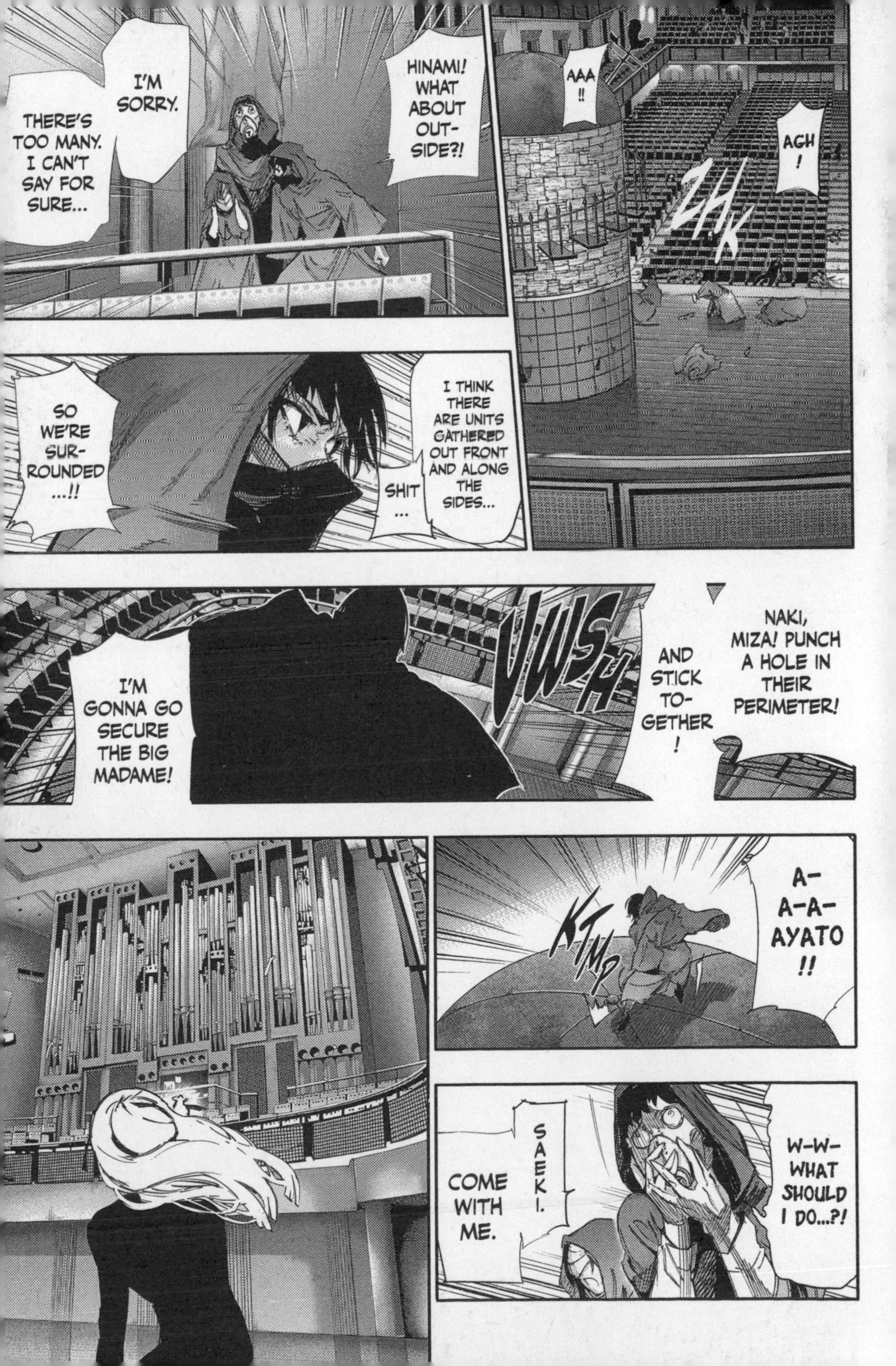
AAA!!
AGH!
ZHK
HINAMI! WHAT ABOUT OUTSIDE?!
I'M SORRY.
THERE'S TOO MANY. I CAN'T SAY FOR SURE...
I THINK THERE ARE UNITS GATHERED OUT FRONT AND ALONG THE SIDES...
SHIT...
SO WE'RE SURROUNDED...!!
NAKI, MIZA! PUNCH A HOLE IN THEIR PERIMETER!
AND STICK TOGETHER!
VWSH
I'M GONNA GO SECURE THE BIG MADAME!
A-A-A-AYATO!!
KTMP
W-W-WHAT SHOULD I DO...?!
SAEKI.
COME WITH ME.

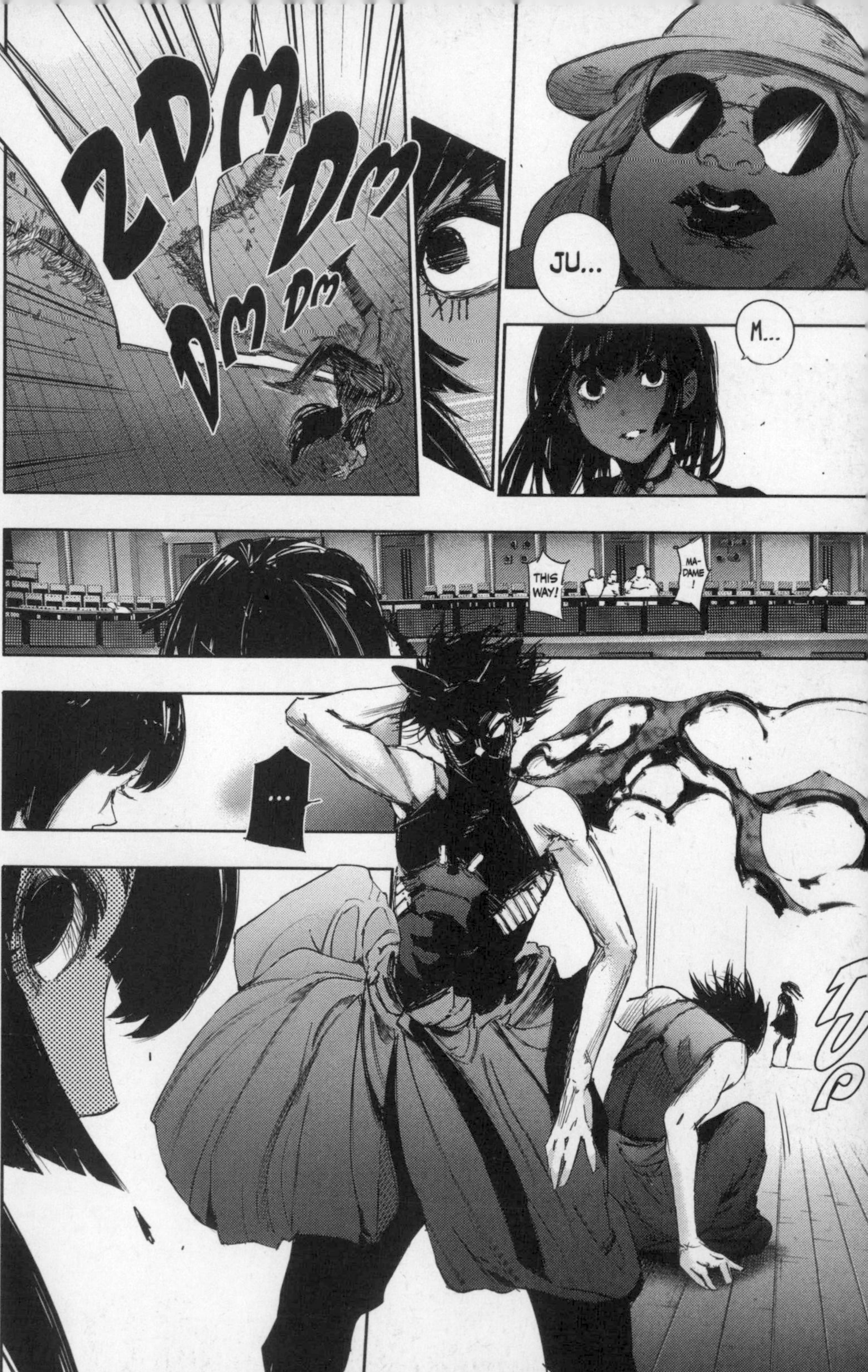
JU...
M...
ZDM DM DM DM DM
MA-DAME!
THIS WAY!
...
TUP

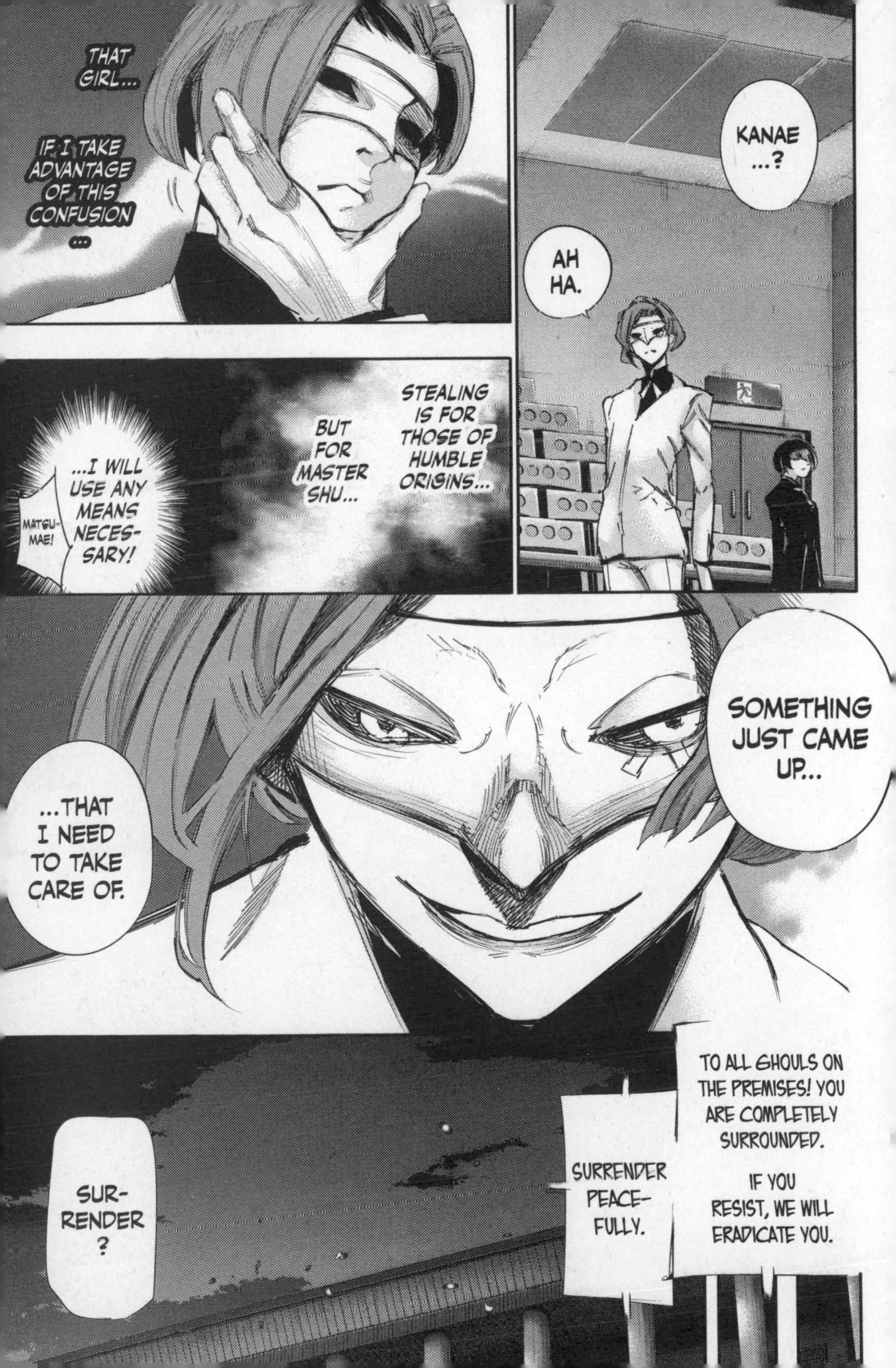
KANAE ...?
AH HA.
THAT GIRL...
IF I TAKE ADVANTAGE OF THIS CONFUSION ...
STEALING IS FOR THOSE OF HUMBLE ORIGINS...
BUT FOR MASTER SHU...
...I WILL USE ANY MEANS NECES-SARY!
MATSU-MAE!
SOMETHING JUST CAME UP...
...THAT I NEED TO TAKE CARE OF.
TO ALL GHOULS ON THE PREMISES! YOU ARE COMPLETELY SURROUNDED.
IF YOU RESIST, WE WILL ERADICATE YOU.
SURRENDER PEACE-FULLY.
SUR-RENDER ?

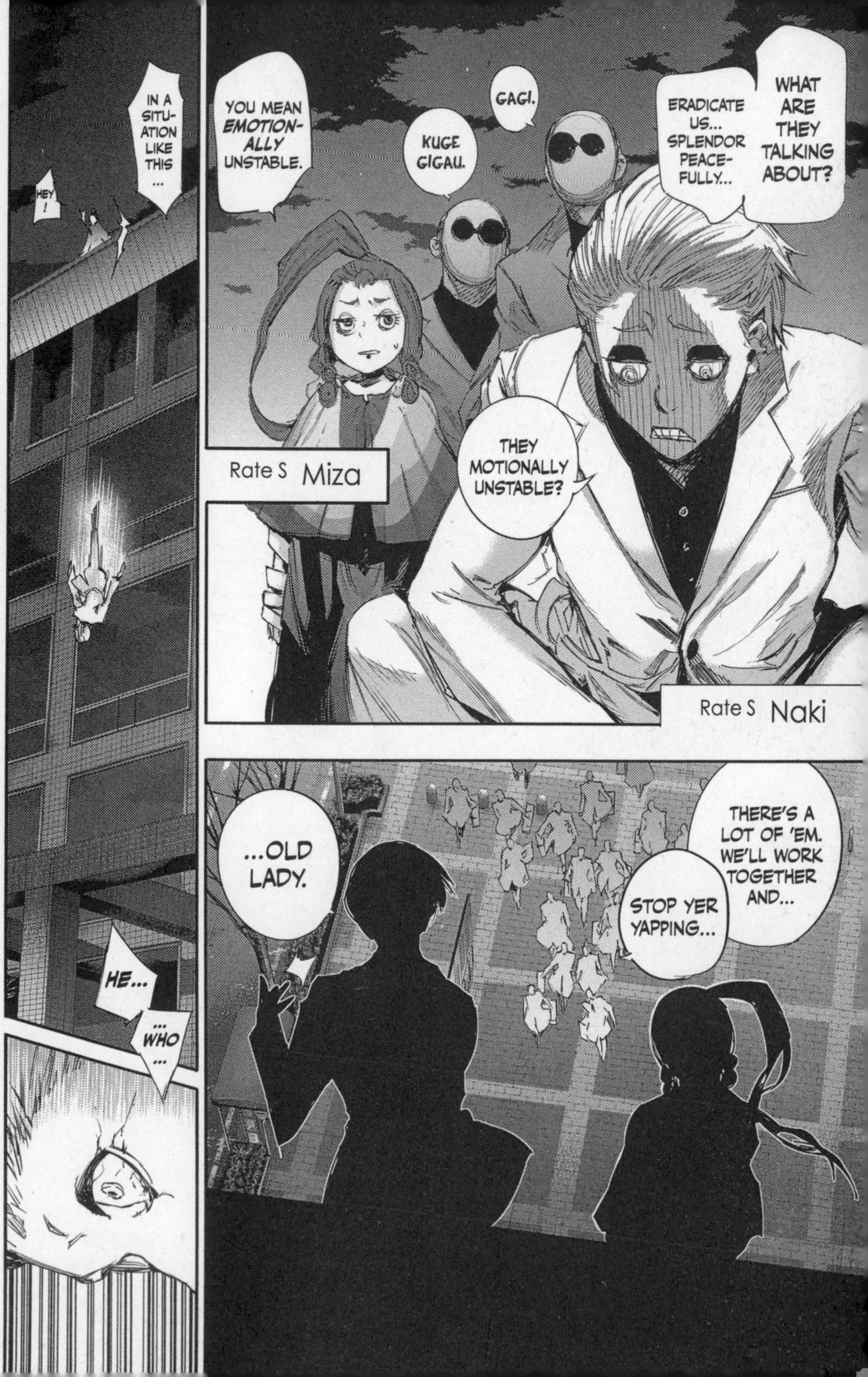
WHAT ARE THEY TALKING ABOUT?
ERADICATE US... SPLENDOR PEACE-FULLY...
GAGI.
KUGE GIGAU.
YOU MEAN *EMOTION-ALLY* UNSTABLE.
THEY MOTIONALLY UNSTABLE?
Rate S Miza
Rate S Naki
THERE'S A LOT OF 'EM. WE'LL WORK TOGETHER AND...
STOP YER YAPPING...
...OLD LADY.
IN A SITUATION LIKE THIS...
HEY!
HE...
...WHO...

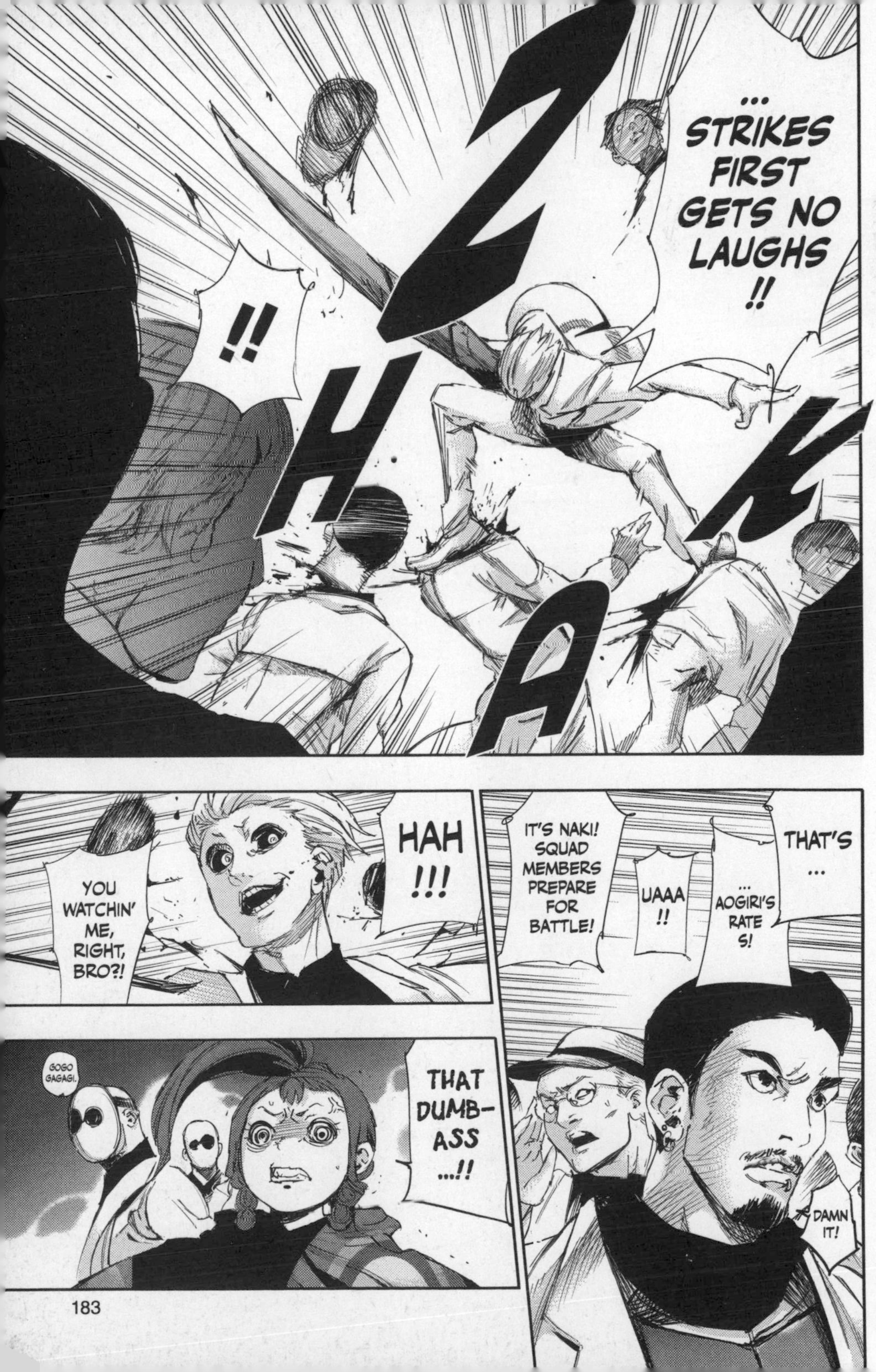
... STRIKES FIRST GETS NO LAUGHS !!
!!
THAT'S ...
... AOGIRI'S RATE S!
UAAA !!
IT'S NAKI! SQUAD MEMBERS PREPARE FOR BATTLE!
DAMN IT!
HAH !!!
YOU WATCHIN' ME, RIGHT, BRO?!
THAT DUMB-ASS ...!!
GOGO GAGAGI.

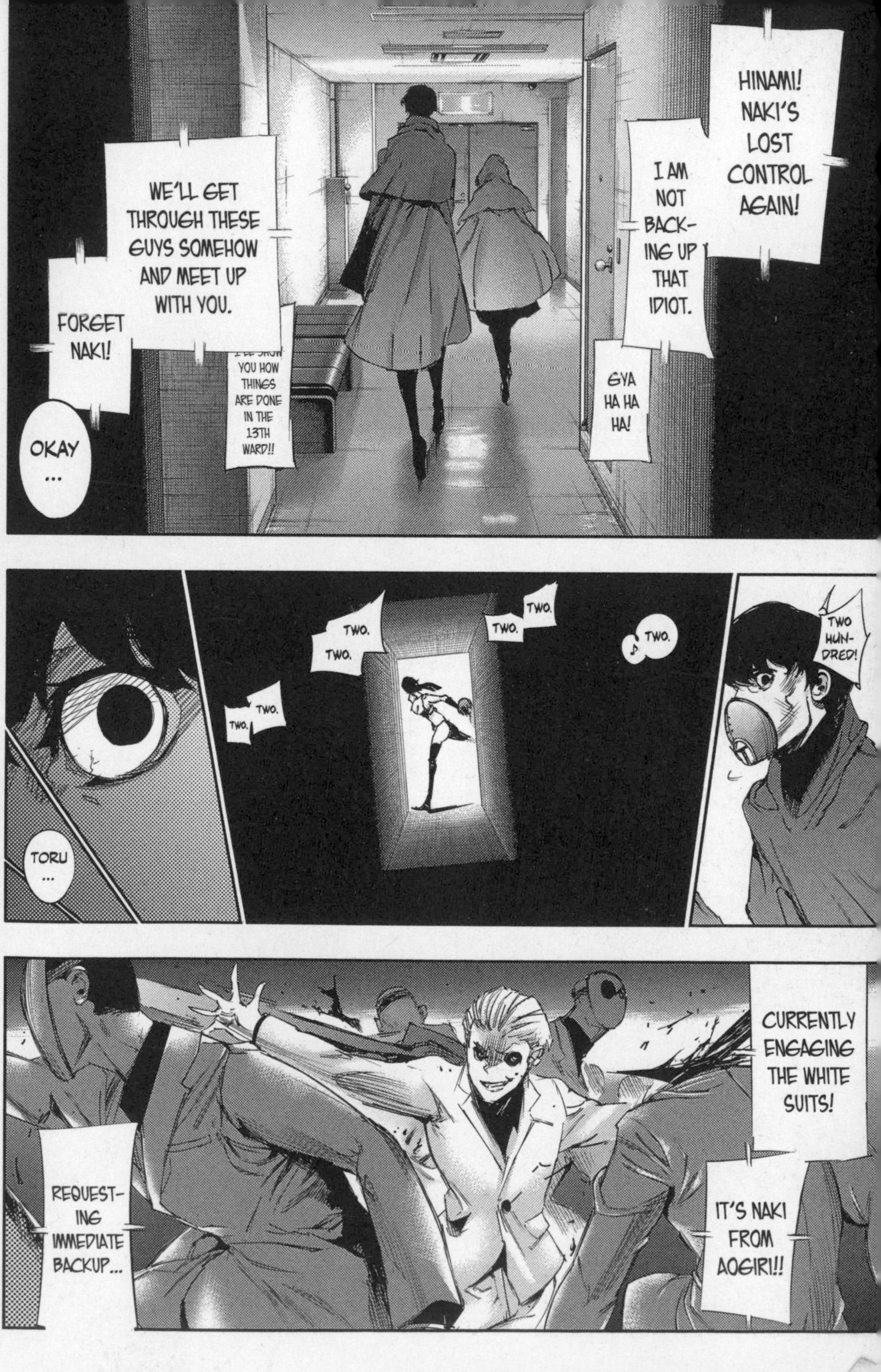
HINAMI! NAKI'S LOST CONTROL AGAIN!
I AM NOT BACKING UP THAT IDIOT.
GYA HA HA HA!
WE'LL GET THROUGH THESE GUYS SOMEHOW AND MEET UP WITH YOU.
I'LL SHOW YOU HOW THINGS ARE DONE IN THE 13TH WARD!!
FORGET NAKI!
OKAY...
TWO HUNDRED!
TWO.
TWO.
TWO.
TWO.
TWO.
TWO.
TWO.
TORU...
CURRENTLY ENGAGING THE WHITE SUITS!
IT'S NAKI FROM AOGIRI!!
REQUESTING IMMEDIATE BACKUP...

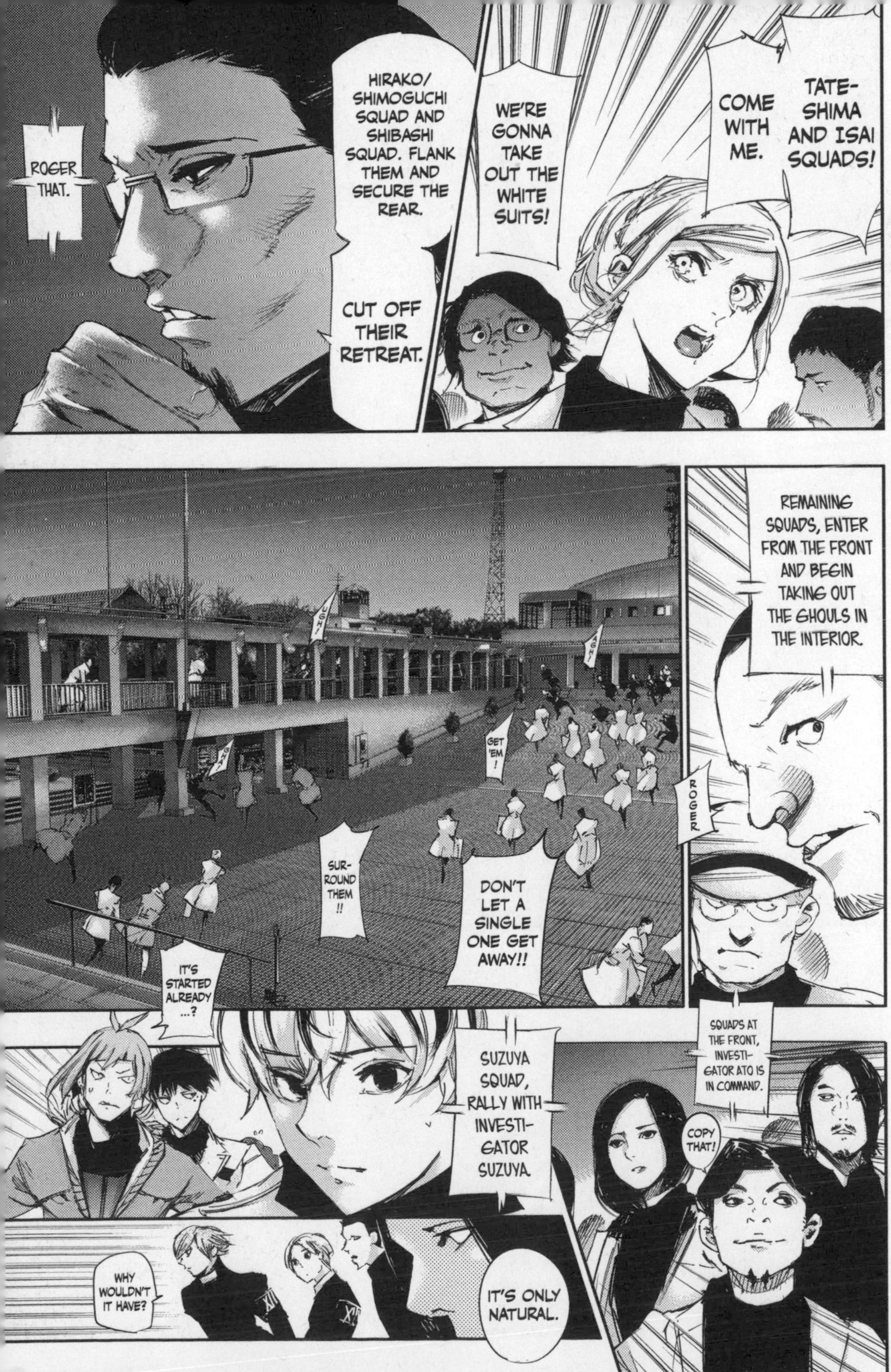
TATE-SHIMA AND ISAI SQUADS!
COME WITH ME.
WE'RE GONNA TAKE OUT THE WHITE SUITS!
HIRAKO/ SHIMOGUCHI SQUAD AND SHIBASHI SQUAD. FLANK THEM AND SECURE THE REAR.
CUT OFF THEIR RETREAT.
ROGER THAT.
REMAINING SQUADS, ENTER FROM THE FRONT AND BEGIN TAKING OUT THE GHOULS IN THE INTERIOR.
ROGER
GET 'EM!
DON'T LET A SINGLE ONE GET AWAY!!
SUR-ROUND THEM!!
IT'S STARTED ALREADY...?
SQUADS AT THE FRONT, INVESTI-GATOR ATO IS IN COMMAND.
COPY THAT!
SUZUYA SQUAD, RALLY WITH INVESTI-GATOR SUZUYA.
IT'S ONLY NATURAL.
WHY WOULDN'T IT HAVE?

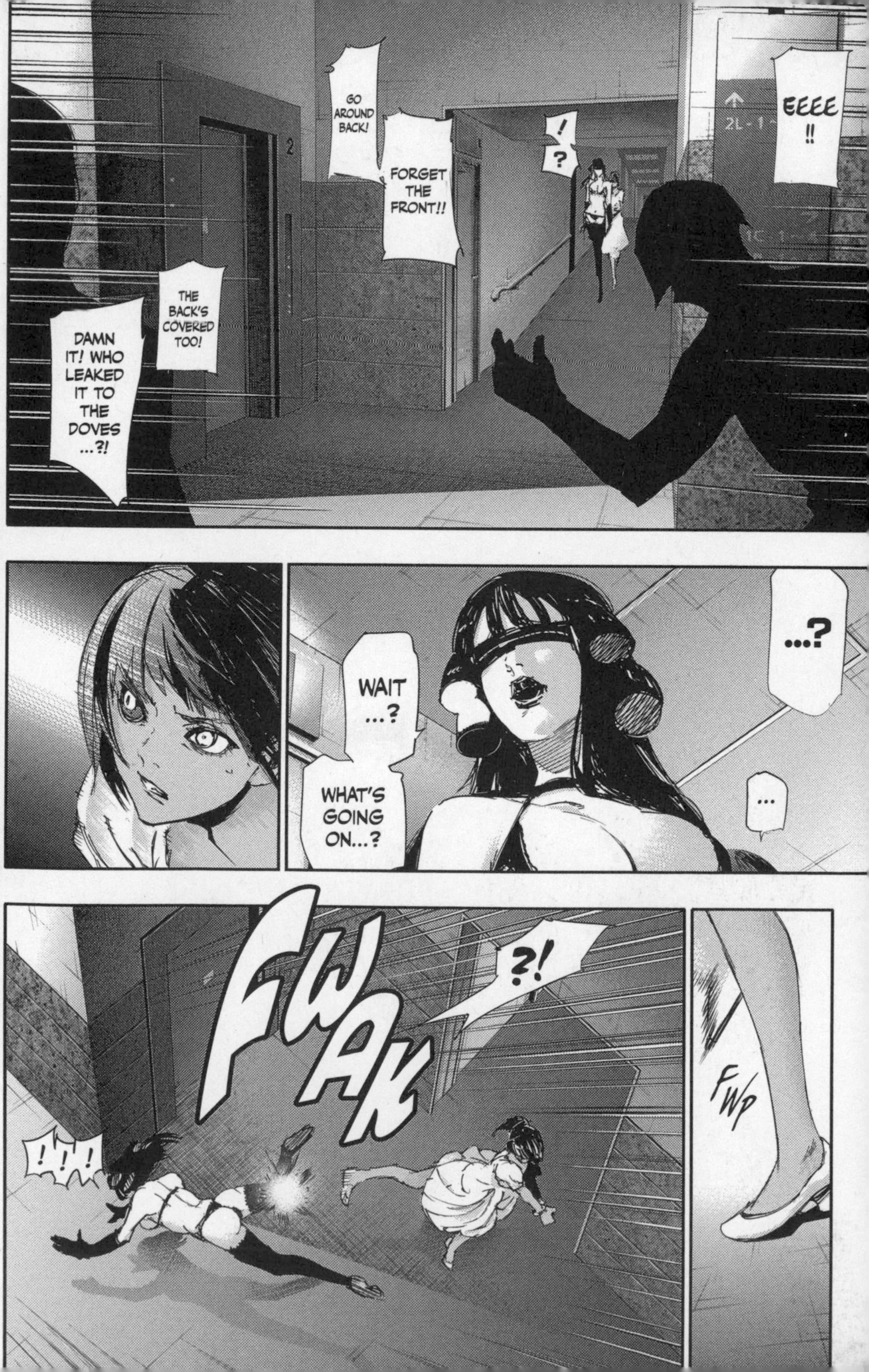
EEEE!!
!?
GO AROUND BACK!
FORGET THE FRONT!!
THE BACK'S COVERED TOO!
DAMN IT! WHO LEAKED IT TO THE DOVES...?!
...?
...
WAIT...?
WHAT'S GOING ON...?
FWP
?!
FWAK
!!!

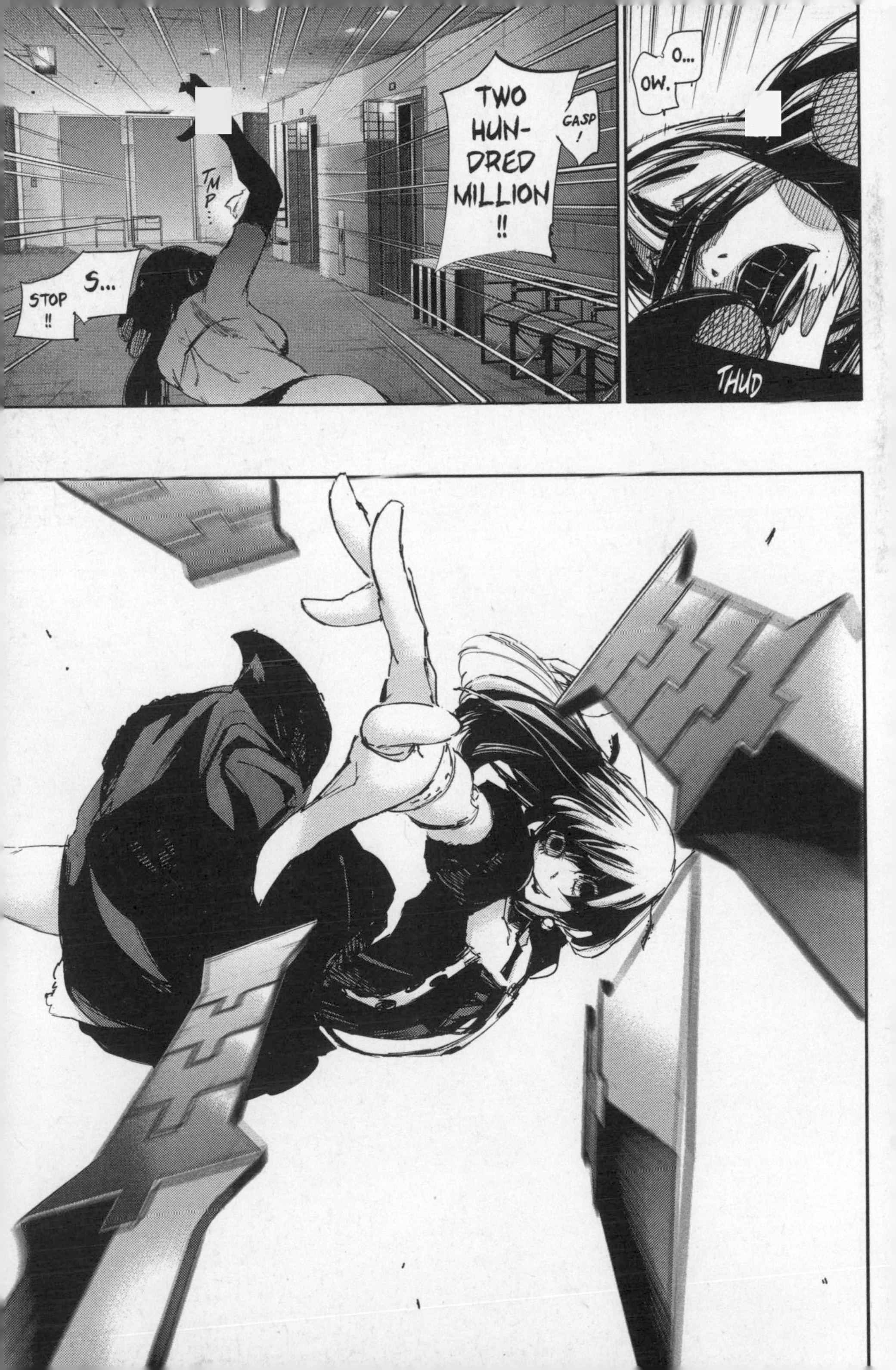
O... OW.
THUD
TWO HUN-DRED MILLION !!
GASP!
TMP...
S...
STOP !!

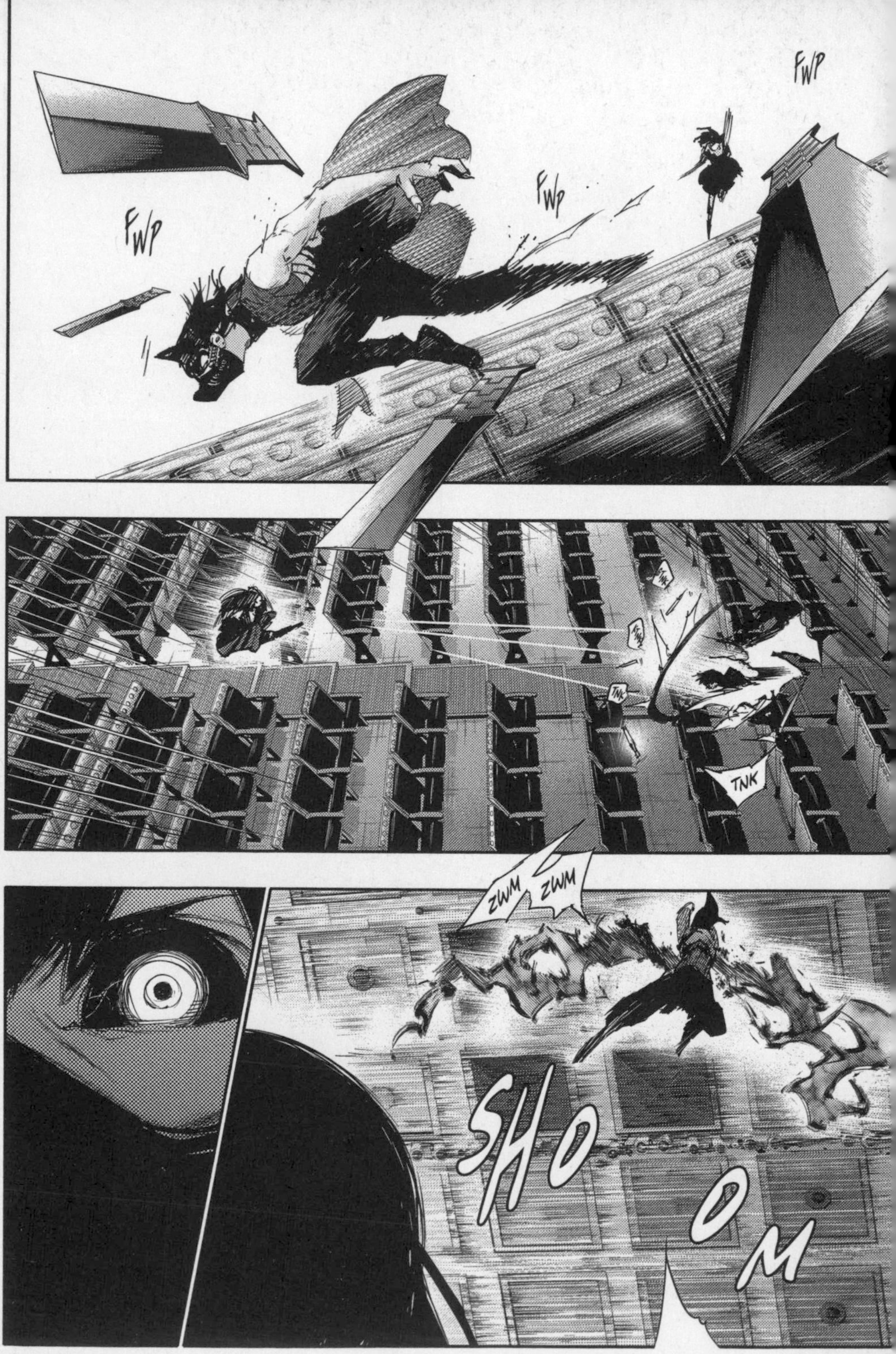
FWP
FWP
FWP
TNK
TNK
ZWM ZWM
SHOOOM

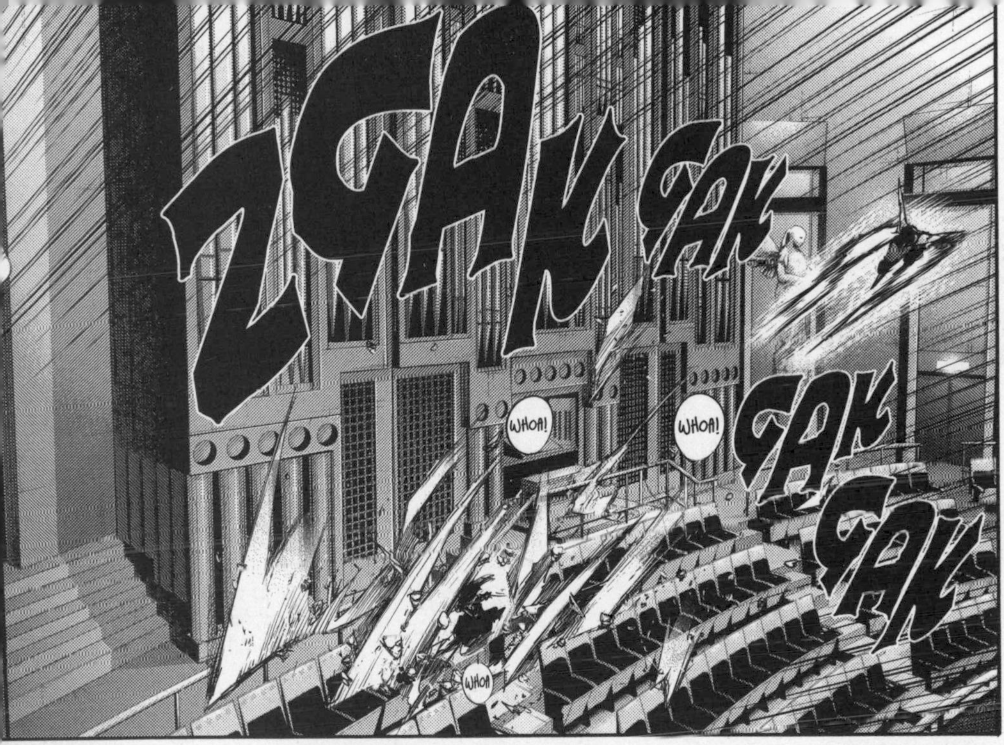
ZGAK
GAK
GAK
GAK
GAK
WHOA!
WHOA!
WHOA

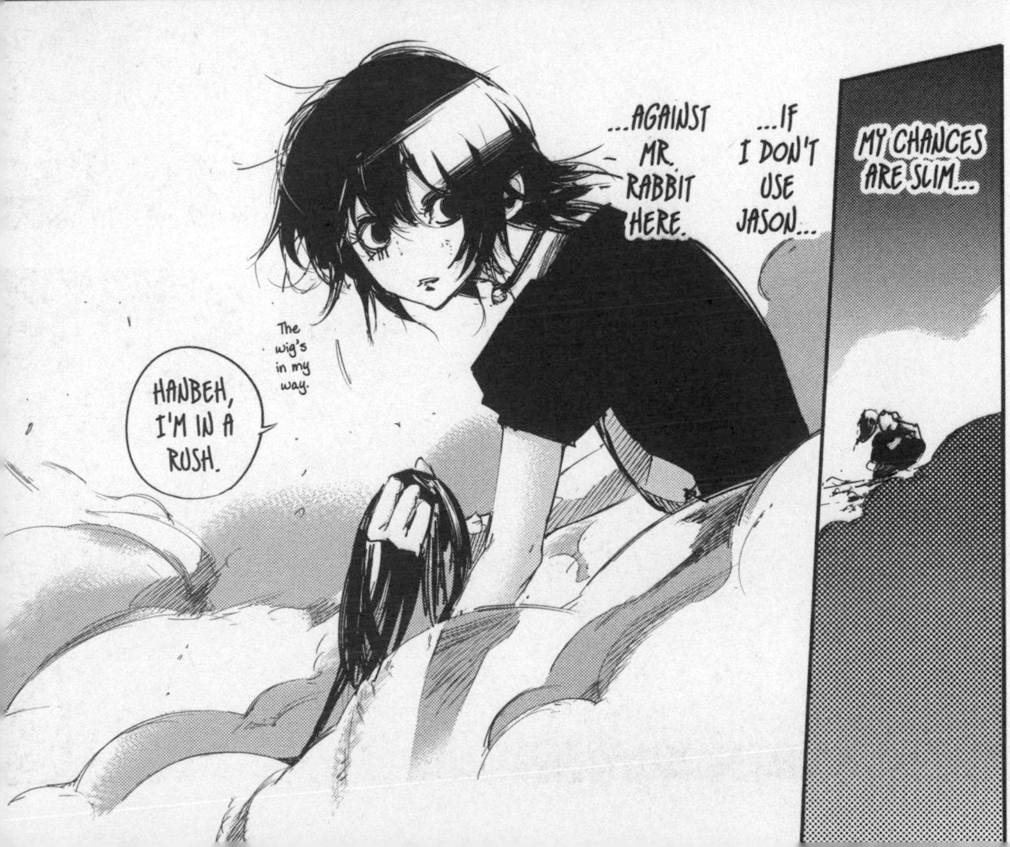
MY CHANCES ARE SLIM...
...IF I DON'T USE JASON...
...AGAINST MR. RABBIT HERE.
The wig's in my way.
HANBEH, I'M IN A RUSH.

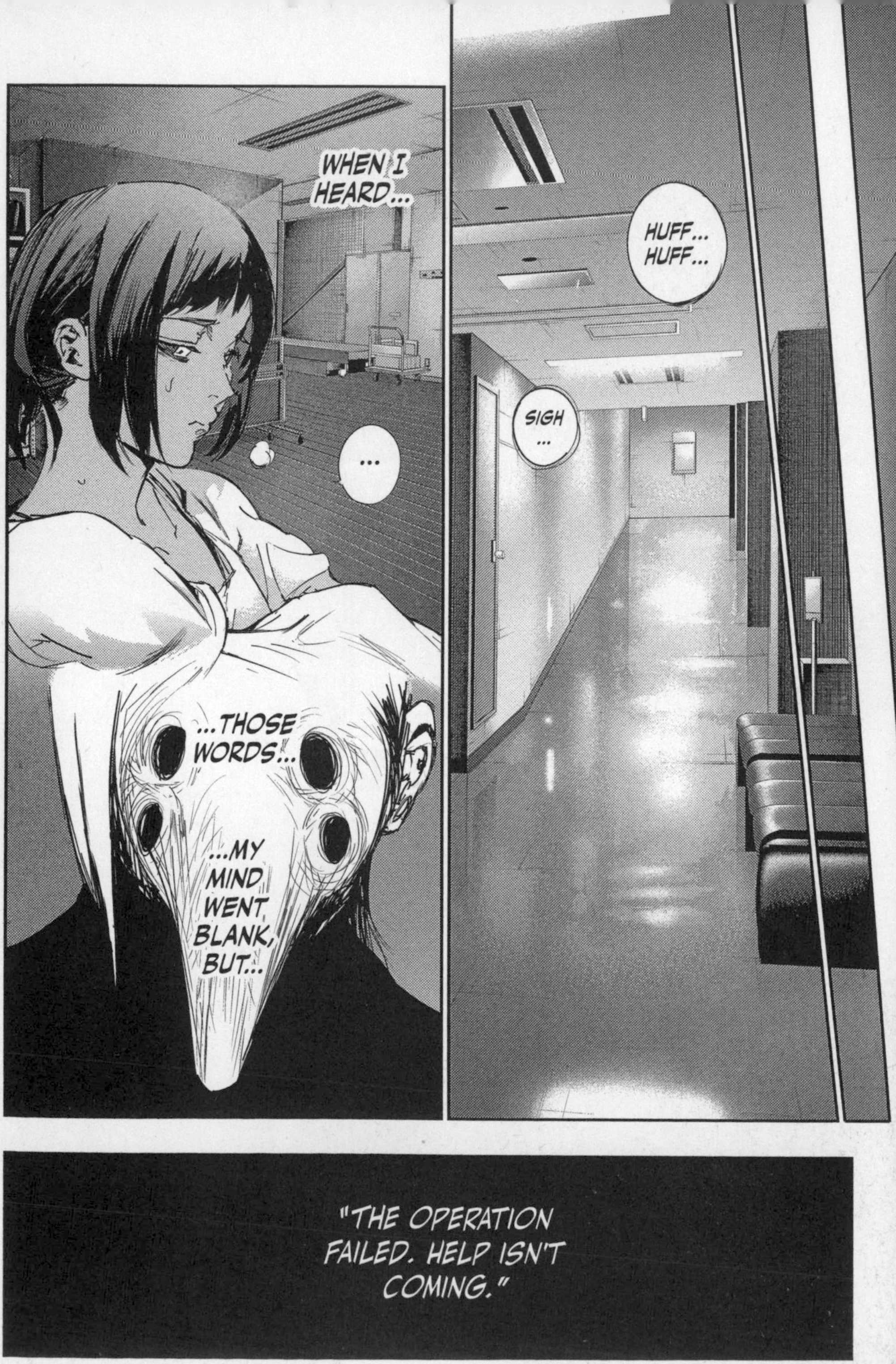
HUFF... HUFF...
SIGH...
WHEN I HEARD...
...
...THOSE WORDS...
...MY MIND WENT BLANK, BUT...
"THE OPERATION FAILED. HELP ISN'T COMING."

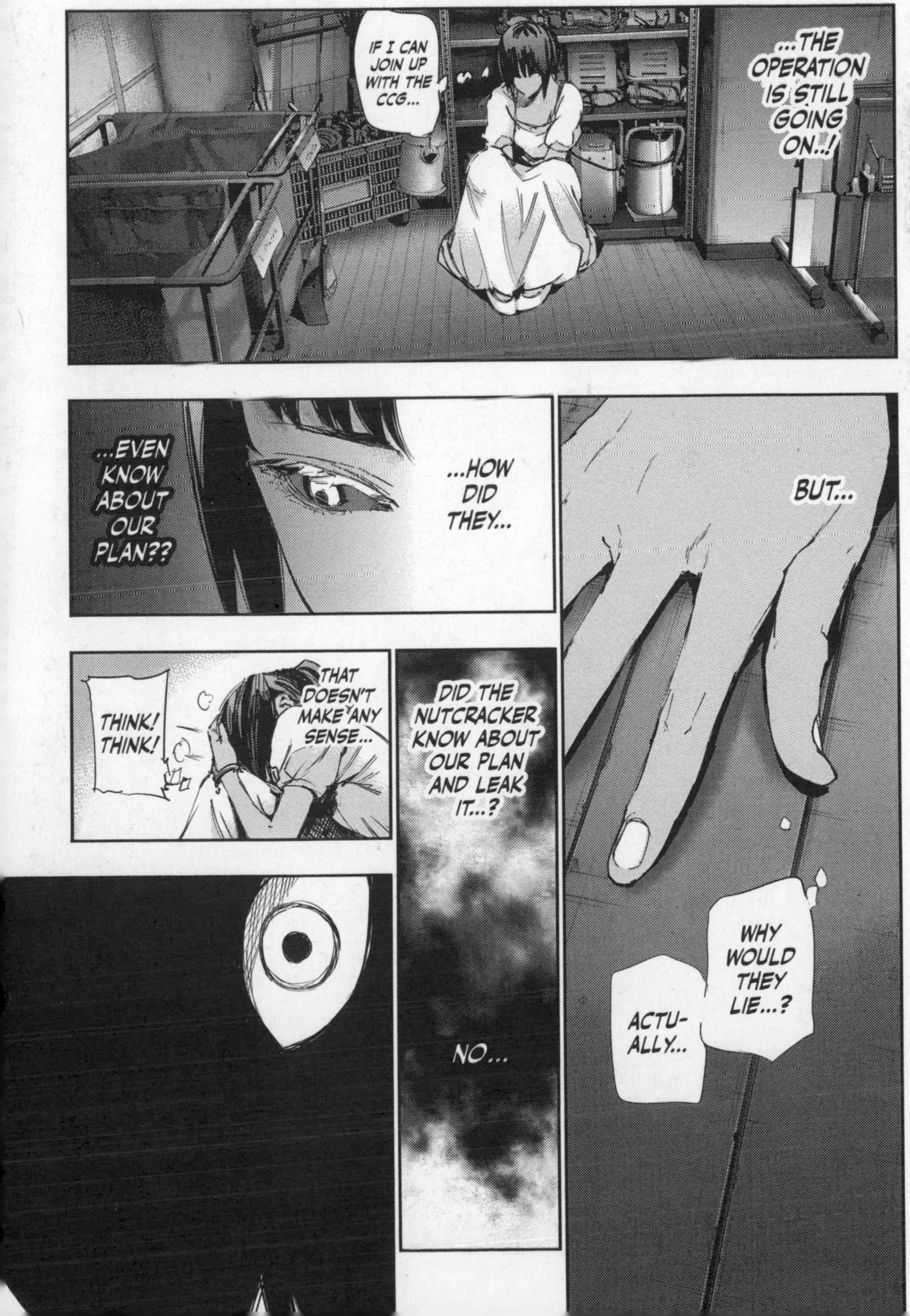
...THE OPERATION IS STILL GOING ON..!
IF I CAN JOIN UP WITH THE CCG...
BUT...
WHY WOULD THEY LIE...?
ACTU-ALLY...
...HOW DID THEY...
...EVEN KNOW ABOUT OUR PLAN??
DID THE NUTCRACKER KNOW ABOUT OUR PLAN AND LEAK IT...?
NO...
THAT DOESN'T MAKE ANY SENSE...
THINK! THINK!

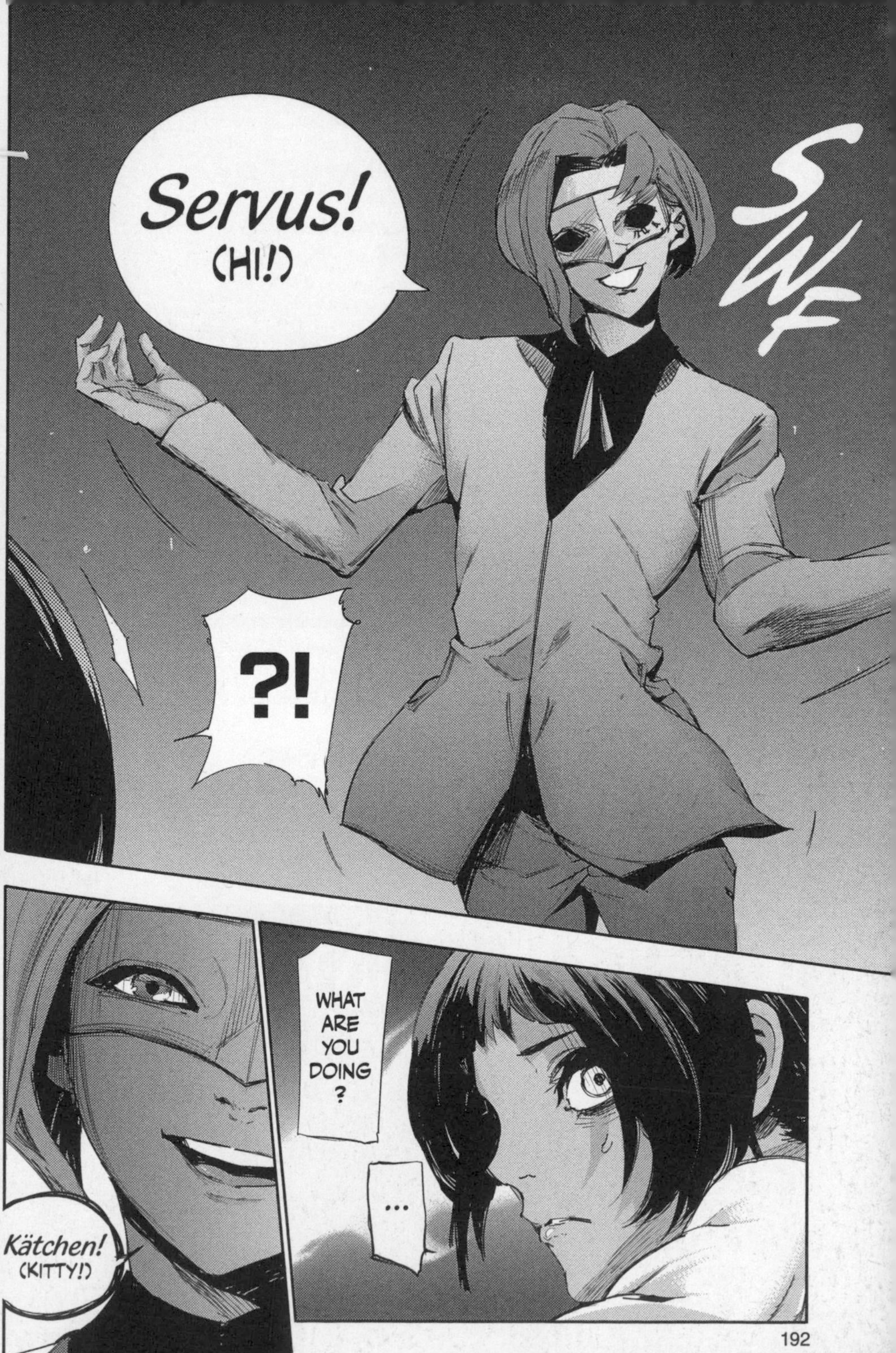
SWF
Servus!
(HI!)
?!
WHAT ARE YOU DOING?
...
Kätchen!
(KITTY!)

Operation Auction Sweep Report #1

Tokyo Ghoul :re Weekly Report

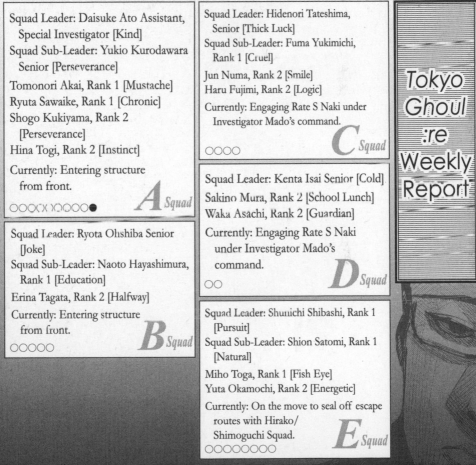

Squad Leader: Daisuke Ato Assistant, Special Investigator [Kind]
Squad Sub-Leader: Yukio Kurodawara Senior [Perseverance]
Tomonori Akai, Rank 1 [Mustache]
Ryuta Sawaike, Rank 1 [Chronic]
Shogo Kukiyama, Rank 2 [Perseverance]
Hina Togi, Rank 2 [Instinct]
Currently: Entering structure from front.

○○○○○○○○○●

A Squad

Squad Leader: Ryota Ohshiba Senior [Joke]
Squad Sub-Leader: Naoto Hayashimura, Rank 1 [Education]
Erina Tagata, Rank 2 [Halfway]
Currently: Entering structure from front.

○○○○○

B Squad

Squad Leader: Hidenori Tateshima, Senior [Thick Luck]
Squad Sub-Leader: Fuma Yukimichi, Rank 1 [Cruel]
Jun Numa, Rank 2 [Smile]
Haru Fujimi, Rank 2 [Logic]
Currently: Engaging Rate S Naki under Investigator Mado's command.

○○○○

C Squad

Squad Leader: Kenta Isai Senior [Cold]
Sakino Mura, Rank 2 [School Lunch]
Waka Asachi, Rank 2 [Guardian]
Currently: Engaging Rate S Naki under Investigator Mado's command.

○○

D Squad

Squad Leader: Shunichi Shibashi, Rank 1 [Pursuit]
Squad Sub-Leader: Shion Satomi, Rank 1 [Natural]
Miho Toga, Rank 1 [Fish Eye]
Yuta Okamochi, Rank 2 [Energetic]
Currently: On the move to seal off escape routes with Hirako/ Shimoguchi Squad.

○○○○○○○○

E Squad

TO NEW GHOUL INVESTIGATORS

We thank you for the overwhelming number of submissions to the Ghoul Investigator Recruitment Project done in collaboration with the job finder website *an*. After strict evaluation, we have chosen the above people to be our fellow investigators. We initially planned to only accept a few applicants, but we selected 20 in response to unfolding events. We received word that the Nutcracker in the 13th Ward, which Suzuya Squad was investigating, had been hired to supply humans to the Big Madame. We speculated that the transaction would take place at the Auction, a place where Ghouls' greed is centralized. We decided to take action when Investigator Mutsuki determined the date and location of the auction. We predict it will be a large-scale operation. We hope the selected investigators will fight hard. We will be reporting their achievements here every week.

We, the CCG, **will** exterminate the Ghouls.

(Operation Auction Sweep) Assistant Special Investigator Matsuri Washu, Commander of Countermeasure II.

*This was originally published in *Weekly Young Jump* 2015, issue 14.

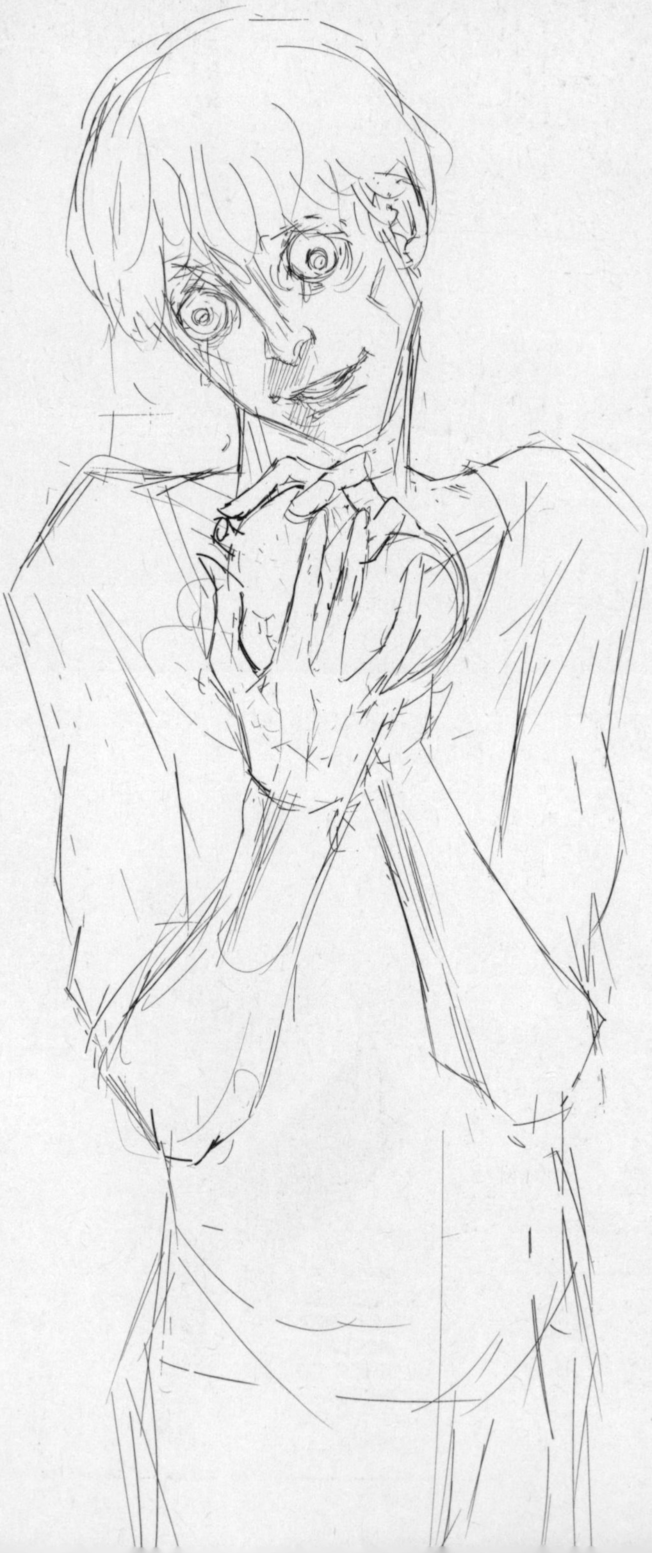

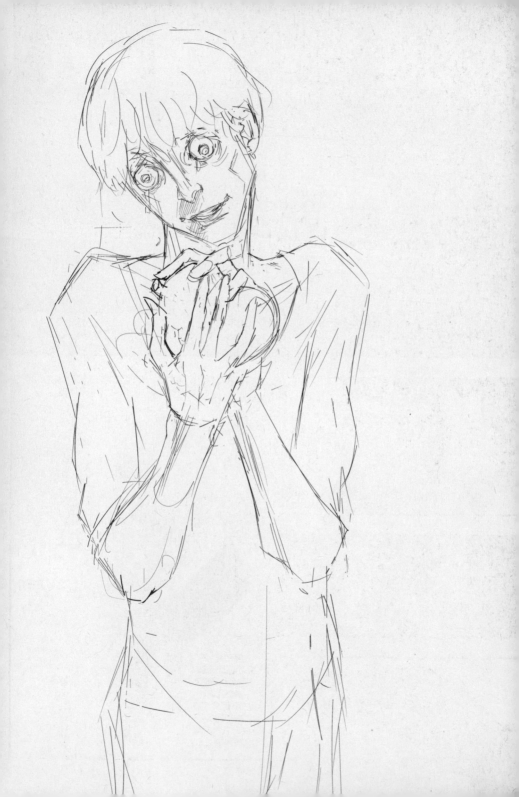

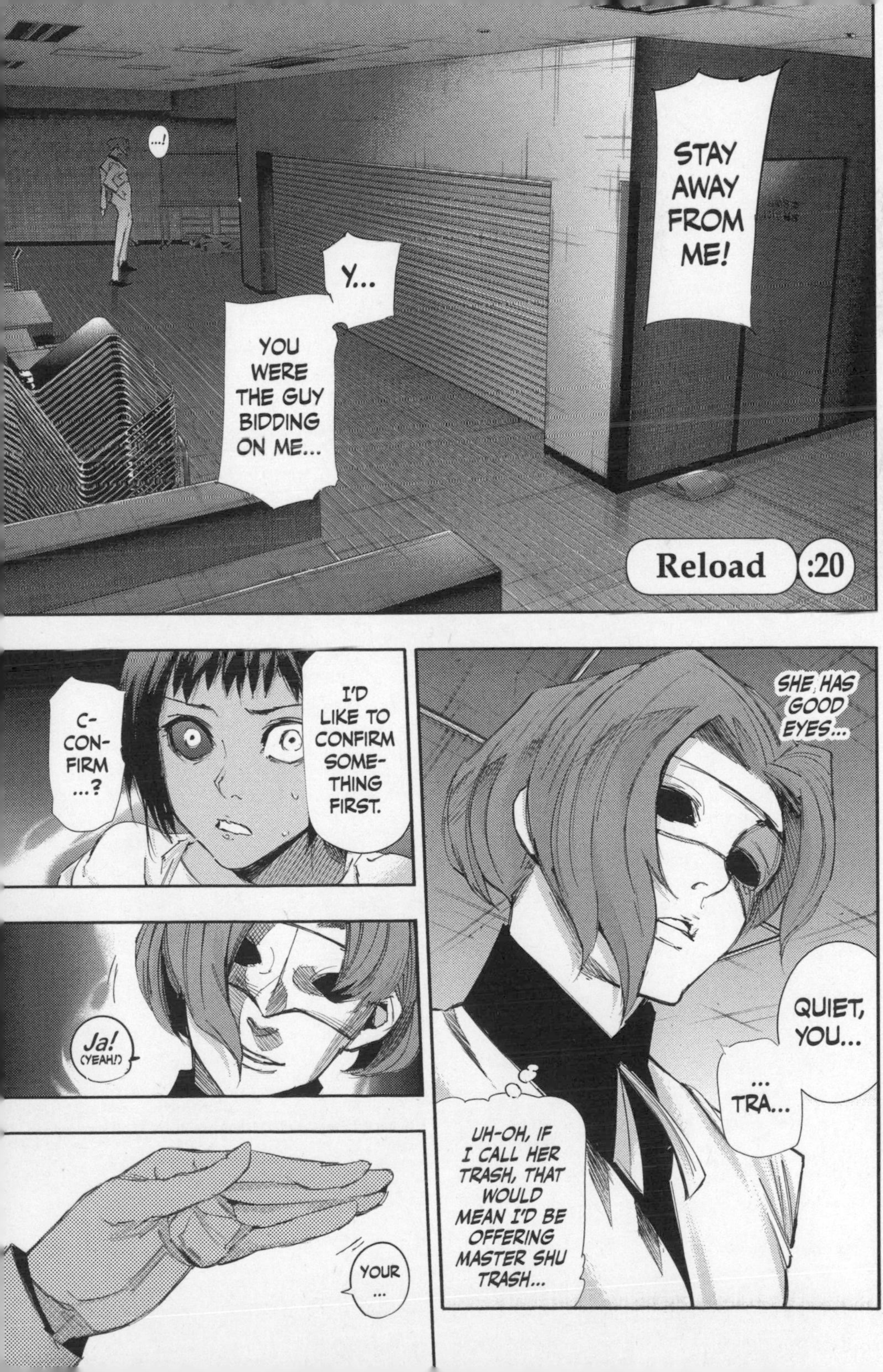
Reload :20
STAY AWAY FROM ME!
Y...
YOU WERE THE GUY BIDDING ON ME...
...!
SHE HAS GOOD EYES...
QUIET, YOU...
... TRA...
UH-OH, IF I CALL HER TRASH, THAT WOULD MEAN I'D BE OFFERING MASTER SHU TRASH...
I'D LIKE TO CONFIRM SOMETHING FIRST.
C-CONFIRM ...?
Ja! (YEAH!)
YOUR ...

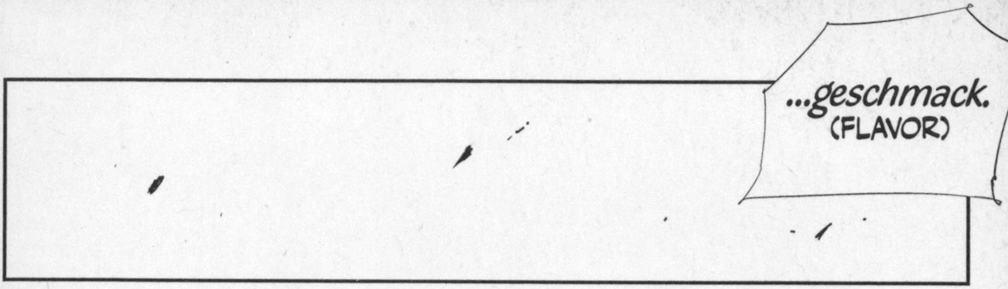
...geschmack.
(FLAVOR)

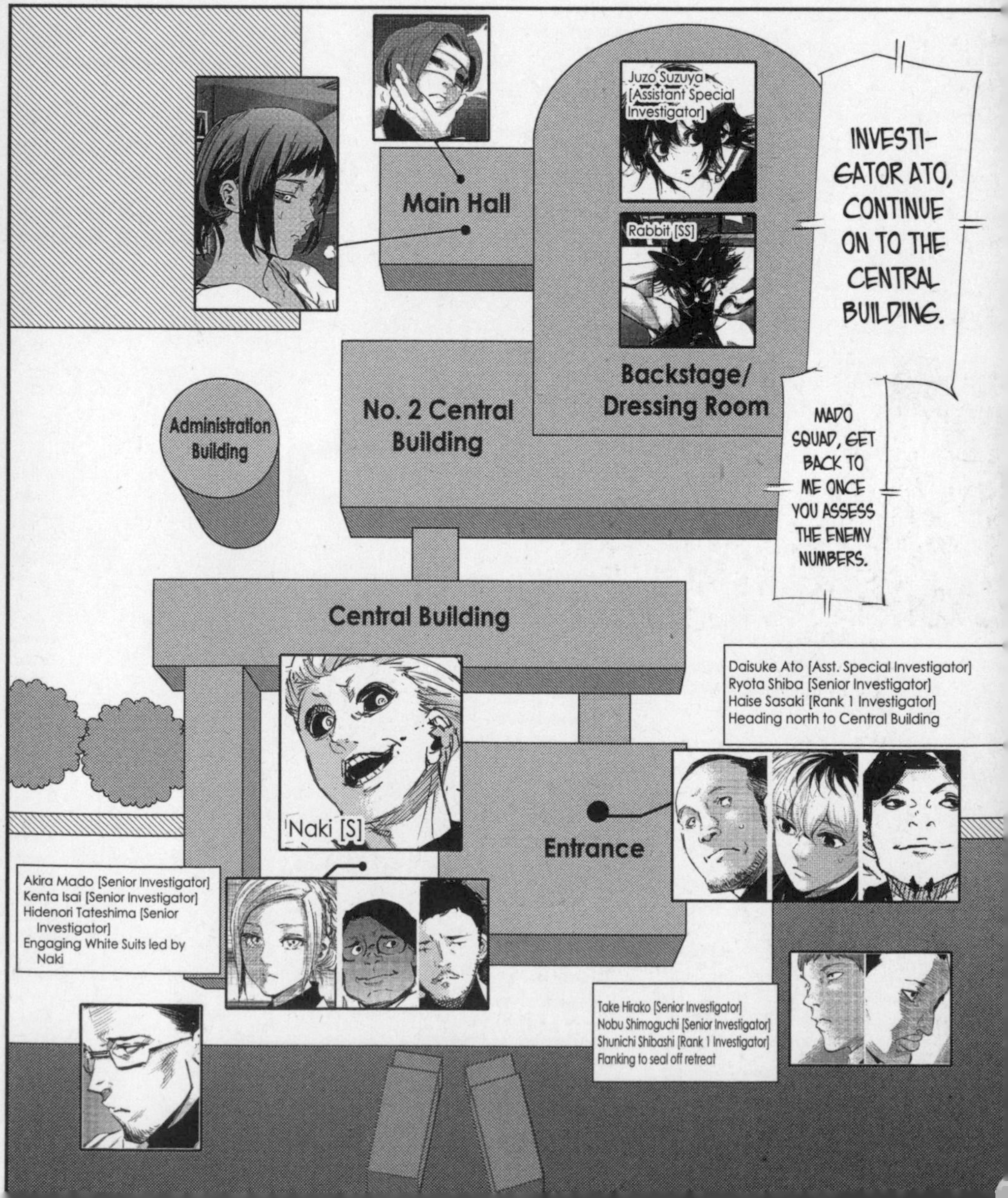
INVESTIGATOR ATO, CONTINUE ON TO THE CENTRAL BUILDING.
MADO SQUAD, GET BACK TO ME ONCE YOU ASSESS THE ENEMY NUMBERS.
Juzo Suzuya [Assistant Special Investigator]
Rabbit [SS]
Backstage/ Dressing Room
Main Hall
No. 2 Central Building
Administration Building
Central Building
Daisuke Ato [Asst. Special Investigator]
Ryota Shiba [Senior Investigator]
Haise Sasaki [Rank 1 Investigator]
Heading north to Central Building
Entrance
Naki [S]
Akira Mado [Senior Investigator]
Kenta Isai [Senior Investigator]
Hidenori Tateshima [Senior Investigator]
Engaging White Suits led by Naki
Take Hirako [Senior Investigator]
Nobu Shimoguchi [Senior Investigator]
Shunichi Shibashi [Rank 1 Investigator]
Flanking to seal off retreat

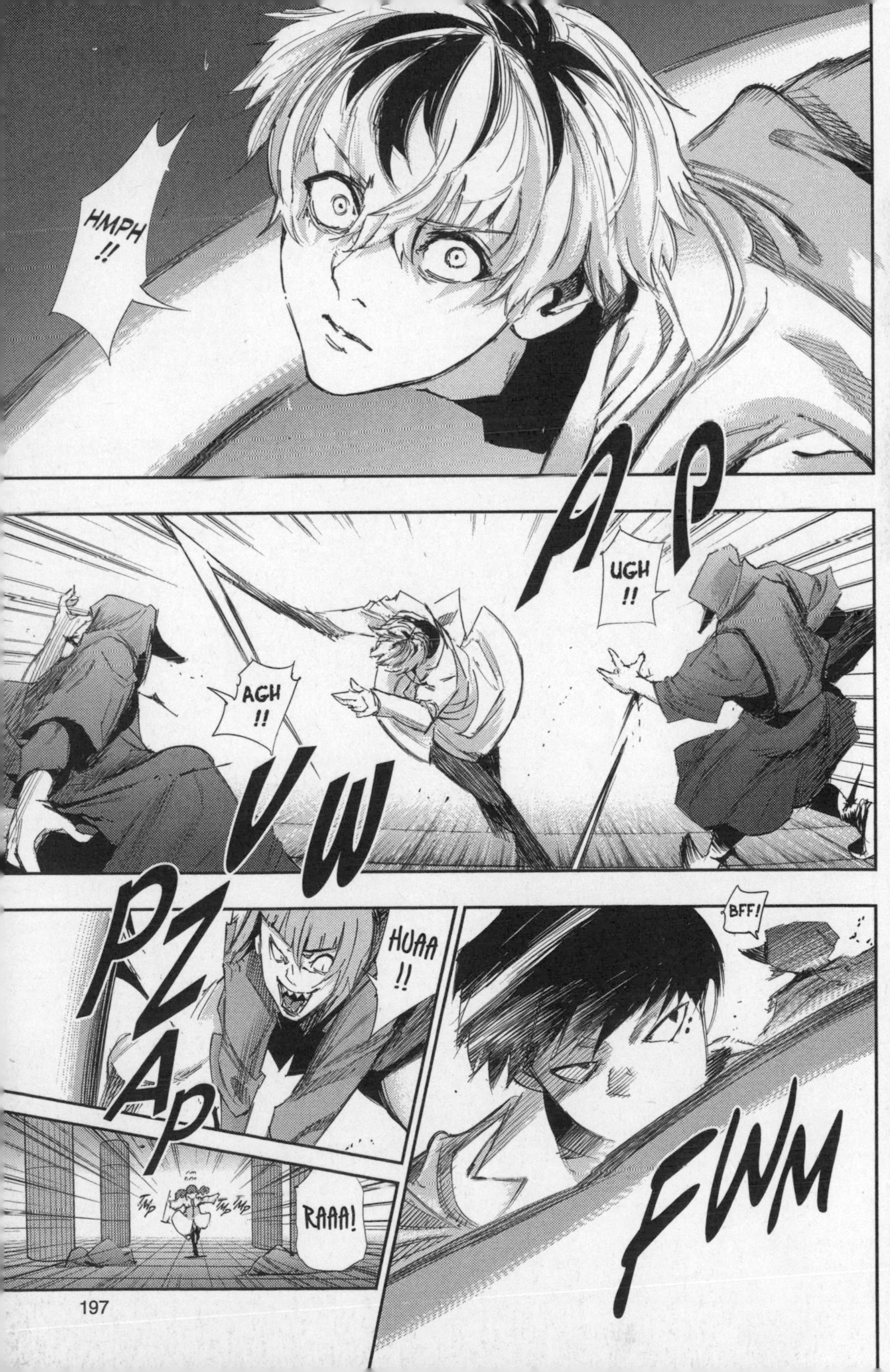
HMPH !!
UGH !!
AGH !!
BFF!
FWM
HUAA !!
RAAA!

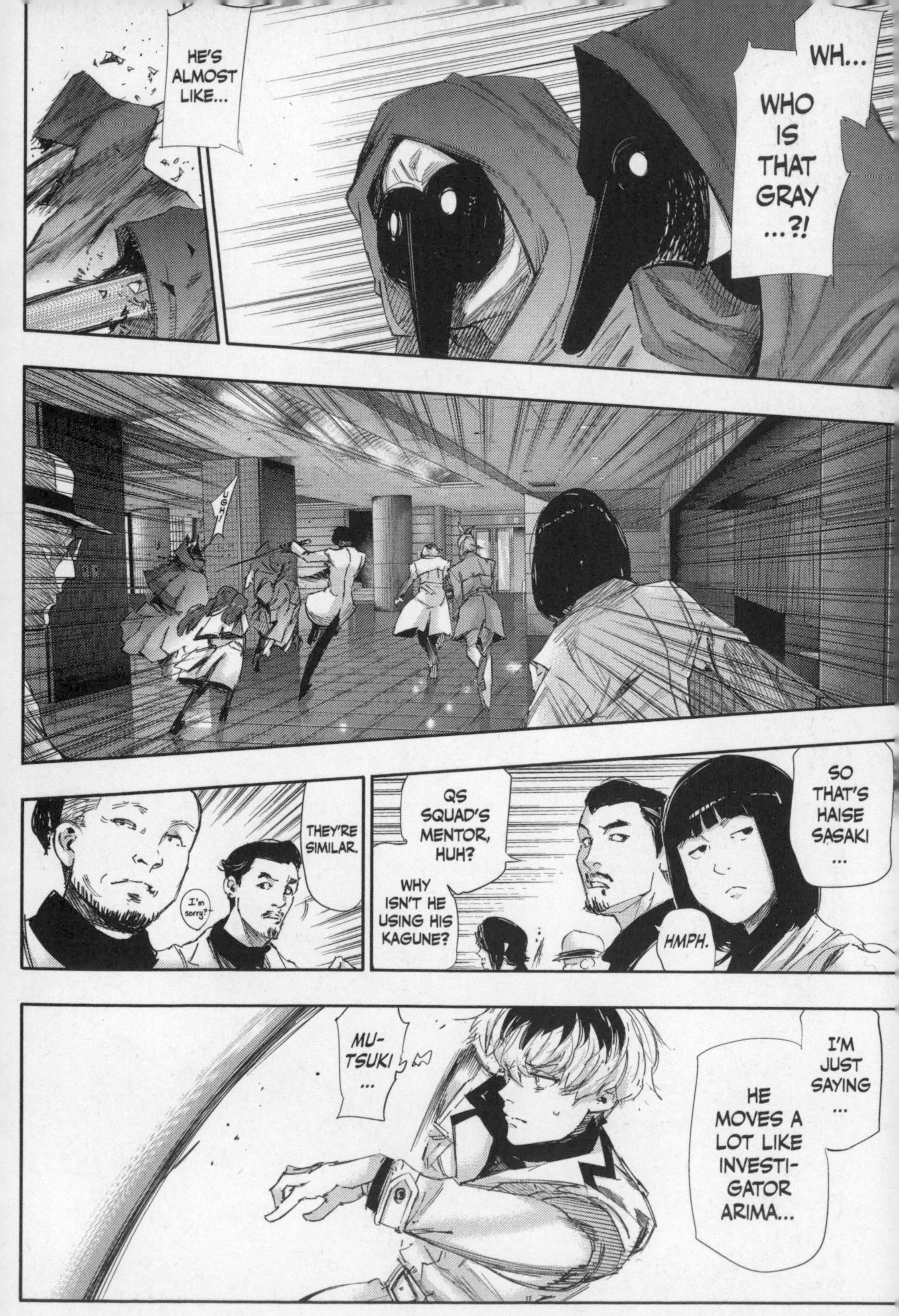
WH...
WHO IS THAT GRAY ...?!
HE'S ALMOST LIKE...
UGH!
SO THAT'S HAISE SASAKI ...
HMPH.
QS SQUAD'S MENTOR, HUH?
WHY ISN'T HE USING HIS KAGUNE?
THEY'RE SIMILAR.
I'm sorry?
I'M JUST SAYING ...
HE MOVES A LOT LIKE INVESTIGATOR ARIMA...
MU-TSUKI ...

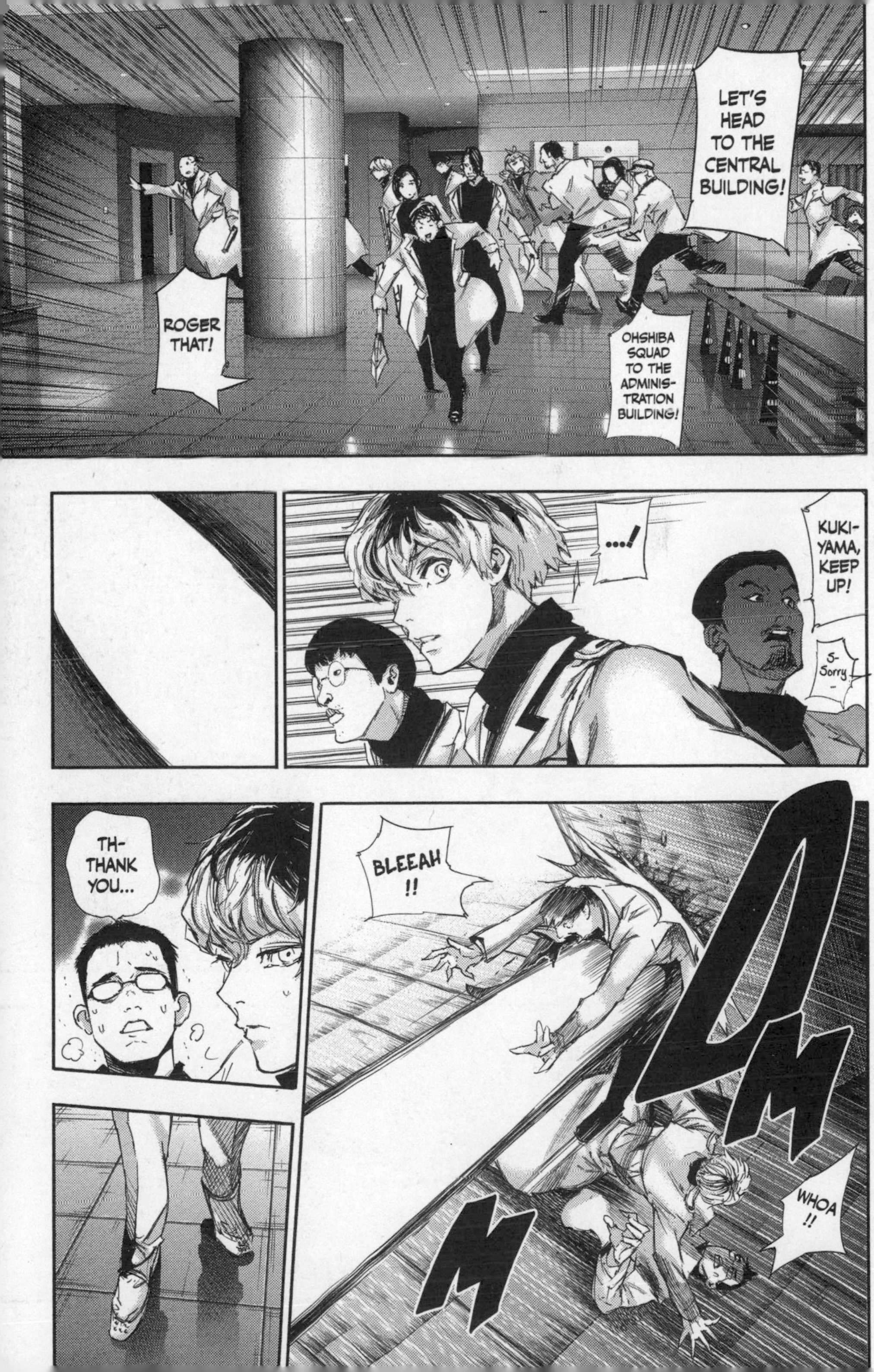
LET'S HEAD TO THE CENTRAL BUILDING!
OHSHIBA SQUAD TO THE ADMINISTRATION BUILDING!
ROGER THAT!
KUKIYAMA, KEEP UP!
...!
S-Sorry...
BLEEAH !!
WHOA !!
TH-THANK YOU...

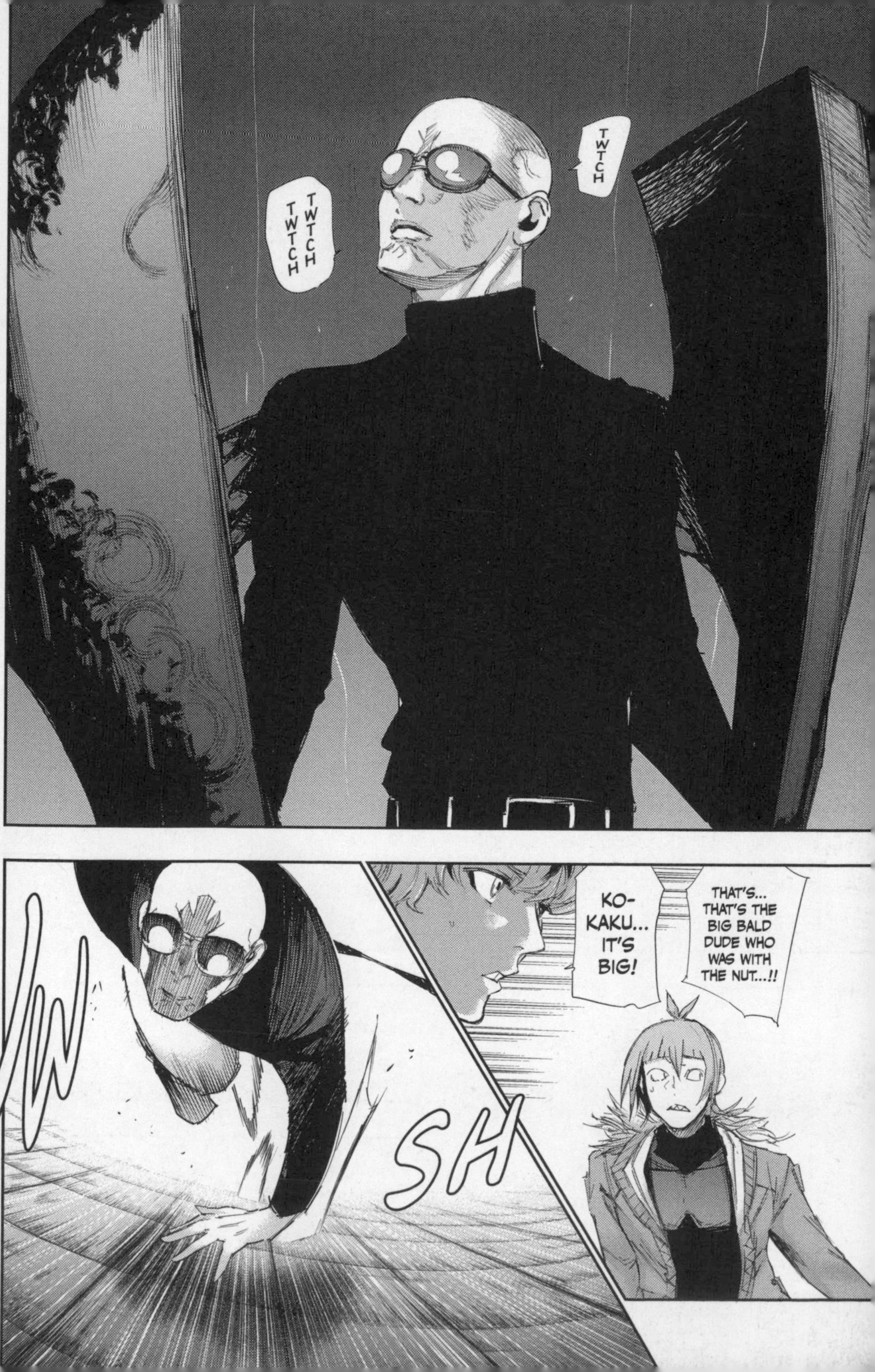
TWTCH
TWTCH TWTCH
THAT'S... THAT'S THE BIG BALD DUDE WHO WAS WITH THE NUT...!!
KO-KAKU... IT'S BIG!
SH
VW

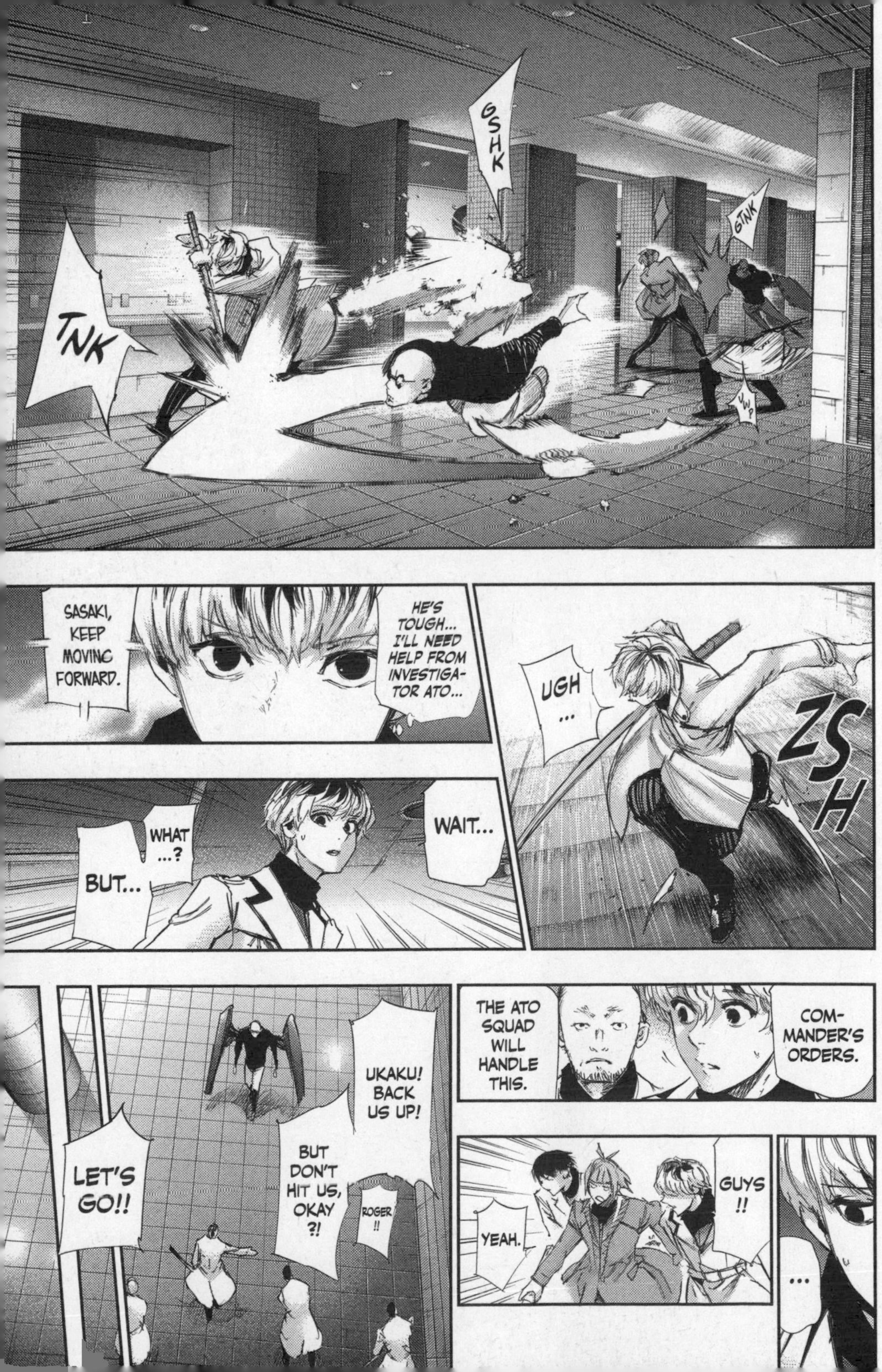
GTNK
GSHK
UWP
TNK
UGH ...
ZSH
HE'S TOUGH... I'LL NEED HELP FROM INVESTIGATOR ATO...
SASAKI, KEEP MOVING FORWARD.
WAIT...
WHAT ...?
BUT...
COM-MANDER'S ORDERS.
THE ATO SQUAD WILL HANDLE THIS.
...
GUYS !!
YEAH.
UKAKU! BACK US UP!
BUT DON'T HIT US, OKAY ?!
ROGER !!
LET'S GO!!

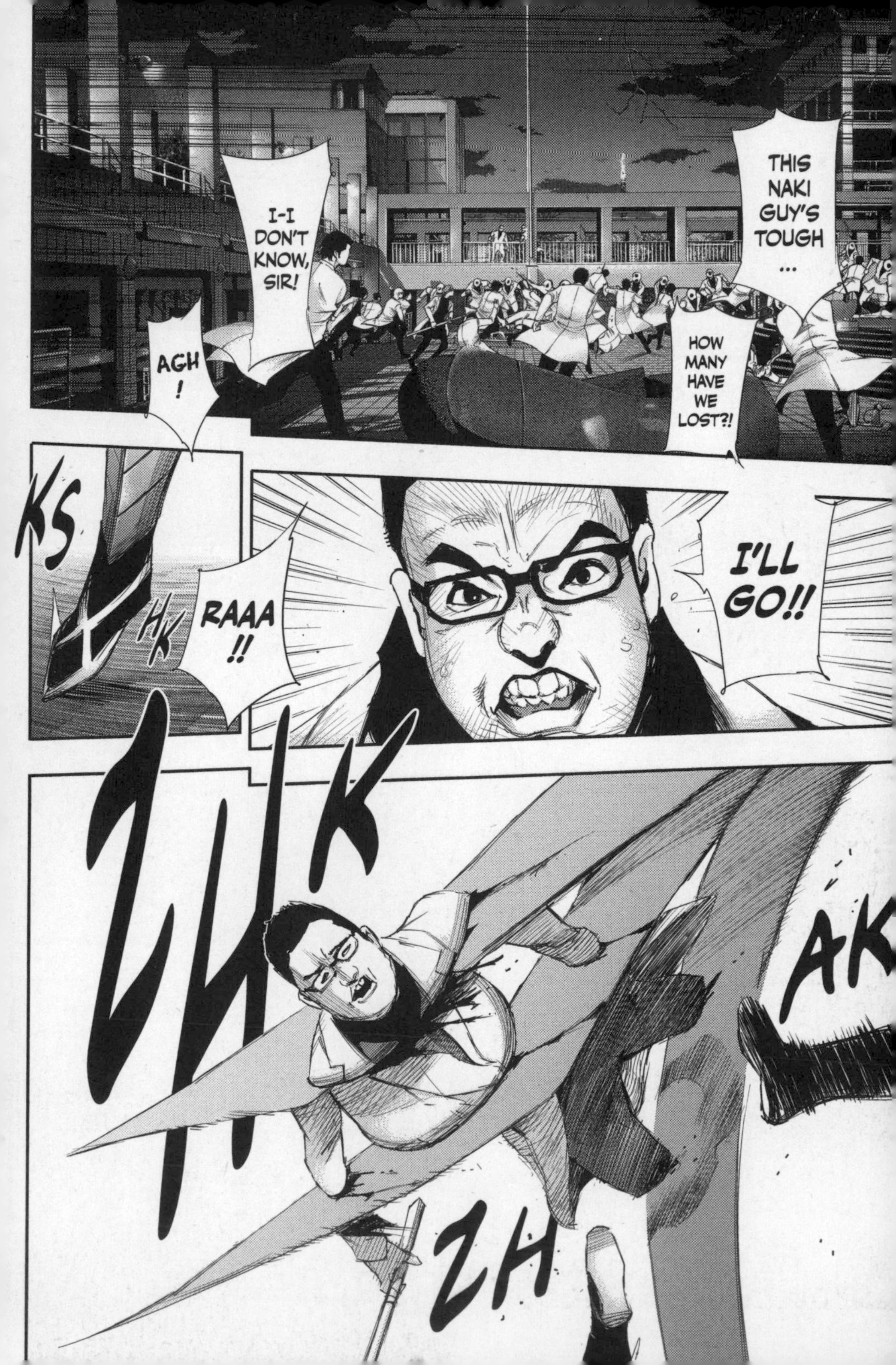
THIS NAKI GUY'S TOUGH ...
HOW MANY HAVE WE LOST?!
I-I DON'T KNOW, SIR!
AGH!
I'LL GO!!
RAAA!!
KS HK
ZHK
AK
ZH

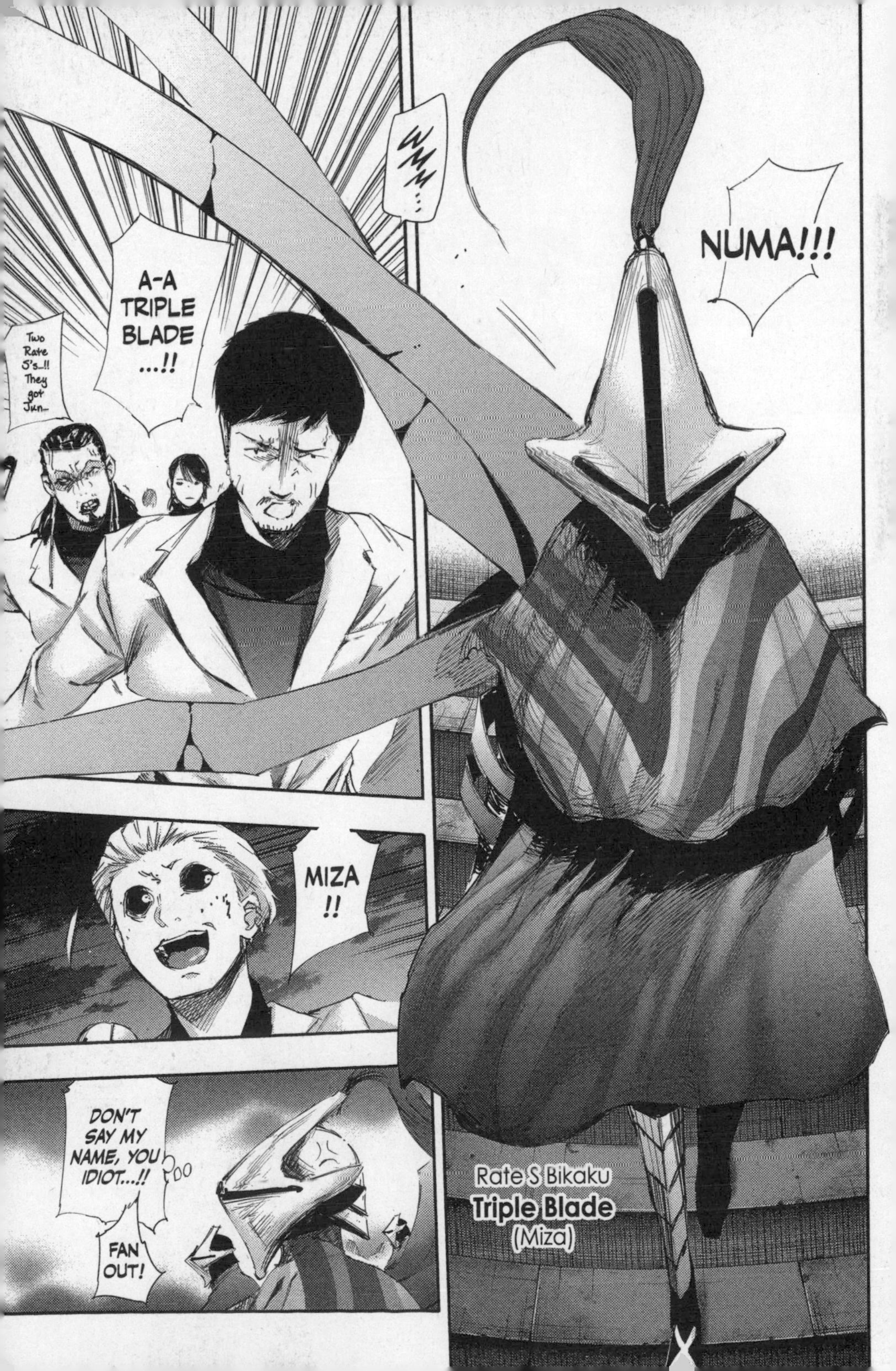
NUMA!!!
Rate S Bikaku
Triple Blade
(Miza)
WMM...
A-A TRIPLE BLADE ...!!
Two Rate S's...!! They got Jun...
MIZA !!
DON'T SAY MY NAME, YOU IDIOT...!!
FAN OUT!

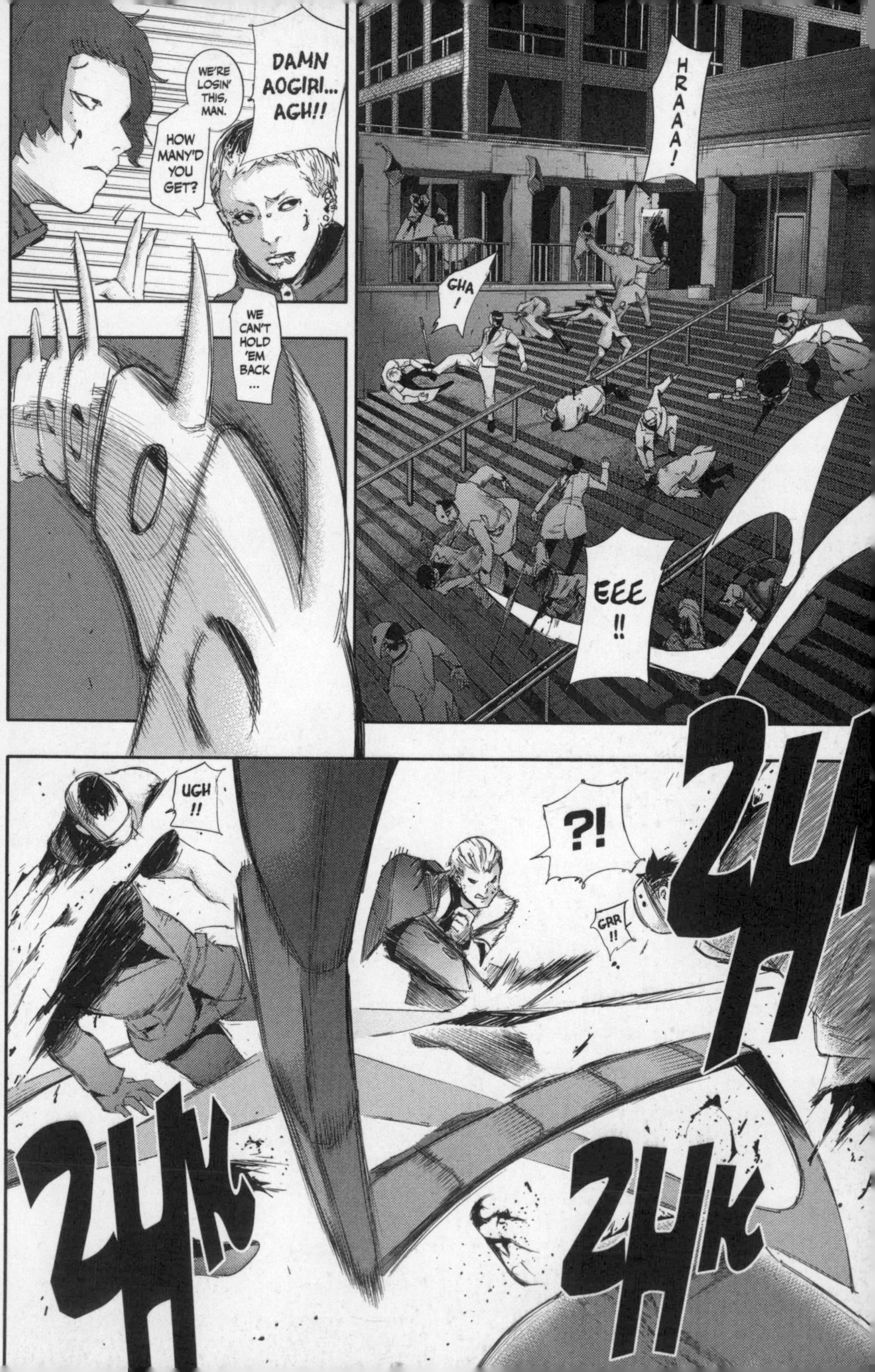
HRAAAA!
GHA!
EEE!!
DAMN AOGIRI... AGH!!
WE'RE LOSIN' THIS, MAN.
HOW MANY'D YOU GET?
WE CAN'T HOLD 'EM BACK...
ZH
GRR!!
?!
ZHK
UGH!!
ZHK

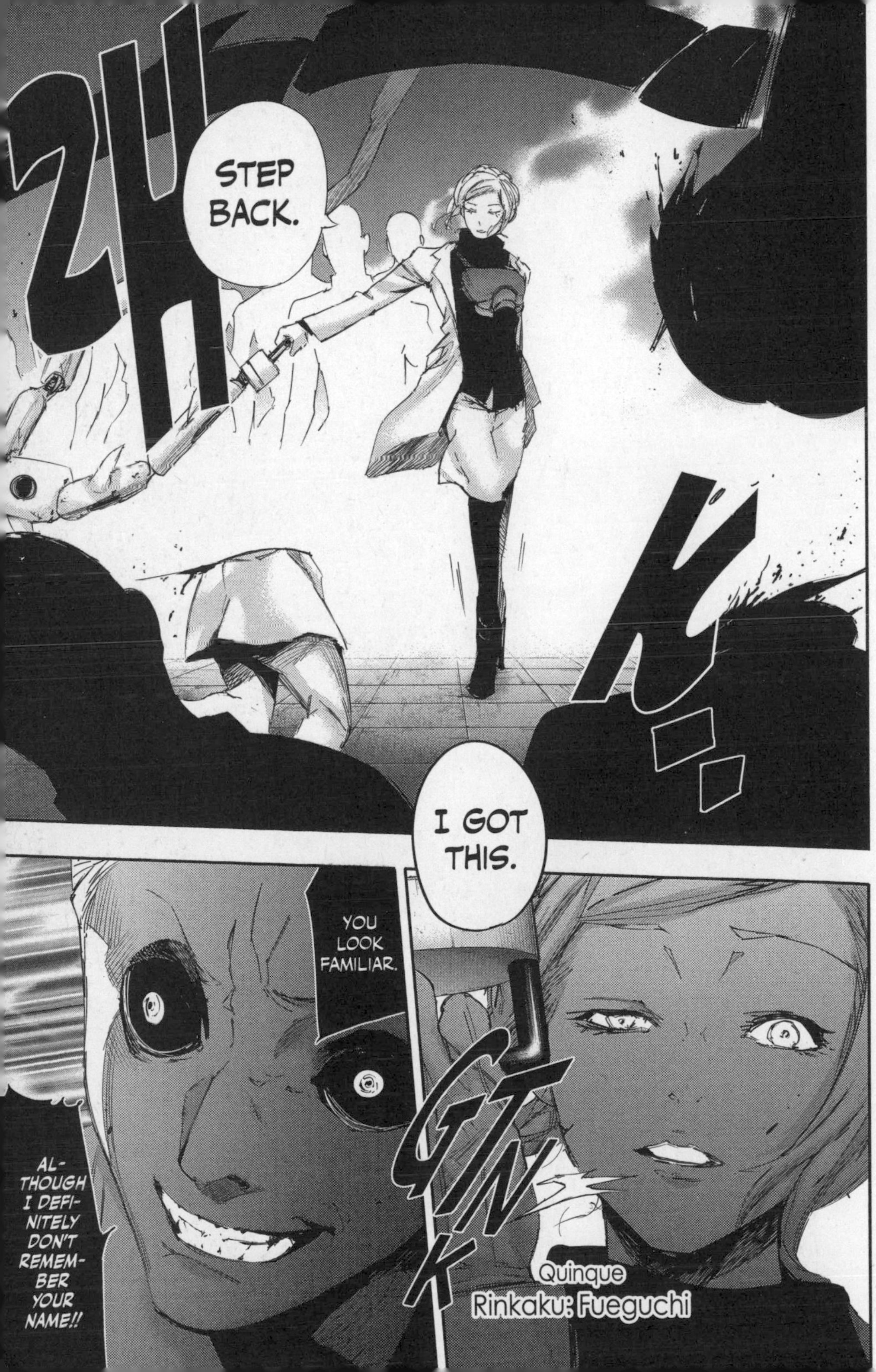
ZH
N..
STEP BACK.
I GOT THIS.
GTNK
Quinque
Rinkaku: Fueguchi
YOU LOOK FAMILIAR.
AL-THOUGH I DEFI-NITELY DON'T REMEM-BER YOUR NAME!!

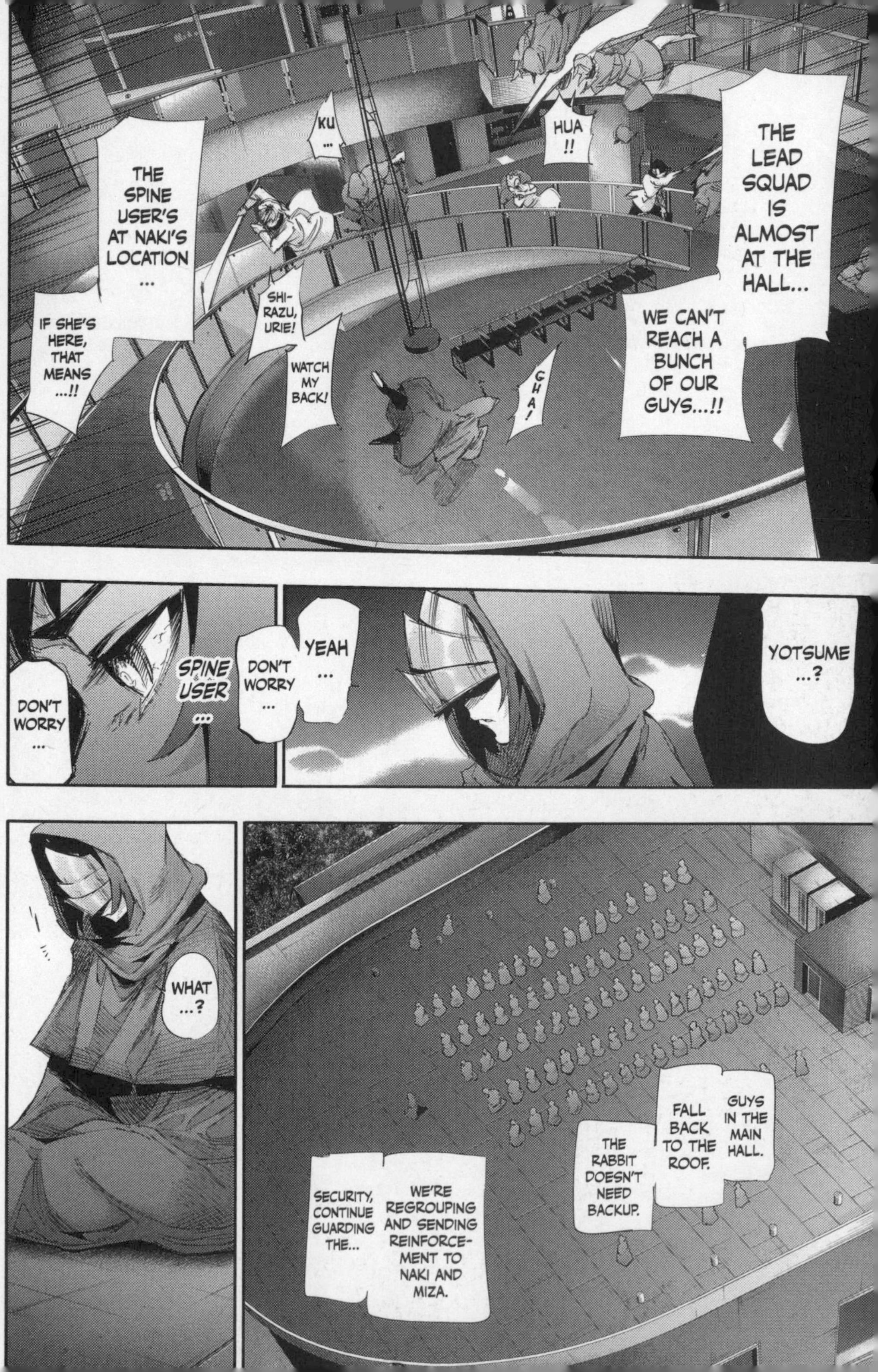
THE LEAD SQUAD IS ALMOST AT THE HALL...
WE CAN'T REACH A BUNCH OF OUR GUYS...!!
HUA!!
GHA!
KU...
SHIRAZU, URIE!
WATCH MY BACK!
THE SPINE USER'S AT NAKI'S LOCATION...
IF SHE'S HERE, THAT MEANS...!!
YOTSUME...?
YEAH...
DON'T WORRY...
SPINE USER...
DON'T WORRY...
GUYS IN THE MAIN HALL.
FALL BACK TO THE ROOF.
THE RABBIT DOESN'T NEED BACKUP.
WE'RE REGROUPING AND SENDING REINFORCEMENT TO NAKI AND MIZA.
SECURITY, CONTINUE GUARDING THE...
WHAT...?

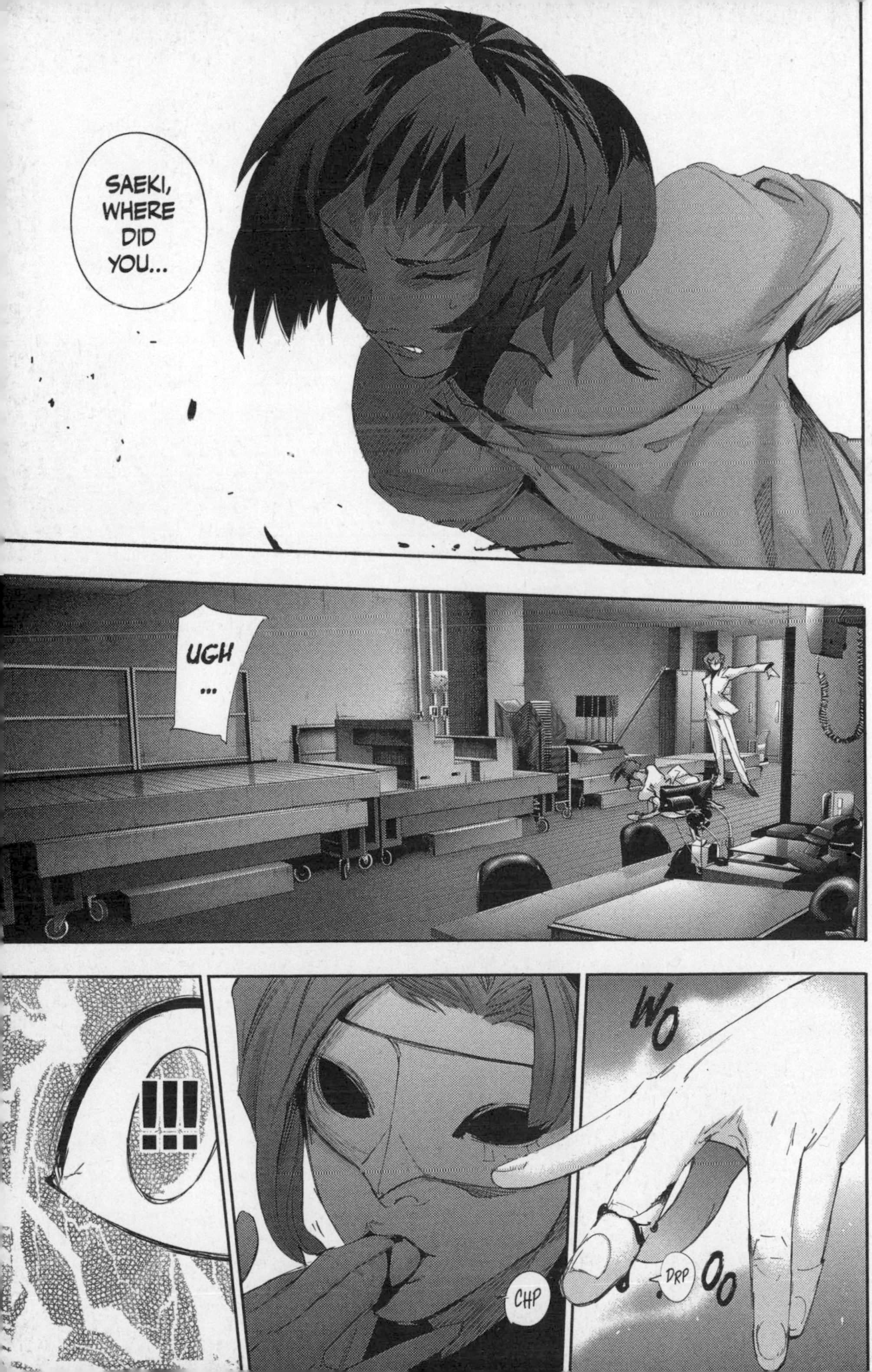
SAEKI, WHERE DID YOU...
UGH ...
WO
DRP
OO
CHP
!!!

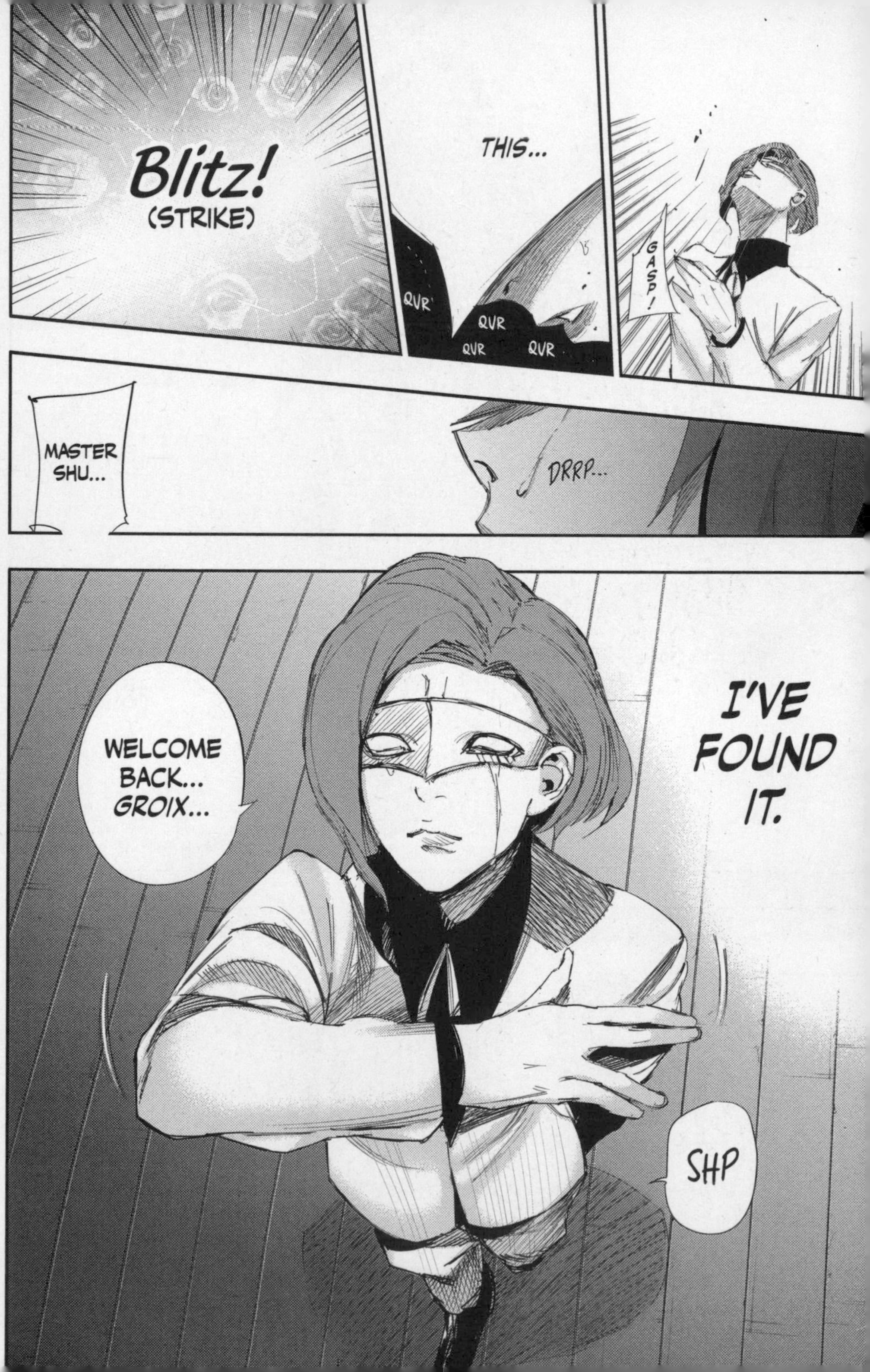
GASP!
THIS...
QVR'
QVR
QVR
QVR
Blitz!
(STRIKE)
DRRP...
MASTER SHU...
I'VE FOUND IT.
WELCOME BACK... GROIX...
SHP

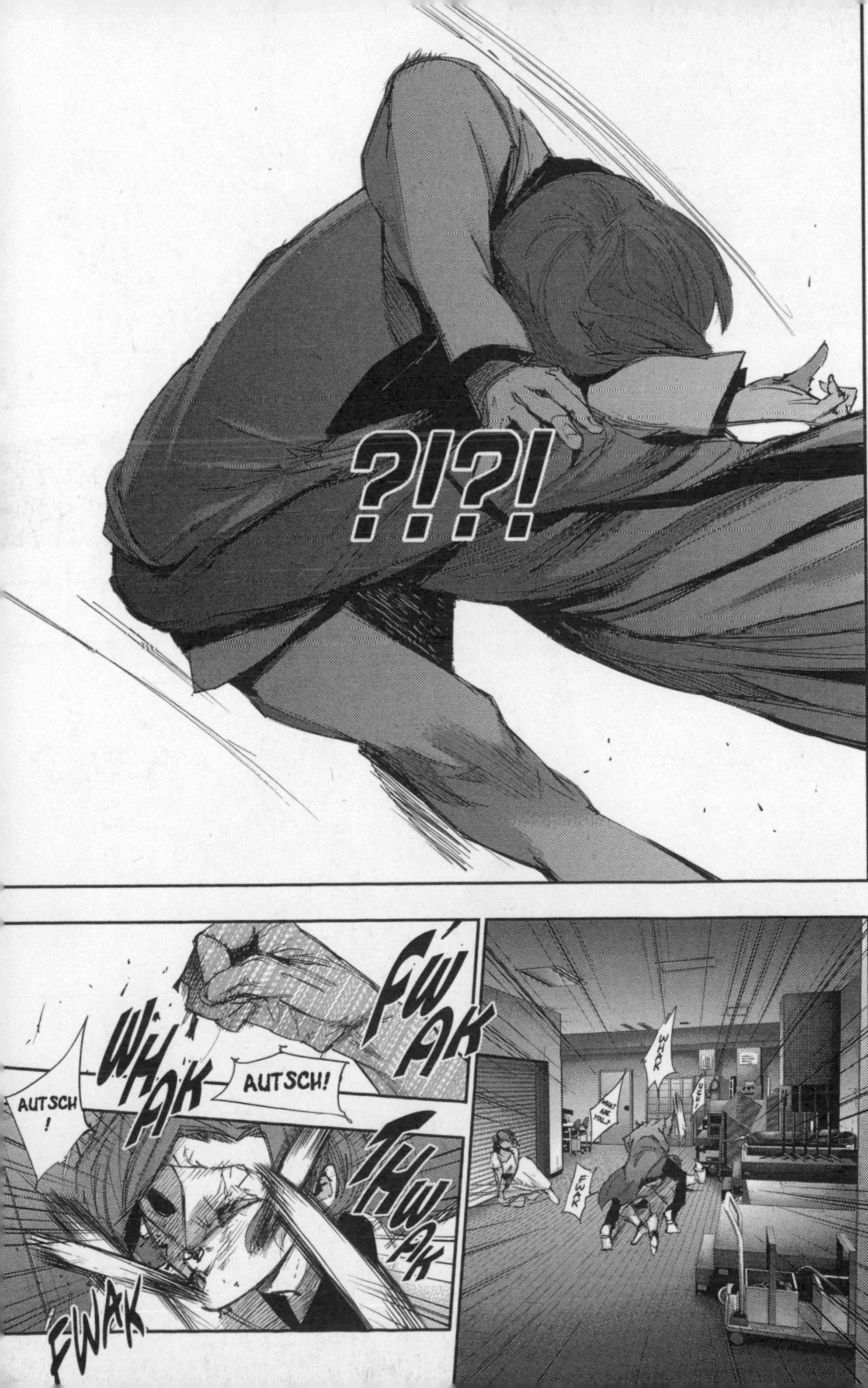
?!?!
WHAK
UGH
WHAT ARE YOU..?
FWAK
FWAK
WHAK
AUTSCH!
AUTSCH!
THWAK
FWAK

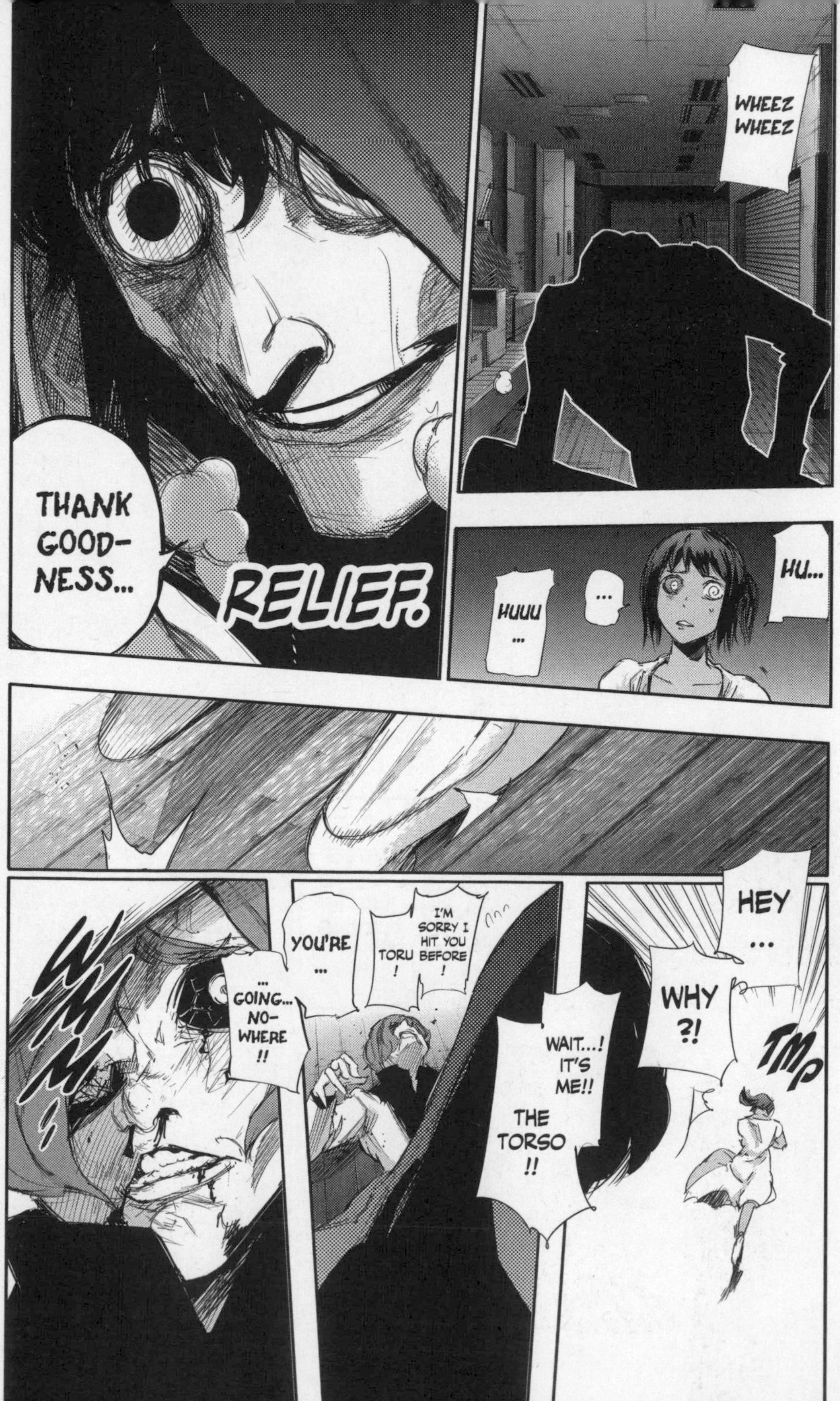
WHEEZ WHEEZ
HU...
...
HUUU ...
THANK GOOD-NESS...
RELIEF.
HEY ...
WHY ?!
TMP
WAIT...! IT'S ME!!
THE TORSO !!
I'M SORRY I HIT YOU BEFORE ! TORU !
YOU'RE ...
... GOING... NO-WHERE !!

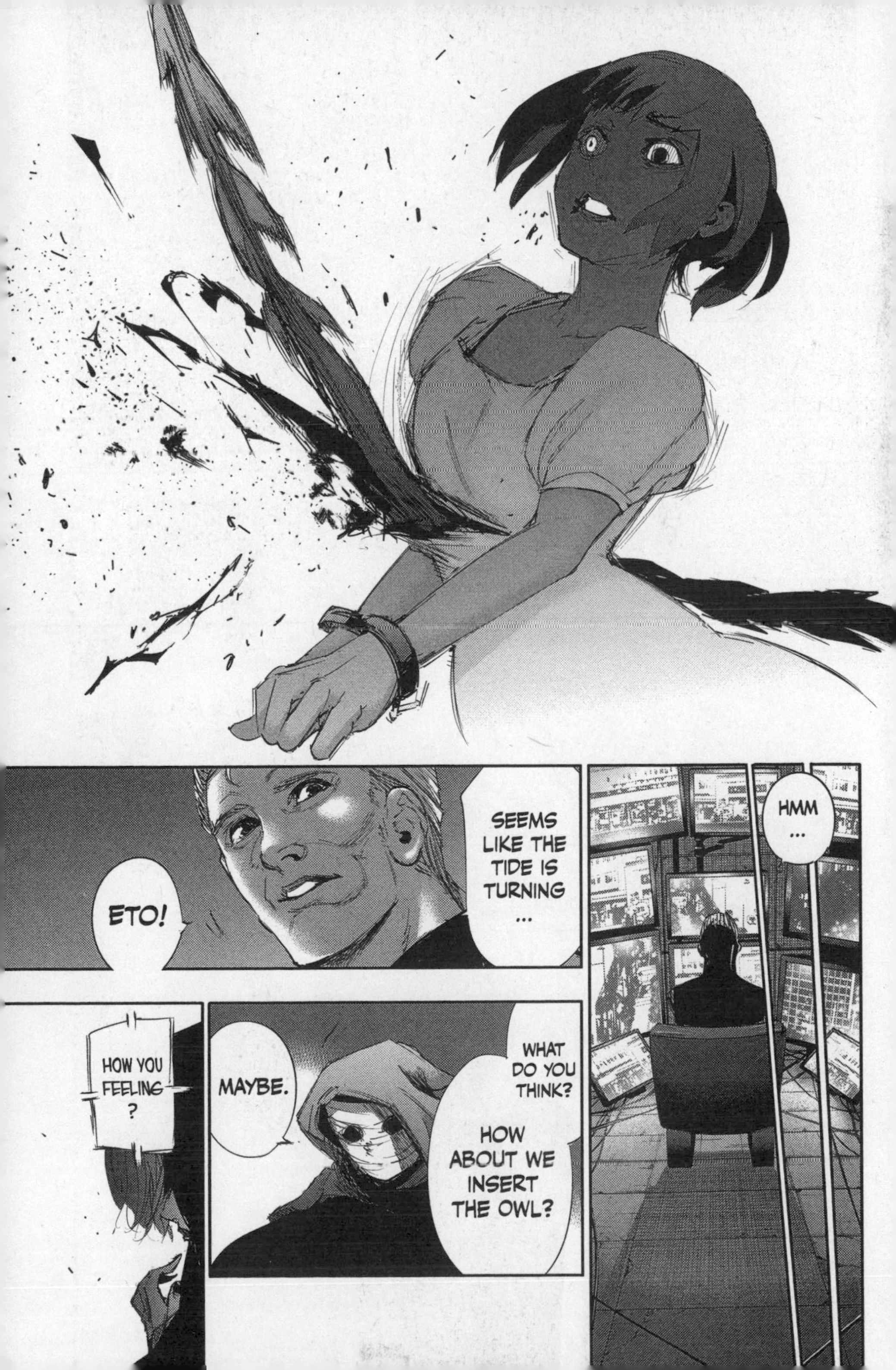
HMM ...
SEEMS LIKE THE TIDE IS TURNING ...
ETO!
WHAT DO YOU THINK?
HOW ABOUT WE INSERT THE OWL?
MAYBE.
HOW YOU FEELING?

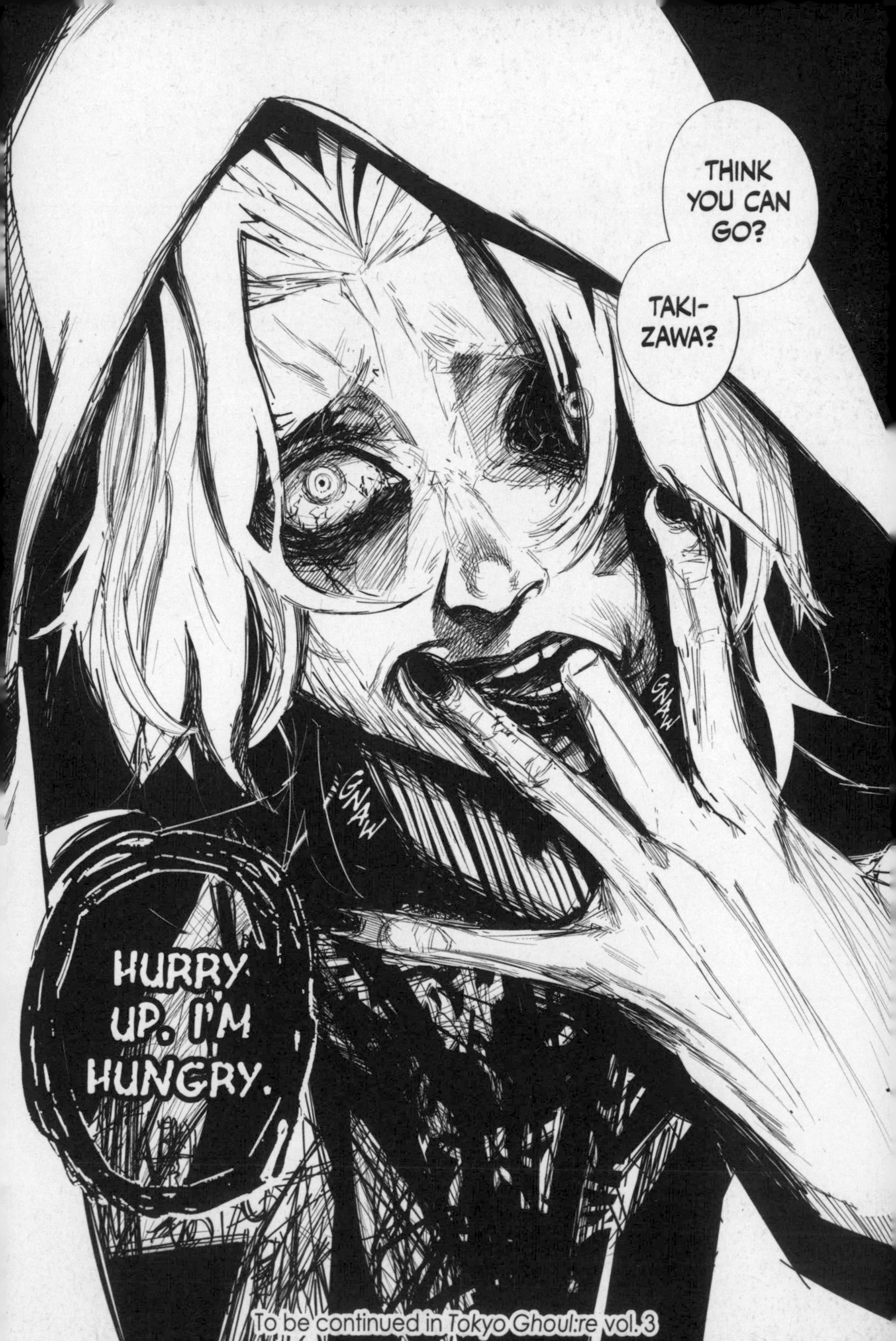
THINK YOU CAN GO?
TAKI-ZAWA?
GNAW
GNAW
HURRY UP. I'M HUNGRY.

To be continued in *Tokyo Ghoul:re* vol. 3

Staff

Mizuki Ide
Matsuzaki
Kota Shugyo
Hashimoto
Kiyotaka Aihara

#15 help

Ryuji Miyamoto
Nakano

Comic Design

Hideaki Shimada (L.S.D.)

Magazine Design

Akie Demachi (POCKET)

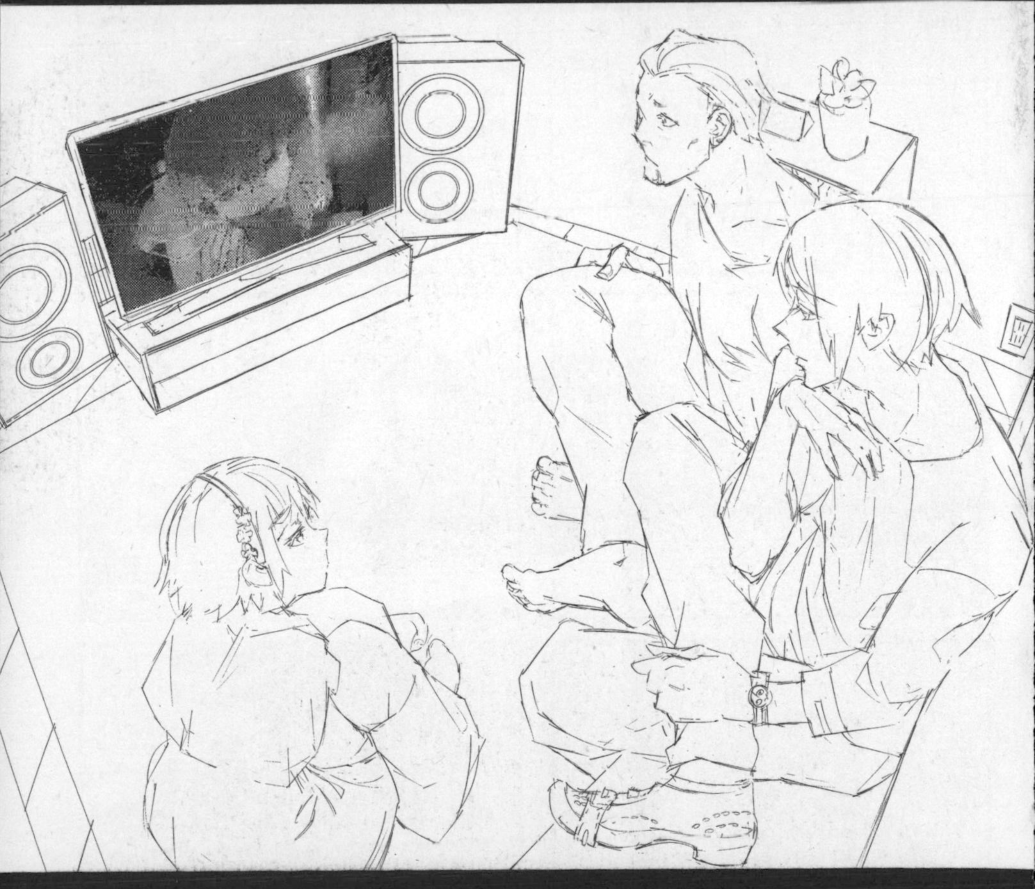

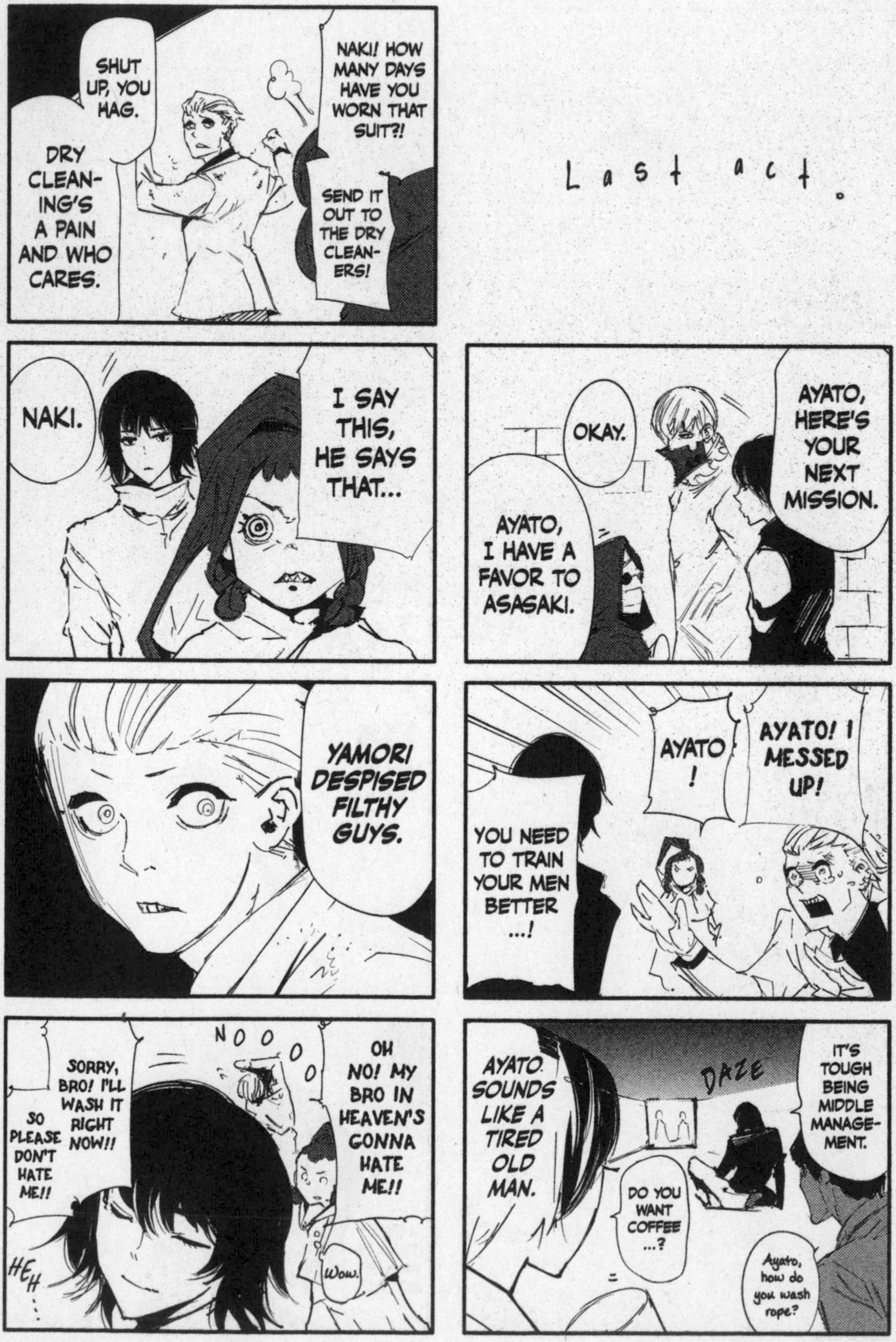

Last act.
AYATO, HERE'S YOUR NEXT MISSION.
OKAY.
AYATO, I HAVE A FAVOR TO ASASAKI.
AYATO! I MESSED UP!
AYATO!
YOU NEED TO TRAIN YOUR MEN BETTER ...!
IT'S TOUGH BEING MIDDLE MANAGEMENT.
AYATO SOUNDS LIKE A TIRED OLD MAN.
DAZE
DO YOU WANT COFFEE ...?
Ayato, how do you wash rope?
NAKI! HOW MANY DAYS HAVE YOU WORN THAT SUIT?!
SHUT UP, YOU HAG.
SEND IT OUT TO THE DRY CLEANERS!
DRY CLEANING'S A PAIN AND WHO CARES.
I SAY THIS, HE SAYS THAT...
NAKI.
YAMORI DESPISED FILTHY GUYS.
OH NO! MY BRO IN HEAVEN'S GONNA HATE ME!!
NOOOO
SORRY, BRO! I'LL WASH IT RIGHT NOW!!
SO PLEASE DON'T HATE ME!!
Wow.
HEH...

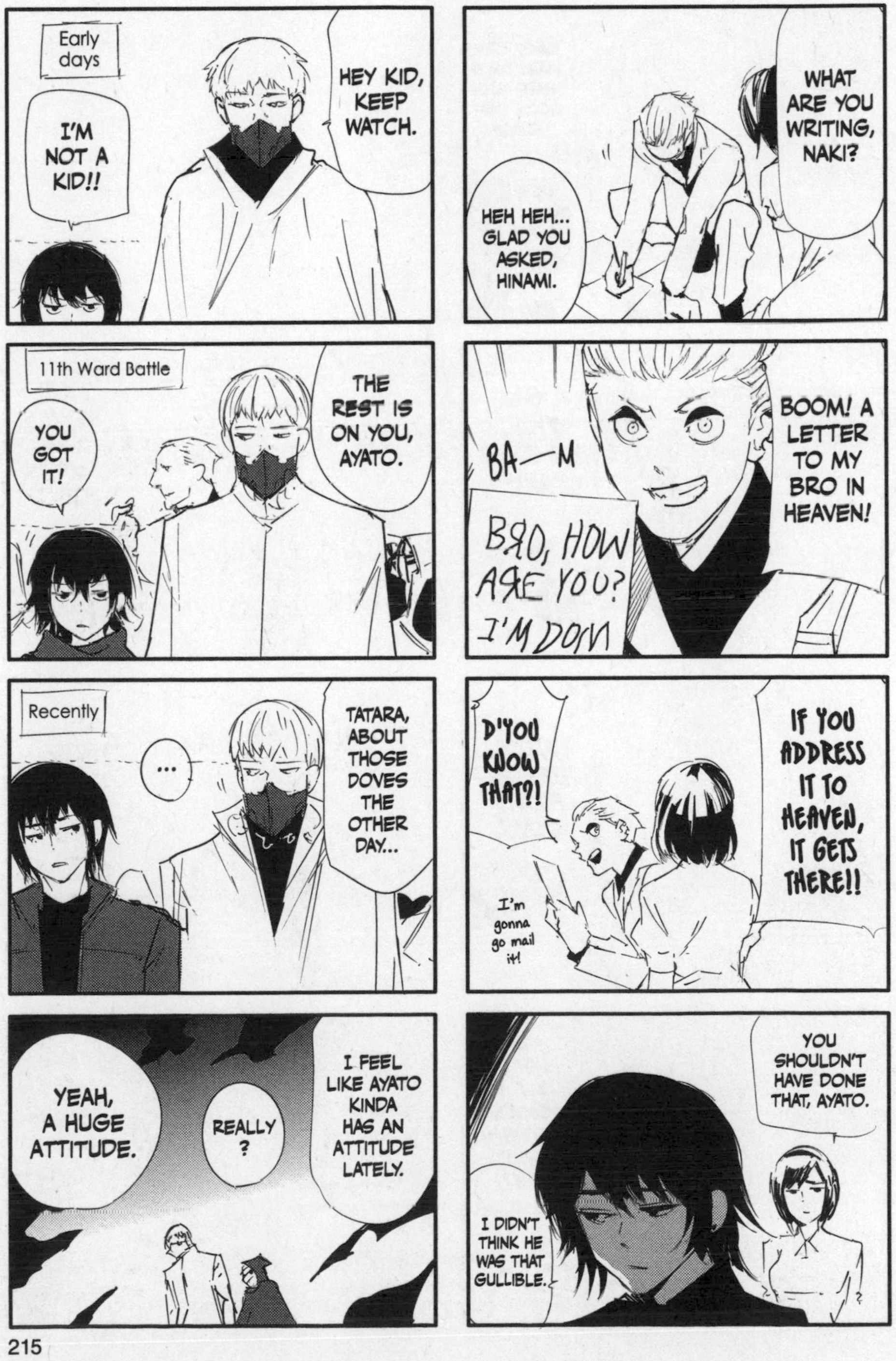
WHAT ARE YOU WRITING, NAKI?
HEH HEH... GLAD YOU ASKED, HINAMI.
BOOM! A LETTER TO MY BRO IN HEAVEN!
BA—M
BRO, HOW ARE YOU? I'M DOIN
IF YOU ADDRESS IT TO HEAVEN, IT GETS THERE!!
D'YOU KNOW THAT?!
I'm gonna go mail it!
YOU SHOULDN'T HAVE DONE THAT, AYATO.
I DIDN'T THINK HE WAS THAT GULLIBLE.
Early days
HEY KID, KEEP WATCH.
I'M NOT A KID!!
11th Ward Battle
THE REST IS ON YOU, AYATO.
YOU GOT IT!
Recently
TATARA, ABOUT THOSE DOVES THE OTHER DAY...
...
I FEEL LIKE AYATO KINDA HAS AN ATTITUDE LATELY.
REALLY?
YEAH, A HUGE ATTITUDE.

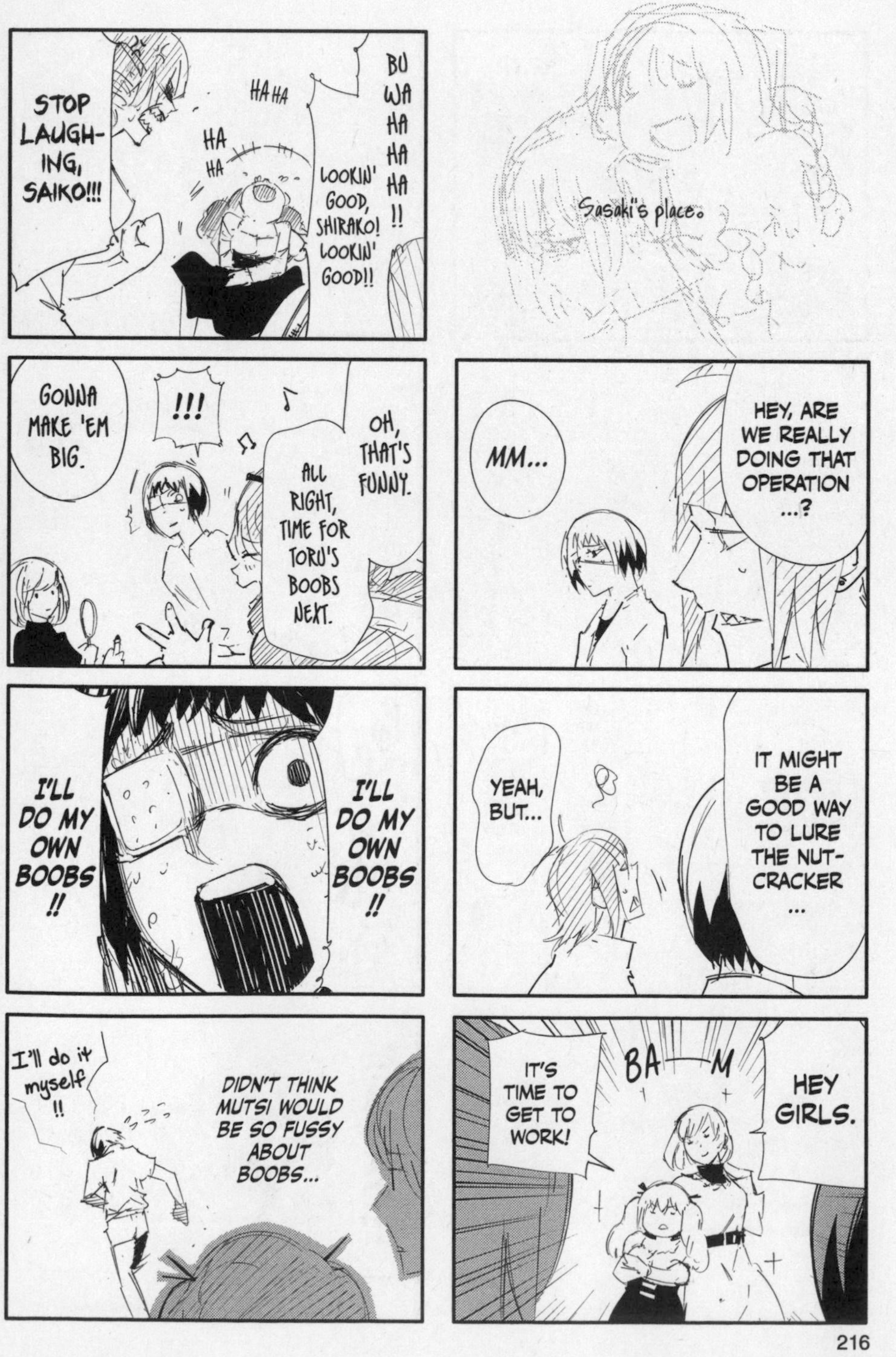
Sasaki's place.
BU WA HA HA HA !!
LOOKIN' GOOD, SHIRAKO! LOOKIN' GOOD!!
HA HA
HA HA
STOP LAUGHING, SAIKO!!!
HEY, ARE WE REALLY DOING THAT OPERATION ...?
MM...
OH, THAT'S FUNNY.
ALL RIGHT, TIME FOR TORU'S BOOBS NEXT.
!!!
GONNA MAKE 'EM BIG.
IT MIGHT BE A GOOD WAY TO LURE THE NUT-CRACKER ...
YEAH, BUT...
I'LL DO MY OWN BOOBS !!
I'LL DO MY OWN BOOBS !!
HEY GIRLS.
BA—M
IT'S TIME TO GET TO WORK!
DIDN'T THINK MUTSI WOULD BE SO FUSSY ABOUT BOOBS...
I'll do it myself !!

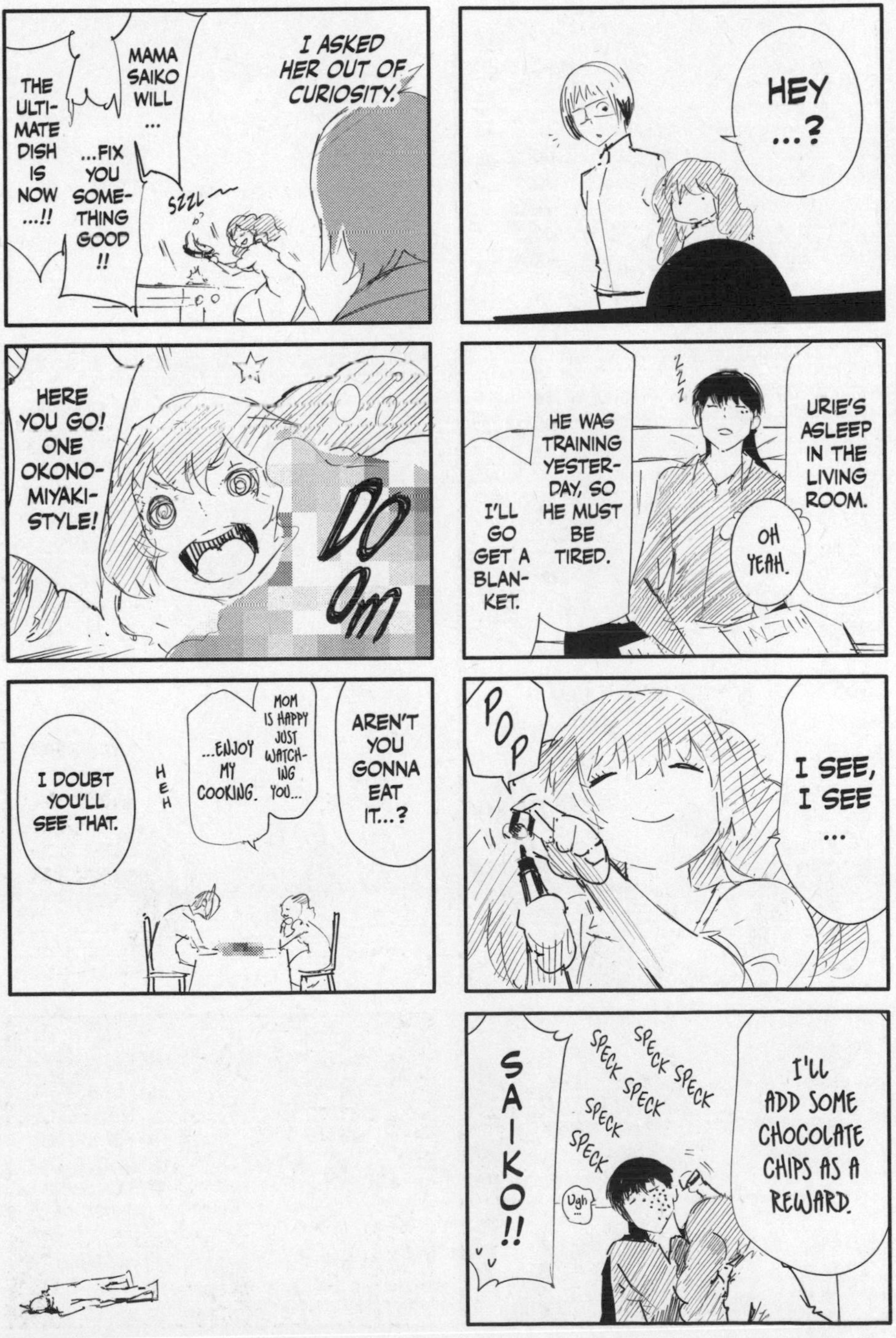
HEY ...?
URIE'S ASLEEP IN THE LIVING ROOM.
OH YEAH.
ZZZ
HE WAS TRAINING YESTERDAY, SO HE MUST BE TIRED.
I'LL GO GET A BLANKET.
I SEE, I SEE ...
POP
I'LL ADD SOME CHOCOLATE CHIPS AS A REWARD.
SPECK SPECK
SPECK SPECK
SPECK
SPECK
SAIKO!!
Ugh ...
I ASKED HER OUT OF CURIOSITY.
MAMA SAIKO WILL ...
...FIX YOU SOMETHING GOOD!!
THE ULTIMATE DISH IS NOW ...!!
SZZL~
HERE YOU GO! ONE OKONOMIYAKI-STYLE!
DOOM
AREN'T YOU GONNA EAT IT...?
MOM IS HAPPY JUST WATCHING YOU...
...ENJOY MY COOKING.
HEH
I DOUBT YOU'LL SEE THAT.

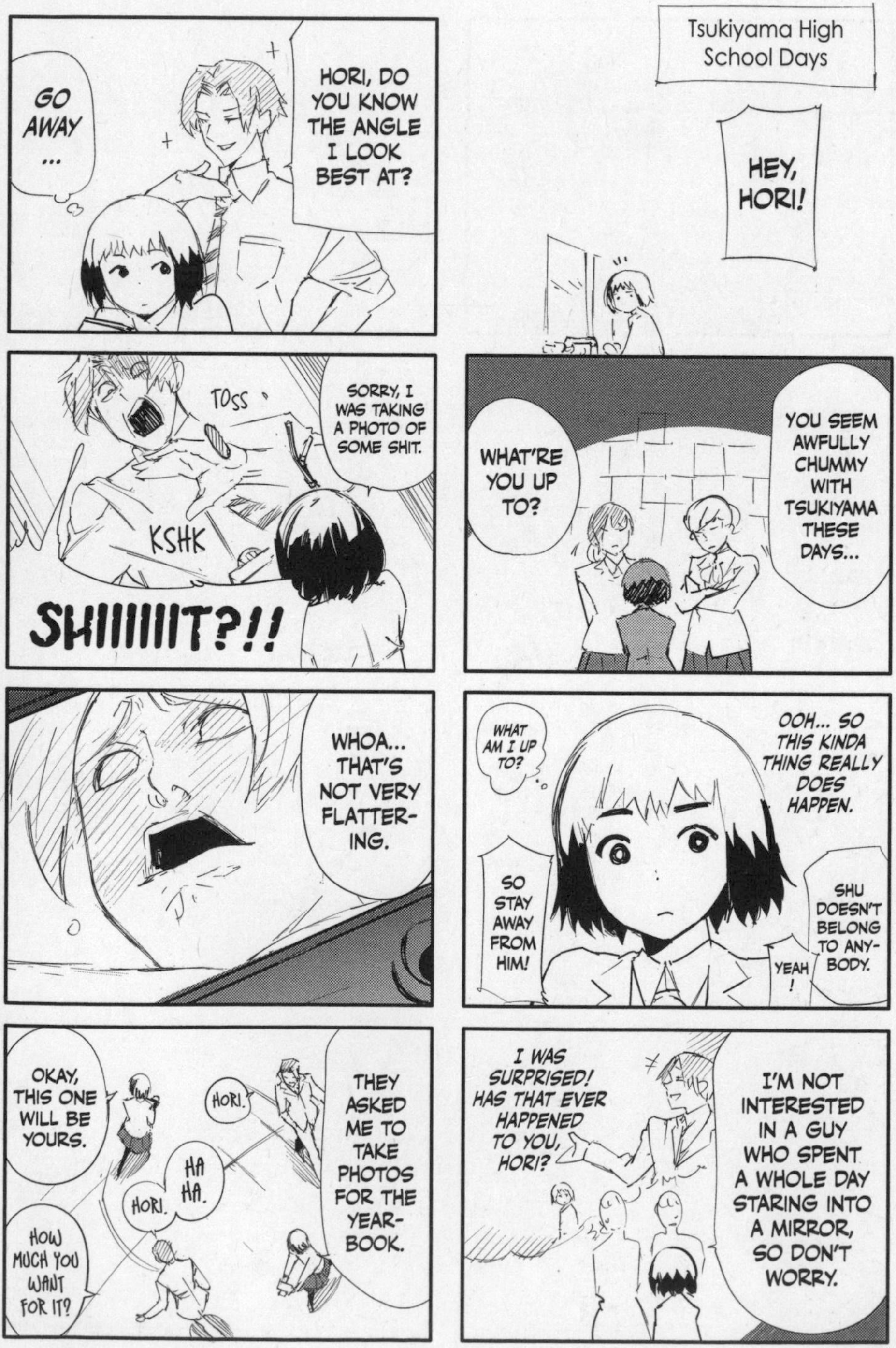
Tsukiyama High School Days
HEY, HORI!
YOU SEEM AWFULLY CHUMMY WITH TSUKIYAMA THESE DAYS...
WHAT'RE YOU UP TO?
OOH... SO THIS KINDA THING REALLY DOES HAPPEN.
WHAT AM I UP TO?
SHU DOESN'T BELONG TO ANYBODY.
YEAH!
SO STAY AWAY FROM HIM!
I'M NOT INTERESTED IN A GUY WHO SPENT A WHOLE DAY STARING INTO A MIRROR, SO DON'T WORRY.
I WAS SURPRISED! HAS THAT EVER HAPPENED TO YOU, HORI?
HORI, DO YOU KNOW THE ANGLE I LOOK BEST AT?
GO AWAY...
SORRY, I WAS TAKING A PHOTO OF SOME SHIT.
TOSS
KSHK
SHIIIIIIT?!!
WHOA... THAT'S NOT VERY FLATTER-ING.
THEY ASKED ME TO TAKE PHOTOS FOR THE YEAR-BOOK.
HORI.
HA HA.
HORI.
OKAY, THIS ONE WILL BE YOURS.
HOW MUCH YOU WANT FOR IT?

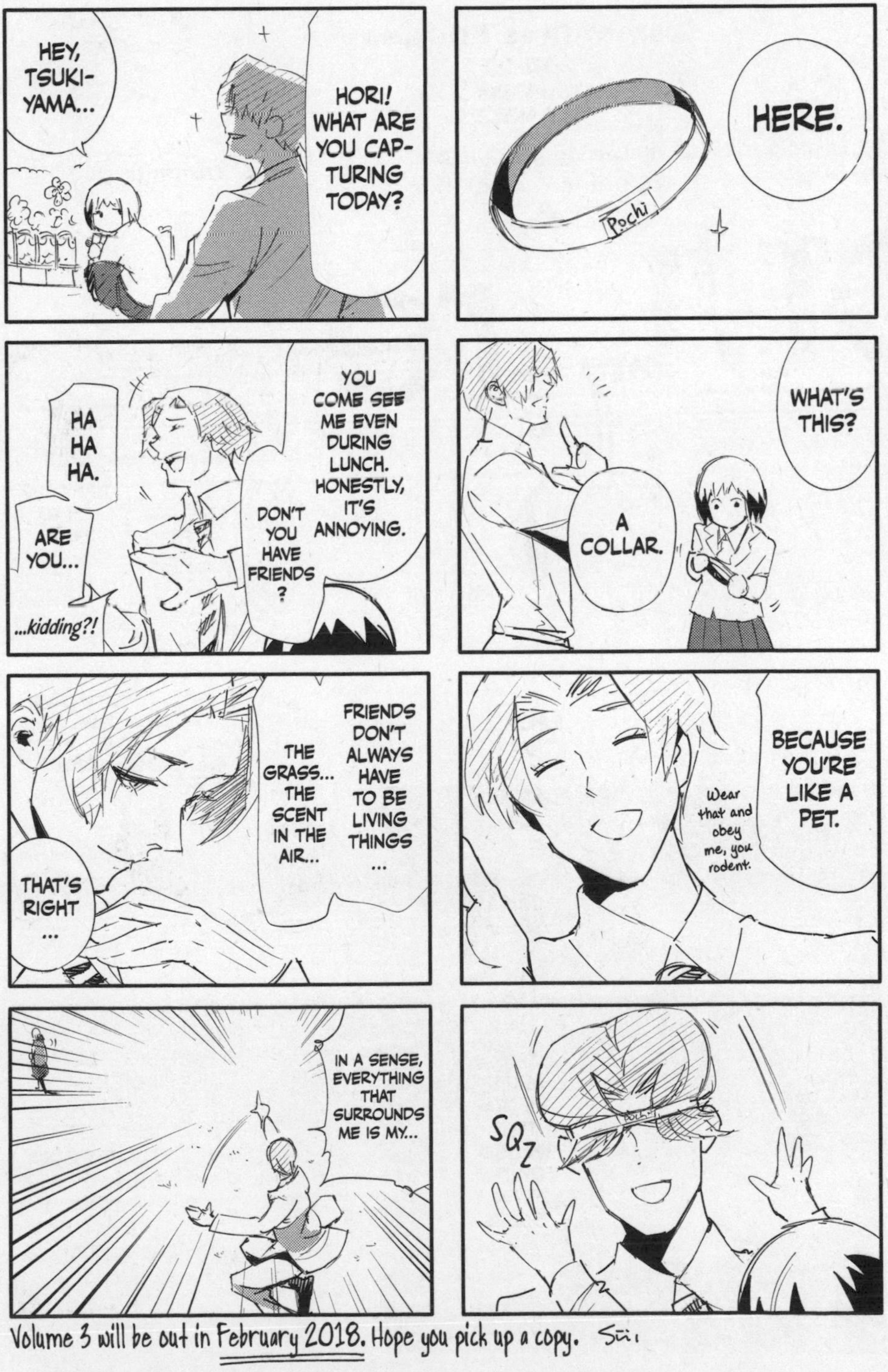
HEY, TSUKI-YAMA...
HORI! WHAT ARE YOU CAP-TURING TODAY?
HA HA HA.
YOU COME SEE ME EVEN DURING LUNCH. HONESTLY, IT'S ANNOYING.
DON'T YOU HAVE FRIENDS?
ARE YOU...
...kidding?!
THAT'S RIGHT...
FRIENDS DON'T ALWAYS HAVE TO BE LIVING THINGS...
THE GRASS... THE SCENT IN THE AIR...
IN A SENSE, EVERYTHING THAT SURROUNDS ME IS MY...
HERE.
Pochi
WHAT'S THIS?
A COLLAR.
BECAUSE YOU'RE LIKE A PET.
Wear that and obey me, you rodent.
SQZ

Volume 3 will be out in February 2018. Hope you pick up a copy. Sui

Osmanthus Badges

Awarded for number of Ghouls eradicated in a year. The emblem is an olive branch, which is also a sign of peace.

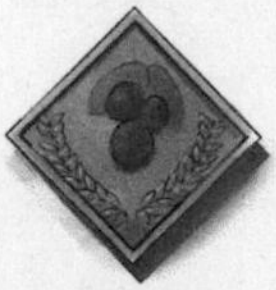

Osmanthus
30 Ghouls/Year

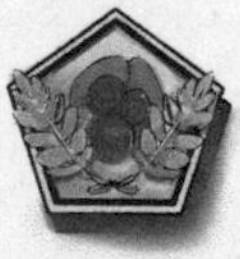

Silver Osmanthus
50 Ghouls/Year

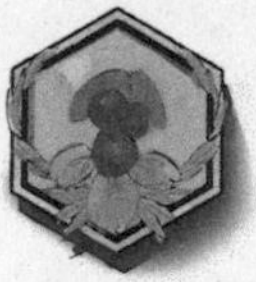

Gold Osmanthus
100 Ghouls/Year

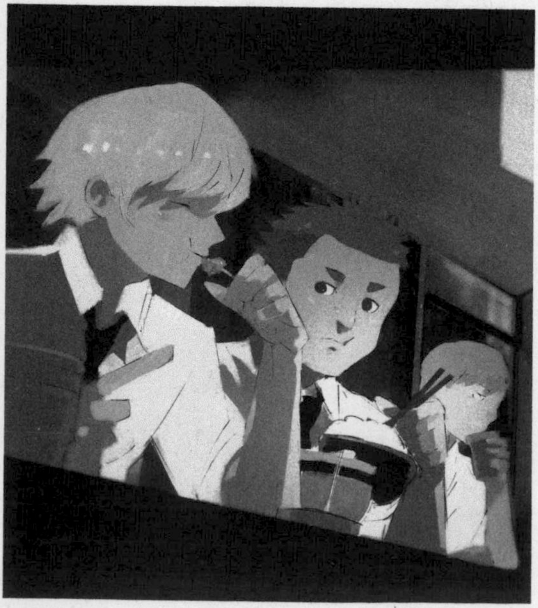

Hirako Squad

- **Take Hirako** (Squad Leader) — Senior Investigator (Class 66)
  平子 丈 （ひらこ たけ） — 3rd Academy Junior
  - Age: 30 (DOB 5/14) ♂ • Blood type: A • Height/weight: 172cm/68kg
  - Quinque: Nagomi (Rinkaku–Rate/A) • Family: Grandparents, dog (Shiba)

- **Kuramoto Ito** — Rank 1 Investigator (Class 71)
  伊東 倉元 （いとう くらもと） — 6th Academy Junior
  - Age: 25 (DOB 11/11) ♂ • Blood type: O • Height/weight: 171cm/60kg
  - Quinque: Senze (Kokaku–Rate/A) • Respects: Take Hirako, Kisho Arima

- **Shinji Michibata** — Rank 1 Investigator (Class 69)
  道端 信二 （みちばた しんじ） — 3rd Academy Junior
  - Age: 27 (DOB 9/23) ♂ • Blood type: A • Height/weight: 175cm/70kg
  - Quinque: Agure (Bikaku–Rate/A) • Nickname: Micchy

- **Masami Umeno** — Rank 2 Investigator (Class 72)
  梅野 雅巳 （うめの まさみ） — 6th Academy Junior
  - Age: 24 (DOB 5/30) ♂ • Blood type: B • Height/weight: 181cm/82kg
  - Quinque: Bull (Rinkaku–Rate/B) • Nickname: Gorimi

- **Yasuhito Nezu** — Rank 2 Investigator (Class 72)
  根津 安人 （ねづ やすひと） — 6th Academy Junior
  - Age: 24 (DOB 8/17) ♂ • Blood type: A • Height/weight: 177cm/75kg
  - Quinque: Melt (Ukaku–Rate/A) • Nickname: Nezu

- **Takeomi Kuroiwa** — Rank 2 Investigator (Class 77)
  黒磐 武臣 （くろいわ たけおみ） — 7th Academy Junior
  - Age: 19 (DOB 9/6) ♂ • Blood type: B • Height/weight: 182cm/77kg
  - Quinque: Tsunagi <hard> (Bikaku–Rate/C) • Honors: Scholarship student

*Ages are from the start of the year.

SUI ISHIDA is the author
of the immensely popular
Tokyo Ghoul and several
Tokyo Ghoul one-shots,
including one that won
second place in the *Weekly
Young Jump* 113th Grand
Prix award in 2010. *Tokyo
Ghoul:re* is the sequel to
Tokyo Ghoul.

TOKYO

Story and art by
SUI ISHIDA

TOKYO GHOUL:RE © 2014 by Sui Ishida
All rights reserved.
First published in Japan in 2014 by SHUEISHA Inc., Tokyo.
English translation rights arranged by SHUEISHA Inc.

Translation Joe Yamazaki
Touch-Up Art & Lettering Vanessa Satone
Design Shawn Carrico
Editor Pancha Diaz

Printed in the U.S.A.

Published by VIZ Media, LLC
P.O. Box 77010
San Francisco, CA 94107

10 9 8 7 6 5 4 3 2 1
First printing, December 2017

viz.com

VIZ SIGNATURE
vizsignature.com

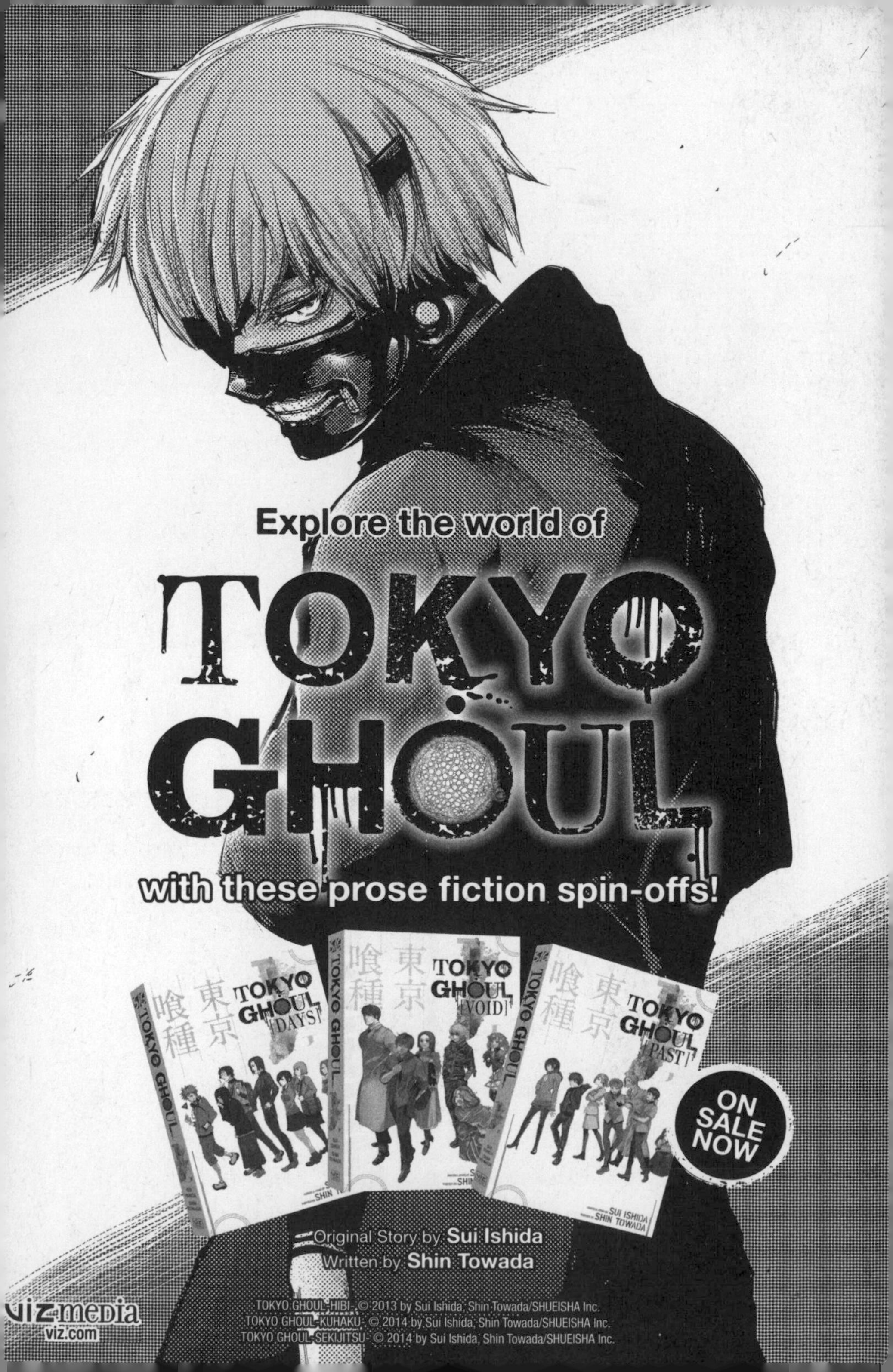

Explore the world of
TOKYO GHOUL
with these prose fiction spin-offs!
TOKYO GHOUL [DAYS]
TOKYO GHOUL [VOID]
TOKYO GHOUL [PAST]
ON SALE NOW
Original Story by Sui Ishida
Written by Shin Towada
viz media
viz.com
TOKYO GHOUL-HIBI- © 2013 by Sui Ishida, Shin Towada/SHUEISHA Inc.
TOKYO GHOUL-KUHAKU- © 2014 by Sui Ishida, Shin Towada/SHUEISHA Inc.
TOKYO GHOUL-SEKIJITSU- © 2014 by Sui Ishida, Shin Towada/SHUEISHA Inc.

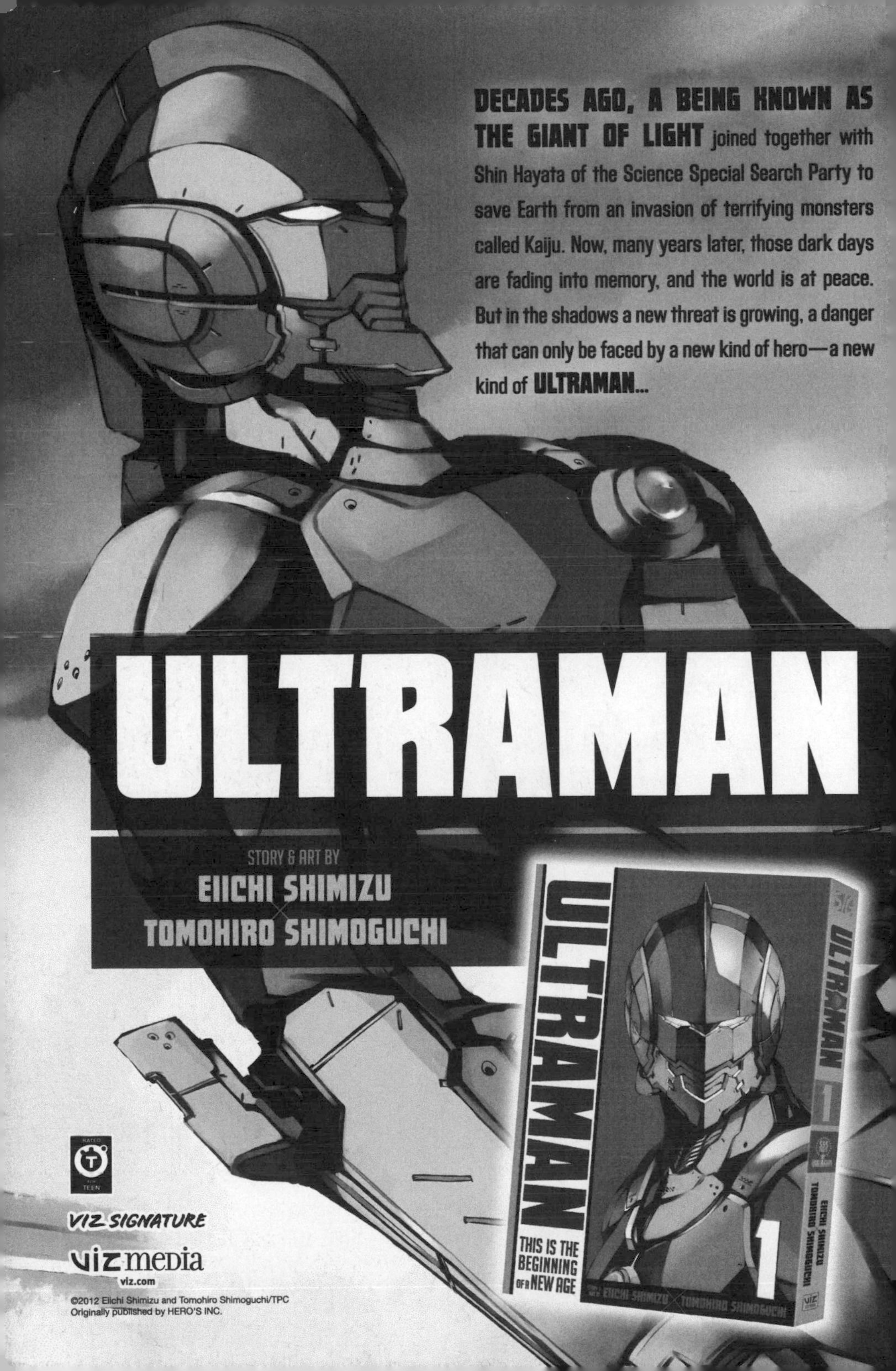
DECADES AGO, A BEING KNOWN AS THE GIANT OF LIGHT joined together with Shin Hayata of the Science Special Search Party to save Earth from an invasion of terrifying monsters called Kaiju. Now, many years later, those dark days are fading into memory, and the world is at peace. But in the shadows a new threat is growing, a danger that can only be faced by a new kind of hero—a new kind of ULTRAMAN...
ULTRAMAN
STORY & ART BY
EIICHI SHIMIZU × TOMOHIRO SHIMOGUCHI
ULTRAMAN
THIS IS THE BEGINNING OF A NEW AGE
EIICHI SHIMIZU × TOMOHIRO SHIMOGUCHI
ULTRAMAN 1
EIICHI SHIMIZU TOMOHIRO SHIMOGUCHI
1
RATED T FOR TEEN
VIZ SIGNATURE
vizmedia
viz.com
©2012 Eiichi Shimizu and Tomohiro Shimoguchi/TPC
Originally published by HERO'S INC.

"Tell me the last time any book disturbed you. When you give up, buy Uzumaki."
– Warren Ellis

UZUMAKI

Story and Art by JUNJI ITO

SPIRALS... THIS TOWN IS CONTAMINATED WITH SPIRALS...

Kurouzu-cho, a small fogbound town on the coast of Japan, is cursed. According to Shuichi Saito, the withdrawn boyfriend of teenager Kirie Goshima, their town is haunted not by a person or being but by a pattern: uzumaki, the spiral, the hypnotic secret shape of the world. It manifests itself in everything from seashells and whirlpools in water to the spiral marks on people's bodies, the insane obsessions of Shuichi's father and the voice from the cochlea in our inner ear. As the madness spreads, the inhabitants of Kurouzu-cho are pulled ever deeper into a whirlpool from which there is no return!

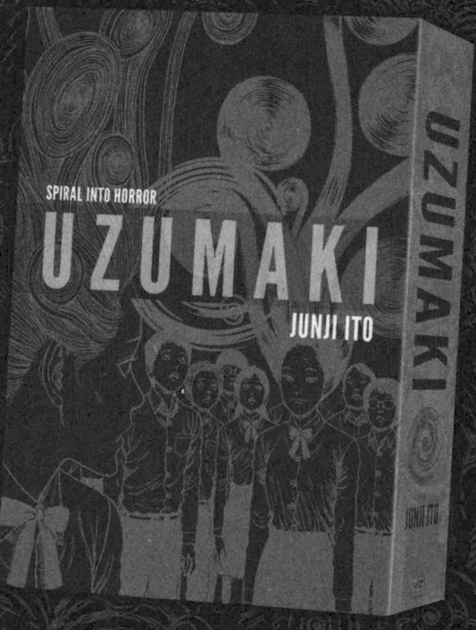
SPIRAL INTO HORROR
UZUMAKI
JUNJI ITO
UZUMAKI
JUNJI ITO

A masterpiece of horror manga, now available in a DELUXE HARDCOVER EDITION!

VIZ SIGNATURE

viz media www.viz.com

RATED T+ FOR OLDER TEEN ratings.viz.com

MOBILE SUIT GUNDAM THUNDERBOLT

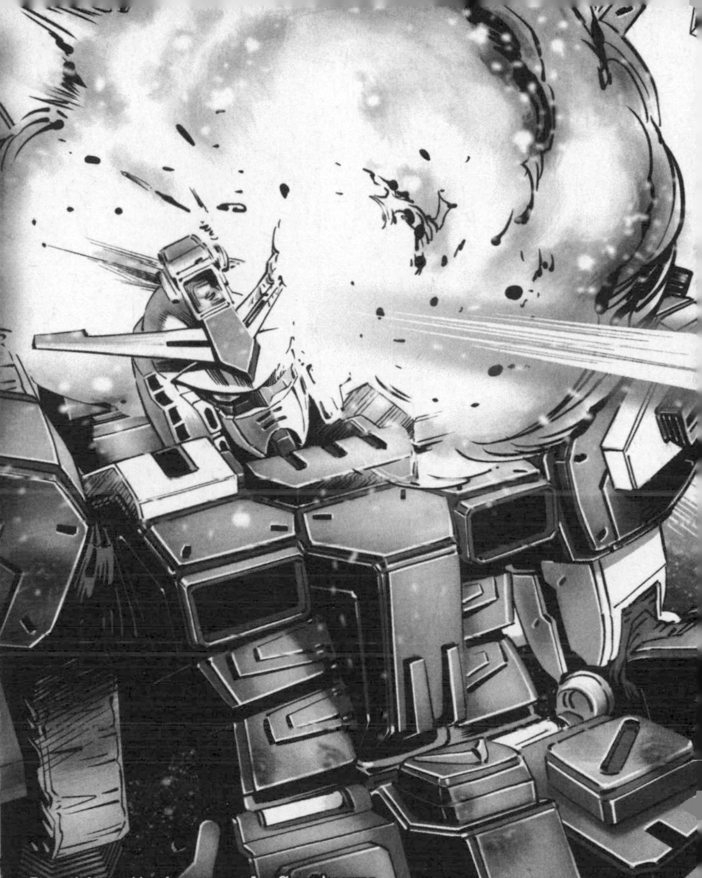

In the Universal Century year 0079, the space colony known as Side 3 proclaims independence as the Principality of Zeon and declares war on the Earth Federation. One year later, they are locked in a fierce battle for the Thunderbolt Sector, an area of space scarred by the wreckage of destroyed colonies. Into this maelstrom of destruction go two veteran Mobile Suit pilots: the deadly Zeon sniper Daryl Lorenz, and Federation ace Io Fleming. It's the beginning of a rivalry that can end only when one of them is destroyed.

STORY AND AR
YASUO OHTAGAK
ORIGINAL CONCEPT
HAJIME YATA
AND YOSHIYUKI TOMI

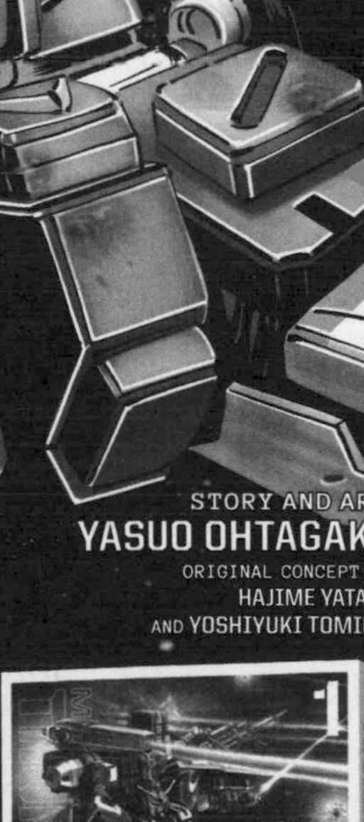
1
STORY AND ART BY YASUO OHTAGAKI
MOBILE SUIT GUNDAM
THUNDERBOLT

RATED T+ FOR OLDER TEEN

viz media
viz.com

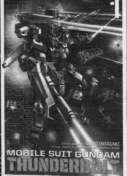

TOKYO GHOUL:re

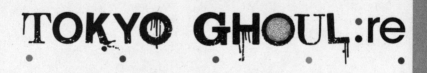

This is the last page.
TOKYO GHOUL:re reads right to left.